Missions Begin with Blood

CATHOLIC PRACTICE IN NORTH AMERICA

SERIES EDITORS:
John C. Seitz, Fordham University
Jessica Delgado, The Ohio State University

This series aims to contribute to the growing field of Catholic studies through the publication of books devoted to the historical and cultural study of Catholic practice in North America, from the colonial period to the present. As the term "practice" suggests, the series springs from a pressing need in the study of American Catholicism for empirical investigations and creative explorations and analyses of the contours of Catholic experience. In seeking to provide more comprehensive maps of Catholic practice, this series is committed to publishing works from diverse American locales, including urban, suburban, and rural settings; ethnic, postethnic, and transnational contexts; private and public sites; and seats of power as well as the margins.

SERIES ADVISORY BOARD:
Emma Anderson, Ottawa University
Paul Contino, Pepperdine University
Kathleen Sprows Cummings, University of Notre Dame
James T. Fisher, Fordham University (Emeritus)
Paul Mariani, Boston College
Thomas A. Tweed, University of Notre Dame

Missions Begin with Blood

SUFFERING AND SALVATION IN THE
BORDERLANDS OF NEW SPAIN

Brandon Bayne

FORDHAM UNIVERSITY PRESS
New York 2022

Copyright © 2022 Fordham University Press

All rights reserved. No part of this publication may be reproduced, stored in a retrieval system, or transmitted in any form or by any means—electronic, mechanical, photocopy, recording, or any other—except for brief quotations in printed reviews, without the prior permission of the publisher.

Fordham University Press has no responsibility for the persistence or accuracy of URLs for external or third-party Internet websites referred to in this publication and does not guarantee that any content on such websites is, or will remain, accurate or appropriate.

Fordham University Press also publishes its books in a variety of electronic formats. Some content that appears in print may not be available in electronic books.

Library of Congress Cataloging-in-Publication Data

Names: Bayne, Brandon L., author.
Title: Missions begin with blood : suffering and salvation in the borderlands of new Spain / Brandon L. Bayne.
Description: First edition. | New York : Fordham University Press, 2021. | Series: Catholic practice in North America | Includes bibliographical references and index.
Identifiers: LCCN 2021037933 | ISBN 9780823294206 (hardback) | ISBN 9780823294190 (paperback) | ISBN 9780823294213 (epub)
Subjects: LCSH: Jesuits—Missions—Mexico—History—Spanish colony, 1540–1810. | Martyrdom—Christianity—History. | Agriculture—Religious aspects—Christianity.
Classification: LCC BX3712.A1 B39 2021 | DDC 266/.209720903—dc23
LC record available at https://lccn.loc.gov/2021037933

Visit us online at www.fordhampress.com.

Library of Congress Cataloging-in-Publication Data available online at https://catalog.loc.gov.

Printed in the United States of America

24 23 22   5 4 3 2 1

First edition

For my mother, Arlene
Paz, Fuego y Luz

Contents

List of Abbreviations	xi
Introduction: Suffering and Salvation	1
1 Seeds: Planting Conversions	29
2 Weeds: Ritual Confrontations	61
3 Fruits: Passionate Expansion	95
4 Deserted: Prolonged Isolation	133
5 Uprooted: Missionary Expulsion	170
Epilogue: Civilization and Savagery	199
Acknowledgments	215
Notes	219
Bibliography	277
Index	311

Abbreviations

AGN   Archivo Géneral de la Nación, Mexico City, Mexico
AHF   Arizona Historical Foundation, Arizona State University, Phoenix, AZ
AHS   Arizona Historical Society, Tucson, AZ
AHPMSJ Archivo Histórico de la Provincia Méxicana de la Sociedad de Jesús, Mexico City, Mexico
AZTM   Arizona State Museum, Office of Ethnohistorical Research, Tucson, AZ
BL   Bancroft Library, University of California at Berkeley, Berkeley, CA
BN   Biblioteca Nacionál de México, UNAM, Mexico City, Mexico
CRC   Chicana/Chicano Research Collection, Arizona State University
HL   Huntington Library, Pasadena, CA
JCB   John Carter Brown Library, Brown University
NL   Newberry Library, Chicago, IL
VSL   Vatican Film Library, St. Louis University
YBL   Beineke Library, New Haven, CT

Missions Begin with Blood

Introduction
Suffering and Salvation

The headquarters of the Mexican Province of the Society of Jesus sits on a quiet street in the charming neighborhood of Del Carmen on the northern edge of Coyoacán, one of the most historic and colorful sections of Mexico City. La Casa Azul, the family home of Frida Kahlo, stands just a few blocks away, now housing a museum dedicated to her life and art. Leon Trotsky's former residence in exile, the place of his assassination, survives nearby as well. Even older histories lie just to the south, where Kahlo's husband/painter Diego Rivera's Anahuacalli Museum displays over 50,000 pieces of pre-Hispanic Indigenous art. In between that museum and the Jesuit Provincial offices, three sixteenth-century churches and the site of Hernán Cortes's colonial palace form the historic center of Coyoacán, a site that had been an Indigenous political and ritual center continuously in use since at least the seventh century CE.[1] To the north of the Province's compound, however, modern hospitals, high-rise apartments, hulking government buildings, and an exclusive shopping mall loom over the bustling highway Churubusco.

Like its headquarters, the *Provincia Mexicana de la Compañia de Jesus* resides in the borderlands between Mexico's past and present. Although the Society first arrived in Mexico City in the mid-1500s, its dramatic expulsion from the Americas in 1767 severed the Jesuits' connection to the spaces, objects, institutions, and relationships that they had forged over the course of two centuries of service in New Spain. Along with the subsequent papal suppression of the Society in 1773, the expulsion meant that the Jesuits lost control of most of their assets in the New World, forfeiting them to other religious orders or the Spanish crown.[2] Ensuing decades of wars and reforms would mean that most of their churches, colleges, writings, and sacred things would be scattered and appropriated by diverse institutions.[3] Still, through networks of loyal allies and elite patrons, they were able to hold onto a few valuables. After their restoration as a Catholic order in 1815, the Society slowly recuperated some of what had been lost. When they finally returned to Mexico in 1840, the Jesuits worked to recover their legacy and secure their place in a nation wracked by ongoing conflicts between church and state.[4] At their offices in Coyoacán, they were eventually able to establish a modest historical archive in the late twentieth century, a small representation of the thousands of letters, histories, catechisms, and other documents produced during their long history in that land.

They deposited other valuable pieces there as well. I had been working in the Province's archive for a couple of weeks in the spring of 2014 before I came to understand the nature of these holdings. Before arriving, a Jesuit friend had told me that the Province maintained a small museum with several historical objects that might pique my interest. Father Elias knew that I was researching martyrdom in the Society's northern missions and that I hoped to find some portraits, sacred vessels, and mission artifacts. With this in mind, I inquired with the archivist, Alejandro, when I first arrived about the existence of a museum. Alejandro demurred and redirected my attention to a catalogue of written sources that they offered.[5] Whether through gradual trust or exhaustion with my persistence, his pliability must have grown in the ensuing weeks, because in the late afternoon of a Friday in March, Alejandro told me to pack up my things and follow him. As we left the archive, he guided me to the back of the complex, past its provincial offices, living quarters, and a garden with a large bronze bust of the famed missionary Father Eusebio Kino. Beside the garden, he showed me a small but striking library named after Kino that housed thousands of scholarly and rare books.

I was impressed with this rich collection and concluded, as I began to browse the stacks, that this must have been what Father Elias had mentioned. But Alejandro prodded me onward to another building. When we neared this final structure, I spotted a sign with the words "Museo Manuel Ignacio Perez Alonso," named for a prodigious Jesuit historian who had passed away in 2007. The archivist then unlocked its two large metal doors and opened them wide. We entered a darkened hall that only began to reveal itself when Alejandro flicked on the lights. Before me opened up two medium-sized white rooms with terra cotta floors. The more distant room held flat screen TVs, chairs, a podium, and audio speakers. At first, I thought these were conference spaces. However, alongside the furniture and AV equipment, I noticed several paintings, including a wall with portraits of all the Society's generals, from Ignatius of Loyola to the father general in 2014, Adolfo Nicolás. As I scanned the rooms, I then took in other canvases, filled with heavenly scenes of Jesuit saints like Francis Xavier, Francis Borgia, and the founder, Ignatius, alongside portraits of renowned Mexican Jesuit intellectuals like Francisco Javier Clavijero and Francisco Javier Alegre.

Despite this curious combination of modern technology, devotional painting, and formal portraiture, a single object drew my eye away from everything else. To the far right in a corner stood a wooden pedestal with an object incased in glass (Figure 1). Approaching, I peered inside the small transparent case and saw what looked like the broken and slightly stained top of a human skull. On closer inspection, I detected a note under the object. The description read, "Head of Father Gonzalo de Tapia, first Martyr and Founder of the Sinaloa Missions, brought by the Father Martín Pelaez, Visitor of those Missions." I froze for a moment because I had already read so much about this peculiar relic and its circuitous journeys. Various Jesuit letters and histories had described how Father Tapia had lost his head during a gruesome martyrdom in July of 1594.[6] Some had written about how his cranium had been varnished in ochre and used as a drinking vessel by the missionary's killers, who had employed it in their "drunken festivals." These perpetrators had reportedly brandished it in mock eucharistic feasts, imbibing from it in a delighted ritual inversal that celebrated the demise of the priest who had attempted to stamp out their traditional rites and dances. Others contended that what Tapia had not accomplished in life, his relics had fulfilled after his death. They attributed this relic with rooting out the Sinaloans' "idolatries" and ending the abuse of alcohol: "The blessed skull extinguished that pernicious and evil vice."[7] And now it rested in the back corner of this odd room.

Several other relics had been gathered to these rooms. Directly above the pedestal hung a large nineteenth-century painting that depicted Tapia's violent death, along with a framed document that narrated the translation of his relics to León, Spain. These items were mirrored in the opposing corner of the same wall by a photograph, clothing, and personal items of Blessed Miguel Pro, a twentieth-century Jesuit who had been executed during the 1920s conflict between the Mexican government and the Roman Catholic Church known as the Cristero War.[8] On a perpendicular

FIGURE 1. The partial skull of Father Gonzalo de Tapia in the modern headquarters of the Mexican Province of the Society of Jesus. "Cabeza del P. Gonzalo de Tapia, primer Martir y Fundador de las misiones de Sinaloa. Trasladó el P. Martín Palaez, Visitador de aquellas misiones," Museo Manuel Ignacio Perez Alonso, Provincia Mexicana de la Compañia de Jesús, Mexico City. Author's photo with permission of the Provincia Mexicana de la Compañia de Jesus.

wall hung gruesome portrayals of sixteen other Jesuit martyrs whose stories filled the history of the Jesuits between the time of Tapia in the sixteenth century and Pro in the twentieth. Most depicted the moment of each priest's murder at the hands of Native people in northern New Spain. Alongside these portrayals of their passions, large maps dramatized a different sort of sacrifice; Jesuit charts displayed the decades of missionary labor spent in exploring, describing, and colonizing the borderlands and its people. In the center of the room, underneath the wall of martyr portraits and maps, a table held an ornamental box that contained the remains of the eighteenth-century Jesuit missionary to the Tarahumara Franz Hermann Glandorf. His decorated ossuary rested alongside his dirty cassock and the worn-out soles of his shoes, which enjoyed the particular reputation of being magical because they had enabled him to travel far and long to rescue other souls.[9]

A combination of conference room, gallery, and museum, this space also operated as a private shrine to the Mexican Province's missionaries and martyrs. Strictly speaking, none of these priests were actually saints of the Roman Catholic Church, with the exception of Miguel Pro, who is a step away. In 1988, Pope John Paul II determined that Father Pro had died in hatred of the faith (*in odium fidei*), which officially designated him a martyr and cleared the path for his beatification.[10] Pro's story mapped easily into established expectations for Catholic martyrs. He had been executed by what the church judged to be an overweening government engaged in widespread persecution of Catholics and evincing clear animosity for the religion that Pro confessed. Demonstrating that the Society's other missionaries had been killed *"en odio de la fe"* had proven much more difficult, since they had died in the process of serving a powerful empire extending its colonial frontiers. Nevertheless, in his twentieth-century account of the Society's martyrdoms in New Spain, the French Jesuit Gerard Decorme connected Blessed Miguel Pro's modern sacrifice to this much longer history of suffering, featuring him as the crowning example of an epic story that marched from the 1566 murder of Father Pedro Martinez in Florida to the fifty-one priests from Sonora and Sinaloa who died during a grueling imprisonment, sea journey, and overland march during the Society's expulsion in 1768. From Decorme's perspective, the Jesuits had purchased their place in Mexico with their sweat and blood. Even their exile and suppression had not thwarted this continuous story of sacrificial labor.[11]

After allowing me to take it all in, Alejandro ushered me to a side room filled with hundreds of smaller relics, some of which were from prominent saints, translated to New Spain from Europe. Many of the items, though, were connected to the Society's unofficial saints, relics that had been gathered from its missions in northern New Spain. There were rosaries and *vitelas*, small sacred images retrieved from Father Hernando de Santarén and his seven "Companions." These missionaries had died in the Tepehuan uprising of 1616 in the Sierra Madre, but somebody had preserved these devotional items as tokens of their sacrifice. More prominently, two wooden boxes sat side by side with plates indicating that the chests contained the remains of fathers Julio Pascual and Manuel Martinez, who had perished in the 1632 rebellion of the Guazapares. Nearby, a broken chalice and monstrance lay strewn beside a stained vestment and stole, recovered from an unnamed mission that "had been raided by an Apache band in the 18th century."

Missions

What was it about these missionary martyrs that remained so enduring after more than four hundred years, making their portraits mirror those of the Society's generals? In their classic portrait of medieval hagiography *Saints and Society*, Donald Weinstein and Rudolph Bell made the ambitious claim that "wherever Christianity encountered a frontier, it had need of martyrs. Whether carrying the faith to infidel and heathen lands, combating the encroachments of kings and princes, or fighting heresy in Europe itself, martyrs there would be."[12] On the one hand, Weinstein and Bell were stating an obvious conclusion about the results of violent encounters in medieval Europe. On the other hand, the authors suggested something more: that Christian stories, relics, and remnants of faithful death did something. They proved socially and politically useful in justifying the conquest and pacification of frontiers. Spiritually, they secured the salvation of new nations, and practically, they fueled the expansion of Christendom.

Death occurred in the colonial Spanish borderlands for a variety of reasons, both mundane and unexpected. Like medieval Christians, however,

Jesuits in New Spain elevated particular missionary deaths into stories of holy sacrifice in order to render them meaningful and useful. Martyrdoms could transform ruinous moments of plague or revolt into mysterious signs of progress. They operated temporally to mitigate setbacks and ensure future salvation. They also worked spatially to bring Christendom into being, sacralizing Native territory with saintly blood. Passion stories, relics, maps, and portraits helped transform Indigenous spaces into Christian places in the European cultural imagination.[13] In this work, martyrdom joined several other naming rituals meant to convert pagan territories by "making the land holy." Like the orthographic practices that endowed Indigenous settlements and sacred places with the names of Catholic patron saints, martyr stories were part of what Daniel Reff has called an "extensive process of inscribing the American landscape with Christian symbols and meaning, rendering it both intelligible and tractable" to Iberian empires.[14] In similar fashion to the atlases, parades, gardens, and performances described by Patricia Seed in her study of "ceremonies of possession," martyrdom operated as a rhetoric and practice that laid claim to Native land and fueled imperial expansion. Missionary and convert suffering marked this space with Christian blood and set it apart as destined for conversion.

The account that follows builds upon this assertion to trace how Jesuits saw their civilizing and Christianizing work through the lens of a powerful agricultural metaphor. Although the imagery of Christian suffering as seed and convert salvation as fruit goes back to the early church, it developed new meaning in the context of the colonization of the Americas.[15] The agricultural metaphor supplied a logic of ultimate productivity even in the face of violent coercion and catastrophic setback. Seeds, weeds, water, fruit, and harvests variously captured stages of investment and return through which Catholic missionaries explained their own trials and Indigenous tribulations as ultimately redemptive. The idea that seeds must die and weeds must be choked out so that evangelism could bear fruit established a redemptive economy that helped priests explain the losses involved with Indigenous resistance or sickness as deposits in a spiritual system that would produce untold profits in the form of future conversion and further colonization.

In northern New Spain, this agrarian metaphor took on a more literal significance. The ultimate goal of the Jesuit missions was to bring semi-sedentary or what they considered "wandering peoples" into Christian civilization through agricultural cultivation and economic production.[16] In this sense, missionary sacrifice and Native suffering not only sowed new Christianity but extended the colonial frontier by appropriating lands inhabited by Indigenous people and repurposing them for European-style agriculture. Several scholars have tracked how gardening, farming, animal husbandry, and viticulture helped European settlers establish dominion over Indigenous territories.[17] In fact, the link between colonization and planting was so strong for English speakers that most of their early colonies were simply called "plantations," a name that survived in the American South in other, related formations.[18] In similar fashion, the preferred term for Jesuit missionary settlements was "reductions" (*reducciónes*).[19] Etymologically, the word referred to the act of convincing or leading back and could be used as a synonym for conversion, but also held the connotation of physical subjection and territorial reclamation.[20] Reduction entailed the clearing away of entangling Native places and practices in order to prepare the ground for evangelization. It also represented the subjection of Indigenous peoples to European religious, spatial, and civilizational practices. Therefore, for Jesuit missionaries in northern New Spain, evangelization was inherently linked to the reclamation of Native land through agrarian development. The Society's missions necessarily entailed the attempted dissolution of existing communal formations and relocation to newly constructed ranches and farms that would supposedly supply their needs and tutor them in the labor, laws, and languages of European colonial settlement.[21]

Blood

Even as Jesuits engaged in real agricultural production and civilizational education, they employed the imagery of "seeding" as an easily comprehensible allegory for colonization and evangelization. Together, pacified frontiers and spiritual conversion represented the twin fruits of their labor. In this story, everyday acts of sacrifice were construed as sweat and tears that watered both types of plants, building up Christendom and filling it with crops of new "Christianities." Similarly, missionary death and convert suffering were recast as seeds and water, bones and blood that enriched the ground and irrigated the fields of the Lord. As Father Antonio

Menéndez, the rector of the Mayo and Yaqui missions of Sonora, assured Father Eusebio Kino after the 1695 revolt of the O'odham and death of the missionary Father Javier Saeta, "It is a good sign, Father, that all those missions begin with the blood of a minister to cultivate it, since it is an indication of their perseverance and good stability."[22] For missionaries in northern New Spain, violent death and widespread disease were not just unfortunate side effects of their evangelistic project but essential deposits in a long-neglected land that would eventually reap harvests of settlement and salvation. Missions begin with blood.

Blood also birthed families. Paternalistic language worked alongside agricultural metaphor to explain the ultimate purpose of suffering and death. Jesuit fathers took Native children as their charges and replaced the authority of Indigenous elders, supplanting blood families with newly seeded spiritual communities. In his genealogy of blood in Christianity and the modern West, Gil Anidjar argues that hematological notions of blood, the idea that blood literally passed on human seed, lie at the heart of modern notions of religion, race, and kinship. Although blood suffuses discursive constructions of family and identity from Aristotle to Ancestry.com, blood as seed found particularly strong articulation in Spanish blood purity laws. *Limpieza de sangre*, or clean blood, established membership in the emerging imagined community of "Spain," and helped secure full rights as a member of its extended family.[23] As mobilized by the Holy Office of the Inquisition, notions of "unclean" blood, or non-Christian ancestry, became particularly associated with dangerous religious practice and the entangling weeds of heresy. Therefore, both *morisco* and *converso* communities represented ever-present threats to Spanish racial and religious communities, liable to taint the Spanish Catholic family with Muslim or Jewish blood.[24]

The Spanish Jesuits who dominated the missions of northern New Spain in its first century focused intently on the effects of this inheritance, worrying that "idolatrous" practices and debilitating vices had been passed down for centuries through blood, along with father's seed or mother's milk. For this reason, they focused their evangelistic efforts on children, hoping to mitigate these effects by early intervention. When disease and demographic collapse took especially heavy tolls on the elderly, missionaries celebrated it as an act of God that cut out the weeds of idolatry and sped a younger generation's embrace of their new fathers. They trusted that the suffering experienced by Native communities over the course of colonization, whether through epidemics or wars, would clear the ground in order to mitigate inherited difference and raise a purer form of Christianity.[25]

This discursive use of blood also speaks to the fraught relationship between suffering and cycles of violence. In an essay on modern suicide bombers, Talal Asad contends that idioms of redemptive death are foundational to the history of Christianity and ultimately Western liberal culture. For Asad, sacrificial death constitutes the necessary foundation for the West's capacity for violence and claim to territorial sovereignty. It also becomes the practice that distinguishes which lives count as fully human and are therefore worthy of saving and which are extinguishable. "Dying to give life" marks these cultural boundaries and authorizes the making of war. Though not exclusive to Christianity, this logic has proved powerful in the Christian West because the conviction that communal salvation requires individual sacrifice lies at the center of atonement theology. Asad argues, "In Christian civilization, the gift of life for humanity is possible only through a suicidal death; redemption is dependent on cruelty or at least on the sin of disregarding human life."[26] When extended to secular iterations of formerly sacred discourse, the critique addresses both the prejudice that somehow only Islam inspires suicidal death and the assumption that modernity has transcended the bloody martyrdoms that marked Christendom in the "Middle Ages." The impulse to ply redemptive meaning from pain pervaded the Christian imagination and still undergirds modern responses to violence.

These discursive strategies help to mark some violence as sacred and other acts as profane. Phillipe Buc has drawn an essential link between bloody sacrifice and bellicosity in the Christian and post-Christian West, from the acts of Maccabean zealots to the French Revolution, from Martin Luther to the American invasion of Iraq after 911. While making wide-ranging comparisons, he focused most closely on medieval Europe, demonstrating how narratives of persecution fueled pogroms and the crusades and set the stage for secular translations in various examples of contemporary genocide.[27] Instead of exceptional moments, Buc argued that tales of redemptive death lie at the root of the Christian capacity to make war, while the ability to mark some violence as sacred and other acts as diabolic constitutes a central method of separating civilized from savage, pure blood from unclean, and holy war from terror.[28]

A similar dynamic drove Iberian imperial expansion and evangelistic enterprises in North America. Practices of martyrdom helped missionaries, soldiers, and magistrates to translate conflict into terms that helped justify the expansion of New Spain's northern borders. At the same time, redemptive death consolidated an imagined Christendom in the minds of those who received their letters, histories, maps, paintings, and relics. These diverse productions were sent to religious superiors, royal overseers, Jesuit colleges, and lay patrons for a variety of reasons, including to support canonization and to explain rebellions. Together, they made the unifying claim that Native bodies, resources, and land would only be secured through the Society's sacrifices.

Beyond being a study of martyrs and their fellow missionaries or the uses to which their deaths were put, martyrdom here becomes a site for competing interpretations of reality, some of which allowed cosmic explanations to override immediate material and physical reasons for conflict. In addition to the deaths of specific priests at the hands of rebellious converts, this book takes up a sacrificial motif that permeated these sources. By tracking that logic, this study offers an explanation for violent confrontations and repositions debates over religious change to focus on space and practice. Jesuit martyr discourse had a symbiotic relation to the attempted conversion of Native peoples and the tranformation of their religious spaces and practices. What should have been the ultimate sign of loving service in the Christian tradition instead helped justify forceful cultural change, physical discipline, and military intervention. In turn, these acts begot further cycles of confrontation, revolt, and attempted reduction. Though not the first to employ sacrificial narratives to sanctify territorial contestation, early modern missionaries of the Society of Jesus mobilized their martyrdoms in a powerful way that ideologically empowered European global ambitions.

Suffering

Scholars of early Christianity have pointed to the central role of martyr discourse in the identity formation and disciplining of Christian communities.[29] Over two decades ago, Judith Perkins highlighted the techniques through which the church cultivated a "suffering self" as a way of connecting to marginalized groups and consolidating a persecuted identity. This suffering self, Perkins argued, paradoxically led to the "triumph of Christianity." She used the language of "triumph" intentionally, with reference to its specific Christian theological connotation.[30] As early as the Second Letter to the Corinthians, New Testament writers had connected apostolic suffering to Roman triumphal processions.[31] Drawing from the Roman practice of victory marches and parades, Christians flipped classical notions of conquest on their head by proclaiming their own deaths as triumphs, just as Christ had conquered through his crucifixion. St. Jerome's pronouncement, "The suffering of the martyrs is the triumph of God," captured this sensibility.[32] Eventually, the adjective "triumphant" came to refer theologically to the Christian dead, and the formal designation of "the Church Triumphant" referred to deceased saints.

In those foundational centuries, Perkins contended, textual representations of persecution "worked not simply to represent a realistic situation so much as to provide a self-definition that enabled the growth of Christianity as an institution."[33] Likewise, in her work on martyrdom and memory in early Christianity, Elizabeth Castelli has analyzed the real-world social contexts of "performing persecution" and unpacked what she called a politics of martyrdom. As Castelli explained, "Regardless of the historicity of the martyr's story, it is a story that can both make an ethical demand and lend legitimacy to other forms of power claims."[34] Several early martyr accounts like those of Peter, Paul, Ignatius, Polycarp, Perpetua, and the martyrs of Lyons variously displayed this conviction, each operating under the logic that Christian victory could come through their victimization and that stories of faithful death would form followers into a disciplined community.

Not everybody has embraced this portrayal of Christian passion stories as politically useful. Notably, the historian of early modern Europe Brad Gregory has argued that such an approach to understanding Christian martyrdom is woefully wrongheaded, obscuring historical difference with theoretical assumptions that are at best anachronistic. Writing about Protestant, Catholic, and Anabaptist martyrs in the sixteenth century, Gregory contended that most contemporary theoretical concerns smack of presentism and only impede us from truly understanding martyrs, the rulers who persecuted them, and the communities who celebrated them.[35] Gregory maintained that martyrs are particularly resistant to critical theory because they cannot be accused of merely "representing" themselves or masking ideologies in order to justify secondary motives. On the contrary, they actually gave up material comforts and political aspirations to die for the very doctrines they confessed. For Gregory, the idea that martyrs were "performing" only obscures the true reasons for their all-too-real sacrifices. When all parties involved, including opponents and proponents, agree that they are killing and dying over their beliefs in ultimate truths and objective reality, how can modern interpreters simply dismiss the martyrs' deaths as performative?

While disagreeing with overtly politicized readings of martyrdom, Gregory nevertheless recognized the social contexts of medieval and early modern passion stories and the devotional literature that shaped its development. He has helpfully charted how pious idioms like the *imitatio Christi* and *ars moriendi* sublimated an ancient ideal of sacrificial death into everyday piety in the Middle Ages. In turn, these practices prepared European believers to die for their salvation when the opportunity came in sixteenth-century wars of religion. At the same time, European missionaries increasingly found opportunity to die for their faith in Asia and colonial America. Allan Greer, Julia Boss, Emma Anderson, Carole Blackburn, Paul Perron, and Timothy Pearson, for example, have reexamined from ethnohistorical perspectives the stories of missionary deaths that punctuated and propelled the post-Tridentine expansion of the Roman Catholic Church in New France.[36] In diverging political, geographical, and temporal contexts, these authors make similar claims about the import of martyrdom in the history of Christianity. Mainly, Christian narratives of suffering and death cannot be extracted from lived realities to be read as devotional set pieces, but instead must be firmly situated in the political, social, and theological locations from which they emerged and traced to the communal contexts for which they were intended.[37]

Salvation

The case of missionary death on Spanish frontiers in the Americas affords a different context for analysis than early Christian persecution, early modern wars of religion, or religious orders in New France. The dozens of priests who died violently on the northern edge of New Spain occupied a more complicated space between imperial expansion and Indigenous rejoinder than did persecuted minorities within pagan Rome, competing

European confessions, or more mobile colleagues in Canada. One way of evidencing the distinctly messy position of colonial missionaries in New Spain is to note that not one of them has ever been canonized, while eight Jesuit missionaries killed in seventeenth-century Canada and New York were made saints in 1930.[38] Many more Catholic missionaries died violently in Spanish North America than in New France, but establishing that they died because of hatred of the faith has proved much more difficult. This is not for lack of hagiographical effort. Jesuits mounted several campaigns to advance the cause of their fallen coreligionists. The letters, reports, histories, and maps cited throughout this book represent the myriad ways that they attempted to establish the sanctity of their brothers.

Still, the only colonial missionary from New Spain ever to be canonized was the Franciscan Felipe de Jesus, who was martyred in Japan in 1597 along with twenty-five Japanese Christians and European missionaries.[39] The fact that he died in Asia under the persecution of a rival imperial state further confirms how the Ibero-American context differed from established martyrological expectations. Far from being persecuted by an emperor, Jesuit missionaries in the Americas served a powerful empire. As a part of the system of royal patronage, *patronato real*, they had been tasked with a multivalent project that involved "reducing" wandering peoples to settled spaces, "pacifying" warring tribes, "civilizing" them to European conceptions of time, language, and law, and "converting" them to the Catholic religion.[40] Ostensibly part of the same process, these twin goals inevitably conflicted, as a coercive approach to *reducción* always worked in tension with an avowed message of divine sacrifice and neighborly love. When Indigenous communities resisted forced resettlement, coerced labor, or restrictions on traditional practices, evangelists were made to parse whether their intended converts had rejected the religion itself or other aspects of colonization. In cases where resistance led to missionary death, hagiographers inevitably insisted that a diabolic rejection of Catholic faith had been the cause and came to embrace the language of martyrdom as a way of understanding their setbacks as paradoxical successes. Nevertheless, material concerns always lay behind these spiritual explanations.

We need not fully accept David Sweet's simplistic claim that European missionaries in Latin America were the "stalwart servants of the state religion of colonialism" to appreciate how the same men charged with pacifying Spain's colonial frontiers also positioned themselves as passive victims when faced with opposition.⁴¹ At the same time, the missionaries' motivations need not be undermined in order to interpret their rhetoric in light of colonial confrontations shaped by asymmetric power relations. Contrary to Brad Gregory's claim that "post-everything" critical theory only blinds interpreters to the motivations of the very martyrs they hope to explicate, this book argues that we cannot understand the missionaries who went out, prepared to give their lives for others, without exegeting the prevailing discourse on holy death that undergirded their aspirations.⁴² Fully understanding missionary beliefs about subjects like salvation, Native religion, conversion, and suffering provides a crucial foundation to interpret these motivations. However, to stop at this would be to tell less than half of the story. While missionaries drew on a long tradition in the history of Christianity as they positioned themselves as martyrs, they also used these Christian discourses of holy death as a means of securing their place in an ever-shifting colonial landscape. They turned to martyrological idioms to assuage doubts about the ultimate success of their efforts and justify sometimes brutal acts of violence. Whether defending themselves against critics, recruiting future missionaries, petitioning superiors, or confronting converts, missionaries found that winning would come through their wounding.

Borderlands

Historians of Latin American missions have long challenged earlier works that memorialized the sacrifices of heroic missionaries without engaging the troubling impact of their conquests, colonizations, and conversions on Native communities or accounting for Indigenous perspectives on these often-violent confrontations. In the context of northern New Spain, scholars have worked to overturn the dominant legacy of Herbert Bolton, the California historian who pioneered the field he called the "Spanish Borderlands." Bolton and several of his students famously hailed Jesuit missionaries like Gonzalo de Tapia and Eusebio Kino as men who sacrificed themselves to bring Christianity and civilization to New Spain's northern frontier and what became northern Mexico and the U.S. "Southwest."⁴³ In tune with larger patterns in social, cultural, and postcolonial historiography, some have urged fellow scholars to reject this older Boltonian program, "remove the missionaries from the center stage," and instead focus on once-obscured Native actors.⁴⁴ For decades now, ethnohistorians have risen to this challenge and mined missionary texts, colonial registers, archeological data, and modern ethnography to supply a rich and compelling account of how the region's Indigenous communities navigated their encounter with the Spaniards and European evangelists.⁴⁵

Several of these studies have crucially intervened to correct Bolton's presentation of what he called the "borderlands." David Weber's seminal treatment of the subject, *The Spanish Frontier in North America*, demonstrated how the older Boltonian school had never theorized the term and almost exclusively celebrated the borderlands as a space of Spanish civilizing work and institution building. Instead, Weber returned to the term "frontier," both because it more closely matched the Spanish cognate *frontera* and because it more honestly captured the substance of his focus upon Spanish attempts at colonization.⁴⁶ Richard White, Daniel Richter, and Kathleen Duval, among others, have demonstrated the great potential of beginning with powerful Native polities and conceptualizing European arrivals and incursions as marginal to more continuous Indigenous governance. For Juliana Barr, for example, the language of "borderlands" has too often assumed that European maps represented actual colonial settlement and occluded the defacto territorial dominance and firmly maintained borders of Indigenous people.⁴⁷

This book dialogues with the work of ethnohistorians who have centered Native communities and displaced older hagiographic accounts of Spanish civilizers and heroic missionaries. Without these studies, it would be impossible to understand how Native groups like the Purépecha, Yoeme, Yoreme, Chínipa, Guzapares, Rarámuri, Tegüima, Deve, Jova, O'odham, Guaycura, Cochimí, Pericú, and Inde worked inside and outside the Jesuit system.⁴⁸ As much as it relies upon this previous scholarship, however, the story that follows does not primarily center the experience of Native people and is not an ethnohistory. It does not purport to relate the events as they happened on the ground so much as the way incidents were packaged and made usable both spiritually and politically. It plums the theological convictions and epistemic assumptions that rationalized colonization and conversion in the minds of settlers, priests, and superiors.

Spotlighting Native actors by removing missionary celebrities from the stage has helpfully corrected an older historiography steeped in hagiography. However, because of the nature of the sources as well as the colonial situation itself, the evangelist cannot be extracted without creating another interpretive problem. How do we tell the history of colonialism without a critical rereading of rituals and practices that served to invent colonial authority?[49] As Pamela Klassen has argued in a meditation on Christian power, Indigenous sovereignty, and the invention of nations, "Colonial nation-states in the Americas depended on faith in the righteousness of their own political power." Klassen insisted that this wedding of imperial power with a conviction in religious virtue "depended on ongoing attempts through colonial laws and rituals to erase or deny many Indigenous sovereignties that claimed the land through stories, occupation, and regular patterns of movement."[50] As much as it operated as a ceremony of possession, martyrdom worked as a ritual of erasure, obscuring the material causes of suffering and rendering it salvific.

Missionary discourse needs to be thoroughly interrogated in order to reveal how it helped justify colonization and territorial appropriation in northern New Spain. This critical rereading of missionary sources provides what Linda Tuhiwai Smith has called a "genealogy of colonialism." By situating them in a longer history of Christian practice, it sets out to map and "locate a different sort of origin story, the origin of imperial policies and practices, the origins of imperial visions, the origins of ideas and values." Tuhiwai Smith has warned that we can no longer tell a "single narrative story of important white imperial figures, adventurers and heroes who fought their way through undiscovered lands to establish imperial rule and bring civilization and salvation to 'barbaric savages' who lived in utter degradation."[51] This book explains how missionaries attempted to do just this: tell a single narrative about their heroism, Native "savagery," and the ultimate sacrificial gift of civilization. It does so in order to reveal the ways in which that narrative lent cosmic import to quotidian confrontations and helped missionaries rationalize violence by imagining themselves to be victims.

In this way, *Missions Begin with Blood* supports the work of decolonization.[52] Without unpacking the discursive traditions that shaped colonial missionary sources, modern interpreters run the risk of missing the concerns that shaped the narratives and often end by repeating some of the sources' assumptions about the "authenticity" of conversion or motivations for rebellion. For example, some studies of Catholic missions have taken for granted colonial reports of revolts that emphasized the burning of churches, sacrilege of holy objects, and defilement of missionary bodies as obvious signs that Native communities rejected Catholicism in preference for older traditions.[53] This study explores, conversely, how Jesuits consistently emphasized the desecration of Catholic symbols in an effort to establish a canonical case for martyrdom. Since official Catholic doctrine demanded proof that perpetrators had killed "in hatred of the faith," missionary letters, histories, reports, encomiums, and *vidas* inevitably emphasized these acts in their accounts of missionary death.[54] This is not to say that churches were not burned and bodies were not defiled. However, a critical rereading means recognizing that canonical requirements demanded that those who wished to proclaim the priests as martyrs always highlighted these facts to demonstrate hatred for the Catholic religion as the primary cause of death. For this reason, they inevitably underreported and deemphasized more immediate material and physical causes or lumped them into the wider spiritual battle.

Better understanding the discourse of martyrdom promises to contextualize these accounts in ways that provide a more nuanced rendering of both Indigenous religious participation and resistance. The uprisings of the Acaxee in 1601 and O'odham in 1695 described in chapters 2 and 3 offer just two examples in which understanding the martyrological genre reveals religious practices that were more complicated than a story of wholesale conversion or outright rejection. That said, this study invokes the term "borderlands" not because it best captures the reality of Indigenous power on the ground but because it conveys the rhetorical and ritual sensibilities that shaped colonial discourse. The missionaries analyzed here believed that they lived and worked at the border between civilization and savagery, in lands caught between the kingdom of Christ and the dominion of Satan. These were imagined borderlands, spiritualized contact zones between Christians and "gentiles" where physical acts of confrontation took on cosmic significance. Throughout, Native communities directly contested European claims to their land and proved their own ongoing territorial power, despite the European maps, missionary reports, and natural histories that claimed them as pacified and incorporated.[55]

Though not strictly chronological, this study moves forward in time and northwest in space to unpack the European logic that the Spanish-Christian frontier was advancing. This narrative follows the expansion of

Jesuit evangelization into what they called northwest New Spain, including the provinces of Sinaloa, Nueva Vizcaya, Sonora, and California. It begins with the arrival of fathers Gonzalo de Tapia and Martín Pérez in the Villa de San Felipe de Sinaloa in 1591 and culminates with the Society's expulsion from the Viceroyalty in 1767–68. This mission commenced in the central valleys and coastal plains of Sinaloa, starting in Culiacán and moving northwest into the Sinaloa, Zuaque, Mayo, and Yaqui river basins during the late 1590s and early 1600s. These valleys and riverine tributaries were the home of ethnically and linguistically diverse people, including Mayo, Zuaque, Tehueco, Sinaloa, and Ahome groups who for a time settled into consolidated *reducciones* along the province's rivers. From these earliest efforts, the Jesuits turned slightly east as they moved up from these coastal valleys into the western edge of the Sierra Madres Occidentales. Beginning in 1600, new missionaries like Father Hernando de Santarén set out to "reduce" serrano people, including the Guazapare, Chínipas, Acaxee, and Tepehuan, attempting to coax them from difficult-to-access parts of the Sierra's ridges and ravines into lower, surveillable spaces near the region's expanding mining operations. Spurred by other mineral discoveries in Sonora and Nueva Viscaya in the mid-seventeenth century, the missions crept north into what became San Ildefonso de Ostimuri, a region of convergence between Sinaloa's lush river valleys, the Sierra's rugged mountains, and the Sonoran Desert to the north.[56]

Around the same time, other conversion efforts began further in Sonora, including work with the Yoeme (Yaqui), Ópata, Jova, Tegüima, and Eudeve. By the late seventeenth century, priests like Eusebio Kino and Juan Maria Salvatierra attempted to open up new operations in California and northern Sonora, an area Kino dubbed the "Pimería Alta," after the O'odham (Pima), whom he targeted for evangelization. The Akimel O'odham who lived near the desert's crucial rivers shared the region with the Tohono O'odham (Papago), Quechan (Yumans), and Pii-Paash (Maricopa), who lived between the San Pedro, Altar, Colorado, and Gila rivers in both Sonora and what today constitutes the U.S. state of Arizona. Shortly after Kino's movement into the Pimería Alta, the latest in several attempts to establish missions in the lower California peninsula finally took root under the supervision of Fathers Salvatierra and Piccolo in the late 1690s. By the mid-eighteenth century, Jesuits like Ignacio Keller, Jacobo Sedelmayr, Gaspar Stiger, Sigismundo Taraval, and Fernando

Consag explored further north and west in a final effort to prove the peninsularity of California and advocate for further missions into what is now the U.S. West.[57]

Although within the ostensible confines of the Spanish Viceroyalty of New Spain, these borderlands were, in fact, contested spaces, where cultural productions and living communities confronted each other in both violent and religiously creative ways.[58] As Cynthia Radding has argued in reference to these spaces, "Borderlands, like all regions, are produced historically through human labor and social practices, with specific ecological, cultural, economic, and political components."[59] Jesuit labor and missionary practice concentrated on the goal of *reducción* in the production of borderlands, convincing and sometimes coercing Indigenous communities to move from intentionally small and dispersed settlements called *rancherías* into larger, centralized "*conversiones*" or missions.[60] In this sense, conversion was always a physical, spatial, and ritual practice, as much as or more than doctrinal, judged by its success in cajoling Natives to move from *monte* to *mission*, from what Europeans considered wild spaces to places marked as civilized. However, any claim that these territories had become fully "Spanish" or "Christian" by the time of the Jesuit expulsion was always rhetorical. If anything, the territorial dominance of O'odham, Quechan, Maricopa, and diverse Apache bands established a functional border in the Sonoran Desert that was always elided by Jesuit maps. This Indigenous power on the ground only grew throughout the eighteenth and nineteenth centuries and strikingly corresponds to the Mexican-American national border as recognized today.

Sources

While this book features Jesuit interpretations of missionary death and convert suffering, religious perspectives were not the singular cause of conflict, nor are they the only sources presented here. Rather, missionaries (themselves quite diverse) were one group among many in a colonial situation replete with competing interests. Soldiers, settlers, and magistrates all had a stake in the rise and fall of the missions. Not all of these groups left the same sort of sources as the Jesuits, who kept superiors consistently updated and therefore have supplied modern scholars with diaries, letters, sermons, ledgers, histories, and maps, as well as cultural and geographic observations. Still, the soldiers involved in investigating and punishing rebels provided their own interpretations of missionary death, sometimes confirming the priests' accounts, but sometimes revealing key discrepancies.[61] In addition, after several Native rebellions, civil magistrates and religious superiors investigated their causes and results. Military diaries, governors' reports, settler histories, and letters from Jesuit rectors, visitors, provincials, and generals reflect crucial additions and sometimes corrections to the missionary letters, histories, and hagiographies that form the foundation of this analysis.

As is the case with most other colonial contexts, the sources for Indigenous perspectives are nowhere near as plentiful. In fact, with few exceptions virtually no surviving documents provide direct explanations of the causes, principal events, and results of their rebellions, let alone specific missionary deaths from Native perspectives. The voices that do survive are inevitably filtered through the lenses of Spanish-speaking translators, scribes, functionaries, soldiers, and missionaries with their own conscious and unconscious biases. Some of these documents have been read critically for what they reveal about Native actions and intentions. Similarly, post-rebellion investigations carried out by secular authorities supply testimonies from both Indigenous allies and captive rebels that sometimes confirm and at other points reveal telling differences from the priests' narratives. Any attempt to "read against the grain" in these texts requires a critical eye for the overall contexts, limitations, and purposes of both those who produced such material and those who collected them.[62] However, ethnohistorians like Daniel Reff, Maureen Ahern, Susan Deeds, and Cynthia Radding have demonstrated the remarkable details about Native communities that can be gleaned from Jesuit, secular, and civil sources. Sometimes the work entails not just reading between the lines but noting what is not in the lines at all, the work of marking silences that Marisa Fuentes has termed "reading along the bias grain."[63] Even when they are not mentioned or occluded, the presence of Indigenous people pervades the missionaries' preoccupations.

Missions Begin with Blood contributes to a growing body of literature about the Society of Jesus, globalization, and colonial encounters in the early modern period. It engages several recent works that have reevaluated previously essentialized notions of missionaries, whether as epic heroes or dastardly villains. This scholarship has begun to offer more complex portraits of Jesuit evangelists in New Spain, struggling for meaning in the midst of rapid change and moral ambivalence.[64] Likewise, new studies of global early modern Catholicism have tracked the transformation of Catholic spirituality and practice in the context of imperial expansion and intercultural encounter.[65] This book joins this conversation by focusing on how martyrdom became an orienting metaphor that helped New Spain's Jesuits make meaning from pain and legitimate their role in colonization.

Chapters

From the earliest years of the mission, Jesuit writers employed the agricultural metaphor to argue for the eventual fruitfulness of both Native and missionary suffering. Though not the first to utilize the imagery, the missionary, historian, and later provincial Andrés Pérez de Ribas invoked it throughout his *History of the Triumphs of Our Holy Faith Amongst the Most Barbarous and Fierce People of the New World*, a work that became the paradigm for many future interpretations of missionary death. Beginning with his account of the 1594 martyrdom of Gonzalo de Tapia in Sinaloa, he argued that, contrary to expectations, New Spain's missionaries had triumphed through their deaths. Pérez de Ribas drew upon earlier Jesuit hagiographers, like Juan de Albiçuri, to argue that missionary bodies were seeds that would one day bring harvests of Native conversions. Alongside the agricultural metaphor, these histories employed the language of cosmic battle. Seeding Christianity through apostolic labors would help reclaim the land from a diabolic lord who had long held sway. In turn, physical reduction, political loyalty, and diligent labor joined spiritual conversion as the first fruits of sacrificial seeding.

Martyrdom not only served as a site for competing interpretations of reality, but also incarnated confrontations latent in colonial encounters. Chapter 2 locates one source of conflict in the competing traditions of the holy dead as practiced by missionaries and Indigenous communities. Taking examples from Sinaloa, Durango, and Sonora, it examines the ironic convergences and predictable conflicts between Native and European treatments of sacred bones. These groups shared similar concerns to recover and revere the bodily remains of their deceased. Occasionally this led to mutual veneration of martyrs, as was the case when Tarascan Catholics requested relics from Father Tapia's body after his murder. Native communities had long valued human remains as potent spiritual objects. Ancestral bone bundles and corporeal war trophies acted as reservoirs of power and sites of cultural revitalization. However, because they were stored away in the rugged terrain outside of the riverine reductions, missionaries feared these sacred bundles and worried about what went on in the *"monte"* (wild). Jesuits depicted these places and practices as rocks, weeds, and thorns, to be mowed down to clear the ground for gospel seed. This conviction fueled brutal "idolatry" extirpation campaigns in the early 1600s that targeted Indigenous funerary bundles and led to the burning of Native bones in dramatic bonfires. In turn, extirpation occasioned new revolts and accompanying martyrs in the decades that ensued.

Chapter 3 charts a transition in martyrological discourse from the framework of cosmic war that characterized earlier histories of the sixteenth and seventeenth centuries to more practically oriented observations and natural histories of the eighteenth century. In contrast to these two orientations, Eusebio Kino's *Innocent, Apostolic, and Glorious Death of the Venerable Father Francisco Javier Saeta, S.J.* mixed trust in the spiritual fruit of martyrdom with realistic assessments of Spanish mistakes and missiological prescriptions for avoiding future conflict. Kino's work, unpublished in his time, set out to explain the killing of Father Javier Saeta and several Indigenous allies during the 1695 O'odham Revolt. When read as martyrdom, Saeta's death presented a practical problem, as it suggested that the O'odham had rejected Catholicism. Kino bridged this gap by arguing that Native Christians, like Saeta, were innocent victims of the diabolic "common enemy." However, he also explained that missionary neglect, military punishments, and rival Indigenous attacks had created an untenable situation that made their rebellion naturally comprehensible, even as it worked for the greater spiritual good. As illustrated in relics and maps, Saeta's martyrdom would produce diverse spiritual fruits and secure the advance of Christendom.

Chapter 4 introduces the rhetoric of "bloodless martyrdom," tracing the term from its roots in medieval spirituality to its application by Father Kino to his North American evangelistic labors. Likewise, Fathers Jacob Baegert and Lambert Hostell described their service in California as a desert exile. Although they were not privileged to die as red martyrs, they embraced this "prolonged" or "white" martyrdom of poverty, suffering, and seclusion. As missionaries moved into the deserts of Sonora and California, the aridity and isolation of the terrain inspired a rhetoric of dry sacrifice that drew upon the spirituality of ancient desert monastics. Some, like Father Lorenzo Carranco, nearly went crazy in the climate, attempting suicide to escape their trials in the wilderness. Nevertheless, hagiographers contended that Father Carranco was preserved from that fate so that he could obtain a full martyr's palm, enjoying a "wet" martyrdom alongside Father Nicolás Tamaral during the Pericú revolt in 1734. Others had to toil in daily exile, far from the families and homes that they had voluntarily renounced. Jesuits like Philip Segesser, Ignaz Pfefferkorn, and Marcos Burriel expressed envy of Carranco and Tamaral but found other ways of explaining their loss. Under pressure from rivals near and far, they used maps and natural histories to argue that their sacrificial labors, as much as their colleagues' deaths, had expanded frontiers and provided invaluable knowledge about North America's landscapes, wildlife, plants, climate, and people. While red martrydoms brought spiritual advances, their white martyrdoms brought scientific, economic, and political progress.

Chapter 5 presents the 1767 expulsion of the Society of Jesus from New Spain as a mirror reversal of this "prolonged martyrdom." While some Jesuits had obtained their reward during the mission, "*enterrados*" in the land of their sojourn, others found themselves "*desterrados*," uprooted from their evangelistic fields and spiritual families. From their later exile in Europe, Fathers Benno Ducrue, Joseph Och, Bernardo Middendorf, Jacob Baegert, and Jaime Mateu wrote natural histories and accounts of the expulsion that they hoped would provoke sympathy for their defeat, painting tearful scenes of Jesuit fathers ripped away from spiritual "children" and shocking moments of mass death during an overland march. Alongside tales of their own trials, they depicted diverse Indigenous communities as suffering, lamenting, resisting, and even dying out of love for their "fathers." These narratives of shared affliction helped exiled Jesuits assure themselves of the lasting value of their work and reconstitute their missionary identity in exile as grieving parents or worried shepherds. When Native Christians shed tears and even blood as they protested the Society's eviction, they seemingly completed the circle of suffering and salvation that had fueled this evangelistic enterprise.

While the expulsion ended the colonial Jesuit evangelistic progress, the rhetoric of redemptive suffering remained. The Epilogue considers how the 1966 discovery of the bones of Father Eusebio Kino revealed the staying power of sacrificial discourse. For promoters like Arizona senator Barry Goldwater, the Jesuit personified the values he hoped to spread from his home state to a national electorate. The story of a tireless rancher, rugged explorer, and successful entrepreneur not only suited Goldwater's libertarian ideals, but more broadly tied Arizona's white elites to a mythic Spanish past. Across the border, Mexican politicians expressed similar optimism about what finding Kino's bones portended. Federal and state leaders cast Kino as the prototypical civilizer, whose work had inaugurated a long process of rendering a savage frontier amenable for development. The power of this rhetoric culminated in 1974, when presidents Gerald Ford of the United States and Luis Echeverría of Mexico held their first international meeting by Kino's mausoleum in Magdalena de Kino and toasted the priest as the harbinger of prosperity and growth in the region. This was a white martyrdom translated into secular form, as they proclaimed that Jesuit missionary sacrifice still sowed the seeds of progress. To the Yaqui, O'odham, and other Indigenous communities who have called the region home since well before Kino's arrival, this legacy evokes something more complex, a difficult mixture of respect for the missionary who brought Christianity and sorrow at the Spanish, Mexican, and American civilizing projects that have caused environmental, physical, and cultural challenges ever since his arrival.

Bones

Like those of Father Kino, Gonzalo de Tapia's bones had been repurposed from their colonial origins for a new cause in the twentieth century. When I encountered them in that backroom of the Mexican Jesuit Provincial headquarters in 2014, I knew some of this history. The earliest reports of their preservation coincided with the account written upon the note I saw under the skull. They stated that Tapia's colleague Father Visitor Martín Pelaez had brought the relics back to the Jesuit college in Mexico City in 1595. Some recorded that part of the skull had been sent, along with his right arm, to Tapia's hometown of León, Spain, in 1622, where it was welcomed by his family and other devotees with a holy procession before being placed in the city's Jesuit church.[66]

Perhaps like the Society itself, the relic had returned across the Atlantic before its restoration to the Americas, but there were also other provenances. According to these, Jesuit superiors charged Father Manuel Piñan in 1906 with traveling to the north and recovering the remains of Tapia as well as those of fathers Pascual and Martinez, who had been killed in the Guazapare uprising of 1632. Father Piñan claimed to have found both Tapia and the Guazapare martyrs' respective burial sites in 1907.[67] He brought back the remains of Pascual and Martinez in reliquary boxes but reported they were missing their skulls. In the headquarters' reliquary, I found a small note attached to a leather pouch labeled "pieces of the martyrs' bones." It confirmed that Father Piñan had located the remains near Conicari, Sinaloa, and brought them, along with other relics, back to Mexico City. Conversely, Piñan could not find Tapia's body but did locate a piece of the cranium. When the priest compared it with the relic recovered by Palaez in 1595, he concluded that it fit perfectly.[68]

Others offered an even more fantastic tale of how the larger piece brought by Palaez had been preserved during the Society's expulsion and other persecutions. The Catholic magazine *Mensajero del Sagrado Corazón* relayed the story of the relic being discovered in a Mexico City convent in 1900. According to this tradition, a sister in the *Casa de las Religiosas de la Compañia de Maria* heard strange sounds coming from a corner room near her own. Since it was located beside a busy street, she first thought the sounds came from wagons, but the noises persisted throughout the night. One evening, the nun reported that something in the wall kept speaking to her "like strange voices from the other world."[69] When she told her superioress in the morning, they decided to call in a stonemason. With the sister's guidance, he removed parts of the wall until he found a hollow chamber containing a decorated box. Surprised, the mother superior then summoned the Jesuit father Laureano Veres Acevedo to come to inspect the container. With everybody gathered around, Father Acevedo opened it up and discovered four pieces enfolded in silk and fine cloth. Unwrapping the object, Acevedo purportedly found the top of the skull and another portion of a human tibia. They also saw a note, which read, "Cabeza del P. Gonzalo d Tapia, Primer Martyr y Fundador de las Misiones de

Sinaloa."[70] If these tales were to be believed, these were the disparate, somewhat conflicting journeys of the martyr's bones.

These relics, however, stood in stark juxtaposition to those of Blessed Miguel Pro. Pro was a single twentieth-century example amidst dozens of sixteenth-, seventeenth-, and eighteenth-century subjects who did not enjoy official recognition or popular devotion and had mostly been forgotten. The prerestoration Jesuit martyrs of New Spain have at various times had their cases promoted but have fallen far short of wider veneration or canonical recognition. Nor were these bones like those of Kino, which had been unearthed by international scholars and the Mexican government and mobilized for regional development, national myth-making, and cross-border cooperation. Rather, the province venerated these in a private and less formal sense, cherishing them as embodiments of a collective sacrificial identity they had cultivated over centuries. Their memories and material remains were placed here to remind modern priests of their legacy and frame their current labors in light of this longer history. Whether returned from Spain, retrieved from Sinaloa, or discovered in a Mexico City convent, the pieces had somehow found their way back into the Society's hands, and now they rested in the Province's small, unadvertised museum on the south side of Mexico City. The blood-stained relics served only a private cause. Far from public memorialization or official veneration, the unofficial martyrs could still remind contemporary Jesuits of their long history in the country and assure them that whatever the suffering, God would use it for good, procuring the salvation of Mexico's people and securing the missionaries' place in that land.

1   Seeds
Planting Conversions

Gonzalo de Tapia arrived in Mexico City in October of 1584. He was a young Spanish scholastic who had only recently completed his education in the colleges and seminaries of the Society of Jesus. Tapia spent most of that initial year in New Spain learning its most widely spoken Indigenous language, Nahuatl, and teaching metaphysics. When he turned twenty-three, he took his priestly vows, which he could only complete once he had reached the canonical age for ordination.[1] During this year, his superiors recognized his intellectual gifts, and New Spain's provincial Antonio de Mendoza inquired whether he would like to study for a doctorate of theology. Tapia balked at this suggestion, explaining that "the only reason why I left my home and family, why I put Spain behind me, was my desire to save the souls of the Natives of these Indies, and to convert them from their idolatries."[2] Relenting, Mendoza agreed to send him west of Mexico City to the Jesuit College in Pátzcuaro, Michoacán, where he could join their ongoing work with Purépecha (Tarascan) communities.

Priests from the Society of Jesus had gone to Pátzcuaro in 1577, just one year after they had arrived in New Spain. Over the next few years, they had started a few churches, begun external missions, and founded a college. In these initial years, the sons of several elite Tarascans had undertaken a Spanish education at Pátzcuaro's Jesuit college, and some had even joined the Society as lay brothers.[3] Father Tapia arrived to this solid beginning in September of 1585, shortly after his ordination to the priesthood. While acquiring a working knowledge of Tarascan at Pátzcuaro's college, he also set out to the surrounding countryside on regular preaching excursions. According to the fellow missionary and historian Andrés Pérez de Ribas, these tours earned Tapia the reputation for linguistic skill, persuasive preaching, and the rigorous enforcement of Catholic practice. At the same time, superiors recognized what they called "a quick temper," rashness, and a melancholic streak that accompanied his evangelistic skills. The rector of Pátzcuaro, Father Francisco de Ramirez, noted Tapia's many abilities but worried about these signs of immaturity and decided to remove him from his preaching mission. In 1586, Ramirez sent Tapia to the nearby Spanish city of Valladolid to complete his tertianship, a capstone year of vocational discernment and spiritual training based upon Ignatius of Loyola's *Spiritual Exercises*, the Jesuit Constitutions, and other meditations on moral and aesthetic theology.[4]

This time of seasoning must have served its purpose, because by 1587 Tapia found himself back in Pátzcuaro, again charged with an external mission to Michoacán's rural Purépecha settlements. This time, the priest quickly gained a name for reduction, "restoring fugitives to their pueblos, which thereby became peaceful and well-populated."[5] In Pérez de Ribas's later retelling, this skill in "reducing" Indigenous converts from the "monte" to the mission engendered a mix of fear and devotion among Purépecha Catholics. Some purportedly marveled at the priest's disregard for his own life, but others bristled at his strict ways. From the perspective of his Jesuit superiors, however, Tapia was becoming exactly the sort of frontier missionary New Spain needed. Despite his earlier tempestuousness, the young priest seemed to uniquely combine intelligence, piety, and an entrepreneurial spirit. For this reason, they agreed in 1589 with his request to leave Michoacán and pioneer a new work among "the wild Chíchimecos" that lived to the northeast near the mining town of San Luis de la Paz, Zacatecas.[6]

The term "Chichimeco/a" was a precontact word that Nahuatl speakers of the central valley of Mexico had used to describe rival groups that moved through the more mountainous regions to Mexico's near north. Spaniards adopted it and gradually applied "Chichimeca" to a wide variety of Indigenous groups that they considered to be irreducible and therefore "barbarian."[7] In the case of Tapia's mission, he had been tasked with ministering to Otomí who lived in rugged climes around San Luis de la Paz. The first step in that mission would mean "pacifying" them after years of conflict and convincing them to settle near San Luis so that they could be Christianized and hopefully utilized to work in the mines. Just as in Michoacán, Tapia's superiors appreciated his abilities, claiming that he not only rapidly learned the Otomí language but quickly succeeded in "reducing" and converting them. The young priest was gaining wider notoriety as a man who converted Natives and opened frontiers.

Confident in his growing skills and bowing to Tapia's restlessness, his supervisors again selected him for a new frontier mission. In 1591, they sent him along with Father Martín Pérez on a journey of hundreds of miles to the northwest to begin a new field in the nascent province of Sinaloa.[8] The Society had been tasked by the governor of Nueva Viscaya with reducing Sinaloa's Natives for the purpose of settling the frontier with ranches and working in the region's newly established mines. Under the system of *patronato real* (royal patronage), the priests would be funded by the crown and put to work in the dual purpose of civilizing and Christianizing these Indigenous communities in preparation for their role as ranch hands and mining laborers.[9]

Tapia embraced this mission and continued his practice of vigorously enforcing Catholic moral practice in the process of *reducción*. He immediately prohibited plural marriage and determined to end what he called *borracheras* (drunken frenzies), his derisive term for seasonal feasts and clandestine gatherings celebrated by the Cáhita-speaking people that he and Pérez had induced to settle along the Sinaloa and Zuaque rivers.[10] The later hagiographer Father Juan de Albiçuri, a fellow missionary in Sinaloa, celebrated Tapia's moral rigor in this pursuit. Albiçuri boasted about how the priest "had taken away the customs and habits of these nations and separated them from the pleasures and entertainments that they had nursed upon since infancy."[11] By Albiçuri's account, the Sinaloans' lack of Christian morality was not inherent, but had been handed down through the teaching of their elders and imparted like mother's milk. For this reason, Tapia was convinced that with the right discipline, he could wean away the younger generation from these imparted "idolatries."

In light of this attempt to separate children from their parents, Sinaloan elders increasingly resisted Tapia's and Pérez's evangelization. Their simmering anger came to a boil in 1594, when an older shaman from the Zuaque town of Tovoropa named Nacabeba began to directly oppose their methods. Nacabeba reportedly argued that the Jesuits' sacraments had been the source of recent diseases and that Tapia had alienated Sinaloans from the ways of their ancestors. In particular, Nacabeba objected to the priests' use of baptism and insistence that adult men take only one wife. Using the occasion of the seasonal *mitotes* (ritual dances) to spread his message, the shaman pledged that if the residents of Tovoropa returned to their former ways, they would not only enjoy their earlier freedoms but be fully restored to health.¹² Nacabeba's message highlighted the ways in which both missionary discipline and European diseases had stressed the community and provoked a moment of crisis.

Father Albiçuri argued for another cause, however, contending that "the old men in particular would not be moved from their pure anger, because the hatred that they had for the Catholic faith was most great."¹³ The Jesuit hagiographer concluded that, rather than a response to epidemic sickness or strained social relationships, animosity for the Christian religion was the real source of their rage. According to him, Tapia took Sinaloa resistance as a matter of proving the power of his faith. Hearing word of Nacabeba's opposition, the missionary went to the *alcalde mayor* of the nearby village of San Felipe, Captain Miguel Maldanado, and asked him to make an example of the elder for the sake of protecting the new conversions.¹⁴ At the priest's request, Captain Maldanado ordered the capture of Nacabeba and after investigation ordered him flogged. Contrary to their expectations, however, this did not stop the agitation, but only steeled the elder's resolve, as he began to call for the priest's murder.

On July 11, Nacabeba and seven others decided to act. Albiçuri maintained that the group initially showed friendship as they entered Tapia's hut. Once Nacabeba had gained confidence, though, he struck the missionary over the head with a war club, or *macana*. According to the Jesuit letters and histories that related the ensuing events, Tapia did not die immediately, but rather remained alive long enough to give several displays of piety.¹⁵ Albiçuri recounted how the priest left his hut, and "seeing himself mortally injured, bathed completely in his own blood, went outside to the patio and called to his God with the sweetest dialogues and tender breaths that could emerge from the depths of his heart." Beyond speaking with his god, Tapia "turned to his very murderers and asked them, 'What is this, my children? What wrong have I done you?'" Nacabeba and his men let the query go unanswered, indicating that the priest who had ordered his flogging, ended their feasts, disciplined their sexuality, and tempted their children should have a decent idea about the source of their discontent.

Albiçuri's narrative nevertheless insisted on a pious reading of Tapia's death. "Seeing that his life was coming to an end, he straightened up and opened his arms wide. Then, he reached for a cross on the ground, intent to die embracing that most holy insignia of our redemption."¹⁶ However,

Tapia was unable to reach the cross, as "the barbarians filled his body with innumerable arrows and a second time fell upon him with strikes from their macanas." Nevertheless, the priest reportedly persisted in his full identification with Christ. Albiçuri described how "the most stalwart Martyr of Christ, struggling still in his final agony and anguish of death and seeing that he could not get to his beloved Cross, instead excellently formed another Cross with the first fingers of his right hand, the index and thumb." The hagiographer interpreted this detail as a sign of Tapia's greater mission as a soldier for Christ, explaining that he expired as "he raised his right arm to heaven in a sign of victory and died under such a glorious standard to bring his sovereign mysteries to the blind gentiles."[17]

With this event in mind, Albiçuri depicted Tapia signing the cross on the frontpiece to his *Historia*. Along with a martyr's palm, a heavenly crown, and surrounding scenes of Christ's crucifixion, the image sealed the pioneering missionary's connection to his savior (Figure 2). In ensuing accounts of Tapia's death, other hagiographers reveled in this detail. They repeated over and over how the protomartyr had perished while signing the cross with his right arm in the air, one of several proofs that he had not died for nothing but instead seeded the gospel in this land with his body and purchased its conversion with his blood.

Seed

Instead of adjusting their missionary method to these moments of violent resistance, Jesuit writers doubled down on their belief in the fruitfulness of both Native and missionary suffering. Though not the first to use the imagery, the Jesuit missionaries and historians Juan de Albiçuri and Andrés Pérez de Ribas employed this agricultural metaphor throughout their accounts of the early missions in this region. Albiçuri's 1633 *Historia de las Misiones Apostólicas* and Andrés Pérez de Ribas's 1645 *Historia de los Triumphos de Nuestra Santa Fe* both featured Jesuit martyrdom and Indigenous suffering as essential precursors that would advance the frontier of Christendom. While Albiçuri's text remained unpublished, it was a key source for Pérez de Ribas's *History of the Triumphs*, which subsequently became the paradigm for most future interpretations of missionary martyrdom in the Viceroyalty.[18] Especially in their description of Gonzalo de Tapia's death in 1594, Albiçuri and Pérez de Ribas agreed that New Spain's

FIGURE 2. Gonzalo de Tapia receives his martyr's crown and palm, surrounded by depictions of the crucifixion of Christ. "Gonzalvus de Tapia, Soc. Iesu, Cinaloa in Mexico pro Christi fide obstruncatus, io. Jul. 1594," Abraham van Merlen, Frontispiece for Juan de Albiçuri, *Historia de las misiones apostolicas que los clerigos regulares de la Compañia de Jesus an echo en las Indias occidentales del Reyno de la Nueva Vizcaya y vida y martyrio del P. Gonzalo de Tápia fundador de las dichas missiones y apostol de Cynaloas, Bamupa*, Mexico, 1633, M-M 7, Hubert Howe Bancroft Collection, Bancroft Library (BL), University of California, Berkeley, courtesy of the BL.

evangelists had triumphed through their deaths. Even as Tapia laid down his life, his body acted as seed and his blood as water that would one day bring harvests of Sinaloan conversions despite present resistance. This helped Jesuit interpreters convert the meaning of missionary deaths from a symptom of obvious setbacks to a sign of imminent success. Instead of grappling with the possible material, social, and political roots of Indigenous resentment of Tapia's methods or the harsh reality of epidemic disease, these writers insisted upon a martyrological claim that Native communities had rebelled because they simply hated Christ.

For centuries Christian writers had invoked agricultural symbols to explain the peculiar relationship between suffering and salvation. This genealogy traced all the way back to patristic writers like Tertullian and Jerome and before that to the synoptic gospels and Pauline epistles. At its root, the seed metaphor proclaimed a mysterious logic hidden inside the shell of violent death. It asserted that even when some intended evil for Christians, God inevitably repurposed their pain for his own plans. Longsuffering missions—especially when they entailed illness, exhaustion, and death—sowed the kernel of salvation and planted Christianity in Native hearts. Indigenous loyalty, sickness, sorrow, and other "cases of edification" provided seed as well. Far from causing them to question their vocation, Jesuits like Juan de Albiçuri and Andrés Pérez de Ribas configured disaster, disease, and death as crucial foundations for conversion. Patient endurance of these trials served as an example to both Native observers and European readers. Likewise, their eventual ascent to heaven transformed them into spiritual patrons who would intercede on the mission's behalf. Together, the first fruits of sacrificed missionaries and suffering converts should not raise concern, but rather portend harvests of spiritual transformation, physical reduction, and political submission.

Agrarian symbols drawn from early Christianity helped explain the enigmatic idea of growth through death. Gospel writers, for instance, had employed this imagery to extol the church's progress in the first two Christian centuries. For example, the Gospel of John relayed how Jesus told his disciples, "Very truly, I tell you, unless a grain of wheat falls into the earth and dies, it remains just a single grain; but if it dies, it bears much fruit."[19] In these words, early Christians provided an explanation for their losses rooted in the example of their lord. While Jesus's crucifixion had appeared to be an end, they understood it to be the beginning of the much larger movement. From this single originating death, a multiplying effect would ensure exponential success in the future. Beyond the gospels, this conviction had roots in both Jewish and Greek connections between sacrifice and fertility rituals of the ancient Mediterranean. Several diverse cultures had developed close analogies between physical seeding and rituals of blood. These rites differed according to time and place but shared a common logic that insisted upon a reciprocal relationship between death and life, blood and blessing, seed and fruit.[20] Blake Leyerle has argued that rituals of blood sacrifice drew upon Jewish, Latin, and African notions of spiritual control, ethnic solidarity, and gendered power. These fertility cults asserted an emblematic correspondence of bodies to seed and blood to water.[21]

While building upon this shared sensibility, early Christians began to develop a particularly strong sacrificial identity.[22] Scholars of late antiquity have argued that they applied these ritual idioms to their own persecution at the hands of the Roman Empire and thereby transformed the meaning of their pain by insisting on its productivity.[23] What was the cross if not a symbol that a single death brought life to many? Likewise, Jesus's disciples' misery would gain significance as it multiplied membership. This growth came on earth as the martyrs' example spoke to new converts, but it also filled the stores of heaven with holy patrons who would intercede for the faithful. By the second century, the idea that Christian suffering and death could expand the church by shaming enemies and securing celestial intercessors had become a powerful way of understanding intermittent persecution.[24] While perhaps less radical than the North African church father Tertullian, many early Christians agreed that "the blood of Christians was the seed of the Church."[25] Sacrifice had become essential to the survival of Christianity.

As much as these earlier traditions explained the persecution of Christians at the hands of the Roman Empire, their immediate applicability to early modern Catholic missionaries presented a challenge. When the emperor Constantine granted toleration to Christianity after the Edict of Milan in 313 CE and Theodosius I established it as the authorized religion of the Roman Empire in 380 CE, Christianity eventually transitioned from a place of marginality and persecution at the edge of empire to wielding authority within it. For this reason, bishops like Ambrose of Milan and Augustine of Hippo were left to reinterpret how to imitate Christ in the context of imperial power.[26] In response to the changed situation, Augustine paired the early Christian language of seeding to a universalist vision of Christian expansion that described the spread of "the seed of Abraham" to all nations through the pairing of evangelistic and political power. The bishop employed a providential logic that trusted that ancient promises to Abraham had been realized in the death of Christ, brought to fruition through the conversion of Rome, and would be gradually fulfilled through the sacrificial labors of the church.[27]

Working with this interpretation, several medieval theologians employed the language of evangelistic seeding to explain their confidence in the expansion of Christian community to all nations.[28] In this context, the "seed of Abraham" became particularly associated with blood, with intersecting connections to kinship, nation, and race. For theologians like Isidore of Seville, the seed that was passed down through blood established consanguinity in a way that linked Christian belonging with political and biological kinship that made them distinct from surrounding Muslims and Jews in medieval Iberia. As Gil Anidjar has argued, this connection of seeding translated ancient notions of kinship to early modern conceptions of Christendom as a racial and political project. In the Middle Ages, an older notion of a mystical body of Christ that would grow spiritually was transformed into a physical notion of seeding through blood, which Anidjar maintains related to "the Eucharist cult and the dissemination of bleeding relics." In this way, the concept of a "community of blood," spread by Christian seed, moved beyond the early church's trust in cosmic triumph to materially based notions of Christendom that closely linked racial identity, state formation, and religious kinship. For Anidjar, the community of blood "no longer signified the *invisible* body of Christ mysteriously found in the sacrament and distinct from other, material, bodies, but rather embodied in the visible members (flesh and blood) of the community."[29] Blood had become central to understanding the constitution of Christendom as well as the borders it constituted with others.

The belief in the advance of Christianity through evangelistic seeding relied upon both this newly exclusive sense of blood as physical community and the older sense that the spiritual kingdom would be expanded through suffering. Both became central to Jesuit self-conception after the order's founding in the 1530s. In his comparative study of early modern Jesuit evangelism, Luke Clossey has argued that the language of seeds, crops, fruits, and harvesting became so prevalent in the Society's missions that it eventually constituted the foundational set of images they employed to talk about their role in global Christian expansion.[30] In some missionary contexts, the metaphor worked directly along the lines of the ancient pattern, where rulers in India, China, or Japan were imagined as oppressive emperors, persecuting comparatively impotent Christian minorities. For those who served in Asia, the notion that missionaries might die powerless at the hand of a ruler directly fit Tertullian's formulation and took on a spiritual meaning beyond the hope of political expansion. Conforming to canonical prohibitions on martyr-seeking, sixteenth-century Jesuit missionaries to Asia were urged to avoid death and do nothing rash to provoke the ire of rulers, whom they ideally would convert along Constantinian models. Although they would have opportunities, martyrdom should be a last resort.[31]

In the case of colonial North America, however, the structures of power were usually reversed. Catholic missionaries found themselves in the position of being "apostles of empire," charged with both converting Indigenous people and advancing colonial frontiers. Recollect and Jesuit missionaries in New France, for instance, appealed to the idea that suffering seeded future salvation as a part of an imperial evangelistic project tasked with securing alliances and guaranteeing access to Indigenous resources. As time went on, the joining of Christian evangelism to French nationalism only grew stronger.[32] And yet, as Emma Anderson has made clear, martyrdom became a way to proclaim victory even when conversions failed or frontiers faltered.[33]

This predicament was not exclusive to Catholic missionaries. In New England, Puritans who once considered themselves elect precisely because they were persecuted had to articulate a new approach to Tertullian's maxim once they gained the mechanisms of government. The colonists who had founded Plymouth and Massachusetts Bay with a strong sense of their own suffering sainthood almost immediately reconfigured martyrdom as a way of explaining challenges from dissenters, Quakers, "witches," and diverse Indigenous communities.[34] Remarkably, the sacrificial idioms proved malleable enough to adjust to new relationships to power in these other North American contexts.

For Catholic evangelists in Spanish America, however, the contrast between the Christian language of oppression and actual authority was even stronger than New France or New England. While wielding control within Massachusetts Bay, Puritans still could imagine themselves surrounded and besieged by rival Catholics to the north, Anglicans to the south and east, Quakers to the west, and "heretics" from within the colony itself. Jesuits, however, served the Iberian monarchs as a part of the system of royal patronage of the church known as *patronato real*.[35] They ostensibly worked alongside colonists and soldiers to induce Indigenous people into colonial settlements and compel their labor into agricultural production. This differed from New France because the Jesuits of Canada were not charged with creating *reducciónes* that depended upon Native work for economic survival. Even mission communities like the Mohawk Catholic settlement of Kahnawake did not require Native coercive labor but were funded by European support. As Allan Greer has argued in his comparison of Native converts in French and Iberian Jesuit missions, "In Canada, unlike the Spanish empire, Indians owed no tribute payments and they had no labor-service obligations." In contrast to New France, "the impulse to secure and exploit Indigenous labor power was central to Iberian colonization of the New World, but it played only a minor part in the French North American empire."[36] Since they were not engaged in these comprehensive settlements and extractive projects, French evangelists did not aspire to the same wide-ranging cultural transformation that marked Latin American reductions. Based on these differences, Greer has concluded that Jesuits in Latin America were much more directly implicated in "violent compulsion" and maintaining a "disciplinary regime" than their northern counterparts. In turn, they had an even murkier claim on a persecuted identity.

Missionaries in New Spain nevertheless embraced the agricultural metaphor as a way to make sense of violent encounters. Far from striking them as incongruous with earlier Christian suffering or other global settings, the Ibero-American context facilitated a transposition in which they understood martyrdom to be essential to colonization. They imagined themselves not primarily as imperial agents, but as suffering servants who laid down their lives in the hope of birthing new members into the family of Christendom. Through this lens, rebellions and missionary death were not interpreted as rejections of the colonial project, but as essential deposits in the land in which Indigenous Christianities would eventually flourish. Likewise, when the Natives of Sinaloa, Sonora, Durango, and Baja California died from epidemic disease, coercive labor, internecine warfare, and colonial reprisal, they partipated in a providential process that would eventually produce settled frontiers and Christianized Natives.[37]

War

Andrés Pérez de Ribas first served as a missionary in northern New Spain in the early 1600s, but had become the provincial, the Society's superior in New Spain, by the early 1640s. In that role he collected letters, histories, passion stories, and other reports sent by frontier priests to the Society's headquarters in Mexico City. Throughout his 764-page *History of the Triumphs*, Pérez de Ribas drew upon these sources extensively to illustrate to European Jesuit readers and their patrons how evangelistic travails actually guaranteed spiritual triumph. His goal was to assure novices in the Society's colleges, superiors in Rome, and sympathetic lay patrons that even though the missionaries of New Spain experienced pain, the mission was prevailing.

The *History of the Triumphs* became a paradigm and source for several ensuing works of Jesuit historiography, including Eusebio Kino's *Favores Celestiales*, José Neumann's *Historia de las rebeliones en la Sierra Tarahumara*, Matthias Tanner's *Societas Jesu usque ad sanguinis et vitae profusionem militans in Europa, Africa, Asia, et America*, Francisco Javier Alegre's *Historia de la Compañia de Jesus en Nueva España*, and most other histories of the Jesuit mission in New Spain.[38] Pérez de Ribas therefore set in place the main thematic features of ensuing studies. For example, his *Historia* established martyrs, relics, and stories of Native piety as central motifs; they were the trophies won in an ongoing cosmic war. In the introduction, he explained that the "Triumphs" in his title referred back to Saint Jerome's dictum "*Triumphus Dei est martyrum passio*," or "The Triumph of God is the suffering of martyrs."[39] Jerome's epigram harkened back to the Apostle Paul's vivid invocation of Roman triumphal procession imagery, which had paradoxically compared Christian suffering to Roman conquest. Citing Paul, Jerome argued that "blood poured out for the name of Christ" (*pro Christi nomine cruoris effusio*) was the only true mark of the apostolic gospel and a sure path to spiritual victory. The Jesuit agreed with the fourth-century exegete that "the martyrdoms of saints" are not the defeats that they seem to be, but instead "triumphs of God and apostolic victories."[40] With both phrases Pérez de Ribas related New Spain's missions to a long Christian history, arguing that Jesuit deaths were sure proof of both the apostolic nature of their work and their advance in a cosmic battle with Satan.

Well before Jerome, martial metaphors punctuated Jewish and Christian discourses on martyrdom. Already in the second-century-BCE account of the Maccabean Revolt called 2 Maccabees, Jewish writers presented stoic death at the hands of oppressors as a spiritual victory over pagan idolatry.[41] Similarly, in his description of Jewish resistance to Rome during Vespasian and Titus's assault on Jerusalem around 70 CE, the historian Josephus portrayed defeated revolutionaries as nevertheless triumphant over the Roman Empire through their willing martyrdom at Masada.[42] After the destruction of the temple, rabbinic Jewish literature and Christian fathers like Ambrose compared and contrasted their communities' martyrdoms to both mark identity and demonstrate their respective triumphs over Rome.[43] Working in this long tradition, Eusebius of Caesarea likened faithful death to cosmic warfare, explaining how even though "the adversary assailed us with his whole strength," the second-century-CE martyrs of Lyons waged war upon the devil with their sacrifice. When the tale of their holy deaths was written and shared with other Christians, its meaning expanded. In retelling, these passion accounts trained followers for similar pursuits and prepared the church for "future movements" to reclaim ground from the evil one.[44]

Pérez de Ribas tapped into these interpretive traditions, in which fathers like Jerome and Eusebius compared martyrdom to militaristic exploit, heroic sacrifice, and celestial battle against pagan and diabolic forces.[45] Tertullian made the martial connection explicit, explaining that "it is quite true that it is our desire to suffer, but it is in the way that the soldier longs for war." Insisting that Christians "conquered through dying," the bishop of Carthage repurposed imagery from the Roman circus spectacle to describe the cosmic spoils reaped from the martyrs' battle.[46] Tertullian drew upon this connection with Roman imperial conquest and argued that shed blood brought spiritual victory, cosmic regeneration, ethnic solidarity, and masculine virility to the Christian movement. Once more, he maintained that Christians triumphed over the empire's idolatry by refusing to eat meat sacrificed to pagan deities and instead offered up their own bodies in a "battle for the truth" of the resurrection of the flesh.[47] As was the case for Jews with 2 Maccabees, the rejection of "pagan idolatry" became intimately tied to the confrontational nature of Christian martyr literature. Sacrificial death constituted an integral advance in a broader war on paganism.

Just as martyrdom became Tertullian's ultimate weapon in the combat against idolatry, Jesuits in northern Mexico recognized an intimate, violent link between their own sufferings and their battle against Native religion.[48] When ancient martyrs died, they not only imitated Jesus's suffering but eventually achieved political and territorial gains through the gradual conversion of the empire. The Society's missionaries emphasized these same themes as they considered their task in northern New Spain. This cosmic contest with Satan over souls and territory pervaded Pérez de Ribas's work.[49] Just as Tertullian presented martyrs as soldiers, "a *militia Christi* whose 'storm troops' (*agonistici*) were formed in the fight against Satan," the Jesuit provincial extolled the "heroic deeds" of his fellow "soldiers of Christ's militia."[50] Slain missionaries were not victims but heroes who spilled their blood to conquer spiritual strongholds and redeem captives. Pérez de Ribas further explained, "These men labored in their apostolic ministry and spiritual conquests to free the souls that God had redeemed with His blood and to destroy the fortresses where the devil held them captive." He connected this warfare not to their direct aggressions, but to their dying passions. "These valiant soldiers spilled their blood at the hands of infidels for preaching the Gospel in these enterprises and missions."[51] While some may have deemed them disastrous, he cast rebellions and death as advances in the cosmic battle for territory.

In one of the most explicit summaries of his history's overall goal, Pérez de Ribas explained how these paradoxical successes worked. He did so through comparison with the Society's other mission fields. Revealing the inherently competitive nature of Jesuit recruiting, New Spain's provincial argued that the mission had triumphed despite the difficulty of the land and its people: "The Principal intention of the manifesto . . . has been to make known how thoroughly evangelical preaching has accomplished its goal among these people, no matter how fierce and barbarous they might be." Even though some may judge North America to be an inferior assignment compared to Europe or Asia, Pérez de Ribas insisted that its soil was equally fertile to other lands. "The goal is to show that these conquests are just as successful and abundant in spiritual fruit as those carried out in those nations of the world that are of greater renown and more illustrious and noble."⁵² By the logic of Christian martyrdom, he argued that northern New Spain presented better grounds for success precisely because it offered more opportunity for misery.⁵³ As he went on to recount numerous examples of Native rebellions, sickness, opposition, and death, Pérez de Ribas understood why potential recruits might balk at working in such a dangerous place. Nevertheless, he hoped to convince Jesuit novices that their sacrifice would be worth the cost.

With this in mind, he insisted that working with people Jesuits considered "savage" merited consideration equal to cultures that they considered more "civilized," like China, Japan, and India.⁵⁴ He argued that the comparative "barbarity" of his missions by no means diminished their glory. Instead, the difficulty of the task made it all the more worthy. Because conditions were more challenging in the Americas than in Europe, Asia, or the ancient world, Jesuit missionaries could reap even more bountiful crops. In this way, *The History of the Triumphs* was a comparative work—one that operated under the assumption that readers had deep familiarity with both ancient and contemporary examples of missionary success.⁵⁵ Pérez de Ribas was convinced that these comparisons gave reason for optimism in New Spain and invoked parallels to biblical and medieval examples to assure his readers that all evangelistic work had costs. This longer view of the established pattern of Christian history should be kept in mind, he maintained, when considering the meaning of colonial violence. From the time of Jesus and the apostles to early modern wars of religion, the Catholic faith had always grown through suffering. Rather than allow laborious journeys or Indigenous uprisings to deter their work, the Society's members should welcome such challenges as an essential part of the divine plan.

From this perspective, Pérez de Ribas concluded that the entire Jesuit mission was an unremitting martyrdom, inaugurated with blood and dependent on ongoing acts of sacrifice for its continued success.⁵⁶ In this way martyrdom became a prime metaphor for all mission work. In an opening dedication to the king of Spain, Philip IV, the provincial explained that while some "courageous preachers of the Gospel ended their lives in such a glorious labor," others who were "currently employed in that labor are none too free of danger."⁵⁷ Still, he explained that his title referred to both types of missionaries, because "both groups have nevertheless achieved very glorious triumphs." These victories, he assured the king, would help secure lands full of silver, oceans with pearls, and people "reduced to the evangelical law."[58] The extension of the Spanish Empire and the rule of Christendom would begin with blood and depend upon sweat.

This conviction structured the entire book. Beginning with his eulogy for Gonzalo de Tapia, Pérez de Ribas paired praise for red martyrs like Tapia with encomiums for "white martyrs" like his companion Pedro Méndez. From there, he alternated each chapter between dramatic stories of "red" gruesome deaths and tales of long-suffering "white" ascetic lives.[59] He explained that this rotating method would provide for the occidental Indies what others had done for "the Indies of the east," giving a full account of apostolic labors in Spanish North America. Even as they competed with rival religious orders and educational institutions for vocations, Jesuits internally vied for recruits with the Society's other evangelistic theaters. Tales and images of suffering helped forge an imagined community of martyrs that united the Society across global theaters. At the same time, they worked polemically to help a provincial establish the relative value of his region vis-à-vis other locations.[60]

Still, Pérez de Ribas made clear that the prospect of red martyrdom was not the only reason Jesuit novices should consider New Spain. Surely, some chosen few of "Jesus's soldiers" had the blessing of "being killed by poisoned arrows or having their heads split open by a *macana* and then being eaten by them." Many others, though, suffered extended passions as "they traveled through the dry and terrible wilderness without any water, or through dense and thorny thickets, or through swamps and burning sand dunes, thirsting for the welfare of these souls."[61] This constant sacrifice should be expected as intrinsic to their vocation, because, he explained,

> It is an illustrious vow taken by the sons of the Company of Jesus, who are well instructed by so many of their holy brothers that when the time comes to give their lives for the profession of that glorious name and the aid of souls, which He redeemed with His blood, they spare no labor, danger, torment, or life until [they have] attained such a noble and glorious objective.[62]

While a death in hatred of the faith might be the idealized culmination of a Jesuit's training, one could never arrive at that end except through daily acts of self-denial expended in the evangelistic cause.

Soil

To establish his case, Pérez de Ribas pointed to New Testament stories of difficulty and adversity that were followed by eventual success. As a prime example, he noted how even "the Apostle to the Gentiles, Saint Paul" had endured "great hardships and dangers for the salvation of souls," risking all to beget spiritual progeny. Quoting from Paul's Second Letter to Timothy and First Letter to the Corinthians, Pérez de Ribas mixed metaphors of tribulation and reproduction to make his case. He explained that the Pauline model proved that those who endured hardship or sometimes death for the sake of the gospel would both secure their own salvation and birth many spiritual children.[63]

In distinction from Paul, however, Pérez de Ribas contended that the opportunity to exchange one's single life for otherworldly progeny was greater in New Spain than it had been in Greece. To be sure, some highly civilized Greeks, like Dionysius the Areopagite, immediately converted and became "very precious fruit," but most elites had mocked the apostle's preaching. Like hard ground, they had resisted the seed of the gospel. From the Pauline example, the Jesuit drew two points of "special solace for the ministers who labor in these nations," one about perspective and the other about potential. First, painful challenges should not be judged for their immediate impact, but rather for their future payoff. Second, more "cultivated civilizations" like Japan, India, and China inevitably yielded less fruit because they lacked the right soil to receive the seed. They had become hardened with their own wisdom, in his opinion. While the Americas might be filled with vines of superstition and weeds of idolatry, once these had been cleared new missionaries would find the soil rich and receptive.

Pérez de Ribas insisted that this pattern had continued to his own time. He pointed out the many obstacles described in medieval hagiographies like the *Golden Legend*, which had become common Jesuit reading through the publication of Father Pedro de Ribadeneyra's widely read 1601 edition of the *Flos Sanctorum*, or *Flower of the Saints*.[64] The lessons he drew from these passion stories and saints' lives were multiple. First, he argued that missionaries should not worry about their present lack of success, for "the fruit of the salvation of these souls should not be measured only in terms of the present harvest." Rather, missionaries should regard resistance simply as neglected soil that would yield itself to cultivation after persistent toiling. The conversion of Europe's barbarians in the Middle Ages should inspire the Society's early modern global evangelism. The particular difficulty of working with "barbarous people" was not the root cause of their lack of productivity, for "even in populous, civilized, and wise nations this fruit seems limited." Instead, the obstacle was the newness of working such difficult ground, and success was simply a matter of time.

As an example, Pérez de Ribas pointed to Santiago (St. James), the martyr and patron of Spain. According to him, Santiago had deposited the seed of the gospel in Iberia during the first century but saw few conversions in his own time. Nevertheless, the small kernel of his preaching and the water of his heroic death eventually had yielded inestimable harvests for "hundreds of years in both the old and new Spains and throughout the entire New World." For his faithfulness, Santiago had been crowned in heaven "with the heroic fruit harvested by Spanish Catholics" and thereby had obtained eternal glory as not only the first sower of the gospel in Spain, but through it the entire world.[65] As the examples of Paul and James illustrated, evangelists had to take a long-term view when looking for the fruit of their labors. They must trust in both typological patterns of the past and the celestial gardener who would superintend the growth well into the future.

In addition, Pérez de Ribas reminded his readers that neither Paul nor James waited for perfect conditions. Rather, they started boldly and let the seed fall where it may. To illustrate the point, he pointed to Jesus's Parable of the Sower as an encouragement toward tireless evangelism. The moral of the parable seemed clear. Some seed might be trampled and some devoured by wild animals; some would fall amongst rocks while other kernels might be choked out by weeds. Nevertheless, if the sowers kept at it, the right grains would eventually find good soil and yield up to a hundredfold.[66] This lesson meant that they should not judge the ground ahead of time. Instead, they should welcome such challenges as inherent to the task.

Likewise, Paul had explained that the wise of the world had deemed their message foolish, but that God had chosen the weak to shame the strong.[67] Pérez de Ribas saw this as descriptive of the North American mission, as it may appear foolish, but would be used to shame the wise. Paul's embodiment of this maxim as recorded in the Acts of the Apostles should console Jesuits who worried that their planting would be wasted in such barren lands. The apostle had not only gone to the rich and powerful, but had also reached out to the humble, even women who worked on the shores of a river, trusting that "the few grains he sowed would produce and yield fruit by the hundreds if they fell on good soil."[68] Good soil could be found in surprising locales, and missionaries could look to the Parable of the Sower and Paul's work for confidence in the ultimate fruit of their work.

In all of these cases, the provincial insisted that even though the conditions might not seem as good as those encountered in places like Judea and Greece in the ancient world, Spain in the Middle Ages, or China in their own time, early modern evangelists sent to New Spain would reap a harvest that was equally "successful and abundant in spiritual fruit" if they were willing to make appropriate sacrifices. In fact, this land offered the best chance of martyrdom and, through that, future conversion, because "among these barbarous nations one still finds crowns of blood shed for Christ and His Gospel and unspeakable toil suffered for His glory."[69] Invoking the metaphor of soil and seed helped explain this momentary suffering and its crucial role in securing Indigenous salvation.

After building the biblical and historical case, Pérez de Ribas applied the logic to northern New Spain, citing personal experience. Speaking of his own evangelistic work among Ahome in Sinaloa, he contended that he actually had found very good soil. He celebrated his relatively good reception and how quickly his "gentle children" learned their *doctrinas* (catechism), songs, and prayers and received "the rebirth in Christ through the water of baptism." His work had grown so quickly, Pérez de Ribas explained, because he found the Ahome pliable, loving, and receptive.

For this good fortune, he took no credit. Instead, he praised the earlier work of an unnamed "blind Christian Indian" from Guasave who tilled the soil before the priest's arrival in each town. Because this Indigenous catechist had gone before him, his sowing seemed easy. At the same time, he contended that the Ahome converts deserved credit, "because divine seed fell on such good soil, the Ahome by nature being pliant, it yielded the abundant fruit that has been discussed." In addition, since they were already living near a river and had developed their own agricultural practices, they had reportedly adjusted to mission life and labor with little resistance.[70] Pérez de Ribas repeatedly described similar scenes in which the kernels of his evangelical instruction found rich ground and quickly sprouted up.[71] The Ahome represented the ideal situation in which evangelists found their hoped-for conversions quickly and easily, while Native assistants willingly joined their cause and prepared the ground.

Nevertheless, the provincial maintained that seed could still sprout from more difficult soil as long as it was softened by the irrigation of blood, sweat, and tears. This conviction allows Indigenous sickness, death, and revolts not primarily as human tragedies but as necessary precursors to eventual salvation. On the one hand, the deceased seeded the ground as they avoided earthly anguish and found their way directly into eternity. On the other hand, the survivors would help cultivate a budding Christianity. These stories of Indigenous suffering served as what Pérez de Ribas termed "Cases of Edification," examples of patient endurance meant to teach the spiritual lessons to Jesuit novices in Europe.

Invoking this logic, Pérez de Ribas argued that children who had been orphaned by epidemics presented a providential opportunity. As evidence, he cited the example of Father Pedro Méndez, Tapia's companion in founding the Sinaloa mission. Faced with a spreading epidemic, Méndez focused his preaching and sacraments on vulnerable elders in hopes that he could rescue them for eternity. "He satisfied himself by winning many of them over in the final moments of their lives." From this perspective, Father Méndez's efforts had freed these older adults from eternal damnation just at the crucial moment. However, the provincial contended that the blessing was doubled because God had left "the youth to be reared as the seed of the Gospel, which produced more abundant fruit."[72] While Méndez had worked with adults to rescue them from judgment, their untimely deaths also presented the Jesuits with the opportunity of raising up Indigenous children without the influence of an older generation attached to hindering customs. Without these obstacles, missionaries would find the ground more amenable to evangelistic cultivation.

Water

In addition to "edifying cases" of Native suffering, Pérez de Ribas placed graphic accounts of missionary martyrdom at the end of each book in the *History of the Triumphs*. The paradigm for all of the narratives was New Spain's protomartyr Father Gonzalo de Tapia. Careful not to overreach by claiming Tapia as a saint before the Holy See had placed its official seal of approval, the Jesuit provincial nevertheless went as far as he could in extolling Tapia's wondrous works, both in life and death.[73] Relying on *Cartas Annuas* and relations from companion missionaries like Father Martín Pérez, he extolled Tapia's physical purity, chastity, and mortification as well as his extensive learning. By his reckoning, Tapia had mastered Latin in Europe and later six Indigenous languages in New Spain. Building upon these linguistic accomplishments, the priest had pioneered new missions, reportedly converting thousands through his scrupulous preaching and pious life.[74]

In his account, Pérez de Ribas also relied extensively upon an earlier unpublished manuscript by fellow missionary Juan de Albiçuri. Albiçuri's 1633 *Historia de las misiones Apostólicas* reported extensively on Tapia's work in restraining idolatry, drunken feasts, and other "vices" in Sinaloa. Albiçuri presented his mission history alongside an extended account of Tapia's life and death, dedicating the second half of his unpublished *Historia* to providing a narrative of the life and "discourse on the martyrdom of the Holy [sic] Father Gonzalo de Tapia." Throughout, the historian worked to present Tapia as a saint, emphasizing how his pious virtues had prepared him for sacrificial labors and holy death. Sometimes his zeal to celebrate Tapia's piety got the best of him and, like Pérez de Ribas, Albiçuri had to curb his enthusiasm. He likely had crossed out the word "*Sancto*" (Holy) in the manuscript's title in anticipation of Inquisitorial censorship.[75] Still, he drove home the point that Tapia lived a life of great holiness and died for hatred of the faith as he confronted Indigenous "sins." Especially as his account became a source for Pérez de Ribas and later Jesuit martyrologists like Mathias Tanner, Albiçuri invoked several hagiographic tropes that would establish the pattern for future passion stories in northern New Spain.

The first specific theme Albiçuri highlighted was Tapia's renunciation of his home and future in Europe. The hagiographer insisted that from the moment of his birth in 1561, Gonzalo de Tapia had been different than most of his aristocratic family in León, Spain. While his father, uncles, and brothers had distinguished themselves as soldiers who earned a noble title by fighting for King Phillip II, young Gonzalo had determined from an early age to fight instead for a divine ruler. In 1571, he entered a Jesuit college at ten years old. Two years later, the adolescent played a key role in rescuing three Jesuit fathers from their captivity in a Calvinist prison in France, paying their ransom with part of his inheritance.[76] This sacrificial act presaged his own vocation, Albiçuri maintained, because at sixteen Tapia would enter the Jesuit college at León and take his first vows in 1578. Seven years later he pledged himself to the priesthood.

Although he was immediately offered several high positions by the very priests he had once rescued, Tapia turned these opportunities down in pursuit of a mission in the Indies.[77] Whereas his ancestors and brothers had achieved fame in war, "the most Blessed Father Gonzalo de Tapia" had the better part because he "would be an Honor to his country and the first of the Company to shed his blessed blood on the ground of New Spain." This, Albiçuri concluded, would lead to more enduring fruit because Tapia "fertilized that land with his precious relics."[78] His family had gained renown for fighting and dying for their homeland; Gonzalo would give his blood and bones to enrich the ground of New Spain. This trope of renouncing family and opportunity for the sake of dying in a faraway land both conformed to earlier patterns and modeled the rhetoric of "white martyrdom" for future Jesuits in Spanish North America. It presented martyrdom as both the ultimate goal of the mission and the metaphor that situated their more quotidian sacrifices.

Albiçuri combined the theme of renunciation with agricultural metaphors in his descriptions of Tapia's life, work, and death. He likened key moments in the missionary's life to seeds, flowers, water, fertilizer, fruit, and harvests. In describing the young boy's early habits of piety, goodwill, love, humility, and zeal, the historian called them the "seed of virtue that later yielded a most copious harvest."[79] This summary sketched the long arc that in Albiçuri's eyes linked the child's holy upbringing with the eventual conversions brought through his work and martyrdom. There were, however, several crucial stages along the way to that fate. In adolescence, Tapia's "heart inclined to the church," and yet he would never reach old age because he would be "cut off by death like a flower." As he entered into the Society of Jesus, the "variety of virtues" he had cultivated as a young man began to "shine like the crop that was harvested in that flowering paradise," and "his soul was transformed by the perfection of Religious life."[80] Later, his martyr's death would make him into "the flower of spring" and become a special noble title, even better than the worldly patrimony he had inherited from his family.[81] From his noble birth and his pious childhood to his religious formation and prolific evangelism, Tapia had forged himself into a flower of Christ, Albiçuri contended, and would produce untold fruits when he was ultimately cut down.

Albiçuri worked to fit Tapia's death into this redemptive framework by suggesting that he had died because of his devout life and faithful preaching. He argued that these traits elicited jealousy from Indigenous elders and invoked a hagiographic trope that Native men hated missionaries. To be sure, Tapia threatened several aspects of their social structure and attempted to replace the influence of male elders. For mature men, the missionaries' specific focus on eradicating plural marriage posed signicant threats, because they typically occupied a higher status and had differential access to both wives and material goods.[82] Martial prowess was also a path to social status. The Cahíta-speaking communities along the Fuerte and Sinaloa rivers had developed practices of redistribution that centered on seasonal feasts and dancing. Since these *mitotes* also served as opportunities to develop martial skill and establish social rank through regulated contests, their prohibition threatened the status of warriors. When the Jesuits proscribed these occasional ritual celebrations, they only increased group tensions and undermined traditional social practices that had facilitated communal life.[83]

Albiçuri, however, traced the correlation between Tapia's prohibitions and growing Indigenous resentment strictly in terms of faith, explaining that as the missionary took away the stumbling block of "many women and making them content with one, as well as rigorously suppressing their drunken feasts and eating human flesh," the elders increasingly refused to participate in the mission. As much as his pastoral work focused intensely upon eliminating supposed polygamy, inebriation, feasts, and cannibalism, it inevitably provoked opposition. In addition to these prohibitions, the imposition of a Christian temporal and spatial regime further raised tensions because "it seemed to them insufferable to come to church at the sound of the bell which called them to doctrine."[84] Tapia's strict enforcement of this program engendered violent reactions.

Instead of condemning his evangelistic methods for their failure, however, Jesuit writers celebrated them as a model. Albiçuri contended that Indigenous communities "attributed so many hardships to Gonzalo de Tapia and made him the object of so much blame." He nevertheless interpreted this fact as a testament to Tapia's piety, courage, and fidelity to his missionary calling. The priest was simply "the first who introduced in those lands that New Law so contrary to their pleasures and savage habits." Rather than highlight the disastrous results, Albiçuri used these stories to demonstrate Native inflexibility, because they "desired nothing else but to drink his blood to satisfy their hatred." From this point of view, the priest was not a zealot who provoked resistance through harsh discipline, but an example of faithful commitment to Indigenous salvation.[85]

Albiçuri also situated the confrontation in a longer arc of sacrificially obeying God. The father had insisted on conformity as an act of paternal charity, because "the priest of Christ had become accustomed to facing similar dangers, taking advantage of the occasion that God had offered him to give his life for his love." Out of concern for canonical requirements, Albiçuri carefully stipulated that the missionary did not go out of his way to find danger "in his desire for martyrdom." To have pursued that fate directly would have necessarily disqualified him from its rewards. Rather, he died because of the "great fervor that arose to defend the party of God and sow his word, which is free and untethered from human fears."[86] By Albiçuri's account, Tapia's exacting enforcement of Catholic moral practice was all part of his sacrificial labor to sow gospel seed.

In life, Tapia's labors culminated in his martyrdom, but Jesuits believed his relics performed greater miracles postmortem. Both Albiçuri and Pérez der Ribas argued that his bones played a crucial role in bringing Sinaloans and Zauque out of their "barbarous customs."[87] In his blow-by-blow description of the missionary's demise, Pérez de Ribas particularly emphasized his killers' purported cannibalism, detailing how they severed the father's left arm and unsuccessfully attempted to roast it. Along with the father's fingers remaining unbreakably locked in the sign of the cross, he highlighted the perseverance of the father's flesh against the flames as a sure sign of Tapia's saintliness. Though dead, his body continued to testify.

As the Zauque celebrations proceeded, however, the perpetrators skinned the arm, stuffed it to the fingertips, donned the priest's black robes, and then "drank wine from the skull of that holy head."[88] While some might take this as a crafty inversal of Catholic sacrament and insistence on Indigenous feasting, Pérez de Ribas stuck with his providential reading. He interpreted the bodily desecration, along with other "dances, drunkenness, and superstitions," as "very clear indications of the motives of the devil and his ministers for taking the life of such a saintly man."[89]

The use of his clothes and body to reenact the Mass, now incorporated into their mitote, indicates a very clear rejection of Tapia's attempted discipline. For Jesuit martyrologists, however, it demonstrated that the Zauque hated the Catholic faith, making a mockery of its sacraments, images, and acts of piety.

In Pérez de Ribas's estimation, even these most gruesome of moments only furthered the Christian cause in Sinaloa. He claimed that the father's decapitation and desecration had actually continued his aim of eliminating vices, because it had the "marvelous effect" of ending drunken celebrations in the province of Sinaloa.[90] He attributed the cessation not to the dead missionary's bold preaching, but instead to the martyr's bodily presence. Tapia's skull had wrought the change "because they used it to drink the wine for their inebriation." Pérez de Ribas explained that, in the midst of their "pagan" celebrations, the Zauque came to a miraculous conviction of sin regarding the murder and their alcoholic revelries. Subsequently, "The blessed skull extinguished and did away with that pernicious and evil vice, and if it was this vice that took the priest's life, then he took its life [in return]."[91] What he could not accomplish in life, Tapia evidently achieved in death, completing the conversion of the Zauque.

In extolling the relics' powers of persuasion, Pérez de Ribas pointed to another key issue. He believed that a chief goal of Jesuit evangelization should be the extirpation of "idolatrous" practices. As such, missionary deaths would be worth the cost if they succeeded in "extinguish[ing] and [doing] away with pernicious and evil vices."[92] He argued that the meaning ultimately transcended the standoff between Tapia and the Zauque because "the devil understood that if he did not stem the course of the Gospel, he would soon be stripped of all the souls in Sinaloa." The later historian framed the confrontations in Sinaloa in cosmic terms. Satan had "realized that Father Gonzalo de Tapia, as captain of the conquest, was the principal person waging war against him. Therefore, he fired all his shots at the priest. It seemed to him that with Father Tapia dead, all the soldiers who accompanied him would lose heart."[93] Pérez de Ribas concluded that "the infernal demon" had hoped to destroy all the churches, altars, and crosses of the "true God" and ensnare Sinaloans once again with drink, dances, and idolatry "until he carried them off to hell." Interpreting the violence as a Manichean battle between God and the Devil helped Jesuits confirm the apostolicity of their mission and bring increased urgency to evangelistic encounters.[94] At the same time, it translated Tapia's

First Fruits

Albiçuri forwarded similar themes in his introduction to his relation of Tapia's martyrdom. The priest's death made sense, he wrote, only insofar as it seeded the gospel in New Spain and watered the ground for future missions. He emphasized this by bestowing several titles and encomiums upon Tapia, "this illustrious man, the First Fruits of the Martyrs that the Society of Jesus has in these Indies of New Spain, the founder and Father of its Apostolic Missions, which to him are owed love and perpetual reverence, as its most pious Patron."[95] Tapia's twin roles as "Founder" and "First Fruits of the Martyrs" meant that he would forever be a heavenly patron that interceded on behalf of all future missions of northern New Spain.

In addition to his role as founder and patron, Tapia's relics had prepared the ground for all future evangelization "because he was the first that preached Jesus Christ and first to water its ground with his blood." Albiçuri argued that the martyr's blood had not only irrigated the soil but combined with his bones to enrich it and prepare it for cultivation. The hagiographer continued, "His precious relics fertilized the earth in such a way that what before had been a closed forest of infidelity, he exchanged (*la trocó*) for a paradise of delights that produced miraculous plants of perfect Christians." His sacrifice had reclaimed the land from its diabolic lord, converting it from a forest of superstition to a garden of delights. This "exchange" lay at the heart of the Jesuit logic of martyrdom. Only through suffering could diabolic forests transform into sacred plants. The sweat of his labors had cleared the ground, while his bones had enriched the soil and his blood had watered the field. Because of his sacrifice, later priests would find this land ready for cultivation. For this reason, to Father Tapia was "owed the growth of such a notable Christianity that these parts have experienced." Not only his death but his strict life would act as an "example that awakens the strength of spirit of his children and successors to attempt the enterprises which they venture and strengthen their arms to complete the work they have begun." Meanwhile, his venerated relics would continue to operate in the extirpation of Native "vices and idolatry."[96]

A few decades later, the German martyrologist Matthias Tanner took up this narrative, featuring Tapia's life and passion as the first and foundational martyrdom in New Spain. Tanner's 1675 account of global Jesuit sacrifice, *Societas Jesu usque ad sanguinis et vitae profusionem militans in Europa, Africa, Asia, et America*, argued that Tapia's combination of an elite background along with his aggressive evangelism and violent demise all exemplified the missionary ideal. The very title of the book, *The Society of Jesus Doing Battle unto the Shedding of Blood and Life in Europe, Africa, Asia, and America*, makes this point clear; the Jesuits were engaged in a cosmic war in which only their martyrdoms would secure victory.[97]

Tanner paired his account of New Spain's protomartyr with a vivid engraving by Karel Škréta (Figure 3). Škréta was an accomplished Baroque painter who had been raised Protestant but converted to Catholicism under the influence of German Jesuits during the height of the Thirty Years War.[98] The engraving not only depicted Tapia's death and decapitation in gory detail but illustrated the deposit of the Jesuit's body and blood in Native ground. At the same time, the severed head and arm would transform into the relics that would inspire future generations. Image paired with narrative and relic to provide a multisensory effect on those who might see, read, and sometimes touch the protomartyr, all of which would ensure other Jesuits that whatever they might give in the missionary endeavor would surely be worth the cost.

Pérez de Ribas similarly argued that the missionary's blood had watered the new Christianity. "Even though this adverse event and the persecution of that primitive Church were a temporary setback, the land bore fruit in time. It was watered with the blood of this apostolic man who so desired the spread of Christ's glory in Sinaloa."[99] This was true for the "bloodstained relics" that Tapia had carried with him from Europe as well. Along with his own body, the priest's cherished saints, the Virgin, and crucifixes had been recovered from the site of his murder in 1594 and venerated as powerful relics. Together, they testified to the missions' ongoing prosperity because his blood would continue to elicit prayers for its flourishing.

In a similar manner, he continued, the ongoing work of Father Méndez, who had survived the uprising, would water what Tapia had planted. Like the account of Tapia's renunciation and dramatic dialogue in death, the trope of twinned sacrifice became a pattern for all subsequent accounts

P. Gundisalvus de Tapia S. I. illustri stemmate in Hispania natus, pro Fide Christi necatus in Mexico A. 1594. 10 Iulij

C. Screta del. Melchior Küsell f.

los cervósque venerantur, nē satis noceant: at venatum profecti, aquilam colunt: & ad bella prodeuntes, novaculam è silice adorant, nè siliceæ sagittarum cuspides obtundantur. Nudi semper incedunt, tenuissimis cinctorijs & floccis sola verenda contecti. Et tamen hæc tam barbara natio, primò omnium à P. Gundisalvo excoli cœpta, ac postmodum à pluribus Socijs Evangelio subacta, tam secundis eventibus semen Cœleste excepit, ut multi ex asperrimis montibus & sylvis ad æquiora loca descenderint, atque à fera ad humanam vitam traducti, Templa domósque fabricārint, ampliùs 5000. salutari baptismo tincti. Ad hæc sublatæ compotationes, idola plus 500. ignibus exusta; tantus autem ad nostros audiendos conciliatus affectus, ut integros dies cibi potúsque expertes consumerent in templis, donec de Fidei dogmatis satis erudirentur: quæ multi post unicum edocti diem, catechesim etiam integram memoriæ captu (tanta est etiam in asperrimis plagis ingenij memoriæque felicitas!) perdiscebant.

Ab his Gundisalvus comite P. Martino Perezio transivit ad Cinaloënses A. 1591. quo nomine plures diversæ linguis & moribus nationes continentur, à Mexico millia passuum ferè nongenta dissitæ: à quibus patet aditus ad montanos populos penè innumerabiles, itémque ad amplissimum novi Mexici tractum, aliásque gentes vel nuper cognitas, vel adhuc incognitas. Ex agris bis in anno fruges & fructus (tanta est glebæ ubertas) colligunt,

FIGURE 3. A Zuaque man holds an axe over Gonzalo de Tapia's corpse. The body's missing head, severed right arm, and the cutting instruments convey both the origin of later relics and the killers' reported hatred of the Christian faith (*odium fidei*). Karel Skréta, *P. Gundisalvus de Tapia S. I. illustri stemmate in Hispania natus, pro Fide Christi necatus in Mexico. Ao. 1594. 10 Iulij* in Mathias Tanner, *Societas Jesu usque ad sanguinis et vitae profusionem militans in Europa, Africa, Asia, et America* (Prague: Typis Universitatis Carolo-Ferdinandeae, 1675), 452, courtesy of the John Carter Brown Library (JCB), Brown University.

of martyrdoms, where bloody deaths paired with sweaty labors to mutually irrigate the fields of conversion. "This apostolic man sowed the seed of the Gospel in this ignorant and savage land, and afterwards the other cultivated it and endured immense hardships." Whereas Tapia had died in a punctiliar offering, Méndez provided daily sacrifices in his ongoing work. Because of their combined red and white martyrdoms, Sinaloa "has borne the ripened fruit that the Church militant and triumphant has subsequently stored in its granaries for heaven and earth to enjoy."[100] In this light, the suffering occasioned by aggressive confrontations and widespread disease was not cause for concern but a way to build up the storehouses of heaven.

Even as they depicted violence and disease as ultimately helpful in seeding future Christianity, Jesuits worried that some communities were so devastated that they faced total collapse. In his narration of the work of fathers Méndez, Velasco, Villafañe, and lay brother Francisco de Castro along the river valleys of Sinaloa in 1601, Pérez de Ribas described widespread epidemic sicknesses that presented more challenging obstacles to their work. Since so many of their intended converts were dying so quickly, he said, the missionaries had to scramble to baptize infants and the elderly in order to give them the saving sacrament before they entered into eternity. Nevertheless, Pérez de Ribas reasoned that the accelerated christenings were all part of a divine blueprint: "because God wishes to take some adults to heaven quickly, it is not only children who enter with baptismal grace and obtain with its flower the fruit of this Holy Sacrament." Although the principal goal of the mission was to plant a flourishing Christianity, if God chose to supersede that process by taking new Christians straight to heaven, they would celebrate the flowering of salvation. The important thing was to reach these lands quickly before these communities disappeared, administer sacramental graces, and thereby usher them into their celestial bounties.

Father Juan Bautista de Velasco emphasized this same redemptive view of sickness in his report for the annual letter (*Carta Annua*) of 1601. Father Velasco began by lamenting the number of Indigenous deaths. However, he reasoned that they ultimately brought eternal life to the deceased and left behind salvific deposits for future generations. Velasco celebrated divine providence as "Our Lord took for Himself a great number of them, but not all, for He also left seed that would bear fruit in the future."[101] He went on to give a specific example of a Native Christian woman who contracted a disease because she had cared for sick neighbors and helped bury their bodies. The priest maintained that he had healed her by sharing sacramental wine and a "Gospel story" with her. Such "cases of edification" reinforced the notion that Christian sacraments redeemed Indigenous sorrow. From this perspective, epidemic disease obtained twin rewards. It pushed Native people toward baptism, the Eucharist, and last rites as the means to procure individual salvation. At the same time, it seeded future conversions, as those who died became heavenly first fruits and those who were healed served as pious examples for future generations.

Conclusion

When Native communities embraced this vision of Christian martyrdom and responded with acts of devotion, Jesuit missionaries celebrated them as the first fruits of conversion and disseminated their stories widely. One of the best examples was an encyclical sent after Tapia's death by "some Tarascan Indians who were working in the mines of Topia" back to their home churches in Michoacán. Written in Purépecha, the letter informed the "residents of Pátzcuaro, Sivina, Navatzín, Charano, Arantzán, and all the other pueblos of the province" that their former priest had died and become "a very great martyr." Reminding them that Tapia had begun his first mission among them in the 1580s, it went on to provide explicit details about his severed appendages, signs of sanctity, and the specific location, time, and manner of death. The letter closed with the pious request that "all of you might pray an Our Father, just as we are all preparing to have a Mass said."

The Jesuits of New Spain delighted in the Tarascan converts' embrace of the martyr and helped spread news of the letter to other Native communities. They preserved it in their annual reports (*cartas annuas*) and several histories, holding up Tarascan excitement over Tapia's martyrdom as the ultimate vindication of their cause.[102] This way the story of the protomartyr Tapia and his Tarascan converts' veneration might be read aloud to both future Indigenous missions and fellow Jesuits in Europe as model cases of edification.

In addition to these stories, Jesuits came to believe that relics and rituals of remembrance demonstrated the fruit of their labors. In 1604, the father general of the Jesuit Order Mutio Vitelleschi described the results of missionary sacrifice as having planted God's "new vineyard," guaranteeing that New Spain would soon produce "abundant harvests."[103] Jesuits on both sides of the Atlantic came to understand this logic as central to their global enterpreise. In particular, they celebrated exemplary Indigenous convert communities who had embraced their priestly passion stories. When Tarascan converts declared Tapia "a very great martyr" and responded with a circular letter that urged memorial masses and other acts of veneration, they demonstrated the final proof of concept. While they popularized the passion stories of fallen brothers as well as the devotions of Native Christians who embraced them, Jesuit evangelists also believed that shared idioms of suffering could stitch converts and European Christians together.

For this reason, they presented converts as long-suffering children, innocently tormented by the diabolic "common enemy." To be sure, some judged the dislocation, disease, and punishments that Indigenous communities endured to be the just punishment of God. Others exonerated their "charges" in various ways, portraying them as everything from ignorant dupes to unknowing victims. Pérez de Ribas depicted the mission as a cosmic war in which most Native lands represented diabolic spaces; its inhabitants suffered under the tyranny of the Prince of Darkness, constantly tempted into drunkenness, adultery, and sedition.[104] But he also mingled stories of convert death and suffering with the accounts of exemplary missionaries, using Native "cases of edification" in an attempt to stitch their cause together with that of their ministers.[105] They shared suffering and glory because "the sons of the Company of Jesus have led many of these nations, albeit scorned and humble, into God's royal palace. Some have entered the palace of the Church militant and others the Church triumphant."[106] Combining these formal theological categories of those who labor against sin in life with those who have already ascended to heaven and now intercede on behalf of the living, the Jesuit pictured the Society's priests and converts as triumphing through their tragedies.

Alongside martial metaphors, Jesuits drew on agricultural images as the primary way to explain multiple trying circumstances. Sickness, suffering, and other setbacks all made more sense when tied to a process that ultimately produced salvation. Examples from both the classical world and early Christianity had established this pattern. Citing Jesus, Paul, Tertullian, and medieval hagiographies, they concluded that God historically expanded Christianity through the suffering of his saints. The symbolism of soil, seeds, water, fruits, vineyards, and harvests invested this language with a sort of commonsense logic. If the natural world brought life through death, then nothing less should be expected in the colonization and settlement of North America. Whereas early Christians had pictured these processes as passive persecutions, early modern Catholic missionaries saw their role in Christendom's growth as active. They were spiritual farmers who labored to uproot rocks, weeds, thorns, and thistles of diabolic vices. At times, these obstacles could develop into superstitious jungles and savage deserts, at once tangled with temptations and devoid of civilization. They could also mean diseases that ravaged their way through harvests and ate away crops of converts. Yet, the sacrificial logic held. Even when Native communities suffered epidemic collapse, their deaths would issue divine fruits like Catholic sacramental rituals and martyrological relics.

Planting Christianity through apostolic labors inevitably provoked resistance. Seeds brought crops, and those crops helped reclaim territory, taken back from a diabolic overlord who had long held sway. In this way, writers like Albiçuri and Pérez de Ribas contended that spiritual cultivation, armed confrontation, and colonial civilization proceeded together as the frontier of Christendom advanced against the kingdom of the diabolic "Common Enemy." The demonization of Native territory and the classification of their cultures as idolatrous helped negate Indigenous sovereignty and authorize missionary claims on their land and labor. When they acted upon these assertions, priests sometimes suffered violence. Rather than reconsider their colonial evangelistic project, however, Jesuit writers looked to an apostolic and patristic past to brand the suffering as sacrifice. Through typological concurrences and historical parallels, they hoped to vindicate themselves by tracing a predestined pattern of victory through victimization. At the same time, this logic occluded the quotidian causes for missionary death—namely, that the Jesuit missionary Gonzalo de Tapia had requested that Tovoropa's *alcalde mayor* whip and tonsure the *cacique* Nacabeba. The Zuaque elder had established the actual points of contention by decrying the ravages of epidemic disease and opposing the priests' preaching against Native supposed vices like polygamy, drinking, dancing, warfare, and sacrifice.[107] While Jesuit writers noted these confrontations as the immediate cause of revolt, they interpreted them as part of a greater celestial battle and necessary for the mysterious process of seeding Christianity on the northern borderlands of New Spain.

2 Weeds

Ritual Confrontations

Father Hernando de Santarén reached Sinaloa the very week of Gonzalo de Tapia's death in July of 1594. His first act as a newly assigned evangelist entailed a visit to the protomartyr's body in the mission headquarters of Villa de San Felipe. Santarén expressed solemn reverence for Tapia's relics but determined to guard against a similar fate for himself, at least until God's providential timing.[1] Santarén's first evangelistic forays took place during the general insurrection and military subjection that followed in the wake of Tapia's murder. His mission began at the same time that the Spanish soldier Captain Diego Martínez de Hurdaide mounted a brutal retaliatory campaign throughout 1594–96. Hurdaide set out to arrest the priest's killers, distribute broad punishments, and pacify rebelling areas of the Fuerte and Sinaloa river valleys. Long term, Hurdaide had determined to work together with the Jesuits, wielding his stick to punish those who would not take the priests' carrot.[2]

For this reason, Father Santarén took comfort in his relative safety compared to his earlier colleague. He also was decidedly less optimistic than Tapia about the encounter with Sinaloa's Natives. While the first wave of missionaries in northern New Spain had emphasized their power of persuasion and ability to win over hearts through languages, preaching, and steady discipline, newer priests like Santarén determined to take an even more confrontational approach.[3] Tapia's death made newer priests anticipate direct Indigenous resistance, and therefore many concluded that they should work hand in glove with the military in the spiritual conquest of Sinaloa's recalcitrant people.[4] With this purpose in mind, Santarén gladly accepted the aid of armed accompaniment as he began his own mission to the Acaxee on the western slopes of the Sierra Madres Occidentales, just to the east of the Sinaloa River.

Beyond self-protection, Santarén actually initiated aggressive attacks on Native material objects and practices. He partnered with the Spanish *encomendero*, Captain Diego de Avila, in 1600 for a pacification and conversion campaign (*una jornada de pacificación y conversion*) as part of a larger plan to reduce communities from dispersed mountain *rancherías* into missions near the Sierra's mining towns of Topia, San Andrés, San Hipóloto, and Las Once Mil Vírgenes de Cosolá. Captain Avila had received permission from New Spain's viceroy to consolidate Acaxee communities into these new *reducciones* and subject them to his governance for the purpose of working in the mines.[5] Father Santarén had his own goals for the operation. The Jesuit set out to uproot what he feared were hidden ritual objects and weed out entangling cultural practices before beginning the work of depositing gospel seed. Like Tapia, he hoped to end drunkenness and polygamy, but he also wanted to eradicate powerful stones and bundles of bones that reportedly had been stashed away in the wilds outside of Spanish surveillance. The Acaxee had fashioned rocks in the form of animals and collected the remains of revered elders as potent tokens of spiritual influence. Sometimes they also took body parts from defeated enemies as trophies and symbols of power.[6] To Santarén the stones and bones represented clandestine "idolatry," which along with other "vices" had kept the Indigenous people of northern New Spain ensnared in the devil's clutch.

With these twin purposes, Avila and Santarén went from town to town in the western Sierra in late 1600 and ordered its people to produce their "idols." When they suspected that a town was not forthcoming, they inspected the nearby hills and forests, looking in caves, ravines, and bushes for hidden idolatries. Santarén especially worried about this terrain of undulating hills and overgrown vegetation that he called *"el monte."* A remarkably flexible term that described everything from mountains to thick brush, in missionary discourse the monte had come to symbolize the veiled, untamed wilderness to which fickle converts inevitably fled when they wished to avoid prying eyes or disciplinary measures.[7] Missionaries in northern New Spain equated these hidden spaces outside the mission with diabolic space, territory where superstition and sorcery still reigned. It could refer to harsh scrubland, dense thickets, overgrown vines, sterile deserts, or rugged mountains, but the monte always represented a forbidden area that existed in opposition to the mission, a place outside of European settlements where Natives hid objects, practices, and their very bodies from supervision.

For this reason, Hernando de Santarén and many fellow Jesuits considered removing both idols and "idolaters" from the monte to be their central objective. As they worked to sow the seeds of civilization in their missions, the monte's weeds and hills had allowed the devil to continue his dominion in New Spain under cover of darkness, holding its inhabitants in bondage to their "idolatries, dances, drunkenness, and superstitions." Once more, the monte facilitated *"hechiceros"* or shamans who ensured the devil's ongoing hold on the land. From the perspective of the Jesuits, these rivals took advantage of the region's clandestine locations to perform rituals, relay visions, and spread "demonic" messages of resistance.[8]

In the case of the Acaxee, Father Santarén believed the Sierra's monte concealed powerful ritual objects. In particular, the priest worried about the "bones of human bodies and . . . statues of brown and red stones, white jawbones both large and small, some figures of people and others of turtles, birds and other things that they said are idols and which they idolize and worship in their way." Santarén contended that Acaxee informants had confessed to venerating both the stones as "gods of the waters, wind, corn, seeding, sickness and other things" and bones as powerful spiritual entities.[9] The caves and hollows in which they concealed these objects might also operate as secret sites for the maintenance of traditional rituals and political organization.

In order to disabuse them of these practices, Santarén staged ritual confrontations in each Acaxee town during their campaign of pacification and conversion. Upon first arriving in a given *ranchería*, the priest ordered residents to bring their idols and place them in a pile at the center of the village. Once the people and objects had been gathered, Captain Avila forced the Acaxee to pay ritual obedience to Father Santarén by kneeling or kissing his hand. They were then made to watch as soldiers broke up the figures and bundles, ultimately grinding them down to small pieces. The Jesuit then delivered a standardized sermon about the bad "fruit that these idols and bones had produced among this barbarous people through which the Devil had held them in blindness." In contrast, the missionary explained that he and Captain Avila would plant good fruit. They had been sent by the two majesties, God and king, to "uproot these vices from your hardened hearts" and replace them with the holy sacraments of the church. This physical and spiritual "uprooting," Santarén insisted, "was only for their good, conversion, and salvation."[10] Then, they burned the destroyed figures and bundles in a large bonfire.[11] Afterward, the inhabitants were forced to leave their settlements in the Sierra and gather in newly consolidated Jesuit *reducciónes* nearer to mining towns or river valleys, where they would be taught to cultivate both physical and spiritual harvests.

These ritual confrontations both followed from and engendered violent resistance in Native communities. Missionary death could be one result of these encounters, when angry Zaque, Tehueco, Acaxee, Guazapare, and Chínipas vented their anger on the priestly extirpators. By labeling these deaths as "martyrdoms," Catholic missionaries inscribed a particular discourse around them, marking them not only for veneration but redemption. These sensibilities engendered practices of memorialization like relic collection and hagiographic promotion. They also assured the missionaries of the redemptive value and ultimate success of their cause by invoking an agricultural metaphor that spilled blood seeded future Christianity.

At the same time, martyrs helped authorize increasingly aggressive measures to achieve conversion, including military pacification, coerced idolatry extirpation, and physical "reduction." In this way, veneration and coercion worked together to mark some places and practices as holy and others as evil and therefore subject to destruction. At times, the violent conflict centered upon the similar but competing traditions regarding the holy dead practiced by the Jesuits and the communities that they targeted for evangelization. These parallel practices engendered both predictable conflicts and ironic convergences. Even as Jesuits in Sinaloa were recovering the relics of martyrs like Tapia, they determined to remove bone bundles and sacred objects from Indigenous communities. This fueled cycles of violent confrontation in the far north as missionary death begot increasingly coercive methods and, in turn, campaigns of pacification, extirpation, and reduction incited new revolts and martyrs throughout the early decades of the 1600s.

Resistance

Despite the physical, spiritual, and material violence of Avila and Santarén's 1600 pacification campaign, Jesuit narrators like Andrés Pérez de Ribas expressed surprise and indignation about a quickly ensuing Acaxee rebellion the following year.[12] Pérez de Ribas directed the blame not on missionary antagonism or military cruelty, but on diabolic sorcerers who were determined to usurp the priests' hard-won ritual dominance. Specifically, he disparaged someone he considered a "lying Indian sorcerer" and "instrument of the devil" who helped ignite a revolt in late 1601. Although he never named the leader in his text, other sources identify the leader as "Perico" (Parakeet).[13] Pérez de Ribas instead called him "the Bishop," because Perico creatively emulated Catholic prelates in his dress and speech. After labeling him greedy, arrogant, "false and diabolical," the Jesuit historian nevertheless detailed the Acaxee Bishop's brilliant program of resistance, clever imitation, and sacramental inversion. Perico had led a revitalization movement that repurposed Catholic practice to directly challenge Santarén and undo the devastating effects of his conversions.

First, Perico timed his movement carefully to coincide with the apostolic visit of the Catholic bishop of Guadalajara, Alfonso de la Mota y Escobar, in late 1601. Learning of Escobar's imminent tour of the region, Perico purposely exploited this moment to mimic the bishop and mount direct opposition to his work. Dressing in clothing that mimicked a cassock and miter, he began preaching throughout the Sierra Madre. Specifically, he targeted the Jesuits and advocated their removal while also encouraging converts to flee their missions and return to the *monte*. This tour acted as a direct reversal of Santarén's pacification campaign the previous year. Perico urged fellow Acaxee to move back into the mountains, away from the Jesuits' missions and the Spaniards' mines. Conversion to his program would mean refusal to be "reduced."

Along with spatial reversals, Perico worked to negate Catholic sacraments, rebaptizing "Indians that had already been baptized by the priests . . . and divorcing them from wives whom they had married as Christians and remarrying them with other women as he pleased." The Acaxee bishop's annulments and weddings demonstrated his own ritual power to sunder and join. Even so, Pérez de Ribas denied Perico agency in these ritual transposals and instead dismissed them as "diabolic hoaxes." By attributing these reversals to the devil, the Jesuit historian blamed "the Common Enemy" and situated the local rebellion within a grand cosmic battle between God and Satan. As such, the material causes of conflict, including endemic disease as well as the coercive measures of Santarén and Avila, could be spiritualized and elided. From this perspective, Perico did not so much represent a direct threat but the means through which the Devil tempted the Acaxee to "return to their former idolatries, superstitions, and barbarity."

However he tried to spiritualize its cause, the Acaxee rebellion of 1601 wrecked almost all of the work accomplished during the previous year. From his place in the monte, the Acaxee bishop had spread a wider revolt that included the killing of several Spaniards, a larger number of Indigenous Christians, and "the destruction of nearly forty churches."[14] As much as the Jesuits emphasized these losses to highlight their own suffering, the uprising also targeted the wider Spanish colonial project, attacking the mining towns of Topia, San Andrés, and Las Vírgenes. Since *encomenderos* and missionaries had worked together in the pacification and conversion campaign, the Acaxee did not distinguish the two in their attacks. Las Vírgenes, for example, was completely burned to the ground, including homes, the church, and the mining operation.

Colonists in the other two towns found themselves similarly under siege. The Jesuit father Alonso Ruiz took refuge in the church of San Andres for nearly fifteen days with a large group of Spaniards, African servants, and Indigenous allies. Although the danger was shared by this diverse group, Pérez de Ribas focused on the brave suffering of the Catholic priest, narrating how Father Ruiz offered his own life to save the others and defend the faith. To prove his sacrificial mettle, the priest "took a crucifix in hand and left the church, encouraging the Spaniards to fight to the death against the enemies of Christ and His Holy Law." Yet, according to the narrator, God determined to preserve Ruiz for the time being, because even though he had "placed himself in full view of that entire rabble whom the devil marshalled and inflamed and even though they shot many arrows at him, amazingly not one struck him."[15] While he had not found martyrdom this time, Ruiz had demonstrated his utter abandonment to that fate and dramatically performed his role in the wider cosmic battle.

In similar fashion, the mission founder Santarén ventured forth several times from the town of Topia to engage the rebelling Acaxee, convinced that he uniquely commanded their loyalty. Unsurprisingly, he suffered multiple rejections, only "escaping at great risk to his life."[16] According to Pérez de Ribas, Spaniards and missionaries together determined that Father Santarén should be sent to broker peace, as they believed he was held with great love and respect. However, when he encountered an Acaxee band holed up in a gorge, the priest experienced the opposite. The group had intercepted a mule train from Culiacán. When Santarén came upon them, they had already "shot a Spaniard who was with the mule train and killed a black man and other mule-drivers who were Christian Indians." Initially, the Acaxee refused to engage the Jesuit until he finally agreed to leave behind his armed escort and descend into the ravine. Once near, he urged them to end the rebellion because "he was their father and that he would look out for them as his beloved children." They completely rejected this paternalistic metaphor, answering that "they were no longer his children" and sent him packing back up the gully.

Although Santarén was unsuccessful, Pérez de Ribas believed the story demonstrated the priest's sacrificial disposition. Switching to his own eyewitness testimony, the former missionary described how "sometime later Father Santarén and I walked through the same gorge," and his fellow Jesuit explained to him that "it was a miracle that he got out alive without being chopped to pieces, given how the Indians' thirst for blood had been so aroused by the prey that they had captured." With the benefit of four decades of hindsight, Pérez de Ribas concluded that only divine providence had spared Santarén from martyrdom, because "on that occasion God saved the priest for another time when he would give his life for the sake of other souls."[17] He emphasized the ever-present threat, as the rebels were "thirsty for blood." Nevertheless, the priest's patient love had won out, he asserted. Santarén ultimately had convinced the Acaxee band to reenter their mission, submit to their *encomendero*, receive baptism, and remain at peace for years to come.[18]

In the Jesuits' 1604 annual report (*Carta Annua*), Santarén insisted that spiritual success had sprung from these setbacks. According to him, the rebellion and subsequent suppression resulted not in ongoing resistance but rather increased repentance and reduction. As evidence, he pointed to the gathering of "more than five thousand people" into pueblos and the "thirty-seven hundred people that have been baptized this year following the uprising." In addition to quantitative results, the missionary hailed the qualitative advances that he observed in their sincere participation in sacraments and devotions. The Acaxee had improved their confessions, developed intense ascetic rituals, and even mounted "a large blood procession" on Holy Week of 1603. Their piety had culminated on Good Friday,

Santarén exulted, when the Acaxee scourged themselves with severe flagellation in imitation of Christ's passion. In case his superiors missed the parallel, Santarén accentuated the symmetry between the previous rebellion and their current blood-soaked repentance. "These people who the year before could not get enough Spanish blood, now shed their own with great sorrow for their sins and a desire to repent of their deeds."[19] By his account, Acaxee acts of Catholic devotion proved the inevitable progression from Jesuit sacrifice and Native suffering to territorial pacification and religious conversion.

For Pérez de Ribas, Santarén's former subordinate, the stories further illustrated his conviction that Catholic fruit grew only after the careful removal of idolatrous weeds. The campaigns to pacify the Acaxee rebels, reduce them from the monte to Spanish missions, and then purify the land of their idolatries had achieved their results—so much so that superiors could send more laborers to "work in the vineyard, where the once-thick weeds and thorns had already been uprooted."[20] If resistance came in this process, so much the better. For him, the deaths of several Acaxee converts, African workers, and Spanish colonists did not represent disaster but more thistles that must be braved in order that the seed find good soil. Once impediments were removed, they would see much fruit, whether through Native conversion or further colonization.

The discovery of new silver deposits in the Sierra Madres throughout the following decade seemed to confirm this interpretation. Like Christianity, Spanish mining operations had grown in the wake of the Acaxee uprising, spreading their "veins like trees—trees whose roots send out many shoots."[21] In the place of previous thorns and weeds, orchards of silver had grown up, ready to be plucked of their riches. By clearing away the monte, the Jesuits believed that the seeds of conversion and colonization were spreading throughout even the Sierra's rugged, mountainous terrain. The attempted killing of Jesuits like Ruiz and Santarén offered the additional possibility of soil enriched with the blood of martyrs.

Brush

Further north and west, the town of Tehueco on the Fuerte River went through a similar cycle of reduction, resistance, and conversion a decade later in 1611.[22] In that year, the small Cáhita-speaking pueblo, nestled in between the Gulf of California and the Sierra Madres, experienced a smallpox epidemic.[23] Five years earlier, the Jesuit missionary Pedro Méndez had "reduced" disparate *rancherías* in the area to form one mission at Tehueco. Méndez maintained that the move from the monte to the riverine mission was voluntary. The initial converts had approached him, offering their children and agreeing to settle in the mission and abandon their Native customs in exchange for Jesuit instruction. In a 1607 letter to superiors, he contended that others had joined as Tehueco's neighbors because they "were so inspired by the baptism of the Tehueco children" that they "crossed the river and came with great enthusiasm." Still, Méndez conceded that christenings and catechisms were not the only motivation for the move and readily boasted about the material advantages the mission brought the community.[24]

Despite these initial worldly motivations, the new *reducción* nevertheless "began to bear first fruits" of a spiritual harvest in the ensuing years. As proof, Pérez de Ribas cited Tehueco willingness to stay in the mission and participate in its agricultural and ecclesiastical life. When spring came, instead of going out to the monte to hunt and gather food, they planted crops and helped Méndez build a church. He boasted that the Mayo of Tehueco had stopped their old dances and "drunken reveling" in the nearby woods. Instead, they chose to stay put, exchanging their bows for crosses, hunts for confessions, and feasts for flagellations. Like the Acaxee, Tehueco reportedly embraced Catholic devotional practices, particularly the Feast of Easter and its accompanying ritual life. Their 1607 Passion Week celebrations reportedly culminated in careful attention to Father Mendez's sermon and an elaborate Lenten procession, complete with careful performance of the Stations of the Cross.[25] Together, Tehueco's spatial persistence and ritual involvement encouraged the Jesuits that they had permanently abandoned the wild and settled into Christianity.

However, this spiritual crop did not remain so healthy. Tehueco's reduction, farming, baptisms, and early embrace of Christian ritual practice had occurred in the wake of an epidemic that had spread along the Fuerte River in late 1606 and early 1607. Four years later, another outbreak of smallpox hit neighboring missions on the Sinaloa River. In response, some of Tehueco's caciques announced that the sickness would no doubt soon strike them. As Catholic sacraments and missionary remedies failed to fend off these plagues, the leaders concluded that they must seek out supplementary methods. Without Mendez's knowledge, the leaders urged residents of Tehueco to begin with a communal dance, or *mitote*. Then, they turned to other objects, practices, and spaces. Pérez de Ribas described how the Tehueco "took a manta, or cotton sheet, by the four corners and threw some of the things into it through which the devil makes his pacts." Clearly equating these actions with a return to "superstitious acts," Pérez de Ribas described in horror how they made masks and "performed other ceremonies, blowing in all different directions, they went to all the houses in the pueblo saying that they were gathering up the illness to take it to the monte, where they also repeated these superstitious acts."[26] While sickness had prompted an initial decision to move into the mission, postpone seasonal hunting trips and dances, and partake in Christian rituals, it also became Tehueco's impetus for returning to the practices and places of the monte.

The failure of Christian practices in the face of disease led them again to try new ritual and spatial strategies. Concerned about what these wanderings in the wild meant for their conversion, Méndez tried to impede the excursions. However, his attempted constraint had the opposite result, compelling Tehueco's residents into a binary choice. Pérez de Ribas summarized Tehueco's response: "All this had the effect of preparing the people to rise up and return to their gentile freedom; to do away with the priests, churches, and instruction once and for all."[27] The Jesuits attributed this turn of events not to the inflexibility of the *reducción* model, but instead to enduring diabolic power residing in the monte. In reference to lingering "idolatry" in Tehueco, Pérez de Ribas claimed that it was well known that when the light of the gospel dawned, the dispossessed demons (*demonios desterrados*) and the "sorcerers" (*hechizeros*) through whom they worked "fled to darker places away from the light."[28] For this reason, the brush surrounding the reduction offered sites of enduring superstition. While missionaries believed that Christian ritual, Spanish architecture, and European agriculture had successfully reorganized Tehueco's time and space, they had to confess that older practices still reigned outside its walls.

Residents of Tehueco in the early 1600s understood their decision to relocate and adopt some forms of Christian ritual and Castilian agriculture in pragmatic terms. The move granted access to key resources, fertile flood plains, Spanish trade, and Christian sacraments. Nevertheless, their subsequent actions indicated that they did not understand this decision as permanent and irrevocable. When a second epidemic came to the Fuerte River Valley in 1611, they made use again of other methods and spaces, gathering up the sickness and taking it out to the monte. Problems only came about when Father Méndez challenged them to remain in the mission and rely exclusively on Christian ritual, European produce, and the priest's crude medicinal treatments. Accustomed to preexisting patterns of both settlement and movement, many resisted during the following year by threatening the missionary's life, burning the mission church, and fleeing to higher climbs. Méndez barely escaped with his life.

Missionaries were quick to highlight the religious aspects of this resistance, emphasizing the violence enacted upon holy objects and bodies as a sign of the fundamental motivation. The Tehueco rebellion of 1612 was ultimately thwarted by military suppression as Captain Diego Hurdaide aided the Jesuits in bringing Tehueco back to submission. Shortly thereafter, two nearby Mayo settlements that were inhabited primarily by "gentiles" joined the mission community. Unsurprisingly, the missionaries maintained that the *rancherías* agreed to the new reduction "in order to govern themselves better and to benefit more from catechism." For Méndez and Pérez de Ribas, this only represented one more cycle in the process of suffering and salvation.

These sources have led modern interpreters to too often view such rebellions in similar terms, as signs of apostasy or revelations of "authentic" religious motivations that persisted beneath feigned accommodations.[29] However, practical strategies of adaptation governed these spatial transitions. Movement between the mission and the monte were not final choices, but strategic arrangements that corresponded to changing seasons and circumstances. In fact, Tehueco achieved some of its goals through the uprising and utilization of the surrounding brushland. They forced the removal of the excessively restrictive missionary Father Méndez and likely averted the continued spread of smallpox.[30] In this light, the uprising reveals less about the supposed authenticity of conversion and instead demonstrates Tehueco's flexible use of diverse rituals and spaces to negotiate dramatic challenges.

Thorns

In contrast to these practical considerations, Jesuits viewed confrontations through the lens of cosmic war. In order to spread the seed of the gospel in such environments, they argued that the land had to be forcefully subdued and returned to its rightful master. Pérez de Ribas described these challenges as thorns and snares plaguing the Natives of New Spain, "who were more possessed by the devil than any others on earth." This, he argued, was because the "tyrant who possessed them" had sown "vices and savage and inhuman customs" throughout his domain. He combined arboreal methaphors with militaristic descriptions about the diabolic master's hold over Sinaloa's terrain. The people lived in an "abyss of darkness," and their land was "a veritable kingdom of Satan that resisted the light of the Gospel." Because Sinaloa and its inhabitants had long lived under "the tyrannical reign of the devil," they had become "hardened in their obstinacy," unable to render physical, intellectual, or celestial fruit. The solution, though, seemed clear to him. At great cost the Society's priests must work to "dispossess him (Satan) of those many nations that he had taken from their Creator" and restore possession back to the Son of God, who had received them "for his patrimony."

The Jesuit historian pictured Indigenous land as a spiritual battlefield, caught in between God and the Devil as they struggled for territorial supremacy. Even if captured for Christ, northern New Spain had been so severely neglected after centuries under diabolic dominion that the Jesuits would have to clear the land before its cultivation. Pérez de Ribas accentuated "the wretched state of this land," not only because it had few Christians, but because of "Satan's heavy yoke." Under his rule, New Spain's inhabitants had become "wild and barbarous, living and dying in misery," while the land lacked "everything necessary for physical life," and the "daily living conditions" were meager, producing only "wild fruits, bitter roots, and locusts" for sustenance. Nevertheless, he contended that the allegedly degraded conditions would only make the fruits of their labor that much sweeter.[31]

At times the weeds were quite literal, as in the case of herbs used for the practice of euthanasia discovered in Sinaloa. Pérez de Ribas decried the consumption of a deadly weed, likely the same one used to poison arrow tips, as a way to escape increasingly frequent sicknesses. Instead of interpreting this as a desperate response to the ravages of epidemic disease, he maintained that the practice had been spread by the devil as a way of impeding evangelization. Missionaries had fought to "banish this abuse," he insisted, and "conquered this gentile nation with good words and speeches." Through example and preaching, "Christian customs and laws became well established in this nation," and this allowed the Jesuits to transform not only hearts, but also the physical landscape. Pérez de Ribas summarized this process of clearing the literal and symbolic weeds: "Once this jungle was razed and the weeds were uprooted, the evangelical seed began to spread and yield happy fruits, as did the divine word and frequent participation in and respect for the sacraments." Contrasting the death that he associated with Indigenous customs and the salvation he contended that the missionaries offered, the historian argued that his fellow Jesuits had removed poisonous herbs and exchanged them for the bread of life.

For the priests, Native burial practices constituted another thorn. Pérez de Ribas noted how the Guasave in northern Sinaloa, like the Acaxee, buried their dead by placing the remains in a cave. Instead of bone bundles, however, they placed the corpse on top of an elevated platform that would prevent it from moving, "in case it attempted to walk." Alongside the body, the Guasave deposited funerary goods, including food and drink, that would accompany it on its journeys.[32] On the one hand, the Jesuits praised this practice because they interpreted it as showing an awareness of an afterlife. On the other hand, they labeled it as "nonsense," because Christian theology contended that corpses had no power to move and that the spirits immediately left the body. As such, these hindrances should be removed and replaced with "the Christian practice of burying the dead."[33] They believed that their success and Native salvation depended upon Indigenous detachment from both these practices and places.

Pérez de Ribas argued that Native "superstitions" must be methodically removed "to better introduce Christian customs and the holy ceremonies of the Church." Like Tapia and Santarén before them, the priests who followed in Sinaloa "were careful to remove from this field the weeds of the monte and the wild grasses of abuse and gentile superstition." However, this process of extirpation must also be approached with caution and care lest revolt lead to total destruction. This would mean "tending to the preservation of this field without neglecting their work." Citing the Parable of the Tares in the Gospel of Matthew, the provincial recalled Jesus's story of a man who had sowed seed in his field, but an enemy had come at night and scattered weeds among the wheat. When his servants set out to uproot them, the man cautioned them to wait until harvest so as not to destroy the wheat along with the tares.[34] The provincial summarized the lesson for dealing with "idolatries" in New Spain: "It is well to pull up the weeds, but do so in due time so as not to harm the good seed."

The idea that thorns and weeds beset Indigenous groups throughout New Spain also helped Jesuits understand why they had not been as successful as they had initially hoped. In a general description of efforts with the Chichimeca who inhabited the Bajio region just north of Mexico City, Pérez de Ribas nearly despaired of their salvation. Because of their semi-nomadic practices, which he characterized as "wandering like savages," these Oto-Pamean relatives of the Mexica had "no hope of salvation." This raised the difficulty of "planting the Gospel in a forest so full of thorns and weeds." Even though they had evangelized "more civilized and populous nations" all over Mexico, the Chichimeca had remained "a fierce and indomitable enemy."[35] He cited various vices facilitated by their mobile lifestyle, including the frequent raiding of Spanish caravans, drunkenness, and clandestine dances in the monte. He also complained that "some murderers among them boasted and bore as a trophy a bone on which they recorded the number of Spaniards and Indian servants they had killed." The keeping of human remains as war trophies expressed the height of their descent into inhumanity in the provincial's mind, but he never acknowledged the irony that the Spaniards also held onto bones as sacred relics and tokens of the divine. Instead, Indigenous bone-collection remained a "superstition," a symptom of the wider problem of ongoing resistance to reduction, remaining with neither "a settled dwelling place nor a king." *Sin ley, sin rey, sin fe*, without law or governance, the Christian religion could never prosper.

In addition to so-called superstitions, sickness represented another thorn in the Jesuits' side. Often the two went hand in hand, as when residents in the missions of Toro, Vaca, and Chois on the Sinaloa River "surrounded their houses with thorny branches," making it impossible for Jesuits or other outsiders to enter. Searching for an explication for this practice, the Jesuit father Cristóbal de Vallalta ascertained that the action was part of a ritual response meant to ward off the "sickness of thorns." The use of thorny branches likely anticipated the arrival of smallpox, measles, or typhus in their towns, but they also helped ward off missionaries and other outsiders with whom the Sinaloans associated its spread.[36] What the Jesuits had spoken of metaphorically as thorns of superstition had taken literal form in the barbs used to fend off the scourge of epidemic.

Father Vallalta reported that Sinaloans in Toro, Vaca, and Chois relied upon ritual specialists to guide these practices. The diseases had been foretold by medicine workers (*hechiceros*) in response to an eclipse that they believed would portend a great battle between the moon and its enemies. This celestial showdown would have dramatic results in the human world if not guarded against with branches and thorns. Vallalta surmised that his intended converts correlated disease and death in these ominous events. For this reason, he concluded that his preaching could only begin after "burning the thorns" by gathering the branches and setting them on fire. He insisted that his converts should rid themselves of the deceptions of the devil, then "should turn to God for relief and the Holy Sacraments" in order to obtain pardon.[37]

Despite having burned away the physical thorns, spiritual snares remained. Residents of Toro, Vaca, and Chois resisted the sacraments, including baptism and confession. Most vexing, they began hiding their sick under woven reed mats in order to avoid the application of extreme unction. They refused this particular Catholic ritual because they connected it to their own deaths and assumed the sacrament had a causal effect on their high mortality rate. In exasperation, Father Villalta tried to persuade them that, "on the contrary, it was often a means of attaining bodily health." Nevertheless, he did so with great difficulty, since "the serpent attempted to place snares in every path and in all the means to salvation, just as he had done with the forbidden tree." According to Pérez de Ribas, the thistles that beset New Spain had grown symbolically into a full tree, a diabolic imitation of the edenic prototype. Instead of recognizing Sinaloan actions as flexible strategies to grapple with devastating illness, the Jesuits read these moves in light of biblical precedent and determined to burn away all entanglements.

Every thorn had its rose. Surely there were challenges in this work, they conceded, but God inevitably brought flowering Christianity out of the bristles of pain. As proof, Pérez de Ribas pointed to the persistent work of Father Santarén with the Acaxee and Xixime over a decade after the first reduction and revolt. The aging missionary had been joined by a younger assistant, Father Diego de Acevedo, to aid in the evangelization of the Sierra de Topia. In his annual letter of 1612–13, Father Acevedo wrote of the numerous challenges the pair faced in this work. He even contended that the devil had been seen roaming the Sierra in physical form, usually as "a child of ten or twelve years of age." According to Acevedo, these "possessed" children focused primarily upon exhorting dying Natives to flee to the monte to die, since "the ancestors did not have the custom of being buried in churches."[38] Over a decade after Santarén's first attempts to extirpate the Acaxee's death and burial practices, the monte still called. In addition to burial, the Indigenous child shamans built up resistance to other Catholic practices, drawing a strong correlation between baptism, confession, last rites, and their people's sickness and death. In a brilliant reversal, they branded Father Acevedo as the "sorcerer" who had cast spells on both children and elderly and made them sick through his rituals.

Nevertheless, Pérez de Ribas assured himself and his readers that all was not lost, because "God well knows how to pick roses from among thorns." He concluded that "this was the case during this time of illness because through Holy Baptism, God harvested infants as His first fruits of heaven."[39] The plagues that devastated mission communities should not discourage the priests as long as they led to baptism and therefore eternal life. The idea that the death of children and the elderly could be interpreted as "roses from thorns" seems inexplicable. Yet, Jesuits believed that they had snatched souls from the clutches of Satan by sacramental grace.[40] Lacking the benefits of contemporary epidemiology and the knowledge that they themselves had brought the plagues and spread them through their concentrated reductions, Jesuits thanked God that they had arrived just in time to rescue converts from hell—particular children that might fall to diabolic temptation—and deliver them to heaven.

Jesuits viewed these deaths as "first fruits," early returns on what would eventually be a celestial storehouse full of new Christians. As Pérez de Ribas put it, "God harvested infants as His first fruits of heaven."[41] In addition, their early mortality helped them achieve salvation, dying in a state of grace before they would ever sin. This gave the children the advantage of never reaching the age of accountability and therefore secured for them the benefits of heaven.

> However, there is no denying that we receive a very tangible reward in the form of fruit so palpable. When I recall that during those years I baptized with my own hands nearly one thousand children who died—

children who were not old enough to sin—it seems to me that I have no right in this life; the consolation is that abundant.[42]

While the children's untimely demises were tragic, the missionary reasoned that it was nevertheless a privilege for him to have baptized so many of them just before their deaths. Pérez de Ribas echoed this sentiment in another similar situation: "The fragrant flowers of infants that are plucked for heaven now grow where once there were thorns."[43] Now in heaven, Indigenous children acted as spiritual patrons, pleading on behalf of their people. According to him, these flowers had manifested through increased sacramental participation and festal devotion. Christenings, confessions, and communions joined "other Christian exercises, including feast days, Christmas, Epiphany, Easter, Pentecost, and Holy Week ceremonies with blood processions," as Indigenous blood evidenced a return on missionary deposits.

Storms

For Father Julio Pascual, who served a decade later in the Chínipa mission, the results were likewise mixed. In the eyes of the priests, the Chínipa ranked highly among the many communities that had been converted since the time of Tapia. Painting an idyllic picture of the mission, Pérez de Ribas described how Father Pascual had imitated the earlier priest by toiling "with fervent enthusiasm to spare no effort, labor or act to remove from the clutches of the devil these souls that were created for heavenly bliss." Eventually, Pascual's labors "produced an abundant harvest of souls converted to Christ," according to the later narrator.[44] Up to that point, everything conformed to the regular pattern of toiling missionary labor compensated with regular harvests of Native Christians.

By the late 1620s, wrote Pérez de Ribas, "Father Julio lived very happily cultivating the tender grapevine that he had planted for the church, whence God was harvesting His fruits." Most of those fruits, though, had only been achieved through sickness and anguish. Several baptized Chínipa had died prematurely of epidemic diseases. Still, the Jesuits understood these tragedies in providential terms. "The souls of children and adults" were actually beloved produce "whom God took to Himself before the storm arrived that nearly destroyed the new Christianity." This fruit had been quickly collected, he reasoned, because God had providentially brought Pascual before the advent of a greater tempest, a storm that would demand the priests join their converts in suffering.

Clouds started to gather in early 1630, when Indigenous shamans began decrying the devastating effects of disease and blaming the Jesuits for spreading it with their sacraments. This led to a series of uprisings that threatened the entirety of Pascual's work. The missionary lamented to superiors that many Chínipa Christians had followed these ritual rivals and threatened apostasy. Invoking the previously mentioned Parable of the Tares and the Wheat, the enemy had sneaked in while the workers slept and sowed bad seed in the field, and now tares were springing up and intermingling with the good fruit. As much as Jesuits were trained to wait for the good to emerge from the bad, they also feared that these bad seeds would threaten their vineyard, entangling new sprouts and choking out the weak. By this reckoning, apostates had mixed with loyal converts in ways that made it difficult to discern the difference and therefore protect "true Christians" from hidden traitors.[45] Even if not in outright apostasy, the priests expressed frustration at what they deemed the fickle choices of converts who initially responded to evangelistic work but later followed shamanic rivals and returned to their "gentile" state. Sometimes the harvests were "not as copious as we had hoped"; at other times, good fruit had turned bad.[46]

At first, Father Pascual thought he could save the crop. When a ritual leader named Cobameai from the nearby and related Guazápare nation began to preach against him, the Jesuit used a combination of military confrontation and evangelistic persuasion to pacify the situation. In late 1630, Cobameai had begun criticizing the heavy burdens of the reductions and pointing to widespread disease as reasons to question Pascual's authority. Like the Zuaque shaman Nacabeba before him, he called upon the Chínipa and Guazápare to wage "war" against the Jesuit and throw off his disciplinary yoke. Holding "illicit meetings" in the forests outside the mission, the shaman used tobacco rituals to forge alliances and allegedly supplied alcohol and other "vices" to tempt them away from Pascual's supervision. In these meetings, he urged his companions to return to their liberties and "kill the priest who had introduced such laws and had changed the people's old ways."[47] Some loyal Christians, however, informed Pascual of the plot, who in turn called a nearby Spanish garrison for help. The soldiers rounded up Cobameai and the principal leaders and brought them to face the priest. Pascual employed prayers, petitions, and preaching in an attempt to calm the uprising, eventually believing he had mollified his opposition, and everything had returned to normal.[48]

But Cobameai's plan had simply been delayed by the arrival of a new missionary, Father Manuel Martínez, along with accompanying soldiers, who had helped Pascual redouble his efforts in the region. Although Pascual and Martínez had temporarily saved this vineyard, the threat had not ended. Rather, Pérez de Ribas suggested, God had only delayed the tempest because "He wished to crown two ministers together with the glorious triumph of death for the preaching of His Gospel."[49] After the soldiers' departure, Cobameai entered the nearby Guazápare town of Varohío on a Saturday morning in early February. There he found the two missionaries working on a small church, along with nine Native builders and "eight little Indian choirboys who served the church." Without much delay, Cobameai and his men surrounded the buildings and set fire to them, declaring their intention to kill the missionaries and "live as they wished." But the Christians were not immediately consumed because the fire burned slowly, "extending their martyrdom" another day.

The hidden blessing of this protracted torment versus a quick death by fire, Pérez de Ribas explained, was that the priests had time to catechize, confess, console, and "prepare the faithful Christians who were with them to suffer death." After praying with their converts and securing their souls, Pascual and Martínez pled with Cobameai and his followers throughout the night, asking them to desist and return to "obedience." When it became clear that this time they would not be pacified, the two missionaries decided to leave the church early Sunday morning, determined "not to die for Christ sadly and with cowardice." At dawn they reportedly exited the building with the boldness of faith. Immediately, they were "struck by thousands of arrows covered with poisonous herb," which "rained upon their bodies until they became two Saint Sebastians."[50] The reference to Saint Sebastian, a fourth-century Diocletian martyr whose well-known passion story included a brutal death by arrows, confirmed the priests' saintly status in the eyes of the narrator.

For further evidence of their holiness, Pérez de Ribas described their suffering during death as well as the subsequent "barbarous" treatment given their bodies by "the apostates."[51] He first explained how two of the

"Indian Christian choirboys" escaped and provided missionaries and soldiers with the details of what happened next. To the provincial, their account only confirmed that the priests had died as true martyrs, suffering for the sake of Christ because "while still alive and after they were dead these blessed priests were tortured by fire, smoke, and insults as well as wounds from arrows, knives, and maces." While their bodies were struck, beaten, and cut, the sacramental vessels were profaned and used in "barbarous dances." As was the case in the Zuaque rebellion and murder of Tapia, the narrative description of the ritual violence against the chalices and patens served to confirm that the killers' hatred was directed not just at the priests but at the Catholic religion, proving that they died *in odium fidei*. The historian invoked typological parallel to drive the point home, recounting how "the rebel Indians ripped the priests' cassocks to pieces and divided them among themselves."[52] Together, the account of their physical torture, mock rituals, and material dispossession symbolized their attainment of a long-hoped-for imitation of Christ.

As he described the abuses performed upon their bodies, Pérez de Ribas also specifically emphasized that the heads were not severed as had been the case with Gonzalo de Tapia. He attributed the restraint of the killers to the intimidation caused "by the clamors of innocent blood," divine will, and the actions of a loyal convert. By referencing these "clamors," he likened Pascual to "the innocent Abel" from the book of Genesis, whose blood cried out from his grave for justice.[53] The example of his blameless life, the hagiographer contended, had the effect of shaming the murderers and condemning their consciences. In addition to the story of Abel, the first of all martyrs, he appealed to historical precedent, noting how the fear of God, "which many times kept the claws of lions and the fangs of hungry wolves from touching the bodies of martyrs," had miraculously intervened to "constrain these ferocious Indians" from severing the heads.

Pérez de Ribas likened the Guazápare to fierce lions, but argued that despite this allegedly beastly nature, they nevertheless recognized that the bodies had become the "relics of holy men." This, he believed, testified to the possibility of moral improvement. As proof of this divine potential, he presented a loyal Chínipa Christian named Crisanto Sivemeai as a case for edification. Sivemeai had risked his own life to fight off the attackers with his bow and arrow, killing five of them and protecting the martyrs' bodies from further damage. Crisanto's actions evidenced the hope that the new Christianity would yet be rescued from these storms. Divine intervention and convert loyalty had warded off further desecration of the corpses and "arranged safekeeping for these holy bodies."[54] To the later historian, this proved that a providential hand had allowed this sacrifice, if only to secure future salvation.

When Christian Chínipa found the bodies still intact the next day, they purportedly considered it a miracle, marveling that the corpses had been protected from dogs and other wild animals throughout the night. Then, they took the bodies from Varohío and back to Chínipa, making two graves behind the altar of their simple church. They combined Catholic burial with their own funerary practices, as they "deposited the bodies and covered them with the mats they use" and displayed elaborate signs of grief. Jesuits savored these tears, as they seemed to confirm the value of their labors. The veneration and mourning assured the priests of the lasting fruit of conversion had survived the storms of rebellion. This persistently redemptive logic also convinced them that fathers Pascual and Martínez had now "become their intercessors in heaven" and therefore would guarantee their Indigenous converts' perseverance in faith and progress, "even though they were persecuted."[55] The narrative of mutual grief and persecution evidenced the core thesis of *The History of the Triumphs*: Native suffering and Jesuit sacrifice worked together to secure the eventual advance of Christendom.

Chínipa attention to the bodies brought further verification of their Catholic piety. When fellow Jesuit father Marcos Gómez later decided to move the corpses from there to his mission at Conicari, the town's residents purportedly expressed "great sorrow" to lose "their relics," since Pascual had "engendered them in Christ."[56] Like the earlier Tarascan Christian embrace of relic devotion in response to Tapia's death, Chínipa longing for Pascual's bones should be a "consolation to all missionary priests," Pérez de Ribas maintained, because they demonstrated the "special love for the ministers who baptize them and transform them from barbarians into Christians." Such recompenses were the greatest dividend possible for Jesuits who deposited their lives in these lands.[57] The Christian Chínipa also mourned the loss of "fourteen or sixteen of their sons along with the priest." Pérez de Ribas related nothing more about these deaths, except that they were loyal Guazápare converts from Varohío and that related Chínipa were "deeply grieved by the death of their sons and relatives." Instead of giving these Indigenous deaths the same attention as the missionary "martyrs," he used the story of their grief to prove their loyalty to the mission and the authenticity of their conversion.

While heartened by Chínipa and Guazápare reverence for the martyrs, the missionaries nevertheless insisted on taking the relics, concerned that Pascual and Martinez's bodies would not be safe in their hands. Once they removed the relics, the Jesuits displayed their own veneration, celebrating a solemn funeral in Conicari on February 14, 1632. After sermons, sacraments, and the singing of a Native choir, the "venerable remains, which had been pierced by arrows, beaten with macanas and clubs, and wounded with knives and hatches—all suffered for Christ and His Gospel—were interred." However, they did not rest in peace for long, as brothers from the Jesuit college in Mexico City requested some relics to remember their fallen companions. Ironically, the brothers "requested the heads of the two priests, which those barbarians beat and wounded."[58] They believed that these blessed tokens of divine presence would encourage the college's novices and serve as an example of their own desired sacrifice of "shedding their blood for Christ."[59] If the parallel of this practice with Indigenous severing of Tapia's head struck any of them as strange, Pérez de Ribas did not let on. Nor did the fact that the missionaries branded their would-be converts as barbaric because they regarded body parts as powerful seem contradictory to the Jesuits' own practice in collecting sacred bones. The phenomenological correspondence of their rituals was beside the point. What marked one as savage and the other sacred were the motives and religious status of the people who acted, not the act itself.

Nevertheless, even these moments of trial conformed to biblical teaching. Citing the Parable of the Sower again, Pérez de Ribas reasoned, "Not all the seed that this evangelical laborer planted bore fruit (as was taught by the Son of God)."[60] Christ had warned them that good seed would mix with bad and that wheat would be inseparable from tares. For this reason, rather than finding insights in temporal facts such as missionary failures or colonial injustices, the situation was understood metaphorically. Germs had infiltrated the field, and some seed had been trampled, neglected, choked out, and burned away. For this reason, the fruit "was not as copious as was hoped." In a lengthy description of the "fruits of illness," the provincial explained that "there was no shortage of the bad seed," but this was something "about which the Son of God preached."[61] Moving from metaphor to lived experience, he described how priests faced "innumerable hardships," ranging from natural disasters like floods, to the preaching of rival shamans, to "vestiges of deeply rooted vices." At the same time, their converts faced rival tribes and epidemic diseases like measles and smallpox. However, he rarely addressed these material causes as worthy of self-reflection or remediation. Rather, colonial violence and Indigenous sickness were transmuted into steps in a supreme plan and read with providential eyes.

In his estimation, a diabolic Johnny Appleseed was to blame for harvests of wheat mixed with persistent tares, as "the enemy of the salvation of souls was sowing this bad seed even in the midst of good seed." However, where evangelistic preaching was stamped out, the blood and bodies of the martyrs purchased new seed and continued watering the fields. This was the result in the case of Pascual and Martínez, he believed:

> Even though his sudden death did not give him the opportunity to cultivate this vineyard, he harvested a fair amount of fruit for himself with the crown of martyrdom. He left this entire Christianity watered with his blood, and it has been bearing fruit and growing ever since the death of these holy men.[62]

The tempests of apostasy and rebellion might cut short the work of an individual missionary, but this did not end their labor. On the contrary, their blood continued to water the seed and guaranteed more seasons of harvests. Even through persecution, God had rescued "many innocent lambs, which were children, to go to praise Him eternally in blessedness, as well as some predestined adults, whom God usually selects and removes from the midst of those condemned to hell." Pérez de Ribas mixed the pastoral metaphors, sometimes speaking of innocent lambs and other times harvests of fruit, at one point conflating the two, "the fruit of the flock, or herds of domesticated sheep."[63] Still, the point was clear. When one considered the devotion of loyal converts, the baptized adults who passed away, and the christened children taken away by the disease, the reader should conclude along with the evangelist that "divine providence nevertheless had its harvest."[64]

Spoiled

More than any other moment in the first century of Jesuit missions in northern New Spain, the revolt of the Tepehuán in 1616 illustrated this paradox. Like their near neighbors the Acaxee to the west and Tehueco to the north, the Tepehuán who occupied the eastern slopes of the Sierra Madres had been induced into reductions in the early 1600s with the promise of accessing Spanish food, tools, and other weapons. However, nearly two decades of epidemic disease had taken a severe toll on them, leading to a massive population decline that may have depleted their numbers by half since the missionary arrival and up to 75 percent since the 1590s.[65] Despite the devestating demographic decline, Jesuit observers expressed optimism about Tepehuán conversion and cooperation, especially in contrast to the more resistant Chichimeca in the deserts to the east. In their first encounters in the 1590s, the Jesuits positively contrasted their settled, agricultural lifestyle with the more mobile groups around them. Two decades later, in the *Carta Annua* of 1615, they argued that the Tepehuán "showed great progress and were in the things of our holy faith *muy ladino*," or very much like other Spanish-speaking mestizos.[66] Noting their use of clothing, cultivation of maize, and development of houses, missionaries deemed them more amenable to life in *conversión*.[67]

However, there were also signs of trouble from the beginning. The Tepehuán's settled lifestyle entailed relationships with powerful spiritual beings that could surround their settlements and sustain agricultural production and hunting. The same letter that celebrated their fitness for reduction also described the Tepehuán's veneration of an "idol" that they believed helped cure sickness and grant victory in war. The Jesuits expressed disgust at the object's appearance, which they admitted was composed of beautiful jasper but had been dressed with dehydrated body parts, likely human brains.[68] Father Nicolás de Anaya connected the relationship between the Tepehuán and these divinities to Mesoamerican practices of reciprocal sacrifice. Anaya reported to his superior that a Tepehuán shaman named Andrés had explained to him that the "idols were spirits" that came from the ground and had the power over life and death. For this reason, they must be continually consulted, placated, and fed in order that they might provide abundant rain, harvests, and prey for the hunt.[69]

This combination of optimism at their propensity for Christian civilization, distrust of their ongoing "idolatry," and fear about the accumulating effects of disease characterized Jesuit reports on the Tepehuán right up until the revolt of 1616. They worried that bouts of sickness would turn the Tepehuán back to their previous ways, corrupting their conversions and spoiling the missionary harvest. While the annual letter of 1615 had spoken in glowing terms about their "muy ladino" embrace of Catholic religion and Spanish customs, Pérez de Ribas expressed unease about the Tepehuán as he traveled through their region en route to Mexico City. He argued that they seemed ignorant of the faith and demonstrated little love for their priests in comparison with his own converts in Sinaloa.[70] When questioned about this, one of the priests working with them, Bernardo Cisneros, confessed that he did not know what "hellish idol" had made them so "restless," but maintained that he and the other fathers had been working to bring calm.

Pérez de Ribas noted that he also had heard fears from settlers in the nearby mining towns, but that nobody took the threat seriously. What they did not know is that the Tepehuán were in the final stages of planning a revolt nearly four years in the making that would take the lives of ten missionaries and hundreds of colonists and last for nearly four years. The rebellion destroyed much of what the Society had built up among the Acaxee, Xixime, and Tepehuán in over two decades of work. More dramatically, eight Jesuits died during the opening days of the uprising.[71]

In a *Memorial* about these "martyrs," the procurator of the Indies, Francisco Figueroa, chronicled the Jesuits' past labors and present losses. Figueroa described how the viceroys of New Spain had entrusted the Society with the discovery, pacification, reduction, and conversion of "Indians of Tepehuán, Topia, San Andres, Xiximes, las Parras, and Sinaloa, one hundred and fifty, two hundred, and three hundred leagues from Mexico in the North toward New Mexico."[72] Following the lead of other hagiographers, he insisted that these missions had only been made possible because of the earlier martyrdom of Gonzalo de Tapia. "The first Religious of the Society who entered, giving a beginning to these missions and reductions, was Father Gonzalo de Tapia, who poured out his blood for our holy Faith." At the same time, Figueroa acknowledged the material causes at the root of his death, "as those Barbarians took his life because he separated them from their drunkenness and the abuse of the many women they had, just as the very murders confessed."[73] Figueroa went on to describe the way Sinaloans not only killed Tapia, but took vengeance upon his body, drinking with the skull of the man who had "impeded their dances and drunken festivities."

Still, he insisted that the martyrdom had provided the foundation of all the missions that followed. Despite gross indignities, "the Lord had been served by the irrigation of this first Martyr and the good labors of the rest of the Society." In fact, Tapia's death had inaugurated "thirty years of the pacification and reduction to our Holy Catholic Faith and the baptism of more than fifty thousand Indians, alongside many children who just after baptism went to enjoy the glory of the Lord."[74] The protomartyr had planted the whole harvest, and Native children taken by disease who now experienced celestial splendor helped it grow through their supplications. His blood and their tears were supplemented by the sweat of the "Fathers who in the season of winter, went by foot through swamps and rivers with water up to their chests at great detriment to their health and danger to their lives." Death, disease, and daily suffering combined to further this new frontier of Christendom.

Figueroa then completed the circle of martyrdom, sickness, conversion, and idolatry, insisting that the fruit of Jesuit sacrifice and Indigenous suffering had been challenged by diabolic jealousy. "From the blessed deaths of the recently baptized, the Devil used an opportunity through his sorcerers to dissuade the Indians from Christianity, convincing them that the water of holy Baptism and the Sacrament of the Extreme Unction (that the Fathers gave them) were the cause of their sickness and death."[75] Like the Acaxee before them and the Guazápare at a later date, Tepehuáns had noted the correlation between life in *conversión* and the regular onset of disease. While most of these groups had long balanced living in the relatively small *rancherías* with seasonal movement in the monte, the missions had congregated them into much larger towns, placed them in close contact, and confined their travels. This constriction made them more vulnerable to failed crops or regular epidemics. Whereas Figueroa believed the devil had used "sorcerers" to spread such "lies and deceptions because he could not prevent the fruit that was being produced," Tepehuán ritual specialists had rightly correlated hunger and sickness with the Jesuits' missions and sacraments.

In addition to directly attacking Catholic rituals, Tepehuán shamans claimed to master the sacraments better than the priests. Figueroa expressed particular frustration with a man who he claimed had come from New Mexico to corrupt the Tepehuán. The procurator described him as an "apostate from our Holy Faith" who had renounced his baptism, embraced idolatry, fled the missions, and preached that others should do the same. With a clay crucifix covered in a black veil and two letters "sealed in the Spanish style," the leader had convinced the Tepehuán that he was "the God of earth, son of the God of the Sky, whom he said was the Sun." As the God of the earth, he came with a message from the Sun that they should liberate their land from those who had commandeered it, taking knives to all of the Spaniards, beginning with the priests of the Society. The leader, whom Pérez de Ribas later identified as Quautlatas, followed the example of the Acaxee Perico, proclaiming himself a bishop, but raised it a level by claiming divinity.

Quautlatas delivered a message common to other Indigenous revitalization movements that if the people would rise up, he could guarantee them victory because of his special powers. He would protect them in battle, resurrect the dead, restore the old to youth, heal the sick, control the weather, and expel the Spaniards from the land. If they refused, however, he would "send upon them hunger, pestilence, and sicknesses" and the Holy Spirit would cause the ground to swallow them alive and consume them in fire.[76] His message took hold first in Tenarapa, on the eastern side of the Sierra Madres.[77] But soon the message spread as he used the shroud of the monte to impart visions and demonstrate power. Moving to the "pueblo of Ozino, in the monte, he appeared to some Indians, transfigured into an Angel of Light, surrounded in splendor and ordered that they gather the rest because he wanted to do important business with them for their common good, growth, and prosperity."[78] Once gathered, Quautlatas shot rays of fire from his eyes and mouth, warning them to prepare themselves for battle with the Spaniards and their priests. From these hidden locales, they would soon divide and attack the European towns and missions, sacking them of their wealth, killing the cattle, burning the homes and churches, and spoiling years of work.[79]

Just two months later, the Tepehuán struck. They waited for the precise moment when all of the region's Jesuits and many Spaniards had gathered at the mission of San Ignacio del Zape to celebrate the Feast of the Presentation of the Blessed Virgin Mary on November 21, 1616.[80] They knew that this particular year the feast would attract even greater numbers because a mule train had arrived from Mexico City and the Jesuits would be installing a new image of Our Lady in the altar of El Zape. Pérez de Ribas sourly noted that they knew this because so many of them had participated in Christian instruction and sacraments and because their missionaries had failed to understand how deeply they had been "corrupted."[81] However, the coordinated attack was preempted slightly by the murder of Father Hernando de Tovar. Five days earlier, residents of Santa Catalina had raided the mule train returning to Mexico City and killed Tovar, who was accompanying its journey. Word spread about the killing of Tovar, quickly mobilizing hundreds in outright revolt. In the following two days, Tepehuán rebels and their allies killed seven more Jesuits, two mendicant friars, and hundreds of European, *criollo*, and mestizo colonists.[82]

The culmination of these events occurred on November 18, when a force of 500 Tepehuán surrounded the mission of Santiago Papasquiaro. They set about burning Papasquiaro's houses and other buildings before cornering the priests, Spaniards, and allies in the church. At first, the revolt's leaders agreed to make peace, and allowed fathers Bernardo de Cisneros and Diego de Orozco to lead a religious procession with dozens of settlers out of the church. Feigning devotion, the Tepehuán approached the fathers on their knees, venerating the Eucharist and an image of the Virgin held high by the priests. Once at their feet, however, a warrior stood up and struck Orozco with a sword. The rest followed him, killing Cisneros and everybody else, with the exception of six survivors.

At the same time, others executed the original plan in El Zape, surrounding that town's church during the festal mass. No survivors lived to recount what happened next, but the following day, soldiers dispatched to aid Zape found the church sacked and burned and one hundred bodies laid out in the nearby cemetery. The two priests who had led the mass, fathers Luis de Alavés and Juan del Valle, were among the dead. A short distance outside the town the soldiers also found the beaten bodies of two more Jesuits, fathers Juan Fonte and Gerónimo de Moranta, likely killed as they approached the town for the festivities and apparently ignorant of the wider uprising.[83]

After the initial violence, news spread to the nearby missions of the Acaxee and Xixime, some of whom joined in the revolt. The superior over those conversions, Andrés Tutino, heard of Tovar's death from loyal Xixime at Coapa, a neighboring town to the Tepehuán. Father Tutino quickly sent notice to surrounding missions, mining settlements, and especially to his fellow Jesuit Father Hernando de Santarén. However, Santarén had already left to attend the feast at El Zape and missed the warning. He arrived at the Tepehuán town of Yoracapa on November 19, presumably unaware of the danger. Hoping for supplies and to provide sacraments, Father Santarén rang the bell to call the *fiscal* to gather its residents to the church, but nobody came. When he entered the church, he found the altar profaned, the images of the saints disfigured, and everything ransacked. The veteran evangelist, who had already survived two rebellions, now knew his imminent danger. Confident in his persuasive skill, however, he mounted his mule and continued on to Papasquiaro.

Just as he departed Yoracapa, Santarén descended into a gully. Tepehuán warriors, who had been watching him, waited until he reached the bottom and then fell around the elderly missionary. Figueroa narrated the exchange that ensued: "Asking them what evil he had done and why they wanted to kill him, the Tepehuán responded that he had not done anything other than be a priest, which to them was extremely evil." Explaining that they needed no other reason, the Tepehuán delayed no longer and "hit him on the head with such a fierce hit that they split open his brains, along with many other wounds." According to Figueroa, Santarén still had time to "call out the Most Holy Name of Jesus," a final identification with Christ before "the good priest joyously ended his journey." While this imagined dialogue bolstered Santarén's claim to martyrdom, verifying that the Tepehuán had killed him out of hatred of the faith, it also conformed to reality. His pacification and conversion campaign fifteen years earlier had inaugurated a traumatic period of dislocation, disease, and demographic decline in the Sierra. As much as they viewed that operation as central to his vocation, it was true that the priests' very presence had brought cascading evils.

Despite the utter nakedness of his death, Jesuits still attempted to clothe it in sacred memory. They did this once again by invoking Native veneration. Figueroa explained that while Tepehuán males had treated Santarén so cruelly, their wives lamented his loss. "The women of the Tepehuán Indians have grieved over the death of these priests from the Society, because they are tired of witnessing the cruelty of their husbands against the fathers, who so peacefully taught both men and women the doctrine."[84] By summoning the example of Tepehuán women, he hoped to evoke sympathy and find a way to still proclaim their ultimate fidelity to Christianity. Like Pérez de Ribas and others who would later hail his sacrificial life, Figueroa insisted that Santarén "had walked apostolically for more than twenty-four years of labor in those missions." As much as he focused on the priest's passionate service and self-renunciation, these encomiums also revealed the root of why Santarén was not regarded with equal love by the Native men who killed him. "Father Hernando de Santarén, born in Huete in the Province of Toledo, had confessed and preached in the lands of the Idolaters for 24 years and was martyred by the same."[85] Santarén's rigorous extirpations in the "lands of the idolaters" had finally earned him his martyr's crown.

Conclusion

While scholars have productively studied idolatry extirpation campaigns in the Andes, Yucatan, and Central Mexico to evaluate the success of Iberian evangelization and the creative resistance of Indigenous communities, they have not always linked these clashes to the discourse and practices of martyrdom.[86] The story of Santarén's campaign and later murder illustrates how increasingly militant cultural invervention fueled cycles of violent confrontation in northwestern New Spain. Extirpation provoked resistance, and these uprisings sometimes led to missionary death. When dressed in the rhetorical clothing of "martyrdom," the murders elicited further hostilities, as new generations of zealous priests went into to these borderlands with the conviction that they would convert them or die trying. The Christian rhetoric of persecution lent celestial import to these ritual confrontations and epidemic plagues, spurring further cycles of violence over the course of the first few decades of the seventeenth century.

A material reality linked the two discourses, as both focused on bones and other spiritually potent objects. Although they treasured the relics of their own dead, Jesuit missionaries did not reflect upon their correspondence to the religious practices of Sinaloa's Indigenous communities. Without a hint of irony, the priests insisted that Native burial goods and sacred bones must be extirpated, even as they cherished the bodily remains of priests like Gonzalo de Tapia and Julio Pascual. However, Europeans and Indigenous communities shared similar interests in recovering and revering the remnants of their deceased. The Acaxee, Chínipa, and Tepehuán valued human remains as potent material and spiritual objects. Ancestral bone bundles and corporeal war trophies acted as reservoirs of power and generators of cultural revitalization.

When stored away in the monte, Native stones and bones occasioned missionary anxiety. The priests interpreted the objects and accompanying rituals of the *monte* as "idols" and "vices," which had allowed the devil to hold onto the vast territory outside of the priest's isolated Christian outposts. As they lamented the situation, they insisted that these "rocks, thorns, and thistles" be weeded out, mowed down, and pruned away to clear the ground for gospel seed.

Conversely, Indigenous communities in Sinaloa and the Sierra Madres made use of the missions to reconstitute themselves in a period of demographic pressure and converted Catholic practices into powerful signs of resistance. Leaders like the "Acaxee Bishop" Perico, the Guazápare shaman Cobameai, and the Tepehuán leader Quautlatas appropriated the evangelists' rituals and repurposed them to urge their people to flee the priests, who had only brought disease and dislocation. These ritual specialists located the source of the problem in the mission and sacraments like baptism, Communion, and extreme unction, which they blamed for spreading sickness. Perico, Cobameai, and Quautlatas all employed practices of ritual inversion and mocking imitation to directly challenge the authority of the Jesuits with the hope of sending them into either exile or eternity.

Santarén's particular attention to extirpating "idols" provoked an especially violent conflict with Indigenous funerary and ritual practice. By gathering stone figures and bone bundles, grinding them up, and burning them in bonfires, the Jesuits had hoped to not only detach the Acaxee from their sacred sites, but emphasize the objects' powerlessness in the face of the Christian God. In 1602, the Acaxee rebelled and came close to killing Father Santarén within the year. For strategic reasons, they relented and let him live another day, a detail that hagiographers construed as providential. As close as the groups were geographically and culturally, the nearby Tepehuán likely knew all the details of his earlier campaign against the Acaxee and their subsequent revolt. Perhaps with that in mind, they killed Father Santarén and seven companions in 1612. Notably, they abandoned the priest's body in a ditch and left it conspicuously without protection from the rough terrain and wild animals. In fact, Figueroa reported that almost a year later, "since then his body has been seen lying naked on the shore of the creek, without burial and without any opportunity of providing one up until this time."[87] Completely ignoring Santarén's naked cadaver represented open disrespect for the man who had shown such contempt to Native ancestral remains.

Francisco de Figueroa's 1617 *Memorial del Martyrio* joined several other hagiographical works produced in the 1630s and1640s to retrospectively clothe the naked death in a sacred narrative. Alongside Figueroa, works like Juan de Albiçuri's *Historia de las misiones apostolicas* (1633) and Pérez de Ribas's *Historia de los triunfos de nuestra Santa Fee* (1645) hoped to gain canonical recognition for Tapia, Santarén, and the other Tepehuán martyrs. In fact, Albiçuri began a sequel to his first history in 1640, this time featuring the life and martyrdom of Santarén as emblematic of the wider mission's success.[88] In addition to letters, reports, passion stories, memorials, and histories, the Jesuit province of New Spain commissioned paintings. In 1617, they quickly drafted several official portraits of the Tepehuán martyrs (Figure 4), sending them to Rome for placement in the galleries of the Society's colleges, rectorates, and houses. These portraits were later copied and expanded to be placed in Jesuit mission churches in Chihuahua, the former novitiate of Tepotzatlan, as well as the Society's college in Mexico City. Much later, they would be reproduced for the provincial headquarter's martyr museum in the twentieth century.[89]

These martyr portraits hung on the walls of colleges in their refectories and recreation rooms. During meals, scholastics and novices would hear tales of martyrs being slain in different parts of the globe and afterward were told to meditate upon the paintings in their free time.[90] Gauvin Bailey has called these displays a sort of "trophy case of Jesuit martyrs" that helped Jesuit novices not only travel imaginatively to global sites of martyrdom but entice them to sacrificial adventures and teach them what was expected in their missions. Less than a year after their deaths, Father General Mutio Vitelleschi was already narrating the passion stories of Father Santarén and the other Tepehuán martyrs to young novices as they ate at the Jesuit Curia house in Rome.[91] After the meal, the students would move to a recreation room, where they could contemplate the eight ink and chalk drawings of the murdered priests. Writing back to New Spain to thank them for the images and explain their devotional value, General

FIGURE 4. One of eight drawings commissioned in New Spain, this depiction of Father Hernando de Santarén's brutal death was sent to the Jesuit Curia in Rome to accompany written accounts of the Tepehuan martyrs of 1616. Artist unknown, Pater Ferdinandus de Santaren, Rome, 1616–17, courtesy of the Archivum Romanum Societatus Iesu (ARSI).

Vitelleschi explained how he had read them "in the refectory with universal consolation by all due to having eight more brothers in heaven." He also relayed that he found the depictions so powerful that he had commissioned copies of "the painting portraits on canvas" so he could place them alongside other martyrs on the Curia's walls.[92] That way, the Jesuits in training could more fully appreciate Santarén's sacrifice as they digested their food and contemplated their futures.

A few decades later, a young Sicilian student named Francisco Xavier Saeta listened to similar accounts of the embattled but expanding Mexican mission as he supped at the Jesuit house in Palermo.[93] At eighteen years old, he wrote to Father General Charles de Noyelle to first request an assignment to New Spain. Over the next decade, he explained to Noyelle and subsequent generals of the Society how daily readings in the refectory had prompted his own desire to serve and give himself entirely for "the missions of the Indies, Mexico, the Philippines or whatever other place they might judge." In six letters to father generals Charles de Noyelle and Tirso González, he pled over and over "to spend his sweat and spill his blood" in this evangelistic work.[94]

After five years, Saeta decided to up the ante and switched from Italian to Castilian in his ensuing letters. The twenty-three-year-old boasted that he had learned Spanish on his own initiative and gently pointed out that no other novice he knew who was asking to go to New Spain had taken a similar step. When the famed Jesuit father Eusebio Kino wrote directly to Sicily from Sonora in 1691 to request workers for his newly pioneered mission to the Upper Pima (O'odham), the rector of Palermo read Kino's pleading letter over lunch at the refectory. Nearly ten years into his campaign, the newly avowed priest Saeta knew this call was divine. He immediately wrote to General González, not once but twice in a row, on September 19 and 20. Just over three months later, on January 24, 1692, he finally received the notice he had prayed for since he was eighteen. Father Saeta was going to Mexico. As he expressed his exhaltation and joy to his superiors, he could hardly know that within three years new depictions and accounts of his own death would be viewed and read by the next generation of Jesuit novices.[95]

3 Fruits
Passionate Expansion

On the Saturday morning between Good Friday and Easter Sunday of 1695, Father Francisco Javier Saeta woke early, eager to prepare for the glorious culmination of Holy Week. Having arrived at his station in Caborca, Sonora, just months before, Saeta had resisted repeated offers from his fellow Jesuits to spend the week with them at the more established missions of the Pimería Alta.[1] He explained that he not only toiled piously with his O'odham converts but had so much physical labor that he could not spare the time. In March, Saeta lamented to his mentor Father Eusebio Kino, "I will not enjoy your favors, for in reality I am swamped both spiritually and temporally." By April, however, he had relented and promised Kino a visit sometime after the paschal celebrations. Thanking him for a care package of letters, bread, and cookies, the new missionary excused his absence by expressing paternalistic concern. He explained that he was presently occupied with his newborn "children" in the faith but would "nevertheless steal a while and like a swift arrow fly to put myself at your feet."[2]

Saeta intentionally employed this image, an obvious play on his family name, which meant "arrow" in the missionary Castilian as well as the native Italian that he shared with Father Kino.[3] Upon receiving the letter, Kino savored the pun. He noted that Saeta invoked it whenever possible: "How many countless times did I hear him say, 'He has made me a chosen arrow,' alluding piously to his name Saeta."[4] In fact, the young missionary had closed a letter to Kino just a few months earlier by apologizing for his penmanship and wryly professing that "I am writing with the strokes of an arrow."[5] Saeta could not anticipate, though, the tragic irony of this earlier witticism or his subsequent promise to fly "like a swift arrow." Weeks later, when he finally arrived at Kino's feet, he did so not swiftly but in a highly ritualized and deliberate procession. The only arrows were those collected in the reliquary that contained his remains.

During the Holy Week celebrations of 1695, Saeta had heard only the first hints of his perilous situation. On the afternoon of Good Friday, he received a distressing letter from Kino with "the news that the Jocomes had attacked San Pedro de Tubutama and killed poor Martín and the boy Fernando," two of Saeta's assistants who had taken Caborca mission cattle to the nearby *ranchería*. After reading the distressing warning, he began a reply, in which he mourned the loss of his Ópata helpers Martín and Fernando and fretted over the fate of Father Daniel Januske, his nearest compatriot on this northwest frontier of the Spanish North American mission. Nevertheless, Saeta tried to carry on with the day's sacred festivities as well as his more quotidian mission chores. In the evening, he heard confirmation of the attack from Caborca's Christians and grew increasingly apprehensive. In a postscript to his reply to Kino, he pled for more information: "For God's sake, dear Father, let me know what has happened and how Father Daniel is faring." Then, after sealing the letter, he mentioned that he was forwarding Kino his vestments and some personal items for safekeeping. He anxiously appealed for protection: "Please don't let me be lost from view."[6]

By the time Kino received the letter just before mass on Easter Sunday, it was too late. At sunrise on Holy Saturday a group of fifty to sixty men from the missions of Tubutama, Oquitoa, and Pitquín had arrived in Caborca. Saeta probably did not know that these O'odham, and not Jocomes or Apaches, as Kino had first warned, had killed the Jesuits' Ópata allies in Tubutama and burned its church. Typology and chronology mix in the diverse accounts of the ensuing events. Nevertheless, soldier, missionary, and Native testimonies all agree that Saeta died soon after the group arrived on that morning of April 2, 1695, suffering at least two initial arrow wounds to his chest and absorbing other blows to the rest of his body.[7] In addition to the missionary, six Native Christians—four Ópata, one Seri, and one O'odham—were killed during Holy Week of 1695.

While the initial uprising was episodic and local in character, cycles of violence spun outward in the following weeks. Indiscriminate Spanish reprisals and disproportionate punishments provoked a wider revolt, eventually leading to burned missions, retreating missionaries, and fleeing Indigenous communities throughout the Pimería Alta. To address the situation, Captain Domingo Jironza Petris de Cruzate, the leader of the newly formed Flying Company of Sonora, mounted a military campaign in May that was tasked with locating the perpetrators, making an example of them, and restoring peace. The Flying Company botched the first task, failing to locate the rebels among the empty settlements, which had been abandoned by their residents. Instead, the soldiers and their allies meted out quixotic and excessive punishments to the few O'odham that they encountered along the way. This only exacerbated the tensions.[8]

In the absence of direct combat, the colonists and missionaries eventually attempted another way. Jironza and Kino reached out to allied O'odham governors and agreed to meet in early June at a marsh called El Tupo to discuss the conditions of peace. Tragically, that gathering went horribly awry. When the O'odham leaders produced some of the men whom they contended had been involved in the uprising, a Spanish Captain named Antonio Solís summarily executed one of them. In response to the sudden extrajudicial murder, several O'odham began to flee. In turn, Spanish soldiers and Ópata Indigenous auxillaries responded by discharging their weapons, reporting that they feared an ambush. Since they had come to El Tupo unarmed and with the assurance of their security, the assembled O'odham endured heavy losses. Forty-eight men and women died on June 9 at El Tupo, a place subsequently known as *La Matanza* (the Massacre). Unsurprisingly, more violent resistance spread throughout the summer of 1695 as angered O'odham attacked the missions of Tubutama, Caborca, San Ignacio, Magdalena, and Irumis. In strategic raids, the rebels killed cattle, destroyed crops, burned churches, and desecrated sacred images.[9]

Grappling with dramatic setbacks, Jesuit writers relished prophetic tidbits like Saeta's "arrow" pledge, eager to point out every sign that the martyred missionary had embraced his trial. To them, Saeta's premonition of death helped demonstrate his sanctity.[10] When placed in letters, *vidas*, histories, and reports the omens transcended hagiographical anecdote and reinforced a shared sense of providential suffering between missionaries, Jesuit colleagues, novices, and the lay patrons who read of their sacrifices from Europe, other parts of the Americas, and as far as Asia.[11] In the face of clear evidence of failure, these signs were meant to assure the surviving missionaries, their supervisors, and their supporters that this was all according to plan. Far from unexpected, the O'odham Revolt of 1695 was just another repetition in the divine pattern in which missionary and Indigenous suffering seeded the future fruits of spiritual conversion and territorial expansion.

This chapter unpacks how Jesuits like Kino claimed that martyrdom produced diverse types of fruit. However, in distinction from earlier accounts that had emphasized providential causes and cosmic warfare, Jesuits by the late seventeenth and early eighteenth centuries increasingly supplemented the spiritual logic with material causes and practical explanations. Faced with grave doubt about the viability of the Pimería Alta mission, its founder, Father Eusebio Kino, marshaled support from fellow missionaries, soldiers, and Spanish colonists to affirm that missionary death had long been the established method through which the Spanish Empire and Christendom advanced in this frontier. Breaking from his predecessors, though, Kino paired this providential explanation with a wide-ranging collection of letters, regional history, maps, and missiological theory to point to more quotidian causes and practical solutions.

To make the argument, he drafted an elaborate defense and future plan for the Pimería mission titled *Inocente, Apóstolica y Gloriosa Muerte del Venerable Padre Francisco Xavier Saeta*. While previous interpreters have either extolled this work as a historical biography of the martyr or dismissed it as irretrievably prejudiced hagiography, comparatively few have recognized how Kino creatively mixed the passion story with cartography, history, and missiology to defend his work and thereby ensure ongoing colonization.[12] This account represented a change in martyr discourse in the latter half of the seventeenth century. Similar to earlier hagiographers, Kino and other writers like the Spanish soldier Lieutenant Juan Mateo Manje and the missionary Father Luis Velarde used the idioms and materials of saintly patronage, relic collection, and canonical expectation to make sense of the uprising. At the same time, he employed historical and material explanations to check these spiritualized justifications and urge practical solutions to endemic violence.

Newly pressing logistical and theological challenges necessitated some of these changes. Catholic missionaries had long served two masters, at once charged by the monarch with pacifying a frontier and by the papacy with evangelizing nonbelievers. In theory, these dual goals worked together as kings directed the missions under the system of *patronato real*, the power of patronage granted to the Castilian monarchs by Pope Alexander VI. Once more, Philip II's 1573 Ordinances Concerning Discovery had forbidden independent "conquests" and instead "made missionaries the primary agents of exploration and pacification."[13] Theoretically, this meant that colonists and soldiers should work in support of the primary goal of evangelism.

However, the cozy alliance between church and state rarely worked out in reality as missionaries, soldiers, and colonists battled for control of Native labor and land.[14] This contest of power escalated in the late seventeenth and early eighteenth centuries. Whereas fathers Tapia, Santarén, and Pascual all had relied upon a close relationship with soldiers like captains Diego Hurdaide and Diego de Avila in Sinaloa, these sorts of relationships were increasingly frayed to the north in Sonora by the 1690s. Kino had developed a close working relationship with some soldiers like Manje, but he also found himself increasingly at odds with others, including Lieutenant Antonio Solís and Corporal Nicolás de Higuera. Soldiers and missionaries blamed each other for revolts and even pointed fingers internally, priests against priests and soldiers against soldiers.

In addition to questions of method, Saeta's death and the O'odham uprising raised other concerns about the sustainability of the northern missions. The Catholic theological argument that proclaimed an eventual spiritual payoff for Indigenous suffering, and missionary sacrifice had started to hold less weight with royal governors and military captains by the late seventeenth century. As the Hapsburg monarchy's ability to control its colonies teetered for decades on the unstable health of the dynasty's last monarch, Charles II, the idea that God would work it all out in the end began to fall on deaf ears. Even before the king's death and the subsequent outbreak of the Spanish War of Succession in 1701, Spain's grip on its colonies had been slipping. This was compounded on the northern frontier by escalating rivalries between religious orders, settlers, and royal officials, as well as the ongoing and assertive power of the region's Indigenous people.[15] Groups like the Caddo, Comanche, Seri, and Apache increasingly exerted their territorial dominion throughout the northern frontier in these decades and signaled to Spaniards that the frontier system of missions and mines would not hold.[16]

Perhaps more than anything else, Spaniards increasingly feared the possibility of an organized pan-Indian revolt. The Pueblo Revolt of 1680 had inspired similar resistance in other parts of the borderlands throughout the 1680s and '90s, including multiple rebellions among the Rarámuri (Tarahumara) in Chihuahua.[17] Simultaneously, increased raiding by Mansos, Sumas, Janos, Jumanos, and Apache bands stoked fear of a larger, coordinated action among diverse Indigenous groups.[18] Some historians have called this uptick of resistance "the Great Southwestern Revolt," though evidence for a united effort is relatively thin.[19] Still, fear of a large coordinated threat led to increased militarization in the region, including the establishment of several new presidios and the rapid response Flying Company of Sonora.[20] The rise of the presidios and *La Compañia Volante* meant new options in the pacification of the frontier.

As many were questioning the state of the borderlands, the martyrological claim that Indigenous converts had rejected Christianity inherently called into question the Jesuits' suitability to rectify the situation. By any measure, Saeta's death, the O'odham massacre, and the wider revolt threatened the viability of the Pimería Alta missions. Kino's religious and secular critics argued for a more aggressive approach. Some missionaries demanded more rigorous pastoral discipline, while soldiers pressed for the increased use of presidios to pacify the frontier. More radically, some suggested transferring responsibility for economic and religious supervision over to miners, settlers, and secular bishops. In response, Kino struggled to make sense of how his supposedly loyal converts had turned first on his handpicked disciple, Saeta, and later on the wider evangelistic project. Similarly, O'odham Christians must have wondered why the alleged preachers of peace joined with the violent soldiers and colonists that brutalized them at every turn. Once more, the priests had employed the nearby Ópata as foremen, catechists, and auxilllaries in this work and failed to realize the tensions this caused for many O'odham, who had frequently competed with the Ópata for resources.[21]

Favors

Faced with such wide-ranging challenges, Kino set out to refute the perception that Saeta's murder represented a fatal impediment to the Pimería Alta mission. In early 1696, he was recalled to Mexico City to report on the revolt. To defend his work with the upper O'odham, Kino drafted the *Inocente Muerte de Saeta* as a thorough apologetic.[22] He did so first by employing the time-tested agricultural metaphor that insisted upon the ultimate fruitfulness of the conversions, asserting that the 1695 uprising was not a sign of rejection, but a necessary pruning and essential seeding in this new ground. As he connected to this enduring logic, he found support in the minutiae of Saeta's life, the longer history of the Jesuit missions in northern New Spain, and the letters of supportive missionaries and soldiers.

To start, Kino recast Saeta's death as one of many "celestial favors," a paradoxical step toward flourishing O'odham Christianity.[23] The title of Kino's later history of the Pimería Alta, *Favores Celestiales*, suggested that these were works performed by God through the intercession of patron saints like the Virgin Mary and St. Francis Xavier.[24] As he explained in his prologue to that work, "We will attribute the spiritual and temporal conquests of these new conversions to the celestial favors of these aforementioned divine protectors of ours rather than human agencies or to the military force of the presidios and soldiers."[25] Contrary to those who were calling for more aggressive martial intervention, the priest insisted that otherworldly intercession was the surest guarantee of success. Within this framework, Father Saeta had transformed from tragic young victim into the region's protomartyr, joining the Virgin and Francis Xavier in heaven as they pled for O'odham conversion. The ultimate success of the Pimería Alta evangelization would not be set back by Saeta's death. Rather, it would depend upon the intercession of this new patron and his celestial favors.[26]

Father Kino worked in the cosmic war tradition invoked by earlier Jesuit chroniclers like Juan de Albiçuri, Andrés Pérez de Ribas, and Francisco Figueroa. The Virgin, Jesuit saints like Ignatius of Loyola and Francis Xavier, and new martyrs like Saeta would provide powerful guidance and aid in the battle to wrest this terrain from its diabolic overlords. He made the parallel clear by charting the providential arc of Saeta's life, tying him directly to holy figures. As previously mentioned, Kino claimed that Saeta often stated that God had "placed [him] as his chosen arrow." By quoting this phrase, he linked Saeta to Isaiah 49:2: "He made me a polished arrow, in his quiver he hid me away." The citation suggested that the younger Jesuit had been perfected and protected for precisely this moment just like the prophet Isaiah.[27]

Since late antiquity this verse had also featured in the mass for the Feast of St. John the Baptist. As a rare Hebrew Bible liturgical reading, "the chosen arrow" would have conjured up not just Isaiah but also John the Baptist for Kino's readers. The image suggested that Saeta both followed these prototypical prophets and served as a forerunner to later evangelists. Once more, since many Christians venerated John the Baptist as the first New

Testament martyr, Saeta's name also foretold his passion. To bring home the typology, the church father Jerome had argued that the image foreshadowed not only John the Baptist, but Christ himself. For Jerome, Jesus was the true "chosen arrow," sent by God to pierce the darkness of the world.[28] In the tradition of Isaiah, the Baptizer, and Jesus himself, the symbol marked Saeta for a prophetic call of suffering service.

In addition to his name, Kino plied redemptive meaning out of Saeta's devotional practice. Specifically, he pointed to the young missionary's dedication to Colette of Corbie. According to Kino, Saeta always carried an engraved parchment, or *vitela*, with her likeness. The significance of the relationship between this devotion and his murder may not be immediately self-evident. The fourteenth-century reformer of the Poor Clares was not a martyr in the strict sense, was not beatified until a half century after Saeta's death, and her death was not associated with arrows.[29] Nevertheless, Kino extracted martyrological meaning from her patronage and image. Santa Coleta had presaged Saeta's ordeal, since she was "represented in paintings with arrows of divine love coming to her from the crucified Christ and with a lamb which holds in its hand a crown of gold bearing this inscription, 'Coronaberis'—'You will be crowned.'"[30]

Kino proceeded to unpack Colette's fourfold association with sacrifice, which together foretold the young martyr's fate. As depicted in the *vitela*, she gladly welcomed the piercing arrows of the celestial caress, she communed with the crucified Christ, she embraced a sacrificial lamb, and she received the promise of a heavenly crown. Colette's endurance of severe opposition and her stringent meditation on Christ's passion had foreshadowed the young missionary's destiny. Just as she had opened herself up to God's piercing arrows and identified with the paschal lamb, Saeta too had embraced his *imitatio Christi*.

In particular, Kino contended that the phrase "*coronaberis*" indicated Saeta's special role in God's economy of redemption. The word came from the second chapter of the Revelation of St. John, in which the resurrected Jesus commands his church to prepare for affliction and diabolic persecution, urging his followers to "be faithful until death." In exchange, Jesus promises, "I will give you the crown of life" and grant victory over the second death.[31] Just as his last name tied him to the words of the suffering prophets Isaiah and John the Baptist, Saeta's devotion to Colette linked him back to the apocalyptic persecution of the early church. Like those

Christian saints, the Jesuit's endurance under tribulation would lead to heavenly returns and eternal life. For Kino, the miniature portrait's survival as a relic acted as a sign that Jesus had extended these promises to the Pimería mission in its own time of persecution. By correlating Saeta's name, life, and manner of death to Colette's *vitela*, Kino painted a multivalent picture of God's provision in the murder. More importantly, the events of 1695 had forged a link with Christian history and secured the celestial favors of divine patrons.

Tokens

Kino could describe the image of *Coleta* in such detail because he likely had it in his possession as he wrote his account of Saeta's death. His regular traveling companion, Lieutenant Juan Mateo Manje, had recovered it "among the rest of (Saeta's) holy things" in the ruins of the Caborca mission. He later gave it to Kino during the martyr's funeral service, and Kino delighted in his friend's gift, having "saved it and venerated it as a special relic."[32]

In his personal diary, later titled *Luz de Tierra Incognita*, Lieutenant Manje related his own account of the *vitela*, explaining how he had recovered "an engraved parchment with a picture of a nun, which bore the name St. Colette." Manje confirmed his gift, noting that Kino "kept it as a relic and an aid in his prayer."[33] Manje likewise mentioned the archery image, detailing how an angel shot Colette with an arrow that "already pierced the Saint's heart and still another one was between her and the angel." Like Father Kino, the relic assured Manje that Saeta had given "his life to enter Heaven triumphantly in eternal glory to celebrate the victory of Christ, receiving the palm and crown of a martyr." Even as God had used Colette's suffering to penetrate her heart with divine love, Saeta's devotion to this patroness confirmed his own divinely pierced passion.

In the rest of Manje's account, a journal begun in the wake of the revolt but compiled and edited over two decades later, he provided additional martyrological details. According to him, the Flying Company of Sonora, which was led by his uncle General Don Domingo Jirónza de Cruzát, had been charged with pacifying the rebels and recovering the martyr's body.[34] As a lieutenant in the Company, Manje had sent the governor of Bosna, an O'odham ally, ahead to Caborca to look out for a possible ambush.

Arriving at a deserted and destroyed mission, the official had discovered Saeta's body. But before the rest had arrived, the governor had decided to burn it, because it had become "swollen and decayed due to poisoned arrows and 13 days" of desert sun. Manje claimed that he had "the blessing of helping to gather" Saeta's charred remains, including "the bones, ashes, and head, which still had some of the deceased priest's hair." Along with the bodily relics, he also gathered the instruments of death, depositing alongside his bones and ashes "the 22 collected arrows (*saetas*) from the floor of the room where the dead priest slept." Finally, he had discovered a singular crucifix that had escaped destruction, which he held onto as a special devotional object.

By adding the detail of Saeta's burning, Manje raised a possible problem in regard to veneration: the corruption of Saeta's body. In terms of devotional expectations, martyrs' bodies should give signs of incorruption as a testament to their sanctity. This was not a hard-and-fast rule, but a hagiographic trope that often bolstered a candidate's claim to beatification. The tradition of unburnable martyrs dated to the time of Polycarp in the early church.[35] It recurred throughout the Middle Ages and peppered accounts of global Jesuit martyrdoms in the early modern period.[36] The conceit had taken on a particularly strong resonance in northern New Spain, as several previous Jesuit martyrs had proven their sanctity when their bodies resisted fires or consumption. Andrés Pérez de Ribas, for example, had delighted in Zuaque frustration when they failed to burn Father Gonzalo de Tapia's arm in 1594.[37] Similarly, he had highlighted the incorruptible bodies of the Tepehuán martyrs Luis de Alavés and Juan del Valle, whose graves were opened years after their death. According to a witness, the bodies not only remained intact, but could still stand and "emitted a very sweet aroma, corresponding to the aroma emitted by their very religious virtues when they were alive."[38] The body of Father Gerónimo de Moranta, who died in the same revolt, similarly remained incorrupt until it was discovered three months after his death.[39] While incorruptibility was not an absolute test of sanctity, it would have been a strong sign of God's favor. Especially as the protomartyr of the Pimería, faithful Catholics would have anticipated that Saeta's corpse would resist decay or destruction.

Each in their way, Kino and Manje both addressed these concerns. First, they pointed to the unique desert environment and duration of exposure.

No body, even a holy one, could last long in the harsh Sonoran heat. Thirteen days of exposure to these elements had taken an inevitable toll.[40] Second, they emphasized that the body had not been reduced during the actual moment of trial, but only slowly afterward. In previous cases, the missionaries' bodies had resisted the burning of the perpetrators, a sign of God's triumph over their evil plans. Kino and Manje contended that they had every reason to believe that Saeta's body had endured the initial attack in the same manner.[41] Rather, the O'odham governor of Bosna who burned the body was a devout Christian and an important ally. They asserted that he burned the body out of necessity but had been careful to first retrieve relics.[42] Beyond practical concerns, Manje went on to assert that the cremation conformed with O'odham funerary practice, as "this nation [burned] the dead bodies of those most beloved and venerated."[43] By claiming this O'odham custom, Manje made the crucial point that Indigenous Christians shared European veneration for Saeta. Rather than hatred, he had been burned out of love, and his relics had been closely guarded by O'odham Christians. He suggested that God was validating Indigenous acts of devotion as much as Catholic expectations of sanctity.

Both Manje and Kino featured another relic prominently in their narratives of Saeta's death, relating how Saeta clung to a Christ figure during his murder. Manje vividly described the evangelist and this "Santo Cristo" in intimate communion during his final moments. According to the soldier, the crucifix had marked the site of the missionary's transition to the heavenly realm. Manje narrated how Saeta fell "to his knees again before his *Santo Cristo*, and offered his soul to the Creator. He departed the body that had been cruelly pierced with 22 arrows (which was his heraldry) and we piously believe he went to glory to sing the Alleluia of the Resurrection of the Lord." As the place of his crossing to splendor, the Santo Cristo connected the martyr Saeta and his celestial home, a crossroads between heaven and earth.

Kino offered a more detailed, if less cosmic, description in his account. According to him, Saeta had met his killers at his door that Holy Saturday morning in April 1695. Realizing their intent, he embraced his fate, "knelt, and opened his arms to receive his most innocent death in imitation of the crucified Christ." After they initially shot him with two arrows, the young missionary retreated to his room and "took up in his holy hands a *santocristo de bulto*." In Kino's retelling, Saeta first sat with the crucifix on a box and then gradually proceeded to his bed, where he lay down with it. The perpetrators followed and finished him off with more arrows and blows from their *macanas*. With this, the Jesuit's *imitatio Christi* was complete. Kino then briefly described the killing of his four Indigenous servants and other robberies and destruction. In particular, he highlighted the perpetrators' profanation of sacred objects, a key detail that would confirm their hatred of the faith. Miraculously, the *santocristo* had escaped this sacrilege because it rested alongside Saeta's head.

Perhaps during the murders and subsequent destruction, Saeta's *cristo* was separated from his cross, because Manje subsequently described two holy objects. He explained that the Christ figure had been recovered by an O'odham Christian and given to Father Agustín Campos, but evidently Manje himself had recovered the burned cross on which the *Santocristo* had been nailed. Along with the *vitela* of Colette, the soldier had rescued it and given it to Kino to hang in his mission at Nuestra Señora de los Dolores.[44] For his part, the senior priest celebrated the gift with a special mass on May 3, 1695, a date they both noted coincided with the Feast of the Discovery of the Holy Cross.[45] At the same time, Father Campos had entrusted the Christ to the Spanish soldier Lieutenant Antonio Solís, who had placed it in Arizpe, Sonora, during the burial of Saeta's relics, where it was ensconced, according to Manje, with "much veneration in a rich golden sepulcher of six crystal moons."[46]

During this latter moment, both sources emphasized the shared reverence displayed by Indigenous, missionary, and military devotees. Everybody showed "the greatest devotion they could throughout the 55 leagues" as they traveled south, first to Kino's mission of Dolores and then to Kappus's headquarters in Cucurpe. As they approached the latter mission, the group arranged itself into two lines, and the caravan of soldiers, *vecinos*, and missionaries aimed to impress allied O'odham and Seris with "harquebus salutes and other demonstrations of affection." Once in Cucurpe, Manje's uncle, General Domingo de Cruzát, got down from his horse in a calculated display of humility and took the reliquary box off the back of the mule to mount it upon his own shoulders as he marched to deposit in the church.

The exhibition was meant to be an example of public piety to the gathered Ópata, Eudeves, and O'odham. The men who would soon lead the pacification campaign against Saeta's killers meant to emphasize the significance that Spaniards attached to the relics. They were tokens that testified to the sanctity of their colonizing project. After the gathered military joined Indigenous Christians and four Jesuit priests for a funeral mass, General Cruzát ordered his soldiers to ready themselves for retribution. For Lieutenant Solís, who had been entrusted with the holy Christ figure, pious reverence would be a prelude to brutal revenge.[47]

Other Jesuits pointed to signs of shared veneration in order to validate Saeta's saintly status. At the conclusion of his *Luz Incognita*, Captain Manje embedded a separate account of the Saeta's death, written by the Jesuit rector Luis Velarde. Father Velarde had taken over the missions of Dolores, Remedios, and Cocócspera after Father Kino's death in 1711. In a 1716 report to the provincial of New Spain, entitled "Relation of the Pimería Alta," Velarde summarized the state of the region in the wake of its founder's passing. From the distance of two decades, he expressed optimism about the results of the revolt, contending that the evangelistic work had progressed well, "despite contradictions."[48] As evidence, Velarde recounted the inspection tour of Father Visitor Luis Mancuso in 1714. The Jesuit visitor Mancuso had come from his own Tarahumara mission to Pimería with the charge of reviewing the rectorate and addressing any problems. In general, Mancuso found that the missions endured and the O'odham remained faithful Catholics, notwithstanding Kino's death and increased raiding from nearby Apaches, Sumas, and Janos.

In addition to this official job, however, Father Mancuso had more personal business on this trip. A native of Palermo, Sicily, he had developed a particular devotion to "the tender memory of his holy *paisano* the venerable Francisco Xavier Saeta." The elderly Mancuso had first traveled from Sicily to the New World with Saeta twenty-four years earlier. Because of this cherished recollection, Mancuso requested that the elderly Father Agustín Campos guide him to the site of Saeta's grave in Cucurpe, Sonora. Since Campos had participated in the funeral nineteen years earlier, he knew where the body was buried.

According to Velarde, Campos and Mancuso entered the church, "opened the sepulcher of the venerable father," and looked for "the place where (Saeta's) bones lay." Hoping to recover substantial relics, Mancuso disappointedly confessed that "they found very few, and it was a lot if they found any at all, since he had suffered such a violent death and been burned." The bones, hair, and skull that Manje had described were gone, perhaps a sign of further decay or maybe of a wider demand for tokens of the region's protomartyr. In resignation, the visitor contented himself with the few pieces of bone that he found and "the sole of a shoe." Mancuso gathered these relics together with a sworn testimony and a letter from Father Campos on the "Life of Saeta." He planned to send them back to Sicily in the hope that the martyr "might gain a singular place in the history of the Company (of Jesus)."[49] Even as he had once listened to stories of New Spain's martyrs and missionary labors, his former college's novices would now hear of Saeta's sacrifice and contemplate his holy relics.[50]

While he gathered these sacred tokens, however, Mancuso chose not to remove another venerated relic from the missions. According to Velarde, he left in place a "*santocristo* of rare material, tender to the touch, preciously and devotionally made," which had been "rescued from the furor and rancor of the murders." Following Kino and Manje, Velarde emphasized the pious role of Indigenous allies in the recovery of the relic. But he provided a different provenance than Manje. Velarde claimed that "a good Indian had hidden it in a box inside of a bag of wheat" and brought it to Father Agustín Campos, handing it to him with sincere devotion "on his knees." With these details, he stressed "the good Indian's" loyalty to the Jesuits and devotion to the martyr.

He also used the relic's recovery to defend the mission and the authenticity of O'odham Christianity. Velarde insisted that the *Cristo's* preservation proved that veneration for Saeta continued nearly two decades after his death. It testified to the missionary's ongoing celestial favors and the enduring fruitfulness of the sacrifice. Velarde attributed this lasting reverence in part to the relic's "wondrous" qualities. Made with a "rare flexible material," Saeta had brought the *santocristo* from his Sicilian home and placed it centrally in his mission. Manje also compared it to a human body: "It was so flexible it seemed like living flesh, transparent in its veins, nerves, and arteries." In the absence of the martyr's human remains, the fleshy *Cristo* transubstantiated both Saeta and Jesus and incarnated the reality of their ongoing protection.

At the time of writing in 1716, Velarde maintained that the lessons of saintly patronage had been effectively communicated to Indigenous converts. He argued that Ópata Christians in Arizpe still held Saeta in highest regard and had ever since employed his *Cristo* and coffin as part of their burial procession each Holy Week.[51] This is why Mancuso had left these relics in Sonora. While fellow Jesuits and lay patrons in Sicily might receive some bones, clothing, and Campos's *vida*, Ópata and O'odham Christians would hold onto these sacred objects as tokens of Saeta's sacrifice. This accorded with the larger point that Velarde extracted from the relics. While his death initially portended trouble, Saeta's spilled blood had actually sealed the relationship between the Jesuits and Native converts. In the years after 1695, "new fathers came who proceeded with fervor cultivating the new vine watered with the blood of the martyr."[52] Saeta had planted the seed, and his brothers cultivated it into a flourishing vineyard of Indigenous Christianity.

However, Saeta's own work had not ceased with his death. Like Kino and Manje, Velarde argued that the martyr had posthumously joined Mary and the saints in their heavenly intercession for O'odham Christianity. Saeta's pleas only multiplied over the years, he explained, as they joined "together with those of many young children who certainly enjoy the eternities of glory." Velarde clarified that the missionary's initial sacrifice had been supplemented not only by the work of Jesuit brothers but by the death of several O'odham children from epidemic disease. Since they had been baptized and thus preserved in innocence, they too now enjoyed eternal salvation and surely worked alongside Saeta in heaven, "moving the Divine Mercy" to bring celestial favors.

Mature O'odham who had died in the following years also helped the cause, Velarde reasoned. Together, they had interceded that Christ "might have pity on these souls redeemed by His precious blood and dispose that all of them be gathered into the gentle fold of Faith."[53] Moving between pastoral and agricultural metaphor, he concluded that the vine had grown through this constant watering and now O'odham Christians had "achieved the fruit of the redemption that his Majesty has predestined for them." Saeta had secured divine access by depositing his earthly relics into Native ground and supplemented these material signs with ongoing cosmic intercession. Sickness had played its own providential role, Velarde concluded with a notably unfeeling tone, because in prematurely taking so many O'odham, the Pimería now had hundreds of patrons joining the protomartyr in heaven.[54]

Blood

In addition to present context and future payoff, these writers contended that Saeta's death should be understood in biblical and historical terms, dating back to the ancient church but replicated in colonial experience. Referring indirectly to the story of Joseph in Genesis, Kino explained that while "evildoers might serve their own causes, ... The Most High permits it with his most divine Providence, because even from evil he knows how to rescue good."[55] This reference to the patriarch Joseph insisted that God redeemed even the vilest of human action. Unsurprisingly, Kino also quoted Tertullian time and again to bolster this argument.[56] He urged his superiors to trust in the belief that blood would seed a new Christianity in the Pimería Alta for "the immense glory and celestial crowns of the holy martyrs, and *Ut sanguis martyrum sit semen Christianorum.*" The pioneer evangelist believed this ancient logic had become the established pattern of redemptive death in northern New Spain.

To bolster that case, Kino cited letters from fellow Jesuits and Spanish soldiers. Throughout, the agricultural metaphor pervaded the epistles of these fellow missionaries and colonists, as all involved assured themselves that Saeta's death and the Pimería's destruction would not be in vain. Summarizing this overall sensibility, Father Antonio Menéndez, the rector of the Mayo and Yaqui missions, optimistically reassured Kino that all "missions begin with the blood of a minister." As evidence, Menéndez cited the martyrdoms of Father Tapia in Sinaloa, "Santaren and the seven glorious Fathers among the Tepehuan," and fathers Pascual and Martínez in Chínipas, as well as fathers Cornelius Beudin, Antonio Basilio, Diego Ortíz de Faronda, and Manuel Sánchez, who had more recently graced the Tarahumara of Chihuahua "with their blood" (*con su sangre*). From this longer view, the Pimería's missionaries should take solace, because "God was pleased that the fervor of Father Francisco Javier Saeta should be the first fruits of that mission."[57]

Likewise, the Slovenian rector of Sonora, Marcos Antonio Kappus, expressed his hopes that bad would ultimately work for good. In the immediate aftermath of the news, Kappus had written to profess his veneration for the region's "glorious protomartyr." He assured Kino that the divine majesty would look upon the sacrifice of the "innocent victim" and work so that "all these evils will fructify greater and greater blessings."[58] Surely, he concluded, the glorified Saeta would work on the mission's behalf and for all of "our protection and benefit."

Little did Kino know; Father Kappus was already working behind the scenes to blame him for the revolt. Nevertheless, his first letter reiterated the widespread conviction that martyrdom produced conversion. Another of Kino's future critics, Father Juan Muñoz de Burgos, also initially praised him for helping bring peace and "staying the fury of those ungrateful people." As the father visitor of the Pimería at the time of revolt, Muñoz de Burgos was tasked with supervising its well-being. While he put the blame on the Tubutamans in the letter to Kino, in letters to superiors he blamed the pioneer missionary and his loose methods.

Nevertheless, in these earliest responses Muñoz de Burgos maintained that everything would work out, because "this watering of that angel's blood will serve the Lord by producing much fruit in the Pimería."[59] To Muños de Burgos, Jesuit blood was the liquid required to loosen the desert's hardened ground. Indigenous rebellion was a "fire" that could only be quenched by the waters of "holy zeal, holy counsels, and holy sacrifices." The visitor reiterated this point in several subsequent letters to Kino, asking, "In what new conversions have we not seen the shedding of blood of apostolic noblemen, whose irrigation has fertilized the crop of many souls?" While blaming "disloyal" converts, Muñoz de Burgos concluded that their hate would providentially give way to love.

Kino drove home the point by including other letters from Father Antonio Leal of Durango and Marcos de Loyola of Mátape. In a June 9 dispatch from the Jesuit college of Guadiana, Father Leal linked the recent violence to the father's earlier success in the region. Citing the hundreds of O'odham who had requested baptism after Kino's last northern voyage, Leal asked, "How could the devil permit so many souls that were once his to escape?" He insisted that the success of the mission, not its failure, had actually caused the revolt, as the diabolic adversary had incited resistance in an attempt to impede the advance of Christendom. Leal pointed to similar setbacks in the time of Christ and his apostles, and yet "every century since then, their successors who still remained . . . have returned to kindle the fire of the Holy Spirit, rising from the cold ashes of the dead." Like a phoenix, O'odham Christianity would resurrect stronger from the smoldering ruins. Saeta would intercede for these souls, and "the blood of our brother will be the irrigation with which more new plants will grow in heaven." Father Marcos de Loyola echoed these sentiments, envying Kino and the O'odham mission for their suffering, as it would surely lead to both territorial expansion on earth and "a great reward in heaven."[60]

Lest superiors ignore these letters as missionary propaganda, Kino included "a few letters from secular men," mostly soldiers charged with keeping the peace in the region. He started with Captain Pascual de Picondo, the lieutenant of the Pimería, who wrote to Kino on May 30 to celebrate that Saeta had been "blessed a thousand times with the gift of having his stole bathed in blood." Captain Picondo insisted that the "reverend Pima Fathers should rejoice and congratulate themselves" now that they had a heavenly intercessor that would ensure their success. Identifying the missionaries with their converts with the phrase "Pima Fathers," Picondo confirmed that the evangelistic work was actually "flourishing" and that its "fruit is ripening for the storehouse of the Church."[61] In Picondo's rendering, the revolt had conjoined the Jesuits with their converts in the work of producing harvests for future maturation.

Kino cited other soldiers to testify to the imminent payoff of the Jesuit work. For example, Picondo's immediate successor as lieutenant, José Romo de Vivar, had written with consoling words of assurance. Unsurprisingly, Kino also cited his friend Captain Juan Mateo Manje, who shared the conclusion that Saeta's death would not bring the end of the mission, but instead a new beginning. "This crop of souls is going to be fertilized by the blood of that most fervent Father and martyr Francisco Xavier Saeta. In time it will flourish, as happens in the fields where the earth is fertilized by means of irrigation so it can vigorously grow crops of wheat."[62] Instead of retreating, the martyrdom should encourage them to explore further, settle new missions, and bring new workers.

Manje also appealed to biblical precedent to conclude that the missionary's death did not demand revenge, but rather prayers for future salvation. Specifically, he invoked the story of Cain and Abel, but did so for both comparison and contrast. "Nor will this innocent blood of our venerable martyr be like that of Abel which cried out for vengeance." By likening Saeta to Abel, he located the Jesuit in a story of sacrificial death that traced back to the biblical account of humanity's very origins. However, he also drew a distinction between the "Old" and "New" covenants. "Rather it will become a flood of supplications and clamors for the conversion of these pagans and for their repentance. They do not know what they have done, as those others who crucified the Lamb, Jesus himself."⁶³ These killings would not operate under *lex talionis*, the ancient law of retaliation embodied by the Cain and Abel narrative. Instead, he argued that Saeta conformed to the model of Jesus, who prayed for his persecutors even from his cross because they knew not what they did. From what Manje observed, "The spilled blood is already beginning to bring forth fruit," as more O'odham were petitioning Kino for baptism and inviting him to begin missions further to the north.

Christendom

This vision of growth through blood was not just temporal but spatial. In his introduction to *Luz de Tierra Incognita*, Captain Manje argued that the logic conformed not only to biblical precedent, but to the Society of Jesus's wider global mission. In imitation of Abraham, Moses, and Aaron, the sons of Ignatius had brought the message of God to foreign lands and secured them with their sacrificial labors. This was especially true in the Pimería, "where these ministers work with such immolation and spirit, to the point of losing their life for love of the one who sacrificed his for us." Because of their martyrdoms, Manje contended the northern borderlands were blessed by God and granted stability for many years. More than just local crops, he argued that Saeta had added a new leaf to the verdant tree of Christendom. His death replicated Jesuit sacrifice throughout the globe and joined the Pimería to "Japan, Ethiopia, the Philippines, Moscow, and China" through a shared story of suffering. Missionary martyrdoms linked their local story to the global advance of Christendom.

Saeta's death was just the newest bud, springing from "24 Jesuit religious in New Spain, as in Florida, Chínipas, Tepehuanes, who with various martyrdoms have given their lives in imitation of the twelve founding sons of the celestial Father."⁶⁴ To make the image clear, the soldier described a lush tree (*frondoso arbol*) that extended across the globe. Ignatius had planted the tree, while the first missionary, Saint Francis Xavier, had begun a branch to Asia, and the second general saint, Francis Borgia, extended an arm to the Americas. Previous martyrs had extended its reach into northern New Spain, while Saeta's blood had engrafted into it the leaves of the "Pima, Sobaipuri and nearby people of the north."

Manje likely had in mind a prominent image from Athanasius Kircher's *Ars Magna Lucis et Umbrae* (The Great Art of Light and Shadow). In his *Horoscopium catholicum Societ. Iesu* (Figure 5), the famed Jesuit intellectual Kircher had pictured the Society as an ever-expanding olive tree, with each new assistancy representing a new branch, provinces as pods, and colleges or missions as leaves. The "Universal Horoscope" meant to map the global work of the Society and serve as a universal clock that when positioned correctly could tell the time in each mission. A banner at the top proclaimed this spatial and temporal effort to be like a "fruitful tree in the house of God (*sicut oliva fructifera in domo Dei*)."[65] By describing Saeta's death as a leaf of this global tree, Captain Manje translated obvious failures into flowering branches in the inevitable universal spread of Christianity.

Kino likewise employed visual means to illustrate his case, preparing two maps to accompany his text. Both would illustrate how martyrdom brought conversion and extended the bounds of Christendom. At the same time, they dramatized the practical accomplishments of Jesuit exploration, cartography, and settlement. The first, "Teatro de los Trabajos Apostolicos de la Compañia de Jesus," or Theater of the Apostolic Labors of the Society of Jesus, set out to tell the wider story of Jesuit labors in the region through a groundbreaking depiction of the region's geography. Kino declared that he drew up a general map of the missions to display the relationship between Spanish territorial advance and Jesuit sacrifice.

In an introduction to a chapter about the previous sixteen "Fathers of the Society of Jesus who gloriously gave their blood for the Faith here in North America," he wrote that he would chart the time, place, and manner of each Jesuit martyrdom in northern New Spain. He further explained that he intended to place "the letter 'M' on it to signify the places where our glorious soldiers of Jesus gave their lives for the Catholic faith." Although he never completed his goal of properly locating each martyrdom, the "Teatro" dramatically displayed the larger point that Jesuit labors (*trabajos*) had transformed Sonora, the Pimería Alta, and California into Spanish Christian space.[66] In this way, Kino joined the work of other Jesuit missionaries throughout North and South America who had marked the sites or manner of martyrdom onto their maps to illustrate the full range of the Society's work to expand Christiantity.[67]

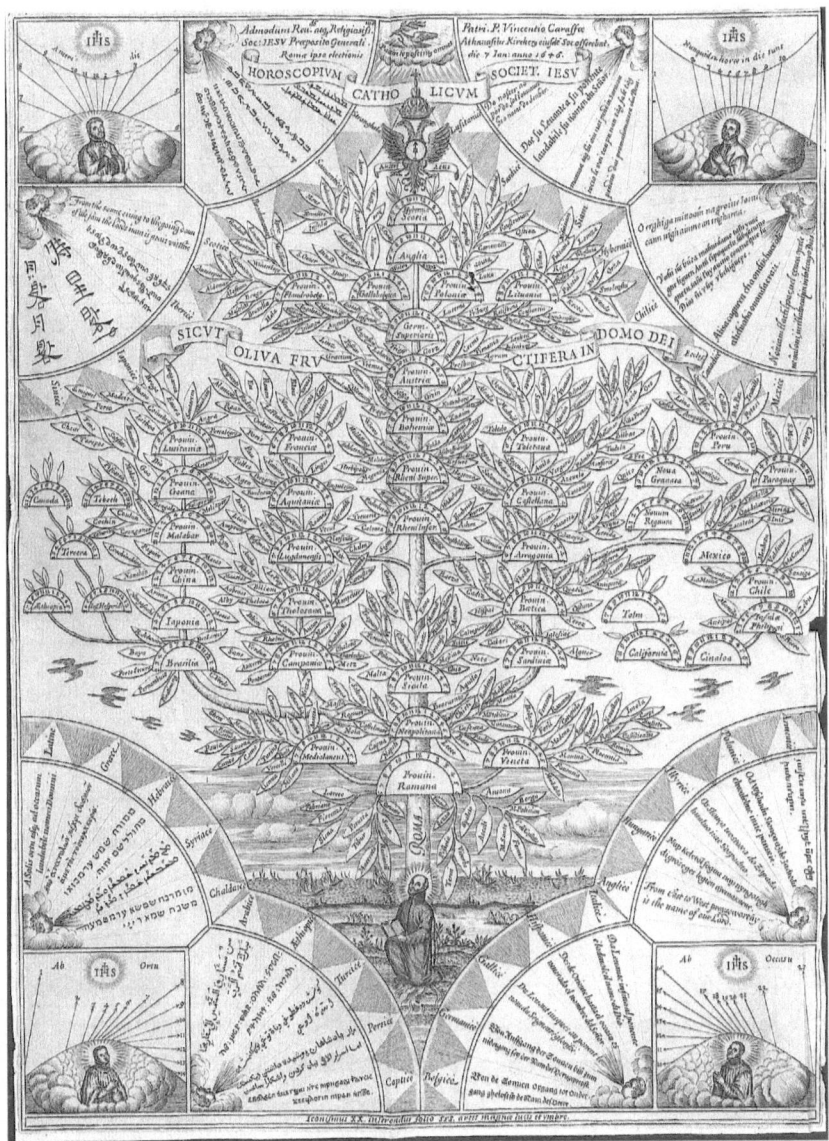

FIGURE 5. Athanasius Kircher's "Universal Horoscope of the Society of Jesus" visualizes the global presence of the Jesuits as a verdant tree. To the right and center, pods for Mexico, Cinaloa, and California join the other missions of Spanish America. *Horoscopium catholicum Societ. Iesu.* in Athanasius Kircher, *Ars magna lucis et umbrae* (Rome, 1646), 553, courtesy Stanford University Libraries.

116 FRUITS: PASSIONATE EXPANSION

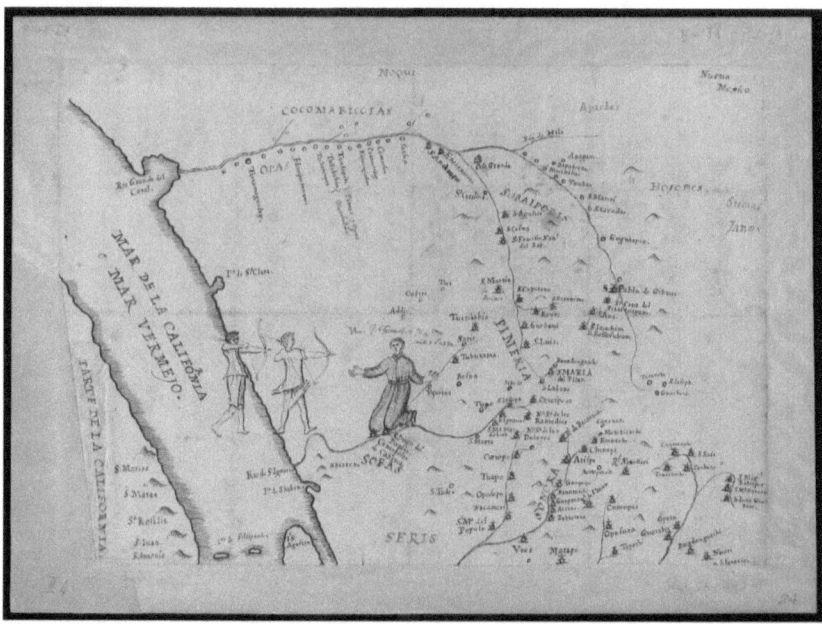

FIGURE 6. Kino created this map of the Pimeria Alta to accompany his account of the life and death of Father Javier Saeta. Saeta is depicted surrendering his life with outstretched arms and his knees on his mission at Concepción de Caborca and the nearby visita of Pitiquín. "Map of the Martyrdom of Father Saeta," 1696, courtesy of the ARSI.

While Kino never realized his intention to mark the time and location of sixteen Jesuit martyrdoms on his "Teatro," he made sure that the theme would not be missed in his second map. In the untitled drawing, Kino focused exclusively on the Pimería Alta, presenting it as a detailed backdrop to Saeta's dramatic passion (Figure 6). Following his written narrative closely, he depicted the young missionary kneeling with arms open in cruciform resignation. Saeta's knees rest on his two missions of Concepcion de Caborca and San Diego de Pitiquín, while two clothed Natives draw back their bows with the resolve of delivering arrows to his chest. The drastically oversized priest looks his persecutors in the eyes and welcomes his fate as his colossal body stretches across the western Sonoran Desert to embrace the frontier. The scene unfolds along the San Ignacio and Altar rivers from Tubutama and Caborca to the coast, at once the location of the uprising and the furthest corner of Spanish presence in

North America. One figure also walks upon water and floats above the Sea of California. This movement from the existing Pimería missions to the sea and on toward the coast of California conveniently linked Kino's existing work to his long-hoped return to the "island."[68] It reminded intended viewers, including the Jesuit provincial Diego de Almonazír and the Jesuit general Tirso González not only of the extensive efforts to pacify and convert the Pimería Alta, but also of the missionary's previous service in California and petition to go back.

Kino's ultimate goal was to not only preserve the Pimería conversions, but to expand the frontier with new missionaries to the north and west. In particular, he believed Caborca and its nearby coast could be the strategic launching point of supplies for the new venture.[69] In the surrounding backdrop, Kino charted his recent explorations to the north to display the many settlements that he had recently explored over the previous year with Manje. Some settlements were marked with only O'odham place names, but he had already added patron saints to others, like San Xavier del Bac just south of modern Tucson. To the north a small illustration of a "Casa Grande" and the telling inclusion of Cocomaricopas, Apaches, and New Mexico hint at Kino's plan of extending the work even further north. Together the message could not be clearer; Saeta's death was strategically located at the northern and western frontier of Spanish North America. His willing sacrifice would not only secure O'odham Christianization but pave the way for the future spiritual and territorial expansion. His blood would help transform both O'odham souls and space to bring both within the bounds of Christendom.

Hatred

Even as Kino, his fellow missionaries, and his military supporters assured themselves that the martyrdom would bring new fruit, they struggled to protect their vineyard from external and internal attack. Both secular and religious critics charged O'odham converts with "barbarity, ungratefulness, cruelty, and hatred of the faith (odio de la fe)."[70] Detractors voiced suspicion about whether these "desolate lands" and semi-sedentary tribes of the north warranted the trouble of evangelization. A few suggested that attention should be devoted to more "worthy" groups, and others ramped up longstanding arguments that spiritual conversions could never pacify the northern frontier.[71] Fueled by the discovery of new silver mines in Chihuahua and Sonora in the 1680s, settlers hoped to appropriate Native land and labor for commercial use and pressured royal officials to focus on the more aggressive means of military conquest, tributary labor, and parochial administration.[72]

Kino expected opposition, since the Jesuits held sway over a wide territory and had access to significant resources. For this reason, he had procured a royal decree before entering the Pimería that granted special exemptions for O'odham Christians. Concerned about past military "violence that had terrorized and caused (Natives) to flee from conversion," the priest had requested immunity from forced labor (*repartimiento*) and military punishments. In accord with a general royal proclamation (*cédula*) that participants in new conversions be protected from tributary labor or taxation for twenty years, the governing audience of Guadalajara issued him the requested order for the Pimería Alta in 1686.[73]

This naturally strained relations with Spanish settlers who desired access to O'odham land and the labor. Kino indicated as much when he indirectly complained of opposition from those who "should have been helping us, but instead hurt us, who were our friends, but became our enemies."[74] Saeta's murder exacerbated this tension and raised an additional conundrum that forced him to walk a fine line in his defense. In order to be recognized by the larger church, any prospective martyr must be found to have died for hatred of the faith or *in odium fidei*. If Jesuits hoped Saeta or any martyr would reach this status, they must demonstrate that the killers perpetrated the act out of anger toward Christianity and not for other causes.

This standard had its roots in the teaching of Saint Augustine of Hippo. According to Augustine, true martyrdom entailed both the victim's willing acceptance of a faithful death and the perpetrators' willful rejection of the Catholic gospel.[75] Centuries later, Thomas Aquinas codified Augustine's teaching in his *Summa Theologica*, arguing that perfect martyrdom could be declared only when an executor took life in rejection of the Christianity and the victim gave life for love of the same. As such, neither death for other causes nor suffering for religion without culminating death could rightly be declared a full martyrdom.[76] Material or political reasons for killing would therefore complicate any martyrological claim.

The martyrological qualifications set by Augustine and Aquinas received fresh articulation in the early modern period. In response to Protestant challenges and Tridentine reform in the sixteenth century, Roman authorities confirmed these standards and used them to increase their control over proliferating martyr cults. Through papal pronouncement and inquisitorial purview, they hoped to vet claims of holy death as a way to produce liturgical unity, limit local devotions, and buoy a shared Catholic identity. In 1625, Pope Urban VIII specifically prohibited publications that urged the public veneration of purported saints without official papal approval. Urban VIII later established the Congregation of Rites to investigate, judge, denounce, or recommend candidates for canonization.[77]

The Inquisition also issued a ban on nonauthorized hagiographies and enforced its censorship in the presses of far-flung colonies.[78] In order to satisfy these interests, Catholic writers included official declarations or "*protestas*" before their works, which carefully explained that their narratives did not impinge on Roman prerogatives.[79] These statements declared that words such as "Holy, Blessed, Venerable" were used provisionally, and the final judgment of all "revelation, prophecy, ecstasy, or miracle" belonged to "the infallible decision of the Holy Roman Apostolic Catholic Church." Still, the authors of these hagiographies and encomiums hoped to supply key details to prove that the potential martyr had died in hatred of the faith.[80]

For example, Juan Mateo Manje cited a 1634 decree of Urban VIII and the later regulations of the Inquisition, "which prohibits the cult of sanctity or martyrs for men who pass from this life without being declared so by the oracle of the Holy Spirit, the Roman Pontiff," in his account of Saeta's death.[81] This did not stop him from arguing that the sacrileges committed against holy objects in Tubutama and Caborca confirmed that Saeta had been killed "*en odio de la fe.*"[82] Father Luis Velarde also pressed the case for Saeta's canonization, because "he gave up his life to enter into glory triumphantly and celebrate the triumph of Christ, received with the palm and crown of martyrdom." Velarde cited Urban VIII to clarify that he called Saeta a "martyr" only in the informal manner permitted by the papacy. Nevertheless, he pointed to "the Indians' complaints, according to what they executed upon the sacred vestments, the holy paintings, the altars, the chalices, the patens," to conclude that "I do not doubt that they killed him *in odium fidei*."⁸³ Manje and Velarde both recognized the prohibitions, but nevertheless emphasized iconoclastic destruction in order to prove that Saeta's killers hated Christianity.

Though he never published his own account of Saeta's passion, Kino similarly hoped that it would make its way to press as a part of Saeta's canonization and as an *exemplum* for the edification of the global Jesuit community. At the same time, he needed it to serve more immediately as an *apologia* for the mission against his critics.⁸⁴ In his presentation of Saeta's martyrdom, Kino anticipated both pontifical and Inquisitorial inspection and offered the standard qualification in his prologue. "I openly declare (*protesto*) that I do not want the least expression in this little work of mine to detract one bit from the holy opinion and judgment of our Holy Mother Church and its holy tribunal, the Holy Inquisition, or from our Holy faith."⁸⁵ In furthering the cause of his young protégé, Kino explained that Saeta had indeed lived a holy life and, more importantly, had died *in odium fidei*. The damage to the church and sacred objects had proven the case.

More precarious than papal censorship, however, the claim of "faith hatred" threatened to undermine all of Kino's work in the Pimería Alta. The notion that Jesuits died because their charges hated the faith ran the risk of convincing superiors to give up on the mission and try another method. After all, why should miter and scepter continue to invest valuable human and material resources in people who violently reject those gifts?⁸⁶ While Catholic martyrological standards meant that Kino must establish faith hatred, the mission's survival demanded that he must also defend O'odham innocence.

Gifts

Kino faced other challenges to a strictly hagiographic account. In the immediate aftermath of the wider revolt, fellow missionaries like Francisco Xavier Mora and Marcos Kappus began making more personal accusations against Kino.⁸⁷ They questioned the pioneer priest's outsized influence in the region and argued that his spiritual negligence had led to both internal dissension among the Jesuits and a rebellious attitude of O'odham converts.⁸⁸ On July 28, 1695, Father Marcus Kappus had written from Cucurpe, Sonora, to inform the Jesuit provincial Almonazír in Mexico City about his own evaluation of the revolt. Like Kino, Kappus had come to the north to serve after previous training in Austria, Italy, and Mexico.

However, he was younger and arrived slightly later to Sonora, just a year after Kino in 1689. Kappus had just been appointed rector of the newly established rectorate of Nuestra Señora de los Dolores, charged with overseeing the interethnic missions of the Pimería Alta. When the revolt broke out, Curcurpe became the center of European operations, serving as both a refuge for fleeing priests and converts and as an organizational center for military operations.[89]

For all these reasons, Kappus had both the intimate knowledge and institutional responsibility to inform the Jesuit provincial Diego de Almonzír about the details, causes, and possible resolution to the O'odham Revolt. And, after customary salutations and a few updates, he wasted little time declaring what he believed to be the root of the violence. Kappus argued that the mission had never been stable because "neither the method of conversion here has ever seemed to me to be well established, nor has the foundation ever been well-laid."[90] Claiming that he had consistently reported this to his superiors, the rector argued that instead of focusing on essentials like preaching and teaching the laws of God, "all of the effort has always been focused on reducing the Pimas by lavishing gifts and meat upon them."[91] Exasperated, Kappus maintained that O'odham adults "are content to have the water thrown on them," but continue in the "ancient ignorance of Gentiles, with less obligations than Christians and without ever obeying because what pushed them to receive baptism was lavishing upon them some gift."[92] According to him, these handouts had led to easy conversions in which the O'odham gladly accepted baptism but went on without any knowledge of Christian doctrine, participation in further sacraments, or intention to "live in a Christian manner."

In the introductory paragraphs, Kappus contented himself with the passive voice, carefully describing the root of the revolt while avoiding the direct accusation. However, on the second page he named names, explaining that "I am not talking about all the Father missionaries that entered up until now the conversions of the Pimería, but instead only Father Eusebio Kino who if he would have had so much determination to teach the Gentiles as his desire, earnestness, and ease to baptize them, this Pimería would have a different look entirely today."[93] Kappus argued that Kino should be blamed directly for the revolt because he had baptized too quickly and pastored too loosely. In so doing, he failed to appropriately teach doctrine or regulate behavior. Unlike the Ópata and Eudeve converts under his personal supervision, Kappus contended that most O'odham were Christians in name only because Kino baptized too widely, throwing water on every random child he saw in his wide-ranging explorations. This had earned Kino international fame in the Society as a prolific evangelist. However, Kappus argued that locally he was not so admired among his colleagues. This was because his "zeal had not been matched with consideration and prudence." The older missionary had encouraged uncountable O'odham to imagine themselves converted through ritual while actually living "50 to 60 leagues away from Christendom" and without any hope of a real priest to come teach them the true meaning and practice of faith.[94]

More specifically, Kappus contended that Kino's success relied chiefly upon his liberal practice of gift-giving. He had earned O'odham loyalty through largess and become a powerful patron in the region. Kino reportedly had developed a large stock of cattle and supply of money to purchase garments and other enticements to baptism. Instead of seeing this relationship as a crucial step in establishing reciprocity with would-be converts, Kappus believed such gifts undermined respect for other priests because the upper O'odham had become "spoiled," always expecting to be "showered with gifts of clothes, meat, etc."[95] Since newer missionaries rarely had access to these resources, they found their people indignant and unwilling to obey them.

In Kappus's explanation we get a rare glimpse of possible O'odham perspectives on the situation. To bolster his case, the priest introduced anonymous quotations meant to signify the general sentiment among O'odham Christians. When new ministers tried to introduce Christian doctrine and moral duties, Kappus wrote, they inevitably protested that "Father Kino does not require these things for those who have asked for baptism." When other priests distributed grain or some garments, they would protest, "Father Kino provided meat more regularly, gave clothes more freely as well as other gifts." What Kappus reported the O'odham saying they also acted upon. He grumbled that many of them came from other missions to visit Kino and "carry away some gift to their house." He reported that even far-away "gentiles" traveled to Kino in hopes of establishing a relationship with him and his material resources. In contrast, the ministers who distributed less and demanded more from their converts were held with "little love, little estimation, and little respect" and found it difficult to keep their charges home instead of moving to Dolores.[96]

What Kappus described as damning evidence against Kino provides insight into why some O'odham decided to participate in the Jesuit missions. Baptism may have been welcomed if it meant reciprocity, balanced with relative freedom to maintain traditional practices. Like many Indigenous groups, gift-exchange and redistribution constituted central elements of O'odham social organization and kinship formation.[97] For example, later studies of the Tohono O'odham who lived in the Sonoran Desert just north of the Altar Valley recorded the practice of *níari*, a form of reciprocal exchange that fostered community cohesion by redistributing supplies of fresh food from those with abundance to those in need. *Níari* encouraged those who had more in the present to distribute it widely instead of storing it up, both to avoid spoilage in the harsh desert environment and to secure future help from allies in changing circumstances.[98] The establishment of such a relationship entailed long-term obligation and familial relationship.

While *níari* may have been particular to the Tohono O'odham, other O'odham communities developed similar gift-giving customs that extended to kinship networks and secured allies. Foodstuff trading allowed groups living in different topographies to diversify their nourishment and insure against famine. These relationships often entailed give-and-take arrangements of submission and benefaction as subordinate groups put themselves at the service of those whose access to food and supplies was steadier.[99] Gift-giving forged bonds of patronage and fealty that, while unequal, established obligations that demanded compliance from each side. When Jesuits entered into this network and offered wheat, meat, clothing, and tools in exchange for settlement in the missions they had little idea of the diverse connotations of these practices within O'odham culture. While they may have missed the varied cultural valences of these exchanges, missionaries like Kino understood that they were initiating a pact that entailed reciprocal responsibilities from both sides rather than a simple conquest characterized by subjugation and obedience.

Abuses

Faced with external and internal challenges like those posed by Kappus, Kino deployed a multipronged explanation of the endemic violence.[100] He conceded that some O'odham may have killed the missionary in resistance to Catholicism. "Many would say that the circumstances and causes of these deaths have been simply the native's barbarity, ungratefulnees, cruelty, and hatred of the Faith."[101] However, he minimized this cause of death as a situation that inherently applied to any new mission field. In other words, initial resistance should be expected in the conversion of "all new and barbarous" people, and the O'odham were not unique. Unless the crown was being asked to give up evangelistic endeavors altogether, this should not be a specific complaint against the Pimería.

Along these lines, he also pointed out that the men he believed to have committed the acts were actually "gentiles," or nonconverts, and therefore not representative of more "docile" O'odham Christians.[102] Therefore, the "*odio de la fe*" that motivated Saeta's murder could not be attributed to the wider community but should be isolated to a small group on the furthest frontier. In addition, he ascribed final agency to the devil, because "it has been publicly known for years that the Common Enemy opposes the advancement of all of them (O'odham) and the coming of the Fathers that so many souls will not be lost; for by tyrannizing them he holds them in his power."[103] By diverting specific blame from O'odham Christians to unconverted "gentiles" and the generalized diabolic opposition, Kino suggested that Saeta died in hatred of the faith in a way that did not impinge upon the innocence of O'odham Christians.

If anything, Kino argued that the violence erupted because Spaniards and Jesuits had not delivered enough missionaries. He contended that some O'odham had killed Saeta not because they rejected Christianity, but rather because they were jealous of Caborca's status as a home (*cabecera*) to the new missionary. According to this interpretation, residents of Oquitoa had initiated the violence in Tubutama and Caborca because they envied their access to resources. The resentment stemmed from the time of Father Juan Maria Salvatierra's 1690 tour as visitor to the Pimería, he explained, because Salvatierra had promised Oquitoa a priest at that time. In preparation for elevation to mission status, the *ranchería* had appointed legal officials ("*governador, alcalde, fiscal mayor, alguacil, topile, fiscales, etc.*") and had their children baptized, only to watch Tubutama and Caborca receive the missionaries first. Always pragmatic, Kino recognized that their decision to accept the mission entailed interest in both "temporal goods and spiritual benefits." In addition to any possible attraction to the Catholic faith, they also sought "clothing, cattle, sheep, goats, horses, mules, farms, cow-hands, pack-trains, and drivers."[104] Not delivering on these gifts had not "spoiled" them as some claimed but caused a serious rupture in the patron-fealty relationship.

Kino went on to make an explicit case for practical supplies as an essential part of successful evangelization. To do so, he placed his argument in the posthumous mouth of Father Saeta as a part of six chapters about the martyr's "apostolic opinions concerning the growth and preservation" of the missions, the qualities of a useful missionary, "the Indians considered as a new people," the best means of conversion, and "goals of new evangelical conquests."[105] Throughout the second half of the *Inocente Muerte de Saeta*, Kino mounted a thorough defense of his missionary method, expressed as convictions that he held in common with Saeta. In this style, he argued that "Father Saeta felt that for a great advance in new conversions, after the Word of God, it is the endearing attraction of little toys and trinkets with which the hearts and souls of a new tribe are won."[106] You must start small as you establish contact. Eventually food, clothes, blankets and other supplies would be required to sustain the mission. While Fathers Kappus and Mora had argued that the O'odham had remained gentiles who only feigned Christianity to obtain such gifts, Kino (à la Saeta) reasoned that sharing goods was an earthly imitation of "the Heavenly Master" who has invited all to the great celestial banquet.[107] If mission status helped secure access to European trade, material goods, and specific lands, then it might be worth participating in some aspects of Christian settlement and sacrament.[108]

However, when Europeans failed to deliver on this relationship, things fell apart. Kino contended that Spaniards were to blame for "various disorders, severities, and cruel and rigorous punishments" in Tubutama. Specifically, up to eight residents of Tubutama had been murdered in the days and months leading up to the murder. The priest provided no further particulars about the circumstances of the deaths but left little doubt that some military leaders and their Native allies were to blame.

Father Kappus's letter to the provincial Almonazír actually supplied more details, stating that Tubutama's missionary Father Daniel Januske had requested soldiers to come and dole out "exemplary punishments" to those who resisted his leadership. Manje mentioned these abuses as well, explaining that Januske had employed a *vecino* named Juan Nicolás Castrioto to instruct the Tubutamans in cattle ranching. Manje contended that Castrioto had commanded an allied Ópata overseer to flog those who disobeyed orders.[109] Worse, Father Januske had called Lieutenant Antonio Solís in October of 1694 to come "make an example" of Tubutama's O'odham *fiscal*, which the lieutenant did by "meting out punishments left and right."[110] These abuses were crucial contributing factors if not the immediate cause of the 1695 uprising.

More generally, Lieutenant Solís and his soldiers had been waging a campaign of terror throughout the northwestern frontier in late 1694. Just a few months earlier, they had killed three Sobaipuri O'odham and whipped two others whom they suspected of stealing horses for meat, only to later discover it was venison that the Sobaipuri victims had obtained through hunting.[111] Kino also mentioned that Spanish soldiers had carried out other ad hoc punishments and unjustly blamed the O'odham for thefts actually committed by Janos, Jocomes, and Apaches.[112] He described one specific moment of abuse during his narration of the murder of Saeta's servants. In his narration, Kino departed from earlier Jesuit hagiographies, which very rarely gave specifics about Indigenous Christian death. To be sure, he provided nowhere near the detail that he supplied for Saeta. However, he did carefully name and highlight the faithfulness of each Native Christian. For example, he prominently mentioned a Chínipa named José, who not only cared for mission cattle as "un buen vaquero," but also had been married in the church and "delighted in the company of the venerable Father."

Accompanying José in the field was Francisco, an unmarried "herdsman of excellent character" from Cumupas. A fifteen-year-old Ópata boy named Tomás had also been killed. Kino gave no specific details about his job, but Tomás likely worked as a *criado*, one of many young men the Jesuits used as household servants. Perhaps for this reason, Kino took care to emphasize his volition in Christian service, writing that Tomás was "very desirous to serve the new Fathers in these new missions."[113] Altogether, Kino described the servants' deaths as willing, like the martyr Saeta, because "they gave their lives" alongside the venerable Father.

Tomás likely arrived in the Pimería with a fourth Indigenous servant for whom Kino provided more background. A fellow resident of Ures, an Ópata named Francisco Xavier had worked as Saeta's interpreter and catechist.[114] Tellingly, Kino noted that Francisco "was married to an Indian girl named Lucía, a Native of Mototicachi." He then went on to describe how in 1688 two hundred men from the Mototicachi had been captured as hostages by soldiers and taken to the presidio at Real de los Frailes. Accused of joining the wider "hostilities and robberies" of the Janos and Jocomes, the Spaniards had brutally punished the town by terrorizing its residents, torturing some, and then taking its adult men. The *ranchería* eventually demonstrated its innocence, but not before "more than fifty Indians were beaten to death."[115]

This massacre at Mototicachi had been led by Corporal Nicolás de Higuera, who later was put on trial, found guilty, and sentenced to death for his role in the murders.[116] Yet Higuera resurfaced to take a prominent role in the 1695 pacification campaign. As was frequently the case in a frontier desperate for capable soldiers, Higuera had somehow made his way back from condemnation to military leadership.[117] Although Kino did not name Higuera in his description of the Mototicachi massacre, the space he took to mention the murders made the implicit point that presidial soldiers deserved significant blame for the revolt.

The abuse was not limited to soldiers, however. Missionaries, too, should have recognized the ways in which they had contributed to an unstable situation. Although he did not specifically call out Father Daniel Januske, Kino implied as much, explaining that Tubutama's converts had complained about their Ópata Christian overseers to their missionary for many weeks. When Januske failed to address their concerns, they took matters into their own hands. Though he came to opposing conclusions, Kino's account closely matched Kappus report of the situation. The harsh discipline of an Ópata foreman (*mayordomo*) had angered the residents. In the same way that Spaniards had used Tlaxcalans and other Indigenous auxiliaries as colonizers and examples of Christianization throughout Latin American frontiers, Jesuits employed Ópata and Tarascan converts to serve as models, manage labor, and catechize new believers in the Pimería.[118] The Tubutamans protested that the Ópata were their enemies and that one particular overseer named Antonio had beaten an O'odham elder (*principal*) nearly to death. Kino recognized that the use of Ópata *mayordomos* had bred resentment and was likely the immediate cause of the rebellion. If Januske himself was not directly responsible for the beatings, he had given free rein to the brutal punishments of the *vecino* Castrioto, the soldier Solís, and the aggressive Ópata *fiscal* Antonio.

Finally, officials should realize that other cruelties had spurred the wider revolt. Lieutenant Solís had presided over the tragic massacre of forty-eight O'odham at El Tupo in June 1695. Kino had convinced several O'odham leaders, including both allies and some rebels, to convene at the marsh near Tubutama to make peace after the initial uprising. As previously described, Solís summarily executed a man he deemed to be a rebel and sparked an outbreak of violence against the unarmed O'odham by both Spanish soldiers and their Native allies. Kino highlighted the Spaniards' guilt in this event by branding it a "massacre" (*la matanza*) and "disgrace" (*desgracia*). Unlike previous Jesuits who had described similar confrontations as inevitable battles in the larger cosmic confrontation between God and the devil, Kino emphasized real-world causes and European cruelties. In light of the abuse of rival Indigenous groups, the punishments of capricious soldiers, and this unprovoked massacre, the general O'odham uprising of 1695 was not only predictable, but a reasonable response to brutal injustices.[119]

Kino believed that such persecutions, and not O'odham "obstinacy," had directly caused the uprising and precipitated Indigenous and missionary deaths. While others blamed their "barbarity" and his laxity, Kino pointed to European "errors, faults, defects, harshness, severity, narrowness, temper, and foolish resentments," which had led to the unjust "mistreatment, torture, and murder" of the O'odham.[120] He lamented the disgraceful killing of "innocent" O'odham and deemed it an "extremely heavy cross."[121] Then, he insisted that all involved shared the cost, "even the palefaces, the very ones who killed the innocent men, and especially the whole Pima nation."[122] Although Kino never precisely equated these O'odham deaths with martyrdom, his emphasis on their innocent suffering and disgraceful Spanish cruelty offered a potent mirror to Saeta's sacrifice. Jesuit evangelists and their Indigenous converts had suffered and shed blood together.

Conclusion

In 1698, the Jesuit visitor Horacio Polici reported to the crown on the "Thankfully Pacified Restless State of this Far-flung Pimería and of the Province of Sonora."[123] Charged with assessing the current situation in the region less than three years after the revolt, Father Polici concluded that things had turned out just as Kino promised. Polici had once joined fathers Kappus and Mora in their criticisms. In 1696, he had written to Mora to pledge his opposition to Kino and affirm that as visitor he had ordered the missionary to amend his laissez-faire ways.[124] However, by 1698 he had changed his tune entirely. He reported to New Spain's provincial and the viceroy that the Pimería was calm, productive, and worthy of further investment. In his explanation of its past he praised the loyal support of O'odham in Spanish wars against various Apache, Janos, and Jocome bands and explained that they had not only defended the frontier but sacrificed their lives as a sign of their love. In particular, he highlighted the town of Mototicachi, which despite the unjust accusations and punishments they had endured, had led the way in protecting the missions.

In making the recommendation, he anticipated the obvious objection. "One might object that the Pimas of Concepción de Nuestra Santisssima de Caborca cruelly spilled the innocent blood of the Venerable Father Francisco Xavier Saeta."[125] He nevertheless insisted that the events should be regarded positively and offered a script for his superiors to reply to critics. "First, you should answer that with this Holy Risk our Lord customarily founds his new Christianities." Unsurprisingly, Polici cited scripture and Tertullian in blended fashion: "He has planted his Church with His blood and the Blood of the Martyrs is the Seed of Christians."[126] Just like Kino, Manje, and later Velarde, Polici was persuaded that the fruit of Christendom would grow from the seed of Saeta's blood.

The Jesuit visitor went on to offer two more practical responses to would-be detractors. In addition to the fruit that would come from martyrdom, all should keep in mind that the O'odham had suffered unjust accusations, punishments, and murders. Like Kino, he placed blame on Spanish abuses and reasoned that some resistance should have been expected. That said, the uprising was small and short-lived. Only "25 or 30 Pimas rebelled and committed the evil while the whole rest of the Pimería totally rejected it." O'odham leaders had confessed their sin, asked for forgiveness, and endured more than their fair share of punishment.

Finally, since the time of the revolt, they had proved themselves to be valuable allies against all of the raiding groups to the north, winning a stunning victory in the northeast against a large Jocome and Apache band on March 30, 1698.[127] Polici assured his superiors that their power in battle had rewarded the Christian hope that ultimate good would come from the original evil. The O'odham had now opened the way to Christian advance "to the north, to the east, to the northeast, and to the northwest in this continent, as well as to the grandest Island on earth, the Great California."[128] For this reason, he recommended sending more Jesuit fathers and materials for the building of churches, farms, and cattle ranches.[129]

Kino likewise celebrated this victory in his own report to headquarters in 1698. Rehearsing the "more than fifteen years in which the Jocomes, Janos, Yumas, Mansos, and Apaches have infested this province with hostilities, robberies, the killing of Christians, and the burning of churches," he delighted in the dramatic victory of the O'odham led by Captain Coro over Captain Copotiari and the Jocomes near the northeastern Sobaipuri O'odham *ranchería* of Quiburi.[130] When he heard of the Jocome attack on the Sobaipuri settlement of Santa Cruz del Cuervo, Coro had gathered several allied O'odham and pursued the band, alongside his newly baptized son, Horacio Polici. Like many O'odham, Coro's son had taken the name of a prominent Jesuit as his Christian name at baptism, a detail that Kino believed attested not only to their conversion but their familial bond with the Society.[131]

Eventually, Captain Coro and the Sobaipuri caught up to the enemy Jocomes. Likening the scene to David and Goliath, Kino described how Coro and Copotiari stepped out face to face in a dramatic showdown. In a rare moment of literary quotation, he narrated how the Jocome captain mocked them, saying that "Coro and all the Pima were not men but women like the Spaniards he had joined because of the Padres. They were not valiant and (Copotiari) had killed many of them, including soldiers." Angered by the taunt, a "strapping young man stepped up and knocked him to the ground, crushed him with such valor that his comrades attacked the rest for two leagues, killing so many that only six escaped." The parallels to the biblical account of David seemed clear. Where once O'odham had suffered indignity and degradation at the hands of the Jocomes, now a young man had come forward, struck their boasting leader, and led them to a glorious triumph. The gendered nature of the dialogue conformed to Kino's argument as well. Opponents had accused the O'odham as being spoiled children or weak "women." On this day, a "*moceton*" or "strapping lad" like King David had proved his manliness along with that of his entire nation.

Still faced with doubters and those "of little affection," Kino called Manje, and they both set off to Quíburi to verify the results. They arrived on April 23 and immediately took the score. Of the Jocomes, "we saw and counted 54 cadavers, 31 men and 23 women . . . while only 5 from the Pima children had died."[132] The difference between his description of the bodies of these "enemies" as "cadavers" stands in stark contrast to his paternal regard for his O'odham "children." The disparity is even more striking with the care Kino had showed earlier for the bodies of both the Jesuit Saeta and his Christian O'odham servants. Where the latter were laden in meaning and power, the former were naked deaths, unadorned with redemptive meaning. Once more, Kino reported on the detail that nearly half of the "cadavers" were women, without the slightest sense that the fact might undermine his depiction of rival warriors on the field of battle. Nevertheless, the events convinced Kino, Manje, and Polici that the O'odham had proven themselves to be not only good Christians, but capable soldiers. Because of their bravery, the Pimería stood open for evangelization and civilization; "ten thousand souls" were ready to enter into "service to the two majesties" of God and crown. Delighted in "such a happy victory," Kino gave thanks to "Our Lord and the Most Holy Mary" for their ongoing celestial favors.

Late in 1698, Kino saw other rewards for his efforts, receiving a letter from the Jesuit general Tirso González in December. In it the general confirmed that he had received Kino's map with the martyrdom of Saeta, although the "eulogy or life, which your Reverence has composed, has not come." General Gonzalez explained that the drawing and text must have been separated in transit. Nevertheless, Kino's map and accompanying letter had greatly encouraged him and convinced him to continue investing the Society's resources in the Pimería Alta. He celebrated the rebuilding of the seven burned churches and pledged his support for Kino's ongoing labors.

Once more, he gave him permission to split his time between Sonora and California, working together with Father Juan Maria Salvatierra to connect the two. General González also thanked Kino for the news that "three Pima chiefs had promised to contribute towards the sepulcher of our Father Saint Ignatius," which the Society was currently building in Rome. Although he confessed that "the expenses have been very considerable," the altar and tomb for their founder would "be among the grandest of their kind in Rome." The O'odham captains' donations greatly encouraged him in that project. From González's perspective, they bore witness to the advance of Christendom into the Pimería and completed the circle of reciprocal giving, ritual participation, and forged kinship. Far from hating the faith, the O'odham had seemingly come to embrace the Jesuits, take Catholic saints, and fight Spanish wars.

Other Jesuits had expressed skepticism about Kino's methods and the fidelity of his Native charges. Fathers Kappus and Mora contended that he had won easy conversions through material gifts and only laxly attended to priestly duties. This, they argued, had spoiled O'odham Christians and made them quick to rebel. In addition, soldiers like Lieutenant Antonio de Solís and Corporal Nicolás de Higuera and vecinos like Juan Nicolás Castrioto had taken things into their own hands and doled out brutal punishments. Contrary to Kappus, Mora, Higuera, and Solís, Kino argued that conversion demanded patient understanding, not increased stringency. They should learn from past mistakes, treat the O'odham with respect, deliver promised resources, and govern with "common sense, prudence, and Christian Charity."[133]

In addition to these critiques of O'odham fidelity, Kino addressed doubts as to their ability to hold the line against Apache, Jocome, and Janos raids. While opponents had argued that the O'odham were at worst dangerous enemies and at best untrustworthy, he countered that they were both loyal Christians and good soldiers, capable of celebrating Christian sacraments and defeating the most threatening enemies on New Spain's northwestern frontier. O'odham converts had demonstrated their loyalty by sticking with missionaries even after suffering unjustly, proving they could be both innocent victims and conquering warriors. By Kino's reckoning, they should be included within what Europeans imagined as Christian civilization and trusted to help them advance the line against "savagery."

4 Deserted
Prolonged Isolation

In response to the 1695 revolt, New Spain's Jesuit provincial Father Diego de Almonazír wrote a circular letter to his northern missions. In the epistle, the provincial acknowledged that Father Saeta's fellow evangelists no doubt longed "with a thousand desires" to join their holy companion in death. However, he urged the missionaries to "prolong their bloodless martyrdom by continually risking their lives and by clinging tenaciously to the ministry despite brute obstinacy."[1] Father Kino relished his superior's commission. Referencing it throughout his writings, Kino argued that while "red martyrdoms" like Saeta's brought special blessings, the "white martyrdoms" reserved for those who remained were the tougher lot, as they were "more laborious, hard, painful, and prolonged" than a comparatively quick death by arrows, fire, or club.[2] The survivors' quotidian sacrifices would prove just as essential to growing the new harvest as the deceased's originating deposits. While Saeta's blood sowed the apostolic seed, the sweat and tears of those who remained watered the plants and ripened the spiritual fruit.

The prospect of dying in hatred of the faith permeated the missions both as an orienting metaphor and an ever-present reality. Kino's very arrival in New Spain had come at a time of large-scale rebellion in the north. As a recently arrived missionary in June 1681, the young Jesuit found Mexico City abuzz with news of the startling revolt of the Pueblo in late 1680. The uprising in New Mexico had left over 400 Spanish colonists and their Native servants and allies dead. Most prominent among the losses for priests like Kino, the rebels had killed twenty-one Franciscans. For most, the targeted murder of over half of the frontier colony's missionaries represented a drastic setback for both imperial and evangelistic causes.[3] It seemed like a complete rejection of Christianity. When Popé and his confederated Pueblo warriors decapitated priests, destroyed churches, and defecated on images of the Virgin and saints, the message seemed unambiguous.[4]

Like so often before, preachers in Mexico extolled the sacrifice of Francis's sons and promised that their death did not presage failure, but instead spiritual and imperial victory. In a March 1, 1681, memorial service held in the Cathedral of Mexico City, for example, the renowned orator and canon preacher Father Ysidro Sariñana y Cuenca explained to his congregants the true meaning of the tragedy. Working with thick biblical and Franciscan typologies, Sariñana y Cuenca insisted that contrary to expectation, "this suffering is joyous—it is the sure road to life; because the better title corresponding to such deaths is to call them lives." Sariñana y Cuenca's quick reversal of meaning, from suffering to joy and from death to life, demonstrated how widely shared the logic of redemptive death was in colonial New Spain. From the episcopal canon to his Franciscan subjects to the diverse congregants, the sermon made clear that the rhetoric of useful martyrdoms traveled well beyond the Jesuit rhetorical imagination.[5]

Just as Kino, along with his military and religious supporters, would later extract providential meaning from Saeta's manner of death, Sariñana y Cuenca contended that the arrows that pierced the Franciscan martyrs ultimately came not from the Native apostates, but from the very quiver of God. The Lord himself had allowed their wounding, the priest insisted, so that Saint Francis's *imitatio Christi* would be fulfilled in their mission. As an *alter Christus*, a Christ figure, Francis had inaugurated the collective martyrdom when he received the signs of crucifixion, the stigmata of divine love. Although Francis had lived a life of poverty and self-abnegation, he had only achieved a white martyrdom and never obtained the red martyr's crown. However, the preacher contended, these sons of Francis now endured hateful murders, thereby securing their founder's full identification with the Lord. In light of these sacrifices, Sariñana y Cuenca argued that the remaining missionaries should stay the course, joining both Francis and their brothers in the long defeat. Instead of retreating, they should finalize the *imitatio* by returning to the place of persecution, for "in no better way can (Francis's) sons show forth this imitation than when, without avoiding the risks through fear, they obediently bare their breasts to the dangers."[6] Like the Jesuit provincial Almonazír after the O'odham uprising, Sariñana y Cuenca argued that the survivors should continue the prolonged martyrdom in fidelity to their calling and surrender to its suffering.

No matter the religious order, most priests working in northern New Spain imagined their vocations as extended acts of sacrifice, commencing with the renunciation of home, stretched out over tortuous travels, plagued by trials, and racked with temptation. In the eighteenth century, missionaries in Sonora and California increasingly equated this suffering with their isolation in rough desert environments. Whereas earlier Jesuits who worked further east and south had described New Spain as overgrown with the weeds of superstition, these subsequent workers characterized the territory and people of the far nothwest as totally deserted.

At the same time, their framing of the sacrifice required of those who worked in such environments shifted toward the turn of the century. Previous missionaries had emphasized diabolic and cosmic oppositions. By the 1700s, however, priests described their suffering with increasingly naturalist and anthropological categories.[7] Jesuit letters home to family lamented the harsh settings, and their published natural histories described the climate, fauna, and flora as dangerous and unforgiving. Their descriptions of the region's Indigenous people mirrored these "*Noticias*" and "Observations"; they represented Native Californians not primarily as captives of the devil, but as children and subhuman brutes whose supposed obstinancy embodied the rocky shorelines and deserts of their habitation. This move toward scientific environmental description paralleled an increasingly racialized view of northern New Spain's Indigenous communities. By uniting the two, Jesuit reports and natural histories highlighted the priests' protracted desert travails even as they naturalized racial differences.

Part of this change was ecological, and part was demographic. The shift in tone in the early eighteenth century coincided with both a renewed effort to sustain a permanent mission in the sterile peninsula of California and the loosening of permission for non-Iberian Jesuits to travel to the Americas.[8] Sorely lacking in water, animals, fruit, and other natural resources required to sustain life in concentrated settlements, California posed several problems. Ignacio del Río has argued that the arid nature of the peninsula consistently forced Jesuits to operate differently there than in the mainland. Partly for this reason, Kino himself had been forced to abandon his earliest evangelistic attempt there, which had lasted under two years, from 1683 to 1685.[9]

However, renewed Jesuit effort, the generous support of wealthy patrons, and constant supplies from the nearby missions of Sinaloa, Sonora, and the Pimería Alta had finally allowed some missions to take hold by the late 1690s. Specifically, aristocratic donors in New Spain established the Pious Fund of the Californias (*Fondo piadoso de las Californias*) in 1697, which allowed the Society to operate there with relative independence, especially after it gained full control of the Pious Fund in 1717.[10] This economic base fundamentally reshaped Jesuit efforts in northern New Spain at the beginning of the new century, redirecting efforts in Sinaloa and Sonora toward supplying expanding missions to the north and west. It also became the source of ongoing tension with colonists and royal administrators, who became increasingly frustrated with the autonomy and control that the fund afforded the Society.

Buoyed by the fund and renewed backing from Superior General Tirso Gonzalez, California's new pioneers, fathers Juan María de Salvatierra and Francisco María Piccolo initially expressed great optimism about their new conversions. Salvatierra and Piccolo were Italians from the arid Milan and rugged Sicily, respectively. Perhaps for this reason, California's desert and rocky shores did not much daunt them. Rather, like their compatriot Kino, they advertised it as a land of abundance and great potential.[11] The Jesuits that followed Salvatierra and Piccolo, however, hailed from more fertile and populous regions in Central Europe. These later priests constantly emphasized the land's severity, sparsity, and seclusion. Compared to the verdant homes or vibrant cities they had left behind, these "German" Jesuits portrayed California as barren and godforsaken.[12] This same attitude eventually took hold across the gulf in Sonora. While Kino, Manje, and Velarde had represented the region as abundant and productive in the 1690s and early 1700s, the missionaries that came after increasingly described it as isolated, unfruitful, and beset with opposition. Jesuits like Lambert Hostell, Wenceslaus Linck, and Jacob Baegert labeled their service in Sonora and California as desert exiles in which they were condemned to lives of continual pain and desperate seclusion. Some, like the Puebla-born Father Lorenzo Carranco, nearly went crazy because of loneliness and deprivation. At one point, Carranco attempted suicide by jumping off a cliff to escape his desert trials. However, hagiographers like Miguel Venegas explained that Father Carranco was fortunately preserved from that fate so that he could obtain a true martyr's palm alongside Father Nicolás Tamaral in the Pericú revolt in 1734.

Surviving Jesuits expressed holy jealousy for Carranco and Tamaral, as well as fathers Tomás Tello and Enrique Ruhen, who later had the good fortune of dying during another O'odham revolt in 1751.[13] Unlike these red martyrs, most preachers toiled in daily isolation, far from the comforts of home and the families that they had voluntarily renounced. Fathers Philip Segesser, Joseph Neumann, and Joseph Och envied the blessed few like Carranco, Tamaral, Tello, and Ruhen who had achieved the final imitation. Still, they stressed that their protracted suffering was the more difficult role because it entailed the sublimation of martyrdom into daily acts of self-denial and abnegation.

Even if it was not as spiritually potent, they maintained that their labors were naturally productive. Under pressure from rivals near and far, they drafted letters, maps, and natural histories to argue that their work had not only expanded frontiers, but provided invaluable knowledge of North America's landscapes, wildlife, plants, climate, and people. These contributions, they believed, had already secured untold scientific, economic, and political progress. Although the early Italian Jesuits in California and the later German priests that served in the northwest differed in their appraisal of the land's productivity and its inhabitants' potential, they shared the conviction that their missions represented prolonged martyrdoms that demanded spiritual desolation, religious submission, visual dramatization, cultural separation, and natural observation.

Desolation

Oscillating between red and white martyrdom, from aspiring for a bloody death to embracing a life spent in renunciation, pervaded Christian spiritual discourse. In many ways, religious orders like the Franciscans and Jesuits traced their very roots to movements rooted in this tension. As described in Chapter 1, martyrdom became a constitutive discourse for early Christian communities, helping them transform sporadic persecution into a collective identity founded upon suffering. However, opportunities for actual martyrdoms dramatically decreased after Licinius and Constantine's Edict of Milan granted official tolerance to the church in

313 CE. Adjusting to this newfound safety, early Christians sought different ways to emulate the pain and anguish of Jesus. Some, like Anthony, Athanasius, Sarah, and Syncletica in Egypt and Awgin in Syria, turned to the desert to test themselves against diabolic temptation and fulfill their imitation of Christ.[14] Eventually communities formed around these desert mothers and fathers as acolytes renounced their earthly families in search of the spiritual communion of desolation. These groups organized around the ideals of rigorous asceticism, familial separation, obedience, prayer, and poverty and began to live under communal rules like those of Pachomius of Egypt and Benedict of Nursia.[15] In their renunciation of earthly pleasures and pursuit of spiritual tribulations, these religious orders not only fashioned their lives as prolonged martyrdoms but became crucial contexts for the reworking, recording, and rehearsing of early Christian martyr stories.[16]

Between late antiquity and the early modern Jesuit missions more than a millennium later, the concepts of red and white martyrdom went through several fluctuations. During Christianity's expansion into Europe and confrontation with Germanic, Nordic, and Muslim armies, opportunities to die for the faith ebbed and flowed.[17] Throughout, an increasingly formal canonical ideal of martyrdom as a pious death suffered "in hatred for the faith" conflicted with more fluid sacrificial idioms in popular culture and practices of everyday devotion. In these less strict iterations, martyrdom mingled promiscuously with other connected practices like poverty, pilgrimage, asceticism, chastity, motherhood, missions, and war.[18] Despite scholastic attempts to narrowly define the term and Vatican efforts to constrain its meaning, expressions of suffering and sacrificial death took on a wide variety of sexual, familial, martial, and spiritual forms.

More immediately, in the century before the formation of the Society of Jesus, diverse Catholic practices reflected this diffusion of martyrological sensibilities. Brad Gregory has charted the transferral of the idealized sacrificial death in the late medieval world into various forms of spiritualized or "white" martyrdom. Gregory argued that while red martyrdom constituted a hagiographic ideal in late medieval Europe, the actual occasion to realize the aspiration had diminished substantially by this period for all but a few missionary friars. As it had with early monasticism, this decline in opportunities for violent death led to what Gregory called a "sublimation" of martyrdom into other sorts of rituals and actions.[19]

Ascetic practice, stoic patience, extreme poverty, and rigorous chastity became core aspects of saints' lives (*vita*), validating a confessor's holy equivalence to previous martyrs. Beyond hagiography, literary genres like *Imitatio Christi* and *Ars moriendi* translated the martyrological ideal into all aspects of life and death. In their reading and shaping of practice, this literature helped Catholics interpret everyday events, sicknesses, and even natural deaths through the lens of redemptive sacrifice.[20]

Vivid meditations on the death of Christ, from personal devotions attached to crucifixes to more public passion plays, established Jesus's martyrdom as a model for more quotidian forms of grief. For example, St. John of the Cross's popular devotional work *The Ascent of Mount Carmel* likened Jesus's desolation in Gethsemane to the author's own experiences of doubt and loneliness. He argued that this prolonged spiritual battle compared favorably to a potential swift death at the hands of "infidels." The mendicant mystic maintained that the pilgrim who died through long-suffering service to God was in fact a true martyr "in the highest and substantial sense," because God bestowed "on that soul the essential love and reward of a martyr, making it a martyr of love, granting to it a prolonged martyrdom of suffering, the continuance of which is more painful than death."[21]

John of the Cross's "prolonged martyrdom of suffering" became not only a widely shared cultural sensibility, but a central facet of Ignatian spirituality. A basic expectation of periods of "desolation" and the pursuit of "consolation" profoundly shaped both Ignatius's *Biography* and his *Spiritual Exercises*. Times of loneliness, doubt, darkness, and isolation must be anticipated as part of the spiritual life. For this reason, Jesuits who began the *Exercises* must be made to fully confront the reality of suffering through their meditation on Jesus's spiritual desolation in Gethsemane. However, if the exercitants persist, they should find consolation in Christ, an overwhelming sense of profound joy that would sustain them in lives of service.[22] One of the primary ways a Jesuit could move out of desolation and to consolation was through a continued meditation on the suffering and death of Jesus.[23] By vividly contemplating the sacrifice of the ultimate martyr, they would eventually be embued with the power secured by his sacrifice that would enable them to endure most anything.

The sustained imagination of Christ and the imitation of his suffering became the discursive foundation for a red martyr "renaissance" later in the sixteenth century. As post-Tridentine Catholic missionaries found new opportunities for actual death on the colonial frontiers of Asia and the Americas, Jesuit training gradually cultivated a desire for such an honored death. From the early days of their novitiate on through the thirteen-year process of discernment, education, and profession of the four vows, Jesuit novices learned daily self-discipline by imagining the embodied suffering of Christ through prayer, fasting, deprivation, and highly focused meditations.[24] In addition, tales of historic sacrifice surrounded Jesuits throughout their education, filling up their senses with both verbal and visual depictions of saints who had suffered and given all for Christ.[25] Even as their founder read the lives of the saints while convalescing after the Battle of Pamplona, so too young Jesuits spent many hours reading collections like the *Flos Sanctorum*, *The Golden Legend*, and other *Acta*, *vita*, and *pasio* of the saints.

The *vitae* were not only biographies, but just as often combined with passion stories, featuring exotic tales of holy death suffered at the hands of diabolic kings or ungrateful apostates.[26] By the 1600s, the Society's novices were just as likely to read accounts of fellow Jesuits dying in mission fields as they were the *vitae* of medieval saints or passion stories of church fathers.[27] Luke Clossey has concluded that descriptions of their deaths so permeated Jesuit letters, histories, classrooms, libraries, dormitories, and churches that the order came to closely identify the missionary with the martyr.[28] Paired together, the long legacy of white martyrdom and newer tales of contemporary afflictions provided a powerful organizing metaphor for early modern global Jesuit evangelization.

As the Society's educational institutions grew over this same period, missionary vocations underwent a substantial decline.[29] In response, Jesuit hagiographers and artists only ramped up their passion narratives and martyr portraits in an attempt to appeal to novices. Surely, some might have second thoughts about their callings after hearing about the great persecutions in Japan during the 1620s. Likewise, the eight Jesuits who died during the 1616 Tepehuan revolt in New Spain left superiors there in a scramble to explain to prospective ministers the transcendent significance of their personal risk.

Such widespread sacrifice had been made possible, at least in part, by the beliefs and practices of faithful death cultivated in the previous two centuries. At the same time, it demanded fresh interpretive work as global provinces competed with each other and European colleges for scarce recruits. For this reason, Jesuit martyr literature and calls for canonical benefits for suffering missionaries increased throughout the 1600s. Heroic passion stories and plenary indulgences could help pry more adventurous novices away from the safe environs of urban universities by lending redemptive value to their life and work. As Clossey has argued, verbal and visual images of sacrifice provided motivation, "pushing them softly toward their duty," but also bridged vast distances between Asia, the Americas, and Europe to forge an "imagined community" of shared purpose and collective suffering.[30]

As early as 1566, Pedro Martínez, soon to be the protomartyr of the Florida mission, had petitioned the Jesuit general Borgia for plenary indulgences and papal benedictions for all missionaries who risked their lives in New Spain. He argued that the spiritual benefits should be extended regardless of whether they died in clearly anti-Catholic violence or as white martyrs who perished during hazardous sea journeys or laborious missions.[31] By the 1640s, Andres Pérez de Ribas employed both kinds of martyrdom as *exempla* to recruit future missionaries to Mexico.[32] Pérez de Ribas highlighted this wider understanding of martyrdom, listing myriad ways a Jesuit could obtain a crown without necessarily being killed in hatred of the faith. As evidence, he pointed out how the church had recognized some who had died while caring for the sick, others who were killed because they defended their chastity, and still more who had died because they "had gathered up the blood, bones, and relics of those whom they considered to be a saint" or gave food and water to martyrs on their way to persecution.

Strictly speaking, they had not been killed out of religious hostility, but the doctors of the church had made them saints by association. Citing Augustine, Ambrose, and Chrysostom, as well as the Jesuit hagiographer Eusebio Nieremberg, Pérez de Ribas argued for an expansion of the concept to include the trials and torments of missionaries. He insisted that they endured "a type of martyrdom that was not with the spilling of blood, that sometimes passes quickly, but another kind of triumph and victory of innumerable prolonged trials, a martyrdom lasting for many years."[33] This recasted martyrdom as a nearly daily experience of desolation, the final meaning of which resided not simply in the destination, but also in the journey.

Submission

Eusebio Kino was one future novice who took these arguments to heart. Accounts of the martyrdom of Father Charles Spinola in Japan and the persecutions of the Jesuits Adam Schall and Ferdinand Verbiest in China had first inspired the young Kino to pursue a missionary vocation.[34] Perhaps the best-known Jesuit of the Chinese Imperial Court after Mateo Ricci, Father Ferdinand Verbiest, had sent a circular letter to the Society's European colleges in 1678 describing a Chinese mission that entailed both promise and peril. As a novice in the Society, Kino read the account of how Verbiest had suffered years of imprisonment, persecution, and near execution. Finally, Verbiest's victory over a rival Chinese astronomer in a showdown of prophetic skills had won him permission to preach Christianity in the empire and to recruit new Jesuits for the work.[35]

With this purpose in mind, Verbiest wrote back to his former companions in the German provinces in his capacity as procurator for the province. He told his junior colleauges that the Chinese harvest was plentiful, but the workers few.[36] Unlike New Spain, he argued that China provided the opportunity to apply the full breadth of Jesuit education to what he deemed a comparable civilization to their own.[37] In order to have success at the imperial court, future missionaries should prepare for years in the best European universities so that they could serve the emperor as astronomers, cartographers, translators, and mathematicians.

Nevertheless, Verbiest worried that the "generous soldiers of the Society of Jesus, most resolute sons of our leader Saint Ignatius and brothers of so many illustrious martyrs," viewed persecution as essential to missions and would see the relative safety of China as less apostolic than the rising danger of the Americas. To this concern, he responded that although their mission enjoyed privilege for the moment, it depended upon the emperor's good will; oppression might return at any moment. In addition, the much longer sea journey to Asia would be its own form of prolonged martyrdom, complete with great hunger, pain, exhaustion, and perhaps death.

Building on Pedro Martínez's earlier argument about the sacrificial quality of transoceanic travel, Verbiest contended that the misfortune of dying en route to China would prove all the more tragic because that empire demanded the Society's very best. Whether through systematic persecution or a tortuous voyage, priests might study languages, mathematics, and science for more than thirteen years and then surrender that training and their lives, should circumstance and the Lord demand. They must be what Florence Hsia has called "mathematical martyrs," ready to serve in the highest and lowest places, in both a life of honor and in death without dignity.[38] While other locales may boast a greater chance of dying, the sacrifice of such extraordinary effort afforded greater human tragedy and commensurate eternal glory to workers in China.

For the young Eusebio, the procurator's letter was like Jesus himself calling him to drop his nets and follow. The novice already had personal connections to the Society's Asian mission. His second cousin Martino Martini had been a famous missionary, historian, and geographer who published a comprehensive cartography of China named *Novus atlas sinensis*. On a 1655 return trip to Europe to defend the Jesuits in the midst of the Chinese Rites controversy, Father Martini had visited his nine-year-old cousin on his way to Rome.[39] Kino attributed this childhood encounter with awakening his initial desire to be a missionary in Asia, and the aspiration only grew subsequently when he saw his theology and geography professors from the University of Ingolstadt assigned to China.[40]

In a later application to be sent to the Asian missions, Kino explained to the Jesuit general Giovanni Paolo Oliva, "From the moment I heard that Fathers Beatus Amrhyn and Adam Aigenler were appointed to China ... desires arose in me of obtaining a similar mission such that I could scarcely be satisfied until the matter had been commended to God and to my most reverend Father."[41] Verbiest's letter the following year served as a confirmation of that vocation, assuring Kino of its divine providence. Following in Martini's footsteps, he had already completed Verbiest's recommended course of training. He had studied and mastered the required languages, cartography, mathematics, and astronomy to prepare himself for the East.

To his delight, part of his request was granted in 1677 when General Oliva agreed to send him on mission. On the eve of his departure, however, he suffered a cruel twist of fate. Oliva had decided to send Kino along with another newly ordained priest from Austria named Father Antonio Kerschpamer. However, only one could go to the Mariana Islands with the idea of eventually moving onto China, while the other would be assigned to New Spain. Oliva left them to determine their own destinies. With practiced humility, each deferred to the other to the point that they decided to pull straws. To his great disappointment, Kino literally drew the short end of the stick and was left with Mexico. For a few months, he took the news hard and prayed regularly for peace.[42]

Eventually, he entrusted the Asian mission to God's superintending hand, concluding that "the Lord would not abandon that Christianity, already seeded with the precious blood of martyrs."[43] Kino consoled himself that, though he would not go, the divine plan would nevertheless be accomplished in China. He resorted to familiar language to explain his own assignment to New Spain, concluding that all missions began with "crosses, suffering, and adversities." By his reckoning, this represented its own sort of martyrdom. He had prepared for so long and turned down so many prestigious opportunities in Europe in pursuit of serving at the Chinese Imperial Court, even giving up a chair in mathematical sciences offered by the duke of Bavaria at the University of Ingolstadt.[44] Now he must take up his cross and accept a mission on the frontiers of Spanish North America.

Kino did, however, make one final attempt to rescue his fate. In a series of letters to his patroness, the Duchess of Aveiro, Kino indirectly pled for her intercession with his superiors.[45] As a Jesuit, he could not insist on a change himself and still fulfill his vow of obedience. So, he stoically resigned himself to his destiny, using sacrificial language. "Only the obedience which *est melior quam victima* ("is better than a sacrifice") could mitigate (my) disappointment that some of us were ordered from Rome for service in New Spain."[46] This was the first time the missionary used what would become a continual refrain for the rest of his life. While some would be actual martyrs, others must demonstrate their worth through lives of obedient service.

In response, Aveiro consoled the missionary by predicting his violent death in New Spain, averring that his chances of obtaining a martyr's palm were better in the Americas than in Asia. Kino responded by trying to look on the bright side; if that prediction were to come to pass, "it would be good for Your Grace and it would be good for me because Your Grace would be a prophet and I would be a martyr."[47] Martyrological aspiration helped him bridge the geographical and emotional distance between New Spain and China. If not in actual service in Asia, he would be joined to his patroness back in Europe and brothers across the Pacific in their mutual longings for a holy death.

Kino also dreamed of more pragmatic contributions to the Asian missions by linking his North American efforts to those in Japan and China through personal, logistical, and even physical bonds. He cited his personal connections to China throughout the *Favores Celestiales*, recalling his relative Martini and his own long-held desire to go there.[48] He also quoted letters between missionaries in Asia and his colleagues in New Spain to demonstrate their common cause. He particularly delighted in correspondance from a former missionary to the Tarahumara, Father Pedro Van Hamme, because he was one of the few workers to transition from an assignment in North America to a post in Asia. Father Van Hamme had written from Haquan (Hong Kong) to Father Guilielmo y Cinzer, a missionary in Chínipas, to update him on the Society's work in China. Van Hamme celebrated the ongoing patronage of the Chinese emperor but complained about the increasing presence of French priests who had engendered opposition at court.[49] More importantly, he reported the progress of a mission by Father Gaspar Castner on Shangchuan Island, the site of the Jesuit St. Francis Xavier's death.[50] Van Hamme buoyantly relayed news of Castner's efforts to build a sepulcher for Xavier and Haquan's natives' reportedly great devotion to the saint.[51]

Kino celebrated this news, because Francis Xavier was not only his personal saint and the patron of the Pimería Alta, but the prototypical white martyr. In both the introduction and conclusion to the *Inocente muerte de Saeta*, Kino connected his own "bloodless martyrdom" to his patron. He had first taken the middle name "Francesco" as an eighteen-year-old in 1663, in gratitude to Xavier, who, he contended, had saved him from an illness in his youth.[52] With this in mind, he strove to imitate the saint and repay his divine protection throughout his life.

No wonder, then, that Kino pointed to the example of Xavier when claiming for himself and fellow missionaries the title of prolonged martyrdom. He concluded in the book, "It should be noted at the same time that the devotees of Saint Francis Xavier ascribe to him the crown of a prolonged martyrdom in his apostolic ventures." Though Xavier had not been murdered by infidels, he had died en route to China. In addition to the crowns of doctrine and virginity, characterized by gold and lilies, Kino explained that Xavier added "the third crown of the roses of martyrdom." More than anybody else, the saint embodied the "prolonged martyrdom," because his practice of self-mortification, worldly renunciation, and evangelistic submission became the ideal Jesuit missionary martyr.[53]

Likewise, Kino explained how his second patron, Nuestra Señora de Dolores (Our Lady of Sorrows), also modeled the bloodless martyrdom. He proclaimed her "Mary the Most Holy Queen of Martyrs," because she had birthed a mission characterized by sacrifice, "even when no blood was shed."[54] As the lady of "Dolores," the Virgin also knew the missionaries' everyday sorrows and pains. Her endurance of doubt and opposition as she birthed Christ and grief as she witnessed his death mirrored Kino's contention that some were ordained to plant new Christianities through death, but others nurtured it through their perspiration and lamentation.

In addition to Van Hamme's letter, Kino quoted from the correspondence between Father Antonio Cundari of the Marianas and Father Francisco Maria Piccolo of California, who had served together in Mexico City before departing to their respective missions. He copied a letter in which Cundari commiserated with Piccolo over the ambiguities of Indigenous conversion, the setbacks of mission building, and the trials of living in the isolation of remote islands.[55] Father Cundari asked Piccolo to continue his support for the Chinese work from across the ocean through his own continual labor and supplications.[56] United by shared evangelists, saints, and frustrations, Kino envisioned the Jesuit work in North America as not only mirroring that of Asia, but connecting directly through a network that transferred spiritual and material goods back and forth across the Pacific.

While he relished the ongoing connections between New Spain and China, Kino came to favorably compare his actual mission assignment to the one for which he had hoped as a young man. He did so with a proviso, admitting the truth of the aphorism that "all comparison is loathsome." Nevertheless, he proceeded to enumerate the benefits or "celestial favors" of "these new American missions of this Unknown North America," as contrasted to "the Asiatic Missions of the Marianas Islands and of Great China." He began by conceding "the greatness and glory of so many and so apostolic, heroic, and holy Asiatic missions with so many glorious martyrs and most sublime triumphs of our Holy Catholic Faith." Yet, Kino listed several advantages of the North American missions.[57] In contrast to Asia, he contended that his mission field boasted plenty of physical supplies and crops, as well as "industrious, docile, and affable Indians," who begged for missionaries. Despite setbacks, the inhabitants of Sonora and

California had opened their towns to preaching and welcomed Jesuits with gifts, crosses, "festive arches, dances and singing, and provisions with the greatest generosity and most singular love and desire to be Christians."

All of this Kino juxtaposed to the difficulty of reaching, entering, and surviving in China and Japan, where the Jesuits had endured official opposition and persecution.[58] He had made his peace with New Spain and, like Pérez de Ribas before him, now attempted to woo new recruits with its comparative advantages. Furthermore, Kino reasoned that these new missions occupied a central role in global Catholic expansion and could forge a crucial link between "Cadiz, Seville, Madrid, Paris, Rome" and the Philippines, Marianas, China, Japan, and Great Tartary. He hoped to bring these territories firmly into Christendom so that "the triumphal car of our Holy Catholic Faith will travel with the sun from east to west, until by the divine grace, all the world shall be converted, *Et fiat unum ovile et unus Pastor.*"[59]

Kino fleshed out this plan in more detail in a letter to the viceroy of New Spain in 1703. Requesting support to expand his work north into what is now Arizona and west into "Upper California," he argued that Jesuit effort would not only convert "this northernmost rim of the empire," but might connect to New Mexico and possibly New France to the northeast, while supplying the Spanish ships along the California coast. If pushed far enough, the priest even hoped they might reach "the land called Yeso (Alaska) . . . and even as far as the territory close to Japan."[60] When realized, the new settlements would play a vital role in supplying the Manila galleons as they made their way from Cape Mendocino to Acapulco. In this way, he would ultimately fulfill his dream of evangelizing Asia by linking geographically and establishing vital North American nodes in the Jesuit transpacific network.[61]

Kino believed that his own prolonged martyrdom, as well as those of his companions, would be crucial in realizing this universal vision. While the Pueblo martyrs or Father Javier Saeta curried favor in heaven, "the rest of the Fathers" had been preserved by the divine majesty that "they may instruct these peoples through the laborious task of their ministry."[62] So those who died performed crucial ritual and spiritual tasks that prepared the way and lent protection. However, the others who continued working could be confident with the knowledge that their toils effected conversions. The priest made this clear in his conclusion to the work.

"Finally, let the blessed crown of a prolonged bloodless martyrdom be the distinguishing motive and special goal of these new missions wherever a sudden and bloody martyrdom like that of Father Francisco Javier Saeta is wanting."[63] As such, white martyrdom should be embraced as foundational for living out their vow of radical obedience.

Dramatization

Memory helped unite the bloodless martyrs to their bloody companions. This is why Kino rehearsed the passion stories of fifteen previous Jesuit martyrs who had died in northern New Spain in his account of Saeta's death. He argued that, far from discouraging the survivors, their memory should inspire further labors and more sacrifice. Citing Pérez de Ribas's earlier argument about the relationship between sudden martyrs and surviving missionaries, Kino argued, "Not on account of all these or even more murders would the apostolic missionaries of the Society of Jesus abandon their flocks." On the contrary, "a new spirit was recognized among all missionary priests—a spirit of dedicating lives to God and of assisting the souls they were teaching."[64]

As mentioned in Chapter 3, Kino made two maps to accompany his *Inocente muerte de Saeta*. The larger of the two, "*Teatro de los trabajos apostolicos de la Compañia de Jesus*," was intended to mark the locations of New Spain's martyrdoms (Figure 7). But by using the now-peculiar word *teatro* to describe the map, Kino made a subtler point. Borrowing a term prominently employed in Abraham Ortellius's 1570 far-reaching cartographic collection *Theatrum orbis terrarum*, Kino's map offered a theater that dramatized the wider story of Jesuit labors in the region. Abraham Ortellius had famously argued that geography was "the eye of history," making a claim on the past in its attention to scientific accuracy and visual appeal.[65] Kino's title established just what claim he intended to make. This would be an exhibition of the Society's *trabajos aposotlicos*, bearing witness to their apostolic work.

Yet, the word *trabajos* carried valences beyond an English translation as "work." It was the word that Jesuits consistently evoked to describe their tribulations and anguished "labors" to bring forth new Christianities.[66] Specifically, the map demonstrated their trials in "reducing" so many dis-

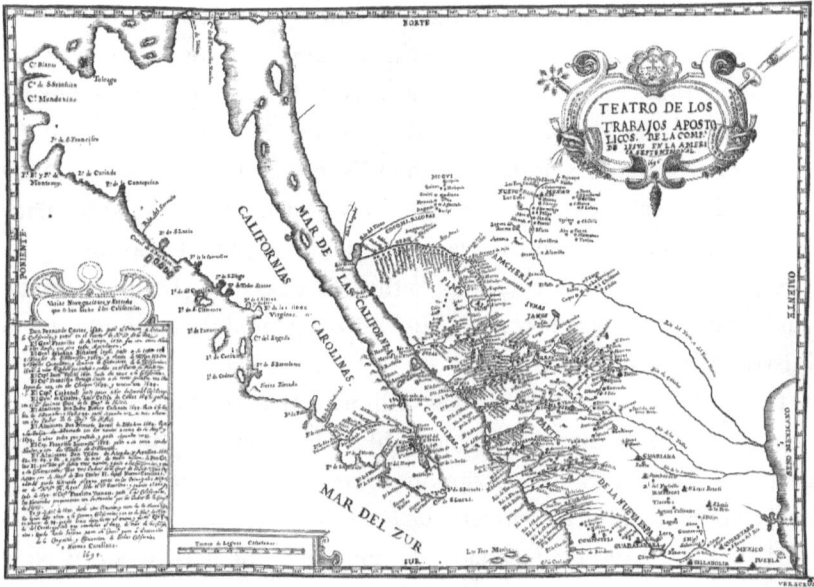

FIGURE 7. Kino designed his "Theater of the Apostolic Labors of the Society of Jesus in North America" to illustrate Jesuit work in exploring, mapping, and evangelizing northwestern New Spain. He also intended to mark all the sites of martyrdom with the letter "M" but, at least in the existing copy, never realized that goal. Eusebio Kino, *Teatro de los trabajos apostolicos de la Compañia de Jesus en la America septentrional*, 1696, courtesy of the ARSI.

parate people into hundreds of *conversiones* in river valleys throughout the north. It also showed the prospect of much more to the north and west, where Kino had recently explored and identified communities that were supposedly eager for missionaries. While populated by O'odham, Quechan, Cocopá, Maricopa, Apache, Yavapai, Havasupai, Navajo, Hopi, and other Indigenous communities, Kino represented this territory as blank space, open for expansion, further reductions, and the eventual realization of the transcontinental dream he proposed to the viceroy in 1703.

Building upon this same vision decades later, the Spanish Jesuit Andrés Marcos Burriel placed two remarkable maps at the beginning and end of his three-volume edition of Miguel Venegas's *Noticia de la California*, published in Madrid in 1757.[67] Burriel's life shared striking similarities with Kino's but ultimately took an opposite path. Unlike the Italian evangelist, Burriel had long prayed to serve as a missionary in New Spain. However, his poor health prevented the fulfillment of this dream. Instead, he resigned himself to an academic vocation and hoped his scholarly contributions in Madrid could aid the cause in Mexico.[68] As he explained to the censors of his edition of Venegas's *Noticia*, "Now that the devil and my sins years ago prevented my destiny to go to California, I desired to help her from here with my pen."[69] For that reason he prepared a comprehensive revision of Father Venegas's long but problematic manuscript *Empresas apostólicas*, including updated details and several illustrative maps.

The first map was a depiction of California that was based on the previous efforts of missionary explorers like Kino, Ferdinand Consag, and Jacob Sedelmeyer. In his description of the *Mapa de California, su golfo y provincias fronteras en el continente de Nueva España* (Figure 8), Burriel argued that it represented exhaustive knowledge of northwestern New Spain, gained through the arduous labors (*trabajos*) of his fellow Jesuits in discovering, describing, pacifying, and converting the region.[70] To make this verbal link visually explicit, he placed several images along the sides of the map, including depictions of California's animals, Indigenous inhabitants, healing practices, and religious practitioners. In addition to these symbols of Jesuit cartography and natural history, he included hagiographic scenes of martyrdom, meant to illustrate the deaths of fathers Lorenzo Carranco and Nicolas Tamaral during the 1734 Pericú Revolt. Placed together, the map and the pictures reinforced the *Noticia*'s key theme: the Jesuits' witness had laid claim to California through both scientific observation and sacrificial testimony. In this, Burriel drove home the second meaning of Jesuit martyr discourse. These martyrs, from the Greek *marturos*, were "witnesses" that corresponded to the original, etymological definition of the term. They testified to the truths of California not only through their deaths, but also through hard-won explorations, reports, and natural histories that bore witness to everyday, prolonged labors.[71]

As a part of this argument, Jesuits in the eighteenth century increasingly emphasized the incapacity of California's Indigenous population and the infertility of the land as a way of highlighting missionary witness. Burriel reiterated this point throughout his reworking of Venegas's *Noticia*, continually juxtaposing the supposed deprivation of California's Natives to the industriousness of the Society's evangelists. He did so in increasingly racialized categories, concerned to mark Native alterity through geneology and environment, rather than cosmic status. He began by arguing that Californians were ethnically nearest to Asians, which according to Jesuit natural histories should make them relatively civilized.[72] According to Burriel, however, they had unfortunately lost all signs of any civilization they might have brought from across the Pacific. The Spaniard argued that their lack of writing and use of oral memory had led to "weak traditions passed from fathers to children by only the living voice," which easily get corrupted in one way or another.[73] Whereas Mexico and Peru had some "cultivation of reason in their Laws, Military, Politics and other branches of Government," Californians had sunk to the lowest social states, living on sparse mountains in the least frequented corners of the earth. Their environment had debased their character, he contended, leaving them in "stupidity, insensibility, lack of knowledge and reflection, unreliability, instability of a will and appetites without check, without light and without object, lazy and afraid of all work."[74]

This viciously negative portrait of California's people extended to their religion, which he characterized as entirely lacking in "Temples, Chapels, Buildings or spaces for the ceremonies of religion." As evidence he concluded, "There were not any religious ceremonies anyway or outward professions of religion in feasts, prayers, vows, acts of atonement or any other practices that recognized God, whether public or private." The good thing, Burriel surmised, was that they had no idols, shrines, or "superstitions" in need of extirpation. He portrayed California and its Indigenous inhabitants as primitive and without resources, but concluded that at least they were devoid of ritual impediments to Christianization.

Overall, this derogatory representation helped Burriel emphasize what he believed were the prodigious struggles of the Society of Jesus. Dedicating the second volume of the *Noticia* to "the reduction of California by the Jesuits and their advance up to the present," the Spanish historian emphasized that everybody had assumed that California was "unconquerable." Nevertheless, Burriel explained that while "men attempted to accomplish this enterprise with arms and power, God wanted this triumph to be owed to the gentleness and frailty of his Ministers, the contempt of his Cross and the single force of his Divine word."[75] These ministers "sought the Kingdom of God in the first place and in second the good of the Monarch." Still, it had not been easy "to reduce those of this country to a life of reason and Christianity, to scold them, to detach them from their customs, to mortify them, and punish the seditious without a general uprising."[76] Yet, he insisted, the sons of Ignatius had risen to the task and established the first permanent missions, which not only gained conversions but aided the Spanish Empire by serving as ports for returning Manila galleons.

Specifically, the work of establishing the missions of La Paz, San Jose, Santiago, and La Purissima, among the Cochimí and Pericú on the peninsula's southern tip, had proven most costly. Deemed crucial to supplying returning ships from the Philippines with water, meat, and fruits to avoid scurvy, these bases had long been a goal for both the Society and the viceroy. However, the Pericú who resided in the southern part of the peninsula had repeatedly resisted any intrusion. Finally, Fathers Nicolás Tamaral, Lorenzo Carranco, and Sigismundo Taraval had established bases in all four by 1734, which immediately paid dividends when Father Tamaral rescued several sailors at his mission in San Jose del Cabo.[77] According to the *Noticia*, this small victory had come at a steep price, since the Pericú of San Jose and the Coras of Santiago resented the fathers because "they denied them the enjoyment of many women and obliged them to live without that brute freedom of their depraved pleasures."[78] Burriel argued that the imposition of Catholic monogomy and "civilization" had constrained Pericú liberty. For this reason, they determined to rise up and kill the ministers, ridding themselves of all supervision and control.

Burriel then went on to describe the organized process by which the rebels coordinated the attacks, separated soldiers from missionaries, and set about killing them one by one.[79] Learning that the elderly missionary Carranco had discovered their plan, they decided to kill him first, striking him and a mestizo servant down as they were traveling in the *monte*, outside the mission on October 2, 1734.[80] Following several other sources, Burriel spent comparatively little time describing Father Carranco's death by arrows and instead emphasized the desecration committed against his body after death. With strongly sexual overtones, the *Noticia* detailed how the rebelling Pericú stripped the missionary's body naked and then committed "unspeakable acts" with it. Burriel drew a connection between their abuse and Father Carranco's earlier control of their sexuality, but,

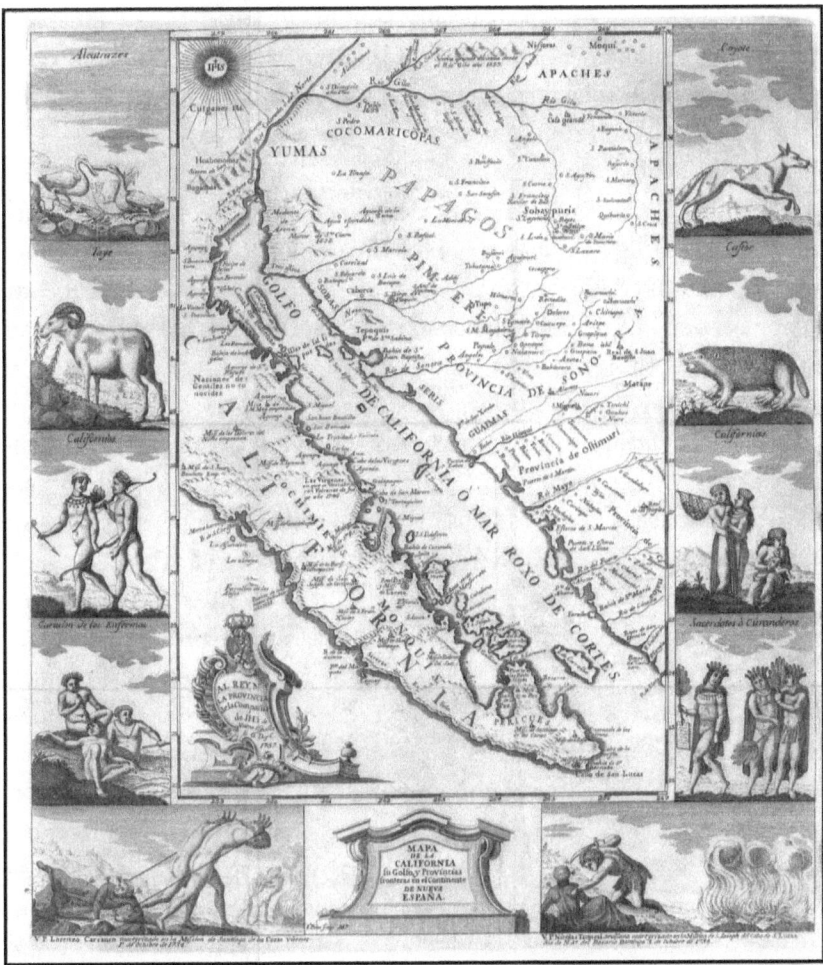

FIGURE 8. This map, made to accompany Andrés Marcos Burriel's edition of Miguel Venegas' *Noticia de California*, depicts Jesuit cartographic and evangelistic labor in Sinaloa, Sonora, and California. Images of the people, flora, and fauna of California surround the central map, along with depictions of the 1734 martyrdoms of Father Lorenzo Carranco and Father Nicolás Tamaral. *Mapa de la California, su Golfo, y provincias fronteras en el continente de Nueva España*, in Miguel Venegas, *Noticias de California*, 1757, courtesy of the JCB.

in accord with martyrological requirement, maintained it was an integral part of Christian faith: "The object of their wrath and rage was only the Faith and Doctrine newly introduced by the Venerable Father that obliged them to chastity and continence."[81]

Like the Sinaloans who had used Tapia's skull in mock Eucharistic celebrations, the Pericú demonstrated the reasons for their action explicitly in 1734. Carranco's attempt to regulate their sexuality and impose monogamy had disrupted kinship and social practice, and his killers made clear their rejection of this surveillance in their treatment of his body. Instead of questioning this method or highlighting Carranco's use of coercion to enforce cultural change, however, the *Noticia* explained the bodily treatment as *odium fidei*. As proof, Burriel pointed out how directly after defiling Carranco, they burned him along with the crosses, saints' images, statues, a chalice, a missal, and other sacred objects in a large bonfire. All of this, he concluded, "testified clearly to their hatred against Religion."

Other sources agreed with this conclusion as they described the martyrdoms of Carranco and then Father Nicolás Tamaral. Their nearby colleague, Father Sigismundo Taraval, detailed both deaths in dramatic fashion.[82] In a diary that he kept from 1734 to 1737, Father Taraval recorded the long process of setting up missions among the Pericú at the southern tip of California. In particular, he highlighted Tamaral's role in pioneering the *reducción* of San Jose del Cabo. In 1734, Father Tamaral had begun so successfully that he was able to resupply that year's returning Manila galleons. San Jose stocked the ships of General Geronimo Montero with meat, fruits, water, and other supplies, and the Jesuit took care of several sick sailors, nursing them back to health.[83]

Taraval later narrated how Father Tamaral shortly thereafter took ill, but decided to stay in his mission even when given warning by a soldier that the Pericú planned to attack in his moment of weakness. Setting the tone for later hagiographies, Taraval told of how his elder colleague preferred to stay and die with his converts rather than flee and abandon them to "gentiles." For his decision, Tamaral suffered a quick death on October 3, but his body endured the same indignities as Carranco's, as it was systematically assualted and then burned along with all of the church's sacred objects. While Taraval reiterated the point of faith hatred, he combined it with an emphasis on the Jesuits' key role supplying the Manila galleons. Their religious sacrifices were paired with practical gains that helped secure territorial advance and facilitated the imperial trade.

Although he extolled Tamaral's willing sacrifice, Taraval took even more time to highlight Father Carranco's prolonged martyrdom. In an extended eulogy, he described Carranco's many sufferings throughout his mission. "He suffered moreover the infinite toil, labor, and the inevitable troubles incident to the planting of a new faith; he was forced to endure injuries, affronts, and false rumors." More expressly, Taraval mentioned how his neighbor had been considered crazy by fellow Jesuits, "even feared and branded as insane, although he had given absolutely no cause for such reports." Although he defended Carranco's reputation, he went on to reveal that Carranco's long trials had led him to consider suicide. The missionary had even confessed "to one of his confidants at this time that for a long time the devil had been constantly persuading him to jump off a mountain, blaspheme, or hang himself." Taraval drew intentional parallels to Jesus's desert temptations, complete with a daring devil who challenges Carranco to put God to the test.[84] In light of his later martyrdom, Father Carranco's early spiritual desolation dramatized his imitation of Christ, because "such were the torments, pains, and sufferings the struggle was costing him, and that to achieve victory entailed so many tears, so much toil, and such effort that he felt faint and bowed down with the weight of his burdens."[85] In the end, death had been a relief from extended trials in the rocky crags of California.

The Jesuit provincial Joseph Barba covered some of the same details as Taraval in a report he made in April 1735 to Viceroy Archbishop Juan Antonio de Vizarrón y Eguiarreta.[86] In particular, Barba emphasized the role of diabolic temptation for the Pericú, who had been "tricked by Our Common Enemy through sorcerers (*hechiceros*) who terrorized them with threats in the name of the false deities that in their Gentile state they worshiped." Like Burriel and Taraval, Barba concluded that gaining freedom from missionary control and returning to their earlier customs motivated the revolt. The Pericú had killed Carranco and Tamaral in order to "return to their ancient barbarous customs and liberty, removing the gentle yoke of Our Holy Law."[87] Following in a long tradition, the provincial displaced blame from the Jesuits' converts onto the "sorcerers" and "Common Enemy" who had tricked them. He also redirected any culpability from the Society by branding its program in colonization and conversion a "gentle yoke." This allowed the provincial, like many before him, to simultaneously proclaim Jesuit sacrifice, while not undermining their evangelistic success.

Like the other accounts, Father Barba made the standard case for *odium fidei*, accentuating the violence against "the saints, the holy vestments, and the churches" that were all burned in a sign of the Natives' "anger and hatred for the Sacred."[88] However, Barba quickly turned to more pragmatic concerns. In the rest of his report, he urged the viceroy to send the necessary supplies and troops to put down the rebellion that had engulfed the missions and spread to other nearby groups like the Guaycura. He stressed that the California *reducciones* had been gained through extensive toil and served a crucial role in the running of empire, since they supplied the Manila galleons. For this reason, Barba urged the viceroy not to abandon the "holy Gospel which has been planted and the Royal Dominions extended three hundred leagues from south to north in this New Word," whose occupants the Society had painstakingly "reduced to the profession of our Holy Church and the obedience of your Majesty."[89] He hoped that Archbishop Vizarrón y Eguiarreta would not "omit all diligence that conduces to the restoration of what has been lost and hope in our good Jesus that he would not permit the wasting of his precious blood."[90] Like Kino, Burriel, and Taraval, the father provincial was translating the martyr motif into a language of a diffused sacrifice that deemphasized cosmic battles and instead highlighted the pragmatic and prolonged accomplishments of the Society's labors. More than mere spiritual deposits, Carranco and Tamaral's deaths represented part of the Society's wider exertions to expand Spain's global empire.

Separation

While Burriel envied the missionaries to New Spain, who had spent their lives discovering new lands and delivering Christianity, those who actually went to that frontier coveted the culminating deaths like those endured by fathers Carranco and Tamaral. The Sicilian father Andrés Tutino, for example, lamented having escaped martyrdom during the Tepehuan revolt of 1616. He blamed his own sins for not obtaining the blessed end of his close companion Hernando de Santarén.[91] While several of his colleagues had obtained their crown, God had not deemed him worthy of the fate. Nevertheless, he comforted himself "with the extraordinary consolation of the fragrance of so sweet a memory as that which lingers from our brothers who so gloriously spent their life's blood."[92]

In a similar vein, the Belgian missionary to the Tarahumara Father Joseph Neumann wrote to his home province of Bohemia to report on the long history of rebellions in the Sierra. Like Kino and Tutino, he regretted that he had not joined those who had died as red martyrs in his region. Still, he prompted his Bohemian superiors to pray that he might one day receive that honor. "Plead for me in your prayers the happy and long thirsted end of my life." He feared that he would not receive this blessing, having "never merited achieving it, even though I have awaited it in three rebellions that I narrate here." Neumann marveled at his bad luck for living through so many uprisings and never being martyred. Nevertheless, he did not despair of some future sacrifice, "because grave and constant dangers surround us here." Like so many others, he rested in the hope that he might yet be a martyr in one way or another. "There may yet be an occasion to offer my life for the glory of God, whether by pouring out my blood or by some other way the Lord disposes."[93] Not every Jesuit could obtain the martyr's palm they desired, but the rest could live vicariously through those who did.

Missionaries in Sonora expressed similar feelings of envy for colleagues who obtained the martyr's crown directly in Indigenous revolts. In a travel report written in the mid-1750s, the German missionary Joseph Och recorded how he and his colleagues had sought out danger. Specifically, they all hoped to be assigned to the northern *ranchería* of Sonoita, because it was the most arduous and remote, in addition to already being the site of several revolts. Stressing its primitive state, Och wrote home that "each of us, as well as those who preceded us, beseeched that he be sent to the missions requested in the previous year by the Indians, even though he be given only a tree under the open sky for a dwelling." In addition to its crude accommodations, he described its isolation: "Yes, each one wished to be sent to Mission San Miguel de Sonóitac, separated by fifty miles around from all other missions and situated toward the Sea of California."

More than the distance and difficult conditions, however, going to Sonoita offered the possibility of a swift passion, because "there in 1751, five years ago, Father Heinrich Ruhen was pitiably slain with clubs by apostates." Och referred to the O'odham revolt of 1751, in which Father Enrique Ruhen and his colleague at Caborca, Father Tomás Tello, had died among several dozen colonists and Indigenous allies.[94] Arriving in the wake of that large-scale uprising, German Jesuits like Och longed to follow in the footsteps of their countryman Ruhen. While resentment still simmered in the settlement, Och maintained that the Jesuits initially believed that Sonoita would welcome new missionaries. However, its residents quickly disabused them of that optimism, as they told the priests that "they would not receive the two fathers, Hlawa and Gerstner, who were sent to them. These missionaries had to return after an eight-day stay, and in this time, they were able to baptize only a few Indian children."[95]

From their actions, it appeared as if the residents of Sonoita still participated in certain sacraments but resisted supervision by the padres. Not unlike the previous generation of O'odham described in Chapter 3, they sought a balance that involved calculated engagement to obtain specific material and spiritual resources, while resisting strict missionary control. Nevertheless, this did not deter Och, who continued in his desire to serve in the town. "Now I, alone, was left and would have liked to be the successor to Father Ruhen, but the superiors did not approve, deeming it inadvisable to re-establish Mission San Miguel, so far distant from the others."[96] Upset about not being able to follow in the martyr's footsteps, Och resigned himself to a prolonged martyrdom that ultimately entailed severe sickness and a lengthy convalescence in Mexico City, separated from his fellow evangelists in Sonora.[97]

Likewise, the Swiss missionary Philipp Segesser expressed his desire to die as a martyr in New Spain. On the eve of his departure, Segesser wrote from Seville to his brother in Lucerne. He meditated on his recent separation from his family and the prospect of never seeing them again. Then, the new priest urged his brother to work for God's glory in their homeland while he, "on the other hand may give maximum effort for the law of God and His glory in the vineyards of Mexico." If each remained faithful to their calling, "after a lifetime of work, we will both be joyfully reunited in heaven."[98] Segesser noted that his brother and family worried for his well-being. However, he reassured them with regard to his eternal state, "Truly, there is no reason to be sad. If I should die, I belong to the Lord. Sooner or later death will come." That said, all things being equal, he preferred to die a martyr. "If I had a choice and it could be without any offense to God, I would prefer to die for the faith, as not very long ago did the two who were killed by Mexican rebels not far from the mission where Father Balthasar is now. The only thing I fear is the manner [of death]."⁹⁹ Referring to the martyrdoms of Fathers Juan Fonte and Gerónimo de Moranta in the Tepehuán revolt of 1616 and the nearby service of their family friend Father Johann Anton Balthasar, Segesser explained that, contrary to their worries, his greatest hope was to be murdered in his mission. Even if he dreaded the actual experience, the end would compensate for the means.

Just three years later, Father Segesser was worried about martyrdom for a different reason. He faced real danger and despaired that he might die a violent death without any accompanying redemptive meaning. In a 1732 letter to his brother, he speculated that if he were to be killed by Natives, it likely would not count, because he served on the far northern frontier in lands subject to Apache raids. Segesser deemed the Apache "far more dangerous enemies" than the O'odham or even nearby Seris because they attacked indiscriminately. Because of their complete disregard for European religion "a violent death would be of little use for a martyr's crown because these enemies know little or nothing about the faith." Dying *in odium fidei* would be impossible because the Apache knew nothing of Catholic religion and did not care to distinguish it from their wider resistance to European colonization. Rather, "they summon up and sharpen all their hatred only not to suffer foreigners in their country and to be able to live in freedom."¹⁰⁰ Because the Apache contested all threats to their territorial dominion without any particular aversion to Christianity, they threatened him with something worse than martyrdom: a death without meaning.

For this reason, Father Segesser's only path would be that of a white martyr, entailing daily resignation to his superiors' orders, "even if something else might seem more necessary and better, because obedience is better than a sacrifice." Echoing the exact language of Kino fifty years earlier, he concluded that a lifetime of faithful submission was actually superior to being a meaningless victim because it demonstrated his willingness not only to die, but to surrender even that goal in humble service. Still, he would die in the mission, telling his brother, "Note well this sacrifice, because on this continent one can very easily fall into the hands of wild Indians whose only desire is to harm the converted Indians, to kill foreigners, and to make a living from that, for if they do not steal, they have nothing."¹⁰¹ This sort of voluntary death was all the greater because he was willing to die for those who had nothing, not even the appropriate hatred that would make him a martyr. Once more, he would do so in a place forever separated from his beloved family and home.

Observation

This sense of separation was compounded by the barrenness of the physical environment. For many Jesuits from German provinces, Sonora and California's lack of water and fertility symbolized its natural and spiritual desolation. For instance, the Bohemian missionary to California, Father Wenceslaus Linck, voiced deep pessimism about its landscape and its Native inhabitants.[102] In a 1762 report to his Jesuit superior, Father Linck complained about the sterility of San Borja, his mission on the northeastern coast of Lower California. "The soil is just as wretched and unproductive as the rest of California. And even if there were any good land here for planting, what it is wanting is water."[103] Linck explained that the lack of precipitation or natural water was the chief impediment to the flourishing of the missions. This meant that it would be forever dependent on supplies from Sinaloa, Sonora, and the Pimería. In addition, San Borja was situated near a mountainous area prone to extreme swings between searing heat and bitter cold, depending on season and elevation.[104] Because of this, very few things could grow, whether natural trees, wild berries, or missionary crops.[105]

In later correspondence with his former superior Father Benno Ducrue, Linck summarized his negative view of California and its climate. Seeking to refute the "numerous accounts of California" that emphasized its "wealth, gold, silver, and pearls" in an effort to "calumniate the Jesuits," Linck insisted that nothing could be further from the truth. While Portuguese, Spanish, French, and English observers in Europe proclaimed the "enchanting magnificence of Lower California," the German missionaries who had actually served there knew the truth. Contrary to tales of abundant natural resources, "there is not one productive field, not a forest; nothing, except the sea to support human life." Linck drove the point home by emphasizing its rough terrain. "There is nothing to be seen except rocks, cliffs, sheer mountains and sandy deserts, whose monotony is interrupted only by stony heights." Father Linck described a pitiful wasteland lacking in any water or ability to produce a harvest. Mincing no words, he concluded, "The peninsula can, in all truth, be termed the most wretched and most unproductive of all lands; for, although one or two of the missions did succeed in producing something, that fact is no indication of the general fertility of the entire region."[106] While it was true that California occupied a strategic position for Spain's trade with Asia and claim to North America, its natural resources were scarce, and occupying it took work.

Linck contended that most European accounts had been based on explorations far to the north in what is now the U.S. state of California. It may be true that lush forests and plentiful fruits characterized parts of that land, but the lower peninsula was nothing but a desert in the midst of a lengthy drought. "Had geographers more carefully distinguished the peninsula from the part of the continent termed California, they would not have spoken so lightly about enchanting meadows and pasturelands, the charming plains, and all the other wonders." Features like *arroyos* had duped them into assuming the land had rivers that could support settlement. Linck conceded that "the dry beds of streams show that perhaps every fifteen, twenty, or thirty years abundant flash floods do occur." These desert washes had only fooled its surveyors: "This has misled many into writing about California what is not true. The long years of drought prove how wretched and sterile the land really is."[107] While the Society's opponents charged them with luxuriating in the abundance of the supposedly sumptuous kingdom of California, Linck laughed at the notion. It was not teaming with prosperity, as some claimed, but empty and harsh. "Such, then, are all the magnificence and rarities of the famous California peninsula, which through its superabundant riches has caused the Jesuits so much hatred!" Only sarcasm could capture his anger over how greatly his desert exile and accompanying feelings of isolation had been misrepresented.

Against these "absurd and ridiculous" accounts of California, Father Linck insisted on his own authority, established through "what I saw and what I experienced." This appeal to direct observation offered a challenge to accounts steeped in Old World mythology and adventure tales. It represented part of a growing contention by the Society's missionaries that they had surer knowledge of most of the world's terrain and inhabitants than European scholars who had never set foot in Asia, Africa, or the Americas.[108] What others theorized about from secondhand accounts, these Jesuits had seen with their own eyes. To this they added tales of suffering, because their suffering bore witness to direct experience and bolstered their claim to have provided the most objective information. In this way, the etymological meaning of "martyr" as "witness" worked in two ways; just as they had testified to Natives about the Catholic religion, they now attested to Europeans about the truth about these distant lands.

At the same time, Father Linck hoped that his blunt description of California's aridity would refute various rumors that the Society had become wealthy through this service.[109] Disputing a common refrain of diverse calumnies against the Jesuits, he insisted that he had left the peninsula just as poor as he had arrived. In the conclusion to his *Observation on Lower California*, he took an oath to attest to that poverty. "I solemnly affirm before the whole world that, just as I landed in California without a cent and lived there in the same indigence, so also did I leave the land without taking a cent with me."[110] Linck repeated the refrain of previous Jesuits who had protested that they had given up everything. Instead, he contended that his only reward had been heavenly and trusted that his converts awaited him in eternity. He still took consolation. Just as he had arrived without a cent, he had left California with "nothing except the comforting memory of labors endured." Echoing Horace, Linck concluded, "How sweet it is to remember my labors (*Dulce est meminisse laborum*)."[111] Even as he presented the mission as isolated, dry, and bitter, he savored the memory of his toil.

Father Linck connected the severity of the climate with the supposed simplicity of the region's Indigenous communities. Describing their clothes as "wretched" and huts as "miserable," Linck summarized his opinion that "the Natives of Lower California know nothing about houses. They dwell on the sand strips along the shorelines of both seas and change the site of their 'homes' every day." As evidence, he pointed to their semi-nomadic lifestyle as a reason that Californians could not be reduced to riverine conversions in the style of the *reducciones* of South American and the rest of northern New Spain. Working with a European notion of civilization and a Jesuit process of conversion that depended on agricultural production, Linck found it hard to imagine that they could ever reach full maturity, either as humans or Christians. What later observers would see as strategic mobility and creative resourcing of the sea for sustenance, he argued, made them a burden to missionaries and incapable of sustaining themselves.[112] "Imagine what effort and care had to be expended on nourishing and clothing the children in a land which produces nothing and all had to be shipped across the sea!" In another letter, he concluded similarly, "Had it not been for the two seas, which sustained my Indian charges, we would all have died of hunger regardless of how much we tilled the soil."[113] In his gross paternalism, Linck hoped to accentuate the Jesuits' labors. Not only had they worked to supply for themselves but, by this rendering, had given everything away to make sure their "charges" did not go hungry.

Fellow Bohemian Jesuit Father Ignacio Tirsch also drove this point home in a series of watercolors he made to illustrate eighteenth-century mission life in California. During and after his time in the peninsula, he painted its people, fauna, animals, and colonists, giving a vivid sense of everyday life. Several of his drawings depicted the practices, dress, and food of Native Californians as a way of complementing Jesuit-written observations, reports, and natural histories. Other paintings, however, depicted the missions Tirsch founded: their churches, farms, and communal life. In all of these, he presented Spanish agriculture and architecture in marked distinction from the rocky, barren, and deserted landscape that surrounded them.[114] One particularly telling scene dramatized the contrast in stark detail. Father Tirsch depicted a family making its way on a path from the monte to the mission. The watercolor dramatizes a progression as son and daughter prompt their parents forward, the young people showing the new way to their older parents. In a description written on the bottom, Tirsch made the lesson clear: "Out of the wilderness a heathen and his wife are coming with their daughters and son to the Mission to be converted." Tirsch's painting presented conversion as a movement from California's dry "wilderness" to a prosperous "mission." He reinforced the point with a subtle shift from black and white drawing to illustrate the sparse surroundings, while he employed vibrant blues and greens to mark the prosperity of the Christian settlement. In Tirsch's representation, the decision to enter the mission meant a movement from the isolated wilderness to the cultivated civilization.

German Jesuits like Segesser, Linck, and Tirsch compared northern New Spain's desolate environments with the imagined vacuity of its Indigenous cultures. In this way, they moved beyond earlier spiritual categories of alterity that stressed their long captivity to the diabolic "Common

FIGURE 9. The Czech Jesuit Ignacio Tirsch painted a series of watercolors to illustrate his time as a missionary in California. In this one he depicts two adolescent California Natives urging their parents to abandon the wilderness and enter the mission. Ignacio Tirsch, S.J., Plate XXX, Prague, Courtesy of the National Library of the Czech Republic.

Enemy" and toward naturalistic explanations that compared the Natives of Sonora and California with animals. Similarly, Father Johann Jacob Baegert depicted Native language as wanting in so much detail that it lacked even the sophistication of beasts. "If foxes were able to speak, they would have a variety of necessary words of which the Californians would not know a thing." This was characteristic of Father Baegert's wider outlook on California, in which he delighted in noting Indigenous deficiency. Like their language, he described Native Californians as lacking all government and religion: "Before they were Christianized, they had no religion at all because they had no law and order."[115] By positing an absence of European notions of civilization, the priests pictured Natives as naturally inferior. Without hesitation, they used dehumanizing language to compare their would-be converts to animals, creatures of the rocky landscape they inhabited.

In his later natural history, *Observations on Lower California*, written from Mannheim, Germany, in 1772, Father Baegert reiterated this point over and over. Like Linck, he hoped to correct the blind optimism and factual errors he detected in other "Observations" and "Natural Histories." In particular, he fumed at several translations of Burriel's edition of the *Noticia de la California*, which had been billed ambitiously in French and English as *The Natural and Civil History of California*.[116] Baegert believed that certain translations of the Burriel/Venegas *Noticia* had furthered the myth of California's natural abundance and fueled the assumption that Jesuits lived lives of profligate luxury and unbridled authority. The text was originally written by Father Venegas in Mexico City and later edited substantially by Burriel in Seville, but neither writer had ever actually been to California. While Burriel had meant to assure authorities of Jesuit success and mission viability in the wake of revolts in 1734, 1740, and 1751, Baegert believed the *Noticia* had actually fueled jealousy and suspicion of the Jesuits and their secret California "kingdom." Especially when translated for readers in nations with strong anti-Jesuit biases, it painted a much-too-rosy picture of the peninsula and its missions.[117] For this reason it had provoked unwanted imperial conflict and unwarranted envy from rival religious orders.

In contrast, Baegert introduced his own account of the peninsula with dismissive cynicism: "Everything concerning California is of such little importance that it is hardly worth the trouble to take a pen and write about it." While insisting that it was nothing to write home about, Baegert nevertheless found enough material to appease readers hungry for news of the distant land. With affected reluctance, he provided thirty substantive chapters, divided into three groups of ten, respectively reporting on the peninsula, its inhabitants, and the "introduction of the Christian Faith." Like so many before him, he emphasized the deserted nature of his mission, begrudgingly giving an account "of the poor shrubs, useless thorn bushes, bare rock, and piles of stone and sand without water or wood."

He was equally contemptuous of the Pericú, Guaycura, and other Indigenous inhabitants of California, whom he belittlingly called "a handful of people who, besides their physical shape and ability to think, have nothing to distinguish them from animals."[118] Earlier Jesuits had emphasized the weeds of culture and the thick proliferation of idolatry that had prevented the implantation of gospel seed with otherwise innocent people. Baegert moved beyond infantilization to dehumanization, characterizing Californians as "a people who occupy themselves with nothing, speak of nothing, think and meditate about nothing, care for nothing but food and other things which they have in common with animals."[119] Likely the most extreme example, Jacob Baegert nevertheless represented an increasing pessimism about northwestern New Spain's land, climate, and Native inhabitants. By the middle of the eighteenth century, a growing contingent of German-speaking missionaries had embraced this skeptical evaluation.

Theoretically, the absence of culture should have cleared the ground for evangelism, but Baegert's extreme cynicism about Native Californians' abilities and scornful dismissal of their humanity prevented him from thinking of them as anything other than wild and untamed. He returned to this theme repeatedly in order to stress the great frustration and difficulty experienced by him and other Jesuits who had the "lot to live" in such a bleak place. Contrary to the "imaginary riches . . . abundance and wealth" reported in other natural histories and reports published in Europe, he set out to correct the record with his own eyewitness testimony. In addition to two appendices in which he explicitly confronted these "False Reports about California and the Californians . . . and the Missionaries of California," the entirety of the account emphasized the authority of the missionary's lived experience and the value of direct observation over the wild rumors spread by others.[120] Like the reports of Linck and Hostell, Baegert's *Obervations* paired this account of California's natural history, terrain, and inhabitants with dismal narratives of long-suffering isolation and dramatic martyrdoms. Even if they had not achieved their goal of converting this frontier, Baegert believed their prolonged sacrifice had prepared the ground for future advance.

The eighteenth-century provincial of New Spain Juan Antonio Balthasar likewise paired accounts of extended missionary exertions with dehumanized descriptions of Native Californians. In a 1752 hagiography of "the exemplary life, religious virtues, and apostolic labors of the Venerable Father Francisco Maria Píccolo," the provincial praised Father Píccolo for his pioneering work among the Cochimí, Guaycura, and Pericú of lower California. Balthasar described Píccolo's grueling travels and patient endurance as he went out into the wild, braving harsh conditions, extirpating "superstitions," and bringing Californians into reductions. To prove the case, he cited an example from a 1708 tour of the east coast mission of Santa Rosalia. In an almost clinical manner, Balthasar related how a devastating smallpox epidemic had depleted Santa Rosalia of its Cochimí residents so that the priest was forced "to go looking in *the monte* in order to catechize and baptize the sick." Father Balthasar blamed the Cochimí flight on "witchdoctors (*hechiceros*) who had been instigated by the devil to persuade them that Píccolo and the other Father Missionaries had caused the pox and was killing their people." In response, they had fled by foot into the forest without any carrying a thing. In addition to the spiritual conclusion that they had apostasized, the Jesuit compared Cochimí relocation to a reversal of the civilizational process, a movement that lowered them back to an animal-like state as they lost homes, tools, clothes, and shoes. This declension, he argued, had immediately changed their behavior so that when Father Píccolo searched for them, they "felt him coming and scattered, fleeing like rabbits."[121] Balthasar argued that their condition of brute existence only subsided when they finally grew tired and hungry and reluctantly returned to the mission.

It is no accident that Balthasar equated the Cochimí of Santa Rosalia to "rabbits." Jesuits commonly associated the effects of "the monte" with animal-like behavior and mission life with "domestication." In a separate letter, he commended Father Nicolás Tamaral for "domesticating" allegedly wild Pericú converts in the far south mission of La Purísima Concepción. Tamaral had arrived a decade after Píccolo, but Balthasar explained that he had learned his missionary method from the older Italian missionary, who had introduced Tamaral to the "art" of reducing Natives from savage to civilized space. From Píccolo, he had acquired the most difficult skill: "He learned the art of arts, which in reality is to domesticate wild Indians (*indios montarezes*), brought up with brute customs and savage properties, reduce barbarians to rational and political life and those who were raised to always pursue their appetite in total liberty."[122]

In his description of Tamaral's work in building up mission San Jose del Cabo, the provincial reiterated the point. Father Tamaral had been tasked with converting thirty-two small settlements (*rancherías*) into a single mission by "grouping and gathering all of the Indians, for this it was necessary to attract them, stroke them, give them gifts, and search them out, as somebody who leaves his home for the wild, for the mountains (*montes*), the bush, and hills, which he could not do without severe labors and imponderable hardships."[123] Balthasar argued that Tamaral himself had to abandon home and enter the wild in order to "stroke" the Pericú into the Jesuit *reducción*. Píccolo's mentoring in this method of entering the monte and coaxing Native communities into missions had been the ultimate model of white martyrdom, a long process of observation in search of redemption. In the case of Tamaral, the training had obtained the ultimate payoff when it culminated in a red martyrdom when the residents in and around San Jose revolted in 1734.

Conclusion

For almost two centuries, Jesuits who went to New Spain as evangelists expressed their hope of serving and ultimately dying for their faith at the hands of infidels. For some, like Gonzalo de Tapia, Hernando Santarén, Francisco Xavier Saeta, Nicolás Tamaral, Lorenzo Carranco, Tomás Tello, and Enrique Ruhen, the hope became a reality as they received their crown and suffered a sudden, red martyrdom, which fellow missionaries cast as death out of hatred for the faith. These wet martyrs planted the seed with their bodies and watered it with their blood. However, countless others never had that opportunity. They wrestled with more quotidian struggles like travel, hunger, climate, language, homesickness, solitude, and sickness. For these surviving missionaries, the notion that everyday ordeals constituted a separate, but equally valid, form of martyrdom became compelling and consoling. By the eighteenth century, sacrificial narratives had become so central to the Jesuit missionary identity that even when fewer died in dramatic rebellions, they still constructed their histories, reports, and accounts of the borderland mission around the motif.

Drawing on the teachings of early fathers like Augustine and Ambrose, medieval devotional traditions like the *imitatio Christi, ars moriendi*, and John of the Cross's *Dark Night of the Soul*, as well as the *Spiritual Exercises* created by their founder, they imagined their sufferings to be like those of Christ, Paul, and the martyrs of the church. While they never spilled blood like these previous saints, they expended sweat and shed tears in bloodless martyrdoms. The "dry martyrs" believed they had lost their lives as they left family, home, and country to serve Jesus and the Society that bore his name. In eighteenth-century California, they increasingly emphasized their desolation as the chief way of realizing this sacrifice. Whereas previous priests had uprooted weeds of idolatry in direct confrontations with shamans or seen abundant harvests of conversion spring from dramatic deaths, these Jesuits imagined themselves in desert isolation without much to show for their labors. Distant from their home culture and disenchanted with the prospect of lasting conversions, these mostly German priests nevertheless made meaning out of their quotidian labors and natural observations. Their discoveries, reports, maps, natural histories, and ongoing reductions had increased scientific knowledge and prepared the way for Christendom's ongoing advance. Though tried and tempted, they believed the desert might still bloom. Critics in Europe increasingly claimed that they luxuriated in the riches of California, but they insisted instead that they had borne witness to its desolate climate, geography, and cultures with their lives.

5   Uprooted
Missionary Expulsion

On July 11, 1767, the governor of Sonora, Juan Claudio Pineda, opened a sealed envelope that had been sent with great secrecy by the viceroy of New Spain, Don Carlos Francisco Marqués de Croix. Inside Pineda found a royal decree that to his surprise ordered the expulsion of the Society of Jesus from New Spain and the seizure of all Jesuit property. More specifically, the *real decreto* instructed him to arrest the thirty-one Jesuit missionaries working in his province, secure their assets, transport them to the Pacific coast, and guard them until arrangements could be made for them to be sent back to Mexico City. Later they would be conducted to Spain and eventually on to the Papal States or their respective countries.[1] The expulsion had already begun in central Mexico in a coordinated action on the morning of June 25. However, these orders had just now reached this northwestern corner of the Spanish American empire.

In obedience, Pineda organized a similarly synchronized operation for July 23. With meticulous planning, the governor commissioned several prominent colonists as captains who would gather the Jesuits of their region, reveal the decree of expulsion, detain them, and march the missionaries toward the Pacific port of San José de Guaymas.[2] Due to the scope of the task, however, things did not go as smoothly as the viceroy or governor had hoped. The captains took weeks to locate and recall each of the priests from their far-flung missions. Once detained, the Jesuits took many more days making their way south. All told, the process stretched out over a month. When the full contingent finally arrived in Guaymas on September 2, Governor Pineda confined the Sonoran missionaries under close guard in a single hut by the coast. There, they awaited twenty colleagues from Sinaloa, who finally joined them in their improvised imprisonment on September 21.[3] Over the next eight months, the fifty-one Jesuits of Sonora and Sinaloa suffered numerous difficulties as they awaited deportation, including swarming insects, rat infestations, spoiled food, salty water, dysentery, scorching heat, and severely cramped conditions.[4] It is no surprise that under these circumstances the elderly Father Joseph Palomino of Sinaloa fell ill and later passed away in April 1768, the first in a series of losses the missionaries would endure during a two-year march toward exile.[5]

In May of 1768, they finally left Guaymas, setting out on a sea journey that took them first across the bay to California and then down the Pacific coast. Because of poor equipment and rough weather, the voyage lasted forty-eight days and led to severe physical weakness and widespread scurvy.[6] When they finally landed in the port of San Blas, Nayarit, the group was forced to move by foot and horseback through the river valleys, swamps, forests, and mountains of central New Spain. First, they moved toward the regional capital of Guadalajara, then on to Mexico City, and ultimately to the Atlantic port of Vera Cruz. Before even departing from the viceroyalty, almost half their number had died, most succumbing during the first days of their overland journey. Specifically, twenty missionaries died in the span of a few days in late August of 1768, near the small village of Ixtlán del Río. After those most deadly moments, the survivors were divided into groups of healthy and sick. Eventually, thirty missionaries made it to the eastern port of Vera Cruz, where in April ships took them first to Cuba and eventually across the Atlantic to Spain. Two years later, on July 10, 1769, they arrived at the port of Cadíz.[7] From there, the lucky ones made their way to their home countries or the protection of the Papal States. The less fortunate lingered in Spanish monasteries, sometimes in solitary confinement, for over a decade before finally being released.[8]

By almost any measure, these missionaries experienced exceptional suffering, enduring harsher conditions and a longer imprisonment than almost any other group of Jesuits during the expulsion.[9] Still, their story formed only part of an unprecedented retraction of the Society globally, as its members were banished first from Portugal and its colonies in 1759, then from French territories in 1762, and finally from the Spanish overseas empire in 1767.[10] In the Spanish case alone, thousands of missionaries were recalled to Spain from as far west as the Philippines and as far south as the Rio de la Plata region of modern Argentina and Uruguay. In New Spain, 678 members of the Society journeyed from northern missions like California and Chihuahua as well as the colleges of central and western Mexico.[11] In addition to the Sonora and Sinaloa missionaries, many others perished during the Atlantic voyage or in the holding cells and hospices of Mexico City, Havana, and Cadíz before the survivors made their way to scattered refuges throughout Europe. Even more crushing for many of these missionaries, Pope Clement XIV bowed to pressure from Portugal and France and issued the papal brief *Dominus ac Redemptor* in July 1773 that formally suppressed the Society of Jesus as a religious order.[12]

Paired together, the expulsion and suppression signified the death of a Jesuit identity as a global missionary enterprise, a self-image constructed in over two centuries of work. At a loss for how to reconstitute their lives and maintain bonds to the wider community of fellow evangelists and converts, the former members of the Society looked to the suffering of Jesus, for whom they had once been named. The men who had once served in the conversions of northern New Spain made sense of these losses through the lens of a familiar metaphor, forged over centuries of evangelistic work. As they had since the beginning, they translated their exile into martyrological terms, trusting that their defeats carried redemptive meaning.

Even if it seemed temporarily like the mission had failed, the expelled Jesuits of northwestern New Spain argued that their sacrificial service would secure their ultimate success. They embedded this conviction in a wide range of writings, penned from their exile in Europe. Former missionaries, Fathers Joseph Och, Benito Ducrue, Johann Jacob Baegert, Jaime Mateu, Francisco Ita, and Bernardo Middendorff wrote natural histories, travel relations, diaries, and other accounts that paired in-demand descriptions of northern New Spain with tales of their sacrifice. These accounts resorted to tried and true metaphors to illustrate the logic of their hope in the midst of grief. Some of the images were paternalistic: Indigenous converts remained "sons and daughters," spiritually orphaned by the removal of their "fathers." Others were more pastoral, emphasizing the danger to their "sheep" now that their "shepherds" had been taken away. But more than anything missionaries felt "*desterrado*" or "uprooted" from the land of their sojourn. Where once they had framed their mission as desert isolation, they now lamented being ripped away from their work in the fields of the Lord, a second unexpected exile. Into this void, tales of their grieving, tortured, and executed Indigenous converts helped validate the mission as Native Christians became the final martyr-witnesses of Jesuit sacrifice.

Exile

Jesuit evangelists had long imagined their vocation as an exile from family and home. They characterized their mission as a series of separations that began in Europe as they entered the Society, continued throughout their education, and culminated in their calling to foreign lands. As they said goodbye to their houses, colleges, and countries, they compared these ruptures to martyrdom, a death to their previous life. As early as 1645, the provincial Andrés Pérez de Ribas had pictured the mission as a life of profound loneliness "in isolation from mankind." Pérez de Ribas explained how he and others had left behind their families and many opportunities, only to dwell "in the company of wild beasts who inhabit hovels along the seashore or in the *montes*, forests, and deep canyons." He compared this state to a prolonged martyrdom, because "in the final analysis, to live among them is to experience a kind of perpetual exile, even though one's life may not be lost." He acknowledged that many thought the Jesuits were crazy for enduring exile and risking their own human corruption, as "the cost of all these continuous and acknowledged hardships would appear to debase dealings with these peoples and to discourage any rational person from undertaking such an enterprise."[13]

By this understanding the priests were forlorn outcasts, living martyrs who had already lost all that a European might conceive of as life. Nevertheless, love and not insanity had prompted their choice, because "all this suffering is endured for the glory of Christ and His redeemed souls." Moreover, the paradigmatic suffering of Christ and his apostles helped make sense of these white martyrdoms, with the Jesuits knowing that their exile replicated Christ's divestment of privilege or that Paul's apostolic anguish "provides an equal amount of consolation to our religious missionaries, who sacrifice and dedicate their lives to God by laboring in exile."[14] For those who never had the chance to die at the hands of persecutors, the daily death of "laboring in exile" became their consolation.

A century later, the German missionary to California Father Lambert Hostell echoed this sentiment. At regular intervals, Hostell wrote home to his family and friends about the sacrifices of leaving European comforts for a thankless and "destitute peninsula." In a 1743 letter to his sister, he told of the difficulty of the work and the pain of being "more than three thousand Spanish miles away from Europe." Nevertheless, he resolved to make himself content in exile, "so much so that I would not exchange this strenuous and needy mission with the pleasantest position and place in Europe." Despite its bleakness, he had determined to "remain in this sterile peninsula and to devote myself to the task of cultivating this evangelical vineyard to the honor of God."[15] For Hostell, an American sacrificial mission could more than compensate for the loss of prestige and the "pleasantest position" in Europe.

The painful separation from Europe often entailed not only physical removal, but also cultural transition, as German, Czech, Swiss, Slovenian, and Italian missionaries struggled to take on Spanish language and customs. In addition, they had to adapt to Indigenous cultures.[16] Some embraced the transitions. Eusebio Kino, for instance, had gone from being a child named Chino to a student called Kuhn to the adult Kino as he moved from Italian to German and then to Spanish-speaking territories. He even showed humor about these transformations. On the eve of his departure to New Spain, he joked to his patroness the Duchess of Aveiro that he was Italian by birth and Austrian by education, only to serve an Iberian empire in the Americas.[17] To Kino, the many transitions struck him as a necessary, if unusual, part of his sacrificial life.

Kino's contemporary, the Slovenian Marcus Kappus, described his time in northern New Spain in terms of familial separation and cultural dislocation as well. Father Kappus's frequent letters to his brother Johann expressed homesickness, reminiscing about his childhood and grieving the fact that he would never see his beloved sibling, parents, or country until eternity.[18] He also reflected on his frustration with Natives in a 1689 letter to his aunt, Lady Francisca Adlmanin, a nun in Skofja, Slovenia. Kappus initially lamented that the Seri, Tapolque, and O'odham with whom he worked supposedly had "no work, religion, or idol" and lived nomadically, "like animals." He compared their customs to the desert that they inhabited, characterized by deficiency and privation. Yet, in the same letter he rejoiced that he had baptized two extremely old O'odham, whom he estimated to be 120 years old. Kappus boasted in God's providence that he had arrived just in time to save them "from the jaws of the devil."[19]

A decade later, in 1699, he still expressed some pessimism about conditions in Sonora, especially the recent rebellions of the O'odham and Tarahumara and accompanying martyrdoms of fellow missionaries in the 1680s and '90s. Nevertheless, he had come to appreciate the Ópata Christians in his missions, as well as many aspects of his adopted country's food, flora, and fauna. To be sure, Kappus missed his brother Johann and closed his note with a touching prayer that he might one day "see his brother again, if not in this world, then in the other world with immortal joy."[20] Such moments are telling reminders that European evangelists usually left their homes without any hope of hearing the voices or seeing the faces of their loved ones again. They also reinforced the Jesuit claim that the mission itself was a martyrdom—a death to a former life that was rooted in country, home, family, and language.

As much as many struggled to embrace their North American context, others complained about Spanish culture in letters to their relatives. Father Hostell, for example, told his sister that he had more trouble with Spanish food and customs than he did Indigenous practices.[21] Similarly, Philipp Segesser, the Swiss missionary to Sonora, emphasized the various culture shocks that heightened his feeling of separation. Upon first leaving home, he wrote his brother to express his sorrow at not saying goodbye to his nephew, whom he "wished (he) could touch with a kiss, whom I am never likely to see again in this life." Even more than fathers Kappus and Hostell, Segesser experienced his dislocation culturally, frequently relating what he considered to be inferior Spanish habits, food, architecture, and education. He even felt these strains amongst the members of the Society, telling his brother that "there is a big difference between German and Spanish Jesuits" as he experienced them at the Jesuit house in Genoa.[22] Yet, his commitment to the mission never wavered. Writing about a sick missionary forced to return to Vienna on the eve of departure to New Spain, Segesser insisted, "As to what concerns me, if nothing else will happen, I am committed rather to lose my life here in Spain according to the will of God than to return home, even if I had to wait my whole life here."[23] Although he bristled at the feelings of dislocation even within diverse European waypoints, he interpreted it as part of the broader surrender to his missionary vocation.

Once in the Americas, Segesser continued to complain of conflict with Spaniards. From Cuba, he wrote to his mother to tell her about tensions with Spanish priests over pastoral practices and the alleged preference of Indigenous and African converts for Germans, or "foreign missionaries," because they were more patient in confession.[24] He later grumbled, in correspondence from Sonora with his brother in 1735, that Spanish superiors discriminated against German missionaries in their assignments, but nevertheless boasted that the church he constructed with central European methods held up better against Apache attacks than did Spanish-built missions. Segesser also told of trouble in civilizing and evangelizing because they had to remove O'odham converts' "deeply rooted habits," not just because of their "savage" state, but also "since they have been instructed in Spanish, not German."[25] Segesser's complaints undermine the notion of any essentialized "European" missionary style, but they also illustrate the ways in which some Germanic Jesuits saw even the Spanish aspects of New Spain as part of their exile.

That said, by the 1740s Segesser showed signs of having planted roots in his adopted home. He still desired news from his family, but now dedicated most of his time to the ups and downs of life in the northwest borderlands. In a telling request to his brother for seeds for his garden, he asked for cauliflower, or "*coliflor*, for I can no longer remember how it is called in German."[26] The home culture he had clung to so tenaciously had fallen away, and in its place, he now thought in Spanish. In the same letter, he recalled fondly how his mission converts at San Miguel de los Ures, whom he always suspected of being disloyal, mourned his leaving when he was switched to another mission.[27] As much as he insisted to his parents and siblings that he recalled them frequently in his prayers and imagination, his heart and mind now rested in Sonora and the hoped-for conversion of its spiritual "children." Likewise, Father Franz Inama of Austria described life without German bread to his sister as one of many reasons, alongside illness, heat, dangerous animals, and Native treachery, that his mission was "perilous and exhausting." Still, he came to appreciate local cuisine like *tortillas*, sharing a recipe with his Carmelite sister for her to try out at her convent in Cologne.[28] While the sons and brothers missed their homes in Europe, becoming "Fathers" to Indigenous "children" seemed to assuage some of their loneliness.

In a letter to his father, Father Lambert Hostell also lamented the hardships of his North American sojourn in "wild, rough, dry, and utterly unproductive" land. Linking the barrenness of the environment with the alleged simplicity of California's Natives, he was pessimistic about his converts. Hostell categorized them as "barbarians" who ranked "below animals rather than be considered equal to other humans" as they "lived without any religion, laws, government, knowledge of divinity, houses or villages" and roamed naked through the wilderness "in accordance with the inclination of (their) sensuous nature."[29] Like the climate and ground, he pictured his potential converts as harsh, obstinate, and lacking in the resources for civilized life.

Yet, Hostell expressed enthusiasm about their eventual conversion and his own goal of "being a capable instrument in promoting the glory of God and effect the salvation of the Christian and pagan California Indians." He explained, "This is and this will ever be until I die my one desire." In another letter to his spiritual mentor, he belabored the deprivation and isolation that plagued him, but he concluded, "Never have I regretted, even for a moment, having exchanged the comforts of my beloved homeland for the misery of this Mexican island."[30] California might be a hot and sweaty mess of a "Mexican island," but it was his miserable strip of land and a material expression of his sacrificial exile. In these letters home, Hostell and his fellow evangelists could never fathom that they would one day grieve their removal from this corner of North America's Pacific coast and sorrowfully return to those very family members across the Atlantic.[31]

Reversal

Depending on the source and criteria, the Society counted around twenty martyrs in northern New Spain by the 1760s.[32] For those who memorialized them, the deaths carried redemptive expectations, pointing beyond the veil of earthly suffering to the final reality of spiritual success. But the expulsion threatened this confidence and called into question two-and-a-half centuries of work. If the Jesuit gardeners were abruptly yanked from their converts, then surely these new plants would wither. If so, then what value were the regular deposits of sweat and blood that watered these North American fields? In light of this threat, they framed the expulsion and suppression as their final and culminating sacrifice, a martyrdom of their missionary identity, and in that way their full identification with Christ. By pairing their own trials with the travails of Native Christians, they sought evidence that even when uprooted from the ground they had fertilized with their pain, their efforts would bring harvests well into the future.

Against this narrative, the Society's opponents argued that they should relish their return to Europe and chided those who grieved their departure.

Even this opposition, however, could be used to provoke sympathy. The German Joseph Och used one such account of antagonism to highlight both Jesuit sacrifice and convert suffering to the European readers of his travel reports. A former missionary to Sonora, Och had returned to Mexico City just before the expulsion because of debilitating arthritis. For this reason, he had escaped the brutal journey of his colleagues from the north before making his way separately to Europe. From his new exile in Germany, he nevertheless wrestled with the meaning of the Society's removal. Och recalled a final sermon preached in Mexico City by the Dominican father Francisco León during their departure. León delivered the address to a diverse crowd that included peninsular nobles, pious *mestizos*, and Indigenous residents of the capitol. This mixed multitude had filled the streets to catch a glimpse of the priests and say goodbye to them in their procession out of the city. According to Och, the people made it clear that they sided with the Jesuits as they surrounded the procession, stroked their carriages, and poured out tears.

The dramatic displays of public grief were too much for the Dominican priest León, however. When he saw the crowds, he immediately announced a "farewell sermon" at the former Jesuit church. According to Och, León began with what seemed like an empathetic rhetorical question: "How long shall this, our unavailing grief, endure?" Quickly, though, he transitioned to chastising his audience. "Cease weeping! You have no reason to do so. You are bewailing an imagined misfortune of the Jesuits." The Dominican preacher contrasted the outcast priests' pretended misery to their actual good fortune. "Do you think these good people will be led to slaughter, or will have to languish in gloomy prisons? You are very much mistaken." León hoped to correct the assumption that the Jesuit expulsion was tortuous or deadly. Rather, it was more like an aristocratic parade. "Don't you see the splendid carriages in which they were driven away like cavaliers?" Far from pitiable, the Dominican contended that the Society's members enjoyed great prestige and privilege.

The Jesuits deserved no pity, León explained to the crowd, as they were going back to lives of luxury, secured by secret treasures that they had absconded from Mexico and their other worldwide missions. "You were apprehensive that they would all be sentenced to death, and have their throats cut or worse. They will be well settled, cared for, and splendidly fed for the rest of their lives. The King will grant them handsome pensions and they will live in the Papal States." They were not persecuted victims, but wealthy aristocrats, he reassured them, covered by lifetime pensions. Passing off a conspiracy theory about the Society's secret accounts, the Dominican preacher continued, "To anticipate the misfortune that would sooner or later overtake them, they have provided for themselves. All of their estates have long been sold and transferred into astonishing sums of money." León assured his audience that the Jesuits had secret wealth and had already remitted it back to Europe, where it rested secure. "This money, many millions, they have already sent overseas and placed in safety. Their accounts lie as credit in Rome, Genoa, Amsterdam and London, perhaps by the hundreds. Hence, they will not be in want. They have enough for their livelihood and will be well off."[33] Far from a curse, he insisted that their return to Europe was a blessing, an unexpected windfall for the Jesuits that guaranteed an easy life of wealth and security.

While León deliberately contrasted their suspected wealth to the popular conception that the Jesuits were being "led to slaughter" or "gloomy prisons," Och used the Dominican's sermon to reflect the crowd's belief that the expulsion was itself a sort of martyrdom. In his final admonition, the preacher León commanded, "Therefore, do not bewail them as future martyrs; rather congratulate them, as great gentlemen who have been removed to your material and spiritual advantage. Dry your tears!" Since almost all Jesuit papers were confiscated during the expulsion, Och likely had few or no notes of the sermon when he wrote his later account; rather, he rehearsed the scene from memory, so the language of martyrdom may come from the later Jesuit narrator as much as the earlier Dominican preacher. Nevertheless, Och used the story to pose a decisive question. Were the Jesuits fortunate to return to lives of luxury in Europe, escaping their difficult mission, or instead condemned to long-suffering exile and final collective sacrifice? The Sonoran missionary argued for the latter, contrasting León's sermon with an extended tale of indignity, deprivation, and tearful farewells.

As evidence, Och depicted Natives of Mexico City bearing witness to this fact by marching alongside the Jesuits "for a distance of two hours," crying and lamenting their departure. Conversely, the preacher León, who had hoped to press "the bishop's miter upon his brow as a reward" for his work in pacifying the people and avoiding a riot, shortly found himself caught up in the Inquisition and punished for his connivance. "We were soon to find the fox in his trap, and instead of a miter there was bestowed upon him the sanbenito (a yellow Inquisition robe)."[34] This narration of an immediate and violent demise had been a common trope in Jesuit martyr narratives for centuries, tracing its origins to the accounts of Judas's death in the New Testament and applied consistently to Indigenous warriors who were said to meet a swift death or providential punishment after dispatching with missionaries.[35] Here, the tale of León's demise served to highlight the injustice of his accusation and the Society's ultimate vindication.

From his place in exile, Och used his *Travel Reports* to provoke sympathy from his European readers and reinforce the tragedy of being uprooted. Although a return to home and family might sound nice in León's telling, it threatened the very *raison d'etre* of the Society and its members. Och, in contrast, framed the expulsion as a dramatic reversal and unremitting loss of both life and calling. In the beginning of his narrative, he recalled the day of May 9, 1754, in Heidelberg, when he had received permission to go to the Indies as "one of the most pleasant days of my life." In his retelling, Och's enthusiasm never waned through his journey across the Atlantic and ultimately to the northern missions of the Pimería Alta.[36] Even though he was beset by hardships—including heat, mosquitoes, poverty, and the difficulty of aquiring the language of the O'odham—he deeply loved his new home. After settling into his mission in San Ignacio, Sonora, Och praised *chocolate, pulque, maguey,* and aloe as Mexican staples that were superior to comparable products in Europe.[37] More personally, he admired the affection he witnessed between the elderly missionary Gaspar Stiger and the O'odham Christians of San Ignacio, expressing his desire to develop similar relationships. There were setbacks, to be sure, notably another O'odham uprising in 1751 that had brought the martyrdoms of Jesuit Fathers Heinrich Ruhen and Tomás Tello. Still, Och trusted that the work was advancing despite momentary setbacks and that Christendom was expanding through their efforts.

Significantly, Och never mentioned in this early narrative that he had developed crippling arthritis during his decade of service, the very reason for which he was ultimately removed to Mexico City. However, the translator of his *Travel Reports*, Theodore Treutlein, rightly notes that the missionary's "point of view seemed to change when he became an *expulso* (exile)." While most of the report emphasized his loving evangelistic labor, the later account of the expulsion makes frequent mention of his illness and that he lay "crippled and lame."[38] The revelation of his severe infirmity late in the text marks a switch from buoyant exuberance about his vocation to tortured anguish about his removal, even though the former represented a separation from his natural family and the latter a return home. Whereas giddy excitement characterized his travel to the mission, a stoic endurance of persecution framed the second half of his account.

His own pain and the travails of other Jesuits formed the substance of the later reports. Och expressed relief to get home to Wirzburg, even if it took "more than twenty-two hundred hours of travel on water and more than eight hundred hours on land, crippled and lame." At the same time, he contrasted his personal reprieve to the sacrifice of his fellow Sonoran missionaries. Och thanked God, "because eighteen of my brother missionaries, all hale and hearty and in the best years of their manhood, died on the voyage in different ships and were buried at sea." He juxtaposed these seemingly meaningless deaths to his own providential preservation: "How I, as a cripple in great pain, came through alive, God alone knows."[39] In Father Och's memory, the mission had been a wonderful blessing, something that made his illness bearable. The tribulation uncovered his anguish as the attacks of rival religious orders, deaths of his colleagues, and loss of the mission itself made his pain more public and less bearable. More importantly, the separation from the mission and loss of the Society itself symbolized a dramatic reversal that threatened the meaning of their long sacrificial work. By positioning it as a collective martyrdom, Och conveyed his trust that God would ultimately make good out of its evil.

Destierro

Like Och, Father Jaime Mateu, a Spanish missionary to the Tarahumara, believed the expulsion completed a cycle of individual exile and communal sacrifice in northern New Spain. The author of an unpublished account of the eviction entitled *Destierro de los misioneros de la América septentrional española*, Mateu also paralleled the surrender of leaving Europe for the Indies and the sorrowful removal from New Spain back to Europe. From the title onward, he invoked the idea of *destierro* (exile) to describe missionary movement in both directions. Echoing the words and themes of his fellow Jesuits, Mateu emphasized the inherently sacrificial nature of the foreign mission. "Trial, sweat, anguish, affliction, and danger—all of these were the cost paid by the Jesuits who exiled themselves voluntarily in those deserts amongst such barbarous people." The Spaniard Mateu used a particular imperfect reflexive form to narrate the difficulty of the northern missions. These priests "were exiling themselves" from home and family to serve on this frontier. This phrase, "*se desterraban*," emphasized their voluntary dislocation from land in a way that the English "exile" does not fully convey. The missionaries literally were "unearthing" themselves, according to Mateu, willingly parting from their home countries and families only to experience severe suffering in deserted spaces on behalf of "savage" people. As Mateu summarized, they embraced being uprooted "for the love of native souls, without hope of reward or any thanks in this life."[40] They unearthed themselves out of love.

Even as he emphasized the missionaries' loving surrender, he underscored what he imagined to be the pitiful objects of their devotion. In highly prejudicial terms, Mateu reiterated the contrast between the priests' opportunities at home and their difficult Mexican exile. "Even if the lands were fertile and even supposing the comforts that they could have had at home, the Jesuits were men of great talent who usually could have done well anywhere." But this best-case scenario did not hold for northern New Spain, Mateu argued, as "they voluntarily left their lands and made trips by sea and land of thousands of leagues to go and be exiled (*desterrado*) amongst those barbarians that resemble animals more than men."[41] Like many other evangelists serving in northern New Spain in the mid-eighteenth century, Mateu depicted the region's Indigenous people as less than human. By emphasizing the supposed lowly state of Native culture, he attempted to play up the extent of missionary loss, the latter growing in inverse proportion to the former. He also hoped to challenge reports of secret Jesuit wealth or hidden kingdoms in California by emphasizing the thankless nature of the mission.

Much like Och before him, Mateu made observations of the frontier's landscape, climate, animals, and Indigenous residents that at once drew in interested readers of Jesuit natural histories and underlined evangelist endurance.[42] In his description, the harsh conditions of northwestern New Spain, with its "deserts" and "barbarous people," made for particularly difficult assignments, as opposed to the usually preferred missions amongst more "civilized" cultures in Asia. In ranking cultures, Mateu and other Jesuits evaluated Native deficiencies according to Father José de Acosta's quadripartite definition of civilization, which judged each culture by its development of cities, law, writing, and gods.[43] Working within this system, these natural histories presented the landscape and inhabitants of northern New Spain in the lowest possible ranking and consistently highlighted its putative absence of urbanization, political organization, literacy, and religion.

The lack of these civilizational markers only added to the pathos of Jesuit forfeiture. The members of the Society went to New Spain only "with hope of so many trials and dangers and without hope of any kind of honor, praise, comfort or any other thing that the world cherishes, yet in their eyes all is misery." Embracing this vocation meant the renunciation of all former ambition and consolation. By drawing this contrast, Mateu worked in the martyrological tradition, contrasting the missionaries' supposedly deserved opportunities with their stoic service in exile. For Mateu and many others who went to northern New Spain before the expulsion, the missionary life constituted a sojourn that entailed great personal, emotional, and physical loss. They consoled themselves with typological connections, turning their exile in savage lands into an imitation of Christ in his desert temptation and deepest misery.

In a dramatic reversal that simultaneously mirrored earlier experience, California missionaries who made their own journey home six months later in 1769 compared the pain of exile with the longer history of Jesuit missionary suffering. In his *Observations on Lower California*, Father Jacob Baegert said relatively little about the expulsion, likely because the Spanish crown had bought Jesuit silence on the matter by providing some exiles a small stipend.[44] Writing on the cusp of the Society's 1771 suppression, Baegert boasted about Jesuit suffering, comparing their "thousands of blood witnesses" and over "30 volumes of edifying letters" to the paucity of Protestant missionary efforts or martyrologies.[45] In particular, the 1734 deaths of Fathers Lorenzo Carranco and Nicolás Tamaral linked the California Jesuits to this wider story, for which Baegert gave "a thousand thanks to God's kindness," because

> he has never failed to give to individuals among the Catholic priests, and particularly to members of the Society of Jesus, even in these days,

the heart and courage to spread the Christian Faith without thinking of personal gain. These men expose themselves to deadly dangers among all kinds of barbarians and are willing to shed their blood when the opportunity for such a sacrifice arrives.[46]

In this telling, all Jesuits stood ready to die when the moment came and face all sorts of "barbarians" to further the advance of Christendom. In contrast to German Protestants, whom Baegert believed basked comfortably in their home parishes, the sons of the Society had proven themselves as Christ's truest followers.

In the conclusion to the *Observations*, Baegert linked this long sacrifice of blood, sweat, and tears to the losses of the expulsion. He started by totaling up all of California's missionaries who were expelled: "We were sixteen Jesuits in all, fifteen priests and one lay brother; six were Spaniards, two Mexicans, and eight German." The multicultural group had formed a brotherhood in their exile, brought from many nations and bound together by their exertions. This communion of suffering extended beyond the living, however, as the exiles had been remarkably matched by sixteen who had died in the mission. "We left behind exactly the same number, that is, sixteen Jesuits (one brother and fifteen priests), buried in California."[47] By linking the *desterrados* to the *enterrados*, the exiled and the entombed, Baegert connected the expulsion to the prolonged martyrdom that characterized seventy years of Jesuit labor in California. Like the accounts of Sonora and Tarahumara missionaries written by Och and Mateu, Baegert's description of the California mission drew strong comparisons between their original exile on the remote peninsula and their startling banishment from their reluctant home. As harsh as California had been, their forced departure somehow seemed worse.

Abandonment

This compulsion to find significance, to redeem the expulsion in light of the longer mission, prompted even bitter malcontents to recall their Native "children" with paternalistic nostalgia. To supply meaning in the face of such an abrupt end, exiles like Baegert, Mateu, and Ducrue pictured Indigenous Christians as hopeless children and untended sheep, abandoned by their fathers and shepherds. This paternalistic language, thoroughly infantilizing in its description of Native converts, helped Jesuits reconstitute themselves as grieving parents even when uprooted from their mission. The metaphor operated as an ironic juxtaposition to their original casting of Spanish North America as an exile from home and family. In exchange for their lost identity as sons and siblings in Europe, the priests had taken up new positions as brothers to fellow missionaries and "fathers" to Native "children." Now they pictured themselves as a beloved community, ripped away from their adopted families and cast back upon the charity of their natural relatives in Europe.

Throughout their natural histories and travel descriptions, the former missionaries regularly complained about the recalcitrance of Native communities and resistance to control. To do so, they often compared them to fickle children, too easily distracted from celestial goals by material desires.[48] Even in this context, however, the gruff Baegert stood out for his pessimism, telling his European readers that "as a general rule, it may be said that the California Indians are stupid, awkward, rude, unclean, insolent, ungrateful, mendacious, thievish, abominably lazy, great talkers to their end, and naïve and childlike."[49] Not one to mince words, Baegert sounded like an exasperated parent, complaining that his kids never listened to him. Of course, this sort of paternalism pervaded missionary discourse. Still, he painted a particularly awful portrait of Indigenous Californians, describing them as simultaneously cunning and naïve, mendacious and lazy.

Yet, Baegert did not know what he had until it was gone. After the expulsion, he switched course and lauded his converts for their loyalty, their sorrows now an unexpected sign of his own success. To do this, he combined paternal and pastoral images, providing detailed relations of how his own converts purportedly grieved his departure. "Their general crying and pitiful lamenting," he insisted, "moved me to tears," so much so that Baegert "could not restrain himself from weeping all the way to Loreto." At this southern port, he related how the peninsula's superior preached to them of Paul's farewell to the Ephesians in the twentieth chapter of the Acts of the Apostles. Like Paul, the rector described the relationship between the Jesuits and their converts as that between shepherds and sheep. By implication, Pericú and Guaycura Christians would be like sheep without shepherds once the Jesuits left, exposed to greedy colonists acting like marauding wolves and left to "rot in their graves" without the benefit of sacraments. From his position in exile, the otherwise crusty Baegart mourned the presumed fate of his former California "charges." "Even now," he lamented, "there are tears in my eyes" as he thought about people he imagined as his unprotected sons and daughters who probably had returned to their sins after their separation from his fatherly guidance and sacraments.

The fellow German father Benito Ducrue described the same final sermon in his account of the expulsion, evoking a similar pastoral ethos. As the superior of Jesuit California, it actually had fallen to him to preach it. Father Ducrue expressed his worry, from his exile with family in Munich, about having left "his flocks without a shepherd, without consolation, without any hope of ever returning to them." Since they could do nothing to stop the separation, the Jesuits left "with the well-founded fear of seeing them scattered after the departure of their shepherds." Ducrue shared Baegert's pessimism over the authenticity and durability of Indigenous conversion. He complained, "Anyone acquainted with the fickle nature of the Indians cannot hope for their perseverance."[50] He likewise mourned the forfeiture of decades of missionary labor. "Who would not grieve to see the efforts and sacrifices of his predecessors through seventy years wiped out suddenly? Who would not weep over the Natives, still victims of their abysmal ignorance pleading for baptism as they returned to the wilderness from which they had emerged?"[51] The same fears that provided apologetic defense of the mission through pity for the Native plight also undermined any pretension to evangelistic success. If the Indians would no doubt return to paganism immediately after the Jesuits' departure, what gains had their seventy years of service achieved? Still, he took solace in Indigenous grief. Like Och, Mateu, and Baegert, Ducrue emphasized Native suffering in order to highlight the Society's redemptive work.

In her study of Jesuit missions in New France, Emma Anderson has argued that the idealization and promotion of martyrdom shored up missionary confidence when their evangelistic work failed.[52] A robust discourse of redemptive suffering meant that all roads led to victory. If Natives converted, good, but if they did not, at least the priests could suffer and die like Christ in the process. The best of all outcomes would be that Natives ultimately embrace Christianity and testify to the authenticity of conversion by embracing their own *imitatio Christi*. This sort of shared martyrdom would stitch the missionaries to their converts, forging a bond of mutual sacrifice that transcended time and place.

Even if missionaries doubted Native Californians' ultimate fidelity to Christian life, they still emphasized their "children's" love of their fathers. To illustrate their connection, Ducrue rehearsed vivid scenes of separation. "Some knelt on the sand to kiss our hands and feet, others knelt with arms outstretched in the form of a cross and publicly pleading for pardon. Others tenderly embraced the missionaries, bidding them farewell and wishing them a happy voyage through loud weeping and sobbing."[53] Through both disciplined acts of piety and spontaneous affect, Ducrue's Indigenous Christians vindicated his work, even while he doubted its endurance.

In the telling, Father Ducrue transported himself from European exile back to his adopted home. A decade and a continent removed, he returned to California in his imagination, switching from past to present tense. "It is time for our departure. The Indians gladly carry on their shoulders the missionaries to the waiting ship in payment for having been brought by them to Christ." Just as earlier accounts had celebrated how Native communities reportedly welcomed new missionaries with triumphal arches and celebratory processions, these dramatic farewells confirmed the mission's meaning. The California superior described the relationship in terms of mutual exchange; the missionaries had deposited their lives, and Natives paid them back with demonstrations of loving gratitude.

Ducrue went on to dramatize the rupture caused by the expulsion as a family torn asunder. "Farewell beloved California, farewell beloved Indians. We leave you not of our own free will, but by a higher decision." He floated from present back to past as he anticipated his absence but insisted on the power of his memory to conquer distance: "True, we are separated physically, but we shall always preserve the memory of you in our hearts, which neither time, nor forgetfulness, and not even death itself will ever efface." The Jesuit superior left his colleagues with a command to turn their tears into laughter, as all forms of Christian suffering find their fulfillment in God. "Cease, then from weeping, cease from all sobbing—they are of no avail. Do not weep over us. We go with joy in our hearts because we have been held worthy to suffer contumely for the name of Jesus."[54] In addition to time and space, the disciplined power of imagination would help bridge life and death, eternally linking the uprooted fathers to their orphaned "children" in their minds.[55]

In similar manner, Father Jaime Mateu frequently pictured his fellow priests as parents who had been forced to abandon their children. For Matue, the expulsion meant the forced desertion of spiritual progeny. In fact, he argued that leaving their Native "children" behind was the greatest sorrow of the entire expulsion. "That the Indians saw their Apostles and Doctors of the Faith in Christ in chains was more tiring and trying than being afflicted with the weight of the exile." Mateu insisted that the abandonment of Native Christians caused greater anguish than their own removal, sickness, or even death. "Even if there were no other affliction, the act of abandoning these Indians, their beloved children engendered in Christ left them with no peace, not even in their afflicted hearts where they carried them with them always."[56] While Baegert, Ducrue, and Mateu frequently expressed frustration with Native Christians, describing them in paternalistic and pejorative terms, now, as exiles, they imagined themselves as shepherds grieving the "sheep" they had been forced to abandon.

Adiós

In the expulsion, the original *destierro* from Europe found its mirror as forged spiritual families faced sudden parting. The Sonoran missionary Bernardo Middendorff drove this home throughout his diary. Written in Germany in the 1770s, Middendorff's diary continually underscored the ruptures the removal caused between missionaries and their Native charges. In the opening pages of the diary Middendorff narrated how his rectorate's Jesuits were surrounded and imprisoned in Mátape, Sonora, on July 25, 1767.[57] Shortly thereafter, the group learned that a terrible plague had spread among "their Indians." By Middendorff's account, the sickness was so severe that the region's ninety Native families decreased to twenty over the course of a year.

In the midst of the catastrophe, the Jesuits pled with Captain Jose Vergara to allow them to return to their conversions, tend to the sick, and administer sacraments. Following strict orders, Vergara denied the request and "prohibited them from hearing confessions, giving absolution, or administering final sacraments, so that our neophytes died without consolation or the aid of their priests."[58] By positioning them as "neophytes" who endured sickness and death without "aid," the diary pictured Sonora's Indigenous people as patients who, without the treatment of their spiritual doctors, risked spiritual death. Like the metaphors of sheep without shepherds or children without parents, leaving the sick behind without aid or consolation elevated the tragedy of expulsion.

Still, Middendorff believed that converts and catechists remained united through their shared pain. While he rarely made explicit theological conclusions in his diary, he nevertheless embedded these tales into his narration of missionary suffering. Moving from the deadly plague in Sonora to describing the Jesuits' subsequent scurvy, insect bites, bruises, hunger, heat strokes, and general misery in confinement, the diarist concluded that they nevertheless suffered "more than anything because of the contagious epidemic that snatched away our neophyte Indians, without us being able to come to their aid." While he complained of the extent and duration of the missionaries' anguish, he insisted that their greatest sorrow was reserved for the region's new Christians. When paired together, the priests' confinement and their converts' deaths mutually reinforced the tragedy of removal.

Middendorff reiterated this theme as he related the first Jesuit death. After three months of imprisonment, he claimed that only three of the fifty-one priests remained healthy. Without adequate shelter, food, or medicine, the elder father, José Palomino, died on April 19. While Middendorff called his death relatively peaceful, the process of burying Palomino proved to be an ugly affair, which "revealed to light all of the hatred that (the soldiers) had for us." The Jesuits requested a proper church burial for the elderly missionary, but the guards decided instead to deposit the body in a manure heap in a horse corral. Horrified, Middendorff and his colleagues pled to send the body back to his mission of Belén to the south so that his converts could bury him, but they were denied. A month later they finally received permission to wrap the body "in an old blanket, sew it together, mount it on a mule and send it with a single Indian to Belén, where his neophytes interred him in the mission church."[59] In the narrative of Palomino's burial, Middendorff further identified missionary sacrifice with Indigenous conversion. The desire of the Jesuits to return the body to Palomino's home mission and the cooperation of Indigenous

Christians in both retrieving and providing ritual services to their former missionary served to validate their work. At the same time, the soldiers' persecution illustrated a new form of *odium fidei*, hatred for the faith from the very empire that they had served.

What follows in Middendorff's diary is an almost daily tally of indignity and sorrow. When his group finally set out in May of 1768, they spent nearly a month at sea simply trying to cross the Gulf of California. Upon landing, they experienced some initial relief when they were allowed to bathe in the ocean and receive supplies from a Spanish official with some sympathy for the Society. Even more heartening, "numerous Indians of California arrived in small boats to say goodbye to their missionaries and gave us many limes and peaches with visible affection."[60] The emphasis on tearful farewells and visible affection recurs throughout Middendorff's writing as he joined other accounts in highlighting the pathos of the departure. The diary also played up the familial metaphor and the notion that the "Indians of California" joined those of Sonora and Sinaloa in lamenting the expulsion.

After this initial respite in California, the group's anguish recommenced when the authorities once again cut off contact with outsiders, and they spiraled back into hunger, sickness, heat exhaustion, and scurvy so that many lives fell back into danger. On July 15, they finally left port en route further south to the mainland port of San Blas, Nayarit. Like their Sonora imprisonment, later sea crossing, and time in California, the following month brought numerous trials, compounded by spoiled food, putrid water, turbulent storms, and even an earthquake.[61] On top of these disasters, Middendorff added ominous foreboding to the narrative, recording how one evening, "the wind howled, the masts creaked, the waves foamed, the thunder resounded, and the sky crashed on all sides with rains of fire."[62] On other nights they lost all light as waves overwhelmed the boat and both sick and healthy prayed silently in preparation for death. In so many ways, these details recalled the woeful voyages they had narrated to their families as they related their original travel to the mission. Now, in reverse, the tortuous winds and waves extended the prolonged martyrdom of expulsion.

When the Sinaloa and Sonora missionaries at last arrived in San Blas on August 9, they found no relief, but instead entered a town plagued by floods, sweltering heat, and swarming mosquitos. The group determined to head east immediately with eyes set on the regional capital of Guadalajara. Although they fled disease, this journey would prove most deadly. Middendorff's ensuing chronicle tells of Indigenous servants leading horses through river valleys with water up to their chests, caimans surrounding the train, dangerous flooding, and increasingly sick fathers. With soaking clothes and dwindling supplies, some of the priests fell off their horses and into the rivers, fainting from weakness.

After five days, they finally arrived in the town of Tepic, where they experienced some hospitality and relief. The residents of Tepic supplied them with food, dry clothes, beds, and fresh horses. Once again, the bond forged between the northwestern Jesuits and the town's Native and *mestizo* inhabitants reinforced the Society's rootedness in New Spain. When it came time to press on toward Guadalajara, the local attachment had grown so strong that, Middendorff maintained, the town's people surrounded them along the road out of town. "The farewell drew tears on both sides. In the villages that we passed through, they produced similar demonstrations of love; many gathered along the borders of the road to tells us 'adiós' with crying eyes."[63] As in Sonora and California, these scenes of tearful departure accentuated the feeling of being separated from children and being uprooted from the fruitful soil of their mission.

After describing the short reprieve in Tepic, Middendorff's diary quickly pivoted back to a story of profound suffering. Within three days, at least twenty of his fellow missionaries died in the neighboring towns of Aguacatlán and Ixtlán del Rio.[64] First, fathers Enrique Kürtzel, Sebastián Cava, and Vicente Rubio had to stay in Aguacatlán because they were too weak to proceed. Kürtzel died on August 23. The septuagenarian father Nicolás Pereira died the same day just as he arrived at Ixtlán. It is not clear what specific illness caused such a large number to die at that juncture. Fellow Sonoran exiles like Father Francisco Ita, whose letter of October 1770 to Father Mateu supplied the latter with the basic details of the journey, concluded that the exhaustion from imprisonment, sea, and land travel had simply been too much for the three, who died in Aguacatlán on August 22. Just as likely, some disease had caught them at this moment of exhaustion.[65]

In what follows, Middendorff delivered a whirlwind account of death. He explained how "in the span of three days another twenty-two followed them on the road to the grave."[66] In another few sentences, Middendorff rattled off how pestilence took hold of the rest of the group, making everybody lose their senses—experiencing instant paralysis, going crazy, falling mute, blind, or simply dying suddenly without a symptom—sometimes in the middle of conversation, sometimes falling straight off a horse as they were riding.[67] Then, Middendorff himself caught the illness. During Confession on August 24, he lost the ability to recognize anybody, even himself. "I spent several days without speech or reason." The bodies of those who died stayed curiously warm days later, sweating even as they were placed in the grave. Meanwhile, survivors like him were "reduced to bones and spent more than a month before rising from the bed." In fact, every surviving missionary except one became so sick that they received last rites, which fell to Father José Lorenzo Garcia, the lone priest in good health.

Eventually, the group was forced to divide and push on to Guadalajara in hopes of escaping the disease environment, regretfully leaving behind moribund colleagues. Even so, four more died in the following days on the road to Guadalajara. Embedded inside of Mateu's relation of the expulsion, Father Ita's account persisted in a providential interpretation of both death and survival. "Those who stayed in Ixtlán died. In all there were 20 dead, having lost their life in the pains of trials suffered for God, leaving 30 alive also to glorify the same God with the arduous lives that awaited them."[68] Like so many Jesuits before him, Ita believed that all the missionaries shared in a suffering identity, whether dying immediately "for God" in Mexico or being chosen by him for more prolonged martyrdoms in exile. In the context of the longer account, Ita's letter forcefully illustrated Mateu's central point that the Jesuits had given all for the sake of their mission, whether through red martyrdoms of death or white martyrdoms of protracted suffering. In parallel form, those who had originally left their homes only to die in their mission had achieved a bloody martyrdom in exile, while the survivors endured a tearful martyrdom of expulsion back to Europe.

While Mateu and Ita lingered on the meaning of these deaths, Middendorff's diary pressed forward. He quickly summarized the mass death, a jolting culmination in the detailed relation of their extended misery. Within paragraphs, his *Diary of Expulsion* moved from almost daily entries to a broad summary of their travel to Guadalajara, León, Mexico City, Vera Cruz, Havana, and finally Cadíz. He only paused to note the support of locals throughout the journey. Middendorff emphasized how they joined in the priests' suffering and embraced them in grief. In the wealthy city of León, for instance, the remnant experienced the opposite of their long deprivation, enjoying luxurious generosity and abundant provision. Once again upon their departure, the whole city gathered at their windows shouting "adiós," running beside their wagons, kneeling beside them, and pleading for blessings. "Many stayed kneeling, crying and shaking their handkerchiefs."[69] Coming as it did in the wake of death, these expressions of solidarity highlighted the tragedy of Jesuit removal—that outside forces ripped them from their home, exiling and uprooting the missionaries from people they regarded as family.

In his narrative of the expulsion, Mateu insisted that Native converts returned the familial affection. As proof, he pointed to the Naáyarite (Cora) who had cared for and then buried the twenty or so Sonora and Sinaloa missionaries who died near Ixtlán del Rio. After the missionaries' deaths, Mateu related Father Ita's account of how Indigenous devotees came from all the surrounding towns "to request the bodies" of the missionaries. According to Ita, each town wanted to take a relic from the holy men back to their church. He relayed that the devotion was so strong that a *"santa envidia"* or "holy jealousy" arose between the towns as they competed for tokens from these new "saints."

This regard for sanctity extended from the Naáyarite to the whole Society: "Men and women, young and old, all with one voice praised these deceased missionaries as saints, and not only them but in great praise for the Company of Jesus, extolling it as holy."[70] They surrounded the bodies with flowers and candles and carried them in procession to their respective villages and towns "to deposit them in their churches." Most requested entire bodies that could become *"su santo,"* their patron saint. But others contented themselves with the deceased missionaries' "images, crucifixes, breviaries, clothes and in a word all the things that had served the deceased, they requested anxiously as requested as relics." When these requests went unanswered, their devotion was so great, the Jesuit contended, that some committed a "pious robbery" of the missionary's bodies or personal effects.

Mateu shaped these stories of Indigenous piety with paternalistic metaphor. At best, this took the form of guarded appreciation for Native communities, such as the devotion that arose in and around Ixtlán del Rio. But more commonly missionaries complained about childishness, picturing Natives as unreliable and dissembling. Even though he praised the residents of Ixtlán for their piety, Mateu elsewhere grumbled that his converts had been plagued with "childish superstition, insincerity, and disobedience." This ambivalence about conversion, whether Indigenous Christians ever really believed and, if so, whether they would hold onto the faith after the missionary departure, plagued Jesuit writers in exile. They grappled with this doubt by appealing to tearful scenes of familial separation: fathers ripped away from spiritual progeny and "children" longing for their parents. When this longing rose to the point of loving farewell or zealous begging for relics, they assured themselves that their losses would be rewarded.

Conclusion

Expelled Jesuits from Sinaloa, Sonora, and California found solace in the Native Christians who accompanied them during their long journey across New Spain. When they arrived at the port of San Blas in Nayarit, they were housed with a group of Otomí prisoners from San Luis Potosi. Like several other Native and creole communities throughout New Spain, these Otomí had risen up in protest of the wider Bourbon reforms, including anger over taxation and monopolies, but also the Jesuit expulsion.[71] Riots in Michoacán, Guanajuato, and San Luis Potosi were met with severe response from the Spanish visitor general José de Gálvez, who imprisoned around 674 people, banished 117, flogged 73, and hanged 85.[72] In the case of the Otomí, the California Jesuits were assured that the principal cause of the uprising was anger at the missionaries' removal. As punishment, authorities had severely beaten and imprisoned these Otomí and sentenced them to hard labor. The missionaries were appalled by the severity of the punishments, in which "some, overcome by their suffering, had died, while others were still paying the penalty of their temerity." At the same time, the priests believed that this torment also provided a confirmation of their sacrifice, a promise of meaning embodied in Indigenous Christians who were willing to give their own lives in a last testimony against expulsion.

Father Benno Ducrue related one particularly gruesome case in his account of the exile. "One of us was summoned to hear the confession of one of them. The skin hung in tatters, torn as it had been by the lashings, naught but blood and bones were to be seen and yet the lashings continued daily." Ducrue grieved the sight of this loyal convert, who had endured brutal torture and had been reduced to a skeleton. "What one of us would not be touched to the quick at such a sight? What source for additional suffering, as the reader can easily imagine, and I shall frankly state. We were moved to the deepest compassion for these unfortunate Natives." Even as the missionaries sympathized with these bloody scenes, they also delighted in them, seeing the Otomí deaths as so many multiplied imitations of Jesus and the Society that carried his name. "They said that it was out of love for us that they endured all this, not that our men had introduced them to revolt but that the love and esteem of the Natives for our men had led them to act as they did."[73] As they had come to die for their converts, now New Spain's Indigenous people had laid down their lives for them. For Ducrue, the Otomí personified the ultimate goal of shared suffering, a mutual victimization that forged a final connection between Jesuits and their converts.

The meaning of those deaths became more plain when read in a wider context. Throughout his account of the exile, Benito Ducrue emphasized the overlap of Christian feasts with Jesuit tragedies. For instance, he noted how the California missionaries first got word of the expulsion decree on the Feast of the Apostle Saint Andrew, a martyr who imitated Christ through his own crucifixion. This convergence, Ducrue believed, "had a providential significance—to recall his cross and to gladly accept the cross in store for us."[74] Later, the fathers had been gathered together by the Spanish governor at Loreto on Christmas Eve, "at the very moment when the Martyrology, according to Spanish custom, was being sung."[75] Then, the decree had been promulgated, Ducrue noted, on the Feast of St. Stephen, the great Christian protomartyr.[76]

After departing San Blas, the California superior presented the rest of the exiles' journey as an extended recapitulation of the gospel crucifixion narratives. He recalled how he and the fifteen other California missionaries were paraded through the streets of Vera Cruz, scorned and mocked just like the Society's namesake. For him, it was no mere chance that they entered their port of departure on the "Day of Palms" at the beginning of Holy Week. Rather, he took solace as he drew parallels between their inglorious exodus from New Spain with Christ's entry into Jerusalem. Noting that they arrived "around the Ninth Hour," the missionaries mounted mules and rode toward the port as soldiers stood guard and curious onlookers crowded the streets.

The convergence of signficant moments with the feasts of Saints Andrew and Stephen, the Martyrology of Christmas Eve, Palm Sunday, mules, and the liturgical hour of None (set aside for meditations on the crucifixion) all associated the missionaries with Jesus's death. Even the departure port's name, Vera Cruz ("True Cross"), reminded them to take up their crosses and follow him. As Ducrue summarized, we were just "like Christ our leader," and they rejoiced in their opportunity to further identify with their lord, because "it was a source of no little consolation for us to memorialize in ourselves a fragile image of His triumphal entry."[77] Ideally, the mimetic sacrifice eventually would produce Indigenous conversion and ultimately vindicate their work. Like so many of his colleagues, however, Ducrue found reason to rejoice in the exile and later suppression, even if those conversions never happened. Because whatever may come, they had imitated Christ in their mission. For that reason, he thanked God that "the Society of His Son" had been allowed to "taste a bit of the chalice of His suffering." His only regret was that they could not have joined their fallen brothers and suffering Native "children" in death and thereby "drink all of it."[78]

Exiled missionaries like Joseph Och, Benito Ducrue, Jacob Baegert, Jaime Mateu, Francisco Ita, and Bernardo Middendorff recorded their losses in the memoirs of the expulsion as well as natural histories, observations, and travel reports. In doing so, they met the demands of European readers, hungry for accounts of North American topography, geography, biology, and cultures. They paired these histories with harrowing narratives of their own trials and tribulations, which joined the story of their expulsion to a longer history of apostolic labors in the service of knowledge and evangelism.

In retrospect, they pictured this ordeal as the final *imitatio Christi*, a typological fulfillment of the suffering servant from whom the Society of Jesus took its name. Indeed, for Ducrue, the greatest loss beyond the expulsion and exile was the eventual supression of the Society, which took away from him the very name of Jesuit. When royal officials in Spain removed "the most Holy Name of Jesus," the Jesuit IES, "from the doors and walls of (his) hospice" in Seville, he worried that the action threatened to erase the memory of their sacrifice. His history of the expulsion needed to bridge the gap and maintain the meaning of their work. Like the crucifixion itself, Ducrue and others insisted that their reversals should not be seen as final. Once, they had severed themselves from their families and the comforts of Europe to serve in a distant and difficult land. Eventually, though, they had made these deserts their home and adopted its inhabitants as "children."

Since the sixteenth century, dozens of Jesuits had obtained their martyrdom during the mission, "*enterrados*" in the land where they served as seeds deposited in once infertile ground. Others found themselves "*desterrados*," ripped away from their families and fields. Nevertheless, their memoirs mobilized a nostalgia for their suffering converts that had more to do with their own needs in diaspora than the material realities of the mission. Indeed, most of them expressed ambivalence about the authenticity of the conversions and the perseverance of Indigenous Christianities. Martyrological discourse filled the gap between those doubts and the Jesuits' desire to believe it was all worth it. Narratives of shared affliction assured them that ultimately, God would use the evil of the expulsion for good. Paired with maps and observations of Native landscapes and cultures, their embrace of martyrological discourse and imagery helped the Jesuits of New Spain reconstitute their missionary identity in exile, whether as grieving fathers or worried shepherds. It also bridged the expanse that separated them from New World converts, if only in their own imaginations.

These dramatic scenes of departure lent a final vindication to the Jesuit sacrificial identity, cultivated over centuries of work in New Spain. When these accounts presented Indigenous Christians shedding tears and even blood as they protested the Jesuit eviction, they sought to complete the cycle of suffering and salvation that had fueled the Spanish evangelistic enterprise in the northern borderlands since their inception in the 1590s. Yet, the Jesuit expulsion was a counterintuitive martyrdom. Whereas earlier Jesuits had pictured their entire mission as a martyrdom—a death to family, friends, and worldly aspiration—the exiles found the discourse of redemptive sacrifice pliable enough to understand the loss of that same vocation as equally providential. From this perspective, the expulsion represented an outstanding reversal of fortune, as the former Jesuits who had renounced kin and country in their embrace of a North American mission now worked to understand their uprooting and return home as their final sacrifice.

Epilogue
Civilization and Savagery

At first, even the *Arizona Daily Star* hedged its bets. "Kino's Grave Believed Located in Magdalena," the cover story on May 24, 1966, began, qualifying the claim in a subtitle, "Confirmation Still to Be Made."[1] The next day the newspaper was less circumspect, proclaiming the "Grave of Father Kino Found in Magdalena" and supplying photos and summaries of the remarkable discovery.[2] Other media outlets in Tucson, Phoenix, and Hermosillo, Mexico, confirmed the event. The *Arizona Republic* misspelled his name, but got the rest of the basics straight, telling Phoenix readers that an interdisciplinary and binational team from Mexico and the United States had discovered the bones of the famous seventeenth-century Jesuit missionary Eusebio Francisco Kino just south of the Arizona border.[3] Then, as now, readers in Mexico saw more graphic proof. Hermosillo's *El Sonorense* provided eight pages of detailed coverage, complete with photos of the discovery team, political dignitaries, and a near full-page picture of the skull. A search for the grave ordered by Mexican president Gustavo Díaz Ordaz in 1965 had taken a binational team nearly a year and entailed 800 yards of trenching, countless hours of archival digging, and numerous rabbit trails into local lore, but had borne fruit at last. Kino's bones had been recovered.[4]

Scholarly, civic, and corporate leaders spoke of the find in miraculous terms. Some expressed wonder. Upon discovering the bones, physical anthropologist Arturo Romano exclaimed, "Extraordinario. Extraordinario."[5] With similar awe, Arizona State Museum archeologist William Wasley declared, "It's like a dream. It's like a dream."[6] Walsley later explained how the search for Kino had defied all odds; it was "like looking for a needle in a haystack, but first we had to find the haystack!"[7] Many echoed his amazement at how fortunate the team had been. Pointing out that the body was unearthed just feet away from Magdalena's 1882 City Hall as well as several other newer constructions, Arizona writer Bob

Thomas marveled at how "extremely lucky" the diggers were to find it undamaged, except by time.[8]

Like those of saints of old, the padre's relics had been preserved and then recovered in nearly inexplicable fashion. Having been brought in to verify the remains, the preeminent Kino expert and Jesuit historian Ernest J. Burrus likewise celebrated the team, for he deemed the discovery to be most propitious.[9] The director of the search, Dr. Wigberto Jiménez Moreno, concurred, pointing to the cooperative work of academic, religious, national, and local authorities whose "fortunate convergence" uniquely permitted the successful breakthrough.[10] They all believed that, whether by luck, fortune, or divine hand, the bones of the beloved missionary had returned at just the right moment. Once more they argued that the discovery of the relics and recollection of the Jesuits' sacrificial labors would inaugurate a new era where civilization would finally triumph over savagery.

Civilization

Some went further, speaking of Kino in near messianic terms. In a speech delivered a few days after the discovery, the governor of Sonora Luis Encinas Johnson hailed the Jesuit as "the constructor of towns and redeemer of Indians," whose emergence from his heretofore anonymous burial spot was a "fortunate event," destined to inaugurate a new era for both the state and its missionary.[11] Governor Encinas Johnson proclaimed Kino as both the civilizer and savior of Sonora, a man whose labor had built its first cities and redeemed its inhabitants. The editor of *El Sonorense* joined the governor in the hope that the padre's civilizing work continued into the twentieth century: "It was not difficult yesterday, hearing the excited words of scientific and civic leaders to those congregated in memory of the remarkable civilizer, to imagine the pilgrim himself mounted on a gentle beast, crossing the desert to complete his final date with Destiny."[12]

Mexican journalist Rubén Parodi similarly endorsed this civilizing mythology, arguing that Kino's spiritual conquest would now pick up where it had left off two-and-a-half centuries earlier. "Kino has returned to conquer with his strong personality the respect and admiration of the men of this Pimería Alta, after so many years being dead."[13] When Magdalena changed its name to Magdalena de Kino later in 1966, Enriqueta de Parodi, an accomplished educator, writer, politician, and mother of Rubén, echoed her son's enthusiasm, praising the Sonoran and Mexican governments for "exalting the memory of the great civilizer" and enshrining "the immortality of the name of Eusebio Francisco Kino."[14] The public intellectual Dr. Joaquin Antonio Peñalosa concurred, attributing the discovery to "the intelligence of love" and comparing Kino to a star whose "light still illumines history."[15] Collectively, Sonora's civic leaders hoped that the priest's remains would renew the Jesuit's civilizing work, which had begun centuries ago.

Still others invoked even more explicitly religious terms. Pledging to protect the bones with his life, prominent businessman Humberto W. López Campbell urged Magdalena's citizens to regard them as sacred relics: "With the serenity that knowledge of his immortality and greatness gives us, let us defend Father Kino who must endure, by God, beyond the ashes of time, beyond oblivion, beyond death."[16] The University of Arizona ethnohistorian Bernard Fontana summarized this same conviction decades later, concluding the fact "that Kino's remains were discovered in 1966 has to be regarded as miraculous. The same might be said for the continuation of so much that he set in motion in northern Sonora/southern Arizona more than three centuries ago."[17]

For these Kino supporters on both sides of the border, the find represented an extraordinary breakthrough that portended a new era. Almost exactly two hundred years after the Jesuits' expulsion from New Spain, their logic of salvation through suffering endured, now translated into a secular discourse of prosperity and progress. But this future could only be secured through increased commerce and governance. The Jesuit missionary, as he was recovered and mobilized in the mid-twentieth century, came to embody the Mexican government's ambitions of finally "civilizing" what they regarded as a still savage northern frontier. Like earlier colonists, soldiers, and priests, they trusted that the missionary's sacrificial labors and material remains would stimulate the full settlement and development of what had been a wild and undeveloped border.

Governor Luis Encinas Johnson descended from a long line of Sonoran settlers who had long dreamed of "civilizing" the state's Indigenous communities. Since the mid-nineteenth century, his family had tried and failed to eradicate the Comcaác (Seri), whose land the Encinas clan had taken for their large hacienda west of Hermosillo.[18] So it is unsurpising that after the find was confirmed, Governor Encinas extolled the missionary's pioneering legacy in a televised speech on May 24, 1966. Encinas celebrated Kino for "teaching Indians the practical elements of civilization" and laying the "foundations of development" for Sonora, Arizona, and both Californias. Then, he called for a monument to be raised over the grave, perhaps with a museum and library that "would make Magdalena a center for cultural and historical research."

Along with the monument, Encinas proposed a Kino Mission Route to encourage tourism, trade, and regional promotion. Union Halls and town offices, which had once been churches and later secularized, would be repurposed again as mission-style churches, easily accessible by modern highways and serviced by new motels. Such attractions would lead to more tourism and commerce and stronger ties with their northern neighbors. The project had special urgency in 1966, Encinas noted, as Mexico was investing heavily in infrastructure in preparation for the 1968 Olympics. The Kino attractions would entice U.S. visitors across the border via the new Mexican Federal Highway 15 and provide a regional attraction as they made their way to the games. The relics would pave the way to progress.

Savagery

Just a year earlier, in 1965, officials in the United States had spoken in similar terms at the official unveiling of a Padre Kino statue in the U.S. Capitol. Presaging the sentiments of his counterpart in Sonora, the recently elected governor of Arizona, Samuel Goddard, expressed numinous enchantment for the pioneer priest. Goddard spoke longingly of the Sonoran desert's "starry skies" and "scales of endless time" as he described the "primitive fear" one feels when confronting its "savage," natural beauty. He marveled at how the bold missionary had ventured forth despite the danger, "a solitary mortal led and protected by the immortal spark of the spirit; the invisible armor of God."

Goddard employed a series of binaries that contrasted the Sonoran desert's untamed wilderness with European sophistication. "Padre Eusebio bore in his person the seeds of change. His maps opened out the distant wilderness for the legions of New Spain; his crusading spirit planted graceful missions whose bells rang with holy sound the fruits of civilization." He specifically hailed the Jesuits, whose missions supposedly had brought gentility and order to the region's Natives. "They called together the solitary savage people; they measured the growing seasons and regulated the new order of cattle growers and farmers; they gentled wilderness."[19] For Goddard and the assembled Kino admirers in the Hall of Statuary that day, the Jesuit represented the arrival of civilization and the taming of savagery in the American southwest.[20]

Leaders on both sides of the border who promoted the memorialization of the Jesuit missionaries were echoing the civilizing claims of colonists and priests that dated back to the sixteenth century. They asserted that because of the region's geography, climate, and mobile societies, it was naturally savage, inherently lacking the law, literacy, settlement, and religion required to form political life according to Greco-Roman and European standards. Yet, evidence of sophisticated Indigenous societies surrounded them nearly everywhere they looked. From Flagstaff to Hermosillo, archeological and historical evidence throughout Arizona and Sonora bore clear witness to the canals, ballcourts, ritual centers, and houses that had constituted powerful Puebloan, Sinagua, Hohokham, and Mugollon cities. In fact, Phoenix itself had been named in reference to the elaborate Indigenous settlements upon which the more recent Anglo-American city had been raised.

Hundreds of thousands of people had lived in these dense urban formations, connected by elaborate irrigation networks only matched in the Americas by the Mexica, Maya, and Inca. These cities not only sustained the cultivation of cotton, squash, beans, and corn, but fostered wide-ranging trade networks that connected them to resources throughout the Americas. Their ritual specialists sought to maintain this power through impressive structures and ceremonies of reciprocity, specifically coordinated to calendric cycles. Extensive legal regulation and political coordination distinguished these societies and allowed them to prosper in the desert. In truth, the region had not only matched, but surpassed the accomplishments of many ancient and early modern European cities.[21]

While those urban networks had declined by the time of Kino, he had nevertheless marveled at their accomplishments as he charted the Casa Grande structures and Gila River canals onto his maps. Their achievements were so evident that the Jesuit was convinced the region's inhabitants had been the ancestors of the Mexica, who he believed had migrated from what is now central Arizona to the valley of Mexico.[22] By the time officials were celebrating his role in inaugurating civilization in the region through his sacrificial labors in the 1960s, however, these histories had been obscured. Still, officials in both the United States and Mexico were well aware of contemporary O'odham communities who practiced many of these traditional ways while adapting to their present: utilizing irrigation, raising cotton, gathering the fruit of the Saguaro, celebrating with chicken scratch and Waila, making pilgrimages to Magdalena, and participating in ritual life both within and without the Christian churches.[23]

The rhetoric of savagery, however, obscured these deeper histories and present communities in preference for celebrating the European civilizers who had supposedly extended the limits of Christendom. In the tradition of Frederick Jackson Turner, Kino's civic promoters bought into the idea of the frontier as a temporal and spatial boundary that marked modernity, a process of progress that could only be advanced by bold European pioneers. As Turner had argued in his famed address to the American Historical Association in 1893, "In this advance, the frontier is the outer edge of the wave, the meeting point between savagery and civilization."[24] For his many promoters in the U.S.-Mexico borderlands, Kino could be refashioned as the pioneer who had not only opened the meeting point but would pave the way for development into the future.

Governor Goddard went on to speak in florid detail in his speech at the U.S. Capitol about Kino's international provenance and suggested that he would become a new model for cooperation with Mexico. "I know Governor Encinas of Mexico shares with me the dream of enriching Padre Kino's pasture with all the fruits of our common history, civilization and the spirit which knows no limits to the brotherhood of man."[25] For Arizona's governor, Kino's sacrificial labors had planted the fields of civilization, the harvest of which would be transborder cooperation and trade. Taking the first step, Governor Encinas of Sonora invited Goddard to join him soon for a formal ceremony the following year to show "the gratitude of the two communities that owe so much of their current progress and civilization to Fray Eusebio Francisco Kino."[26] Encinas told Goddard that Secretary of Education Agustín Yañez, Director of Tourism Agustín Salvat, and Director of INAH Eusebio Dávolos Hurtado would visit within the week to begin plans for the museum, memorial, and mission route and that he would be delighted to work with Goddard to promote tourism to these new Kino shrines.[27]

Dávalos Hurtado arrived in May, and when Salvat and Yañez joined him the next month an initial tribute was organized for June 9, 1966. In his speech at the event, Governor Encinas built upon the themes of his earlier televised address, arguing that Kino's agricultural, architectural, educational, and cartographical work had planted the seeds of modernity in the north, the fruit of which was the economic growth and development that characterized Sonora and Arizona. Thanks to the localization of his remains, the whole world could now recognize their mutual progress, "because before men like Kino borders disappear." Encinas suggested that Kino's bones should not be a symbol of death, but rather of life. Indeed, the Jesuit's "shining example" meant that the priest still "continues his untiring civilizing work today." The harvest of his colonial sacrifice would grow exponentially into the future because "the fruit of his extraordinary effort will keep multiplying century after century, meriting the appreciation of all humanity, without distinction to borders, creeds, or ideologies."[28] Although Kino was dead, his labors continued, not through Christian evangelism, but through the gospel of capital investment, transnational cooperation, and expanding civilization.

At the same ceremony, Secretary of Education Agustín Yañez picked up Encinas's agricultural rhetoric in his public speech, using the long-invoked metaphor to describe how Kino worked to transition "savages to civilization." Secretary Yañez declared that the "fundamental lesson of Father Kino is that of being a great and indefatigable worker who converts enormous deserts into lush gardens and teaches primitive groups a better level of life and rewarding cultivation." He suggested that Kino was a representation of a moral and economic excellence "constitutive of the grandeur of Mexico" and "an example of work and education for entire humankind."[29] Conveniently, this image coalesced precisely with two major initiatives that President Gustavo Díaz Ordaz had been pushing throughout the 1960s in border cities like Juarez, Tijuana, and Nogales. Ordaz believed that the northwest should rapidly industrialize by encouraging U.S. commercial investment. In turn, economic advancement demanded a new era of openness, one that abandoned old conflicts and emphasized free trade of Mexico's agricultural products. In Yañez's rendering, Kino's frontier labors symbolized both initiatives. The Jesuit was both a good worker and goodwill ambassador, a model of Mexican industry and flourishing international relations.

In terms of working with Arizona, Governor Encinas delivered on his desire for a binational gathering in August 1967 when he traveled to Phoenix to dedicate a 12½-foot, 8,000-pound bronze statue of Kino that Sonora gave to Arizona. The large equestrian figure was made in Mexico City by the sculptor Julian Martínez, who created two sculptures, one each for the sister state capitals of Hermosillo and Phoenix. Encinas unveiled the gift in a ceremony, conducted mostly in Spanish, in front of the Arizona Capitol building. Emphasizing the two countries' shared history, geography, and commercial interests, Encinas declared that Kino would be a symbol of cooperation and strengthened relations. From his perspective, the missionary preached a gospel of prosperity and democracy that Encinas insisted could transcend the border. He prophesied that "we may form with the same prosperity of all and with the same ideological goals in all the American continent, the most solid and inexpugnable front of liberty and democracy."[30]

However, Goddard was not present to echo Encinas's call. He had been defeated in his bid for reelection the previous year, part of wave of GOP victories that would transform Arizona's politics. The newly elected Republican governor of Arizona, Jack Williams, nevertheless reciprocated the sentiment and exhorted both states to fraternal love because "God has made us neighbors. Let us not only be good neighbors, but good brothers."[31] They ended the ceremony by depositing a time capsule that contained objects representing the shared values of commerce, cooperation, and civilization. In the context of an escalating war in Vietnam, an increasingly confrontational Fidel Castro in Cuba, and lingering American fears of Mexican socialism, Encinas's pledge of "friendship in all of Latin America" and a "front of liberty and democracy" were not just sonorous language, but coded assurances that Sonora sided with the United States. Dedicated to both this national cause and Arizona's economic growth, Williams surely received the memo.

The *Arizona Republic* took an additional message out of the gift. In an editorial called "Sonora and Arizona," it argued that "no other man so intimately reflects the intertwined spirit of Sonora and Arizona as Father Eusebio Francisco Kino"; as such, the statues in Hermosillo and Phoenix "will remain a permanent reminder of the friendship and co-operation of the two states, and two nations, which share a common heritage and abiding respect for each other." In fact, the states had "ties between the two that were closer than their respective ties with Mexico City or Washington, D.C." They contended that Sonora was wealthier and more technologically innovative than the rest of Mexico, while Arizona boasted more Spanish culture and self-determination than the rest of the U.S. The discovery of Kino's bones had inaugurated the dawn of a new era, they reasoned, arguing that the states should work on easing trade restrictions and fostering immigration to create an example for both nations. In this way, the priest would serve as a missionary of free trade and unrestricted mobility.

The next year Ordaz's interior minister, Luis Echeverría Álvarez, visited Magdalena to dedicate the Kino mausoleum. Echeverría returned to Magdalena in 1971 as the new president of the Republic. On this later occasion, President Echeverría dedicated the recently finished neocolonial plaza and celebrated the city as an economic and cultural gateway, a portal for northward-bound exports and southward-bound tourism from North America. In his speech, Echeverría connected Magdalena's new shrine and plaza to wider regional efforts to better economic and cultural relations with the United States.

This aspiration found highest confirmation on October 21, 1974, when President Gerald Ford made his first foreign trip to meet President Echeverría in Sonora. Coming just months after Nixon's resignation, Ford emphasized "that closer cooperation and friendly relations between our peoples and governments" would be a top priority of his presidency. Ford landed in Nogales, Arizona, before crossing the border on foot and placing a wreath on a monument for former Mexican president Benito Juarez. The president then took a helicopter to Magdalena de Kino (Figure 10). Arriving at the grand central plaza, Ford donned a sombrero that had been given to him by a woman from Magdalena and spoke to a raucous crowd of near 40,000. He then walked with Echeverría to Kino's mausoleum, where he viewed the missionary's bones. Along with Secretary of State Henry Kissinger and his Mexican counterpart Emilio Rabasa, the two presidents laid a wreath on the crypt. Afterward, they proceeded into Magdalena's remodeled Palacio Municipal, where they entered into ninety minutes of what Ford characterized as "straight-talk diplomacy" on oil prices, the border free-trade zone, Cuba, immigration, human rights, drug interdiction, and a Mexican-proposed U.N. charter protecting developing countries from the predation of multinational corporations.[32]

Later in the afternoon, they helicoptered back to a country club in Tubac, Arizona, where they dined and continued discussing the issues raised throughout the day, as well as Kino's significance. In a formal toast that evening, Ford thanked Echeverría for his choice of location, extolling the Mexican president's "sense of history, your understanding of the great role that Father Kino played in the history of this part of the world, made it an ideal setting for the discussions that we had on very important matters." Ford cited the shrine and statues as testament to the missionary's ongoing meaning as a stimulant to progress among the inhabitants of the region. Addressing Echeverría, Ford contended,

> Mr. President, the Jesuit priest whose statue is in the United States Capitol and whose statue is in the state capitol of Sonora and the capitol of Arizona, lived and worked here almost three centuries ago. His efforts gave the first great stimulant to progress among the people of this part of the North American Continent, and we are all proud of his contribution to this flourishing part of our Nation as well as yours.

Ford continued by explicitly citing Kino's farming and ranching, in addition to his spreading his religion, as markers of European civilization. "Mr. President, with the horse, the cross, and the plow, he explored this area of your country as well as ours. He not only served his faith, Mr. President, but he also introduced agriculture, livestock to the inhabitants of this area."

To Ford, Kino's evangelism and husbandry worked together to secure the advancement of Christianity and commerce among Sonora and Arizona's Indigenous people. He continued, "And all of these ingredients, Mr. President, are vital to the progress of your country as well as ours." Once more, the U.S. president insisted that the Jesuit's mission continued into his own time as his legacy propelled cooperation. "Father Kino lives in the memories of those in the town that we visited this morning. On both sides of the border we owe him a very great debt of gratitude. The heritage of Father Kino is an inspiration for all of us to continue the work that he started three centuries ago."[33] Kino embodied the sort of "straight-talk di-

FIGURE 10. U.S. president Gerald Ford meets Mexican president Luis Echeverría in Magdalena de Kino. After speaking to a massive crowd in the new town plaza, both presidents went to visit the newly constructed mausoleum for Father Kino. October 21, 1974, public domain, courtesy of Gerald R. Ford Presidential Library and Museum.

plomacy" that Ford hoped would be a marker of his presidential foreign policy. The evangelist's knack for intercultural communication and industrious civilization could also be a model for both countries.

The Mexican president shared these sentiments, stressing Kino's fruitful labors as the reason he had selected Magdalena for their summit. Replying to Ford in a second toast, Echeverría explained, "When you and I, Mr. President, explored the different possibilities of meeting along the border area, we decided to meet in this vast region which was at that time a desert and which Father Kino discovered and civilized." Echoing Ford's emphasis on cooperation and progress, Echeverría stressed Kino's conversion of desert into city and savagery into civilization, which he had accomplished through indefatigable toil. "Father Kino's untiring work, Father Kino's great foresight and vision and all his dedication are examples that are to be followed in the work that needs to be done in this very vast desert area in which we are at present." In President Echeverría's estimation, the missionary's sacrificial labor had encountered an empty expanse and rendered it amenable to development.

The president of Mexico also took inspiration from the bi-national team that had come together to search for Kino's bones. He argued that just as admiration for the Jesuit had brought both countries together to work on a common goal, the researchers' work should stimulate broader collaboration. "In researching the work that was done by Father Kino, many students of the United States and many students of history of Mexico participated, and similarly to the way in which they joined forces and participated, we can join forces in order to solve the problems of the United States and Mexico."[34] Together, the presidents held up Kino as a symbol of the type of international partnership that would usher in a more civilized borderland future.

This present optimism and imagined future effaced the presence of contemporary Indigenous people that lived in Arizona and Sonora long before the regions ever had those names or had been incorporated into the U.S. or Mexican nation-states. In reference to twentieth-century memorials, Lisa Blee and Jean M. O'Brien have argued that they always tell one story at the expense of another. When it comes to monuments and statues of pioneers, the effacement operates as a key part of establishing settler-colonial territoriality. "Most memorials in the United States, when they mention Native Americans at all, often serve to underscore frontier mythologies and celebrate the dispossession of the nation's Indigenous inhabitants as a measure of progress." By solely focusing on the European civilizer, the poisonous myths of inherent Native savagery and the "tragically disappeared Indian" become firmly fixed in collective memory and historical assumption.

In rare cases where images of Natives are featured, such as the proliferating Massasoit statues that Blee and O'Brien interrogate or James Earle Fraser's 1918 "End of the Trail" equestrian piece that I encountered as a student every year on elementary school field trips to Oklahoma City's "Cowboy Hall of Fame," these sculptures usually dramatize the predestined defeat of "the noble savage." As Blee and O'Brien explain, "American memorial practices involving Indigenous history often invoke an ambivalent narrative that combines remorse with nostalgia to punch up the emotional appeal."[35] This exercise in colonial melancholy bolsters the charm of individual figures like Bartolome de las Casas or Father Kino, paternalistic pioneers who offer Christianity and civilization, while lamenting the supposedly inevitable demise of Indigenous communities.

Roxanne Dunbar-Ortiz connects this fundamental ideological distinction between European civilization and Native savagery to the collective memory-making that undergirds the taking of land. Into the mid-twentieth century, the necessity to baptize Native suffering with European sacrifice remained fundamental to Manifest Destiny and the nation's claim upon Indigenous territory, even "seventy years after the Wounded Knee Massacre, when the conquest of the continent was said to have been complete, and with Hawai'i and Alaska made into states, round[ing] out the fifty stars on today's flag."

Once more this belief in a divinely guided mission fueled global aspirations of spreading democracy, economic development, and international cooperation because "an exceptional U.S. American people" had been "destined to bring order out of chaos, to stimulate economic growth, and to replace savagery with civilization—not just in North America but throughout the world."[36] The assertion of the United States' divinely sanctioned imperial destiny rests firmly on this notion that Euro-Americans brought order, progress, and civilization through their sacrificial labors and selfless suffering. By recovering Kino and the Jesuit missions as symbols of that sacrifice, promoters in both the United States and Mexico were able to mobilize the claim in service of new civilizational projects in the borderlands. At the same time, the O'odham, Comcáac, Yoeme, Yoreme, Quechan, Apache, Maricopa, Yavapai, and other Native communities, their cultures, and their deep histories could be ignored or erased.

Conclusion

I grew up surrounded by images of white cowboy heroes celebrated in "Halls of Fame," while Indigenous representations (where they appeared) dramatized Native Americans' inevitable defeat by the inexorable churnings of modernity. Each year in my elementary school, I looked forward to Land Run Day, where we would dress up as pioneers and reenact the 1889 Land Run that gave over former Creek and Seminole treaty lands in central Oklahoma to white settlers. Many Saturdays, I chanted "Boomer" for Oklahoma Sooner football or shagged foul balls at the Triple A, 89'ers baseball games, each in its way memorializing the day Anglo-Americans inaugurated the modern state.

I finished writing this book in a different context, in the American South, where memorials to redemptive violence have for over a century shaped the landscape in an attempt to fix a collective memory of the Lost Cause. This, too, is a tale of sacrificial heroes and civilizational labor. This narrative countenances the suffering of enslaved African Americans only insomuch as it can be redeemed as necessary to secure Christian salvation and democratic progress. The enshrinement of fallen white heroes and erasure of black torment attempt to consolidate certain ideals about social belonging and group identity while marking those who can never be included. As Fitz Brundage has argued about these efforts, "Collective remembering forges identity, justifies privilege, and sustains cultural norms. For individuals and groups alike, memory provides a genealogy of social identity."[37] At the same time, the work of collective memory necessarily effaces the suffering of others because those in power are "colonizing public spaces with their version of the past."[38]

However, there is a longer genealogy to this practice than most contemporary historians recognize. These statues, memorials, and mausoleums are translations of the martyrological discourses, practices, and material objects traced in this book. David Chidester and Edward Linenthal have argued that for contemporary spaces to be regarded as "sacred" they must exist in dialectic relationship to the "modern" and "the profane." Even as monuments and memorials to soldiers, pioneers, and missionaries incorporate centuries-old traditions and ritual patterns, they are also implicated in political and economic processes, from tourism and commerce to nationalism and the marking of borders.[39] When they become regional or national shrines, these objects and spaces serve as practices and places employed by large institutions with the capacity to produce a narrative of sacredness—in this case about the predestined triumph of progress, modernity, civilization, and commerce.[40]

Colonial Jesuit missionaries would have eagerly embraced this logic. As this book has argued, redemptive death became a central interpretive tool for them as they sought to make sense of both their own sacrifices and Native suffering in the missions of northern New Spain. They contended that their martyrs' bones and blood sowed seed that bore spiritual harvests and would lead to the civilizing of the frontier. Their broken bodies and prolonged labors, they believed, sanctified and thereby civilized this section of North America. The language, idioms, and practices associated with the recovery, display, and memorialization of Kino's body remind us of those longer trajectories. Kino's relics gave the borderlands of Mexico's north and the U. S. Southwest a patron saint who embodied a longer story of the triumph of European civilization over imagined Indigenous savagery.

The language of civilization and barbarity, center and periphery, sacred and profane were constant themes in the recovery of Kino and representation of Jesuit missions in the late twentieth century. This discourse also marked a new moment in the appropriation of Indigenous land and ritual practice. As civic leaders promoted Kino Mission tours, they also marketed new regional festivals that celebrated the Jesuits' legacy. The Society's prolonged martyrdom, therefore, still operated as a foundational mythology that secured civilization and paved the way to prosperity. Since the arrival of the Spanish Empire in this region, this sacrificial Christian logic served the cause of colonization. Mexican and U.S. officials hoped that the holy relics of a martyr figure, translated into secular forms, would finally bring this far-flung frontier into modernity. As was the case in earlier centuries, this was still a unifying narrative purposely fashioned in order to rationalize a much more complex and aggressive process of colonization. On the ground, these spaces were contested, challenged by the tactics of individuals, and hybridized by communities who brought their own practices, interpretations, and memories into that place.[41] The Indigenous communities targeted for evangelization always engaged these teachings and practices on their own terms.

A few years ago, I had the opportunity to talk with several O'odham elders at the Office of Ethnohistory at the Arizona State Museum. I went with the goal of hearing what they thought about this Jesuit martyrological rhetoric. As a part of a reciprocity agreement with the office, I had agreed to provide the elders with translations of several Spanish documents about the 1695 O'odham rebellion, many of which formed the substance of Chapter 3.[42] As we sat down on a sweltering day in June 2013, I introduced myself and my research to the group, eager to ask them for their perspective. Before I could ask, however, they interrupted me and told me that first we must pray and then we must eat. The history could come later.

Through their prayers, the meal, and the ensuing conversation, I learned that there were many different viewpoints on the texts I had given. There were also diverse religious dispositions represented in the room, from traditionalists to Catholics to Presbyterians. There were Tohono O'odham, who still lived in the same Sonoran Desert as their ancestors, but joining them were Akimel O'odham, Gila, and Salt River Pima, some of whose predecessors had lived in the river valleys where Kino had established his missions, and others came from the north, where Kino had only explored and only dreamed of evangelization. They offered no shared story about Kino or the Jesuit missions, at least nothing they were going to share in that particular meeting with me. Still, once we delved into the colonial records, an elder aptly summarized to me his sense of the documents I had shared. "I guess those Jesuit missionaries figured no pain, no gain."[43] Others reminded me that much of that supposed European gain had only come through real O'odham pain for which no imagined success could make amends. Then, one elder pointed out what he saw as a surprising convergence between the account I had presented and their own beliefs about their Elder Brother, I'itoi. He told me that I'itoi participates in both destruction and creation, both death and life. Without one, you cannot have the other, he said. "These missionaries brought death and destruction," he told me, "but we also took what they gave and made life."

Acknowledgments

It would be easy to imagine a book as its own sort of "prolonged martyrdom," a daily renunciation of most all else in the hope of producing something lasting far away in the future. As much as what follows traces that sort of logic, I do not embrace it. To be sure, this work entailed moments of discipline and disavowal, but ultimately what follows witnesses to life. It testifies to the lives of so many friends, family, colleagues, and students who encouraged me along the way. When I think of this book, it will be with that community in mind and the relationships that filled its labors with joy and meaning.

This project originated at Harvard University, where I would like to thank the faculty in both the Divinity School and Committee for the Study of Religion, especially David Hall, who tolerated my move away from the Puritans to their bitter rivals, the Jesuits. Davíd Carrasco, Patrick Provost-Smith, Harvey Cox, and David Hempton all provided insight and help at key moments. When I ventured out, Dana Robert at Boston University modeled a life of scholarly excellence, moral conviction, and global perspective. I owe special thanks to the members of the North American Religions Colloquium for the patient feedback and collegial environment they afforded during the first drafts of this work. Adrian Weimer, Heather Curtis, Rachel Gordan, Lauren Brandt, Eliza Young Barstow, Angela Tarango, Samira Mehta, Zack Matus, David Charles, Christopher White, Stephen Shoemaker, Curtis Evans, Katherine Gerbner, Jon Roberts, Wallace Best, Bob Orsi, Ann Braude, Marla Frederick, and so many others who came through the colloquium offered inspiration and counsel. Linford Fisher probably read more versions of this project than anybody over the years, and for his caring advice and constant friendship I am most grateful. Funding from the Divinity School's Dean's Fellowship, the David Rockefeller Center for Latin American Studies, and the William R. Hutchison

American Religion fellowship provided for writing and archival research in Arizona, California, Texas, and Mexico.

Claremont School of Theology, Phoenix Seminary, Indiana University, and Fordham University gave me my first opportunities to teach and begin to ply my ideas with students. As I passed through these places, new colleagues and friends like Esther Chung-Kim, Sarah Imhoff, Matthew Suriano, Joshua Paddison, Constance Furey, Candy Gunther-Brown, Brenna Moore, Franklin Harkins, Benjamin Dunning, John Penniman, and Kathryn Reklis expanded my intellectual and cultural horizons. In similar fashion, Ronnie Hsia and the members of the Mellon Seminar on Early Modern Global Catholicism at Penn State—Veronica Gutierrez, Danny Wasserman, Leon Garcia, Frederick Vermote, Jared Staller, Chris Wisniewski, Adina Ruiu, and Pablo Aranha—not only stretched my understanding of early modern global Catholicism, but beautifully modeled scholarly community in a moment when that was lacking. Nicholas Canny and the participants in the NEH–Folger Library Seminar on Early Modern Religion and Natural Histories prompted me to think more carefully about how these histories braided religious and scientific discourse.

More recently, the Young Scholars in American Religion program offered a vibrant space for critical thinking and communal sustenance. Though I was not so young by the time I found my way to YSAR, Katie Lofton and Leigh Eric Schmidt never let me feel it. Their vital input, along with inspiration from Cara Burnidge, Emily Clark, Brett Grainger, Rachel Gross, Cooper Harriss, Tina Howe, Elizabeth Jemison, Nicole Myers Turner, and Dan Vaca reinvigorated this project and helped me see its importance in fresh ways. Thank you to Phil Goff, IUPUI, the Center for the Study of Religion and American Culture, and the Lily Endowment for making this place possible not only for our plucky crew, but for so many generations in our field. Although he was in the cohort right before mine, T. J. Tomlin has always been the best example for me of the love, joy, loyalty, work, brilliance, and mutuality that the program promotes.

As I made my way through the archives, I depended heavily on the guidance and aid of librarians and staff at the Arizona Historical Foundation and Chicano Research Collections housed in the Hayden Library of Arizona State University in Tempe, the Huntington Library in Pasadena, California, the Bancroft Library at the University of California at Berkeley, and the Nettie Lee Benson Library of the University of Texas at Austin, as well as the Biblioteca Nacionál de México, Archivo Generál de la Nación, and Archivo Histórico de la Província Mexicana de la Sociedad de Jesús in Mexico City. My hosts in Mexico, Jonathan and Rocio Mikes, opened their home and lives during those months as just one act of hospitality in a friendship that extends across nearly three decades. Special thanks to Dale Brenneman, Michael Brescia, and Diana Hadley of the Office of Ethnohistorical Research of the Arizona State Museum, who not only allowed me to scan microfilm in their office, but constantly provided welcome help and essential insights. Dale Brenneman also facilitated conversations with O'odham elders, who read some of my work and offered invaluable feedback. Equally, I would like to acknowledge the Arizona Historical Society in Tucson, which funded the work for the epilogue with a research grant. AHS archivist Kate Reeve pointed me to the papers of Jane Ivancovich, who for decades faithfully collected articles and artifacts from both Mexico and the United States on the search, recovery, and celebration of Padre Kino.

The Department of Religious Studies at the University of North Carolina at Chapel Hill has been a wonderful place to begin a career as a teacher and scholar. Laurie Maffly-Kipp, Randall Styers, and Barbara Ambros supported both vocations and offered consistent encouragement. I could not have asked for better colleagues than Yaakov Ariel, Jessica Boon, Jonathan Boyarin, Andrea Cooper, Bart Ehrman, Carl Ernst, Juliane Hammer, Harshita Kamath, Joseph Lam, David Lambert, Lauren Leve, Jodi Magness, Evyatar Marienberg, Hugo Méndez, Todd Ochoa, Zlatko Plese, and Brendan Thornton. Funding from the William D. McLester Fund for Faculty Excellence and Sutton Family Fund for Catholic Studies, as well as financial and program support from the Institute for the Study of the Americas and the Institute for the Arts and Humanities, helped me settle into North Carolina and advance the manuscript. My counterparts on the other end of Tobacco Road, Grant Wacker, Kate Bowler, Lauren Winner, and Joseph Winters, never made that rivalry feel real and offered nothing but love and light.

When I began this research, I soon realized that Cynthia Radding knew more about these places and people than I could ever hope. I never imagined that she would become my colleague, editor, neighbor, and friend. Cynthia's careful reading saved me from several mistakes, and the *Saberes*/Indigenous Pathways Working Group she organized offered critical feedback. Similarly, Kathleen Duval and the Triangle Early American History Seminar provided a valuable environment to workshop the last chapter and helped me think more broadly about this project in the context of vast early América. It has been an honor to participate in the American Indian and Indigenous Studies faculty discussions and seminars, and I thank Dan Cobb, Andrew Curley, Emilio del Valle Escalante, Kathleen DuVal, Ben Frey, Valerie Lambert, Malinda Maynor Lowery, Jenny Tone-Pah-Hote, Theda Perdue, and Keith Richotte for making AIIS such a dynamic presence at UNC. Chris Teuton was the first friend I made at UNC, and it has been an honor and privilege to accompany him as he works to recover and pass along Cherokee literary and spiritual practice. I want to thank the anonymous reviewers of this manuscript, as well as Fred Nachbaur at Fordham University Press, who patiently guided this book. John Seitz has supported this project from its earliest iterations through its final publication, and, for that as well as his constant friendship, I am most grateful.

Finally, my deepest appreciation is reserved to Nidia Flores Bayne, who has held and holds our little world together. My father, Brett Bayne, ignited my intellectual curiosity from my youngest days. My mother, Arlene Bayne, modeled real sacrificial love throughout her life. She edited all my writing, including stumbling drafts of this book. It was a grace to tell her it was dedicated to her as I said my final goodbyes to my mom in early 2020. To all these that memory allows me to record here and those whom only my heart knows, *mil gracias*.

Notes

Introduction: Suffering and Salvation

1. Rebecca Horn, *Postconquest Coyoacán: Nahua-Spanish Relations in Central Mexico, 1519–1650* (Stanford, Calif.: Stanford University Press, 1997), 1–24.
2. Eva Maria St. Clair Segurado, *Expulsión y exilio de la provincia jesuita mexicana, 1767–1820* (Alicante, Spain: Publicaciones Universidad de Alicante, 2005); Magnus Mörner, ed., *The Expulsion of the Jesuits from Latin America* (New York: Knopf, 1965).
3. Alma Montero Alarcón, *Jesuitas de Tepotzotlán: La expulsión y el amargo destierro* (Mexico City: Plaza y Valdes, 2009).
4. Perla Chinchilla Pawling, "Jesuit Restoration in Mexico," in *Jesuit Survival and Restoration: A Global History, 1773–1900*, ed. Robert A. Maryks and Jonathan Wright (Leiden: Brill, 2014), 433–49.
5. Personal names of living people have been anonymized, and conversations are shared with the interlocutors' permission.
6. Mathias Tanner, *Societas Jesu usque ad sanguinis et vitae profusionem militans in Europa, Africa, Asia, et America* (Prague: Typis Universitatis Carolo-Ferdinandeae, 1675), 451–54.
7. Andrés Pérez de Ribas, *Historia de los Triumphos de Nuestra Santa Fee entre Gentes las mas Barbaras, y Fieras del Nueuo Orbe*, ed. Alonso de Paredes (Madrid: Alonso de Paredes, 1645), 139.
8. On the Jesuit collection, translation, and promotion of Father Pro's relics, see Marisol López-Menéndez, *Miguel Pro: Martyrdom, Politics, and Society in Twentieth-Century Mexico* (Lanham, Md.: Lexington, 2016), 119–40.
9. According to the Jesuit historian Peter Masten Dunne, Glandorff was known by the Tarahumara as "El Padre de los zapatos magicos"; Dunne, *Las antiguas misiones de la Tarahumara* (México, D.F.: Editorial Jus, 1958), 2:293.
10. López-Menéndez, *Miguel Pro*, 24, 159, 169.
11. Gerardo Decorme, *Mártires jesuitas de la provincia de México* (Guadalajara: Editorial Acevez, 1957).
12. Donald Weinstein and Rudolph Bell, *Saints and Society: The Two Worlds of Western Christendom, 1000–1700* (Chicago: University of Chicago Press, 1982), 160.

13. On the practices of mapping Indigenous spaces in European cultural imagination, see Walter Mignolo, *The Darker Side of the Renaissance: Literacy, Territoriality, and Colonization* (Ann Arbor: University of Michigan Press, 1995), 259–313.

14. Daniel T. Reff, "Making the Land Holy: The Mission Frontier in Early Medieval Europe and Colonial Mexico," in *The Spiritual Conversion of the Americas*, ed. James Muldoon (Gainesville: University Press of Florida, 2004), 17.

15. On blood, seed, and fertility in Second Temple Judaism and early Christianity, see Blake Leyerle, "Blood Is Seed," *Journal of Religion* 81, no. 1 (January 2001): 26–48.

16. Cynthia Radding, *Wandering Peoples: Colonialism, Ethnic Spaces, and Ecological Frontiers in Northwestern Mexico, 1700–1850* (Durham, N.C.: Duke University Press, 1997), 34–35; Susan M. Deeds, *Defiance and Deference in Mexico's Colonial North: Indians under Spanish Rule in Nueva Vizcaya* (Austin: University of Texas Press, 2003), 18–21.

17. Frieda Knobloch, *The Culture of Wilderness: Agriculture as Colonization in the American West* (Chapel Hill: University of North Carolina Press, 1996); Daniel K. Richter, *Facing East from Indian Country: A Native History of Early America* (Cambridge, Mass.: Harvard University Press, 2001), 57–59; Kathleen Duval, *The Native Ground: Indians and Colonists in the Heart of the Continent* (Philadelphia: University of Pennsylvania Press, 2006), 179, 228–29.

18. Patricia Seed, *Ceremonies of Possession in Europe's Conquest of the New World, 1492–1640* (Cambridge: Cambridge University Press, 1995), 16–40; Nicholas P. Canny, "The Ideology of English Colonization: From Ireland to America," *William and Mary Quarterly* 30, no. 4 (October 1973): 575–98.

19. On colonization as spiritual gardening in New England and New Spain, see Jorge Cañizares-Esguerra, *Puritan Conquistadors: Iberianizing the Atlantic, 1550–1700* (Stanford, Calif.: Stanford University Press, 2006), 178–214.

20. "Reduzir," in Sebastián de Covarrubias Orozco, *Tesoro de la Lengua Castellana o Española* (Madrid: Luiz Sanchez, 1611), 1252, http://fondosdigitales .us.es/fondos/libros/765/1252/tesoro-de-la-lengua-castellana-o-espanola/, accessed on May 8, 2017.

21. Charles W. Polzer, *Rules and Precepts of the Jesuit Missions of Northwestern New Spain* (Tucson: University of Arizona Press, 1976), 39; Nicholas P. Cushner, *Jesuit Ranches and the Agrarian Development of Colonial Argentina, 1650–1767* (Albany: State University of New York Press, 1983), 1–20; José Gabriel Martínez Serna, *Viñedos e indios del desierto: Fundación, auge y secularización de una misión jesuita en la frontera noreste de la Nueva España* (Monterrey, Mexico: Museo de Historia Mexicana, 2014); Steven W. Hackel, *Children of Coyote, Missionaries of Saint Francis: Indian-Spanish Relations in Colonial California,*

1769–1850 (Chapel Hill: Omohundro Institute and University of North Carolina Press, 2005), 65–78.

22. Eusebio Kino, S.J., *Kino's Biography of Francisco Javier Saeta, S.J.*, trans. Charles W. Polzer, S.J., ed. in Spanish Ernest J. Burrus, S.J. (Rome: Jesuit Historical Institute; St. Louis: St. Louis University, 1971), 131.

23. Gil Anidjar, *Blood: A Critique of Christianity* (New York: Columbia University Press, 2014), 180–92.

24. Jonathan Boyarin, *The Unconverted Self: Jews, Indians, and the Identity of Christian Europe* (Chicago: University of Chicago Press, 2009).

25. On the devastating effects of European disease on the Indigenous populations of northwestern New Spain and the ensuing cultural changes, see Reff, *Disease, Depopulation, and Culture Change in Northwestern New Spain, 1518–1764* (Provo: University of Utah Press, 1991); on disease and demographic collapse in Native America more generally, see Noble David Cook, *Born to Die: Disease and New World Conquest, 1492–1650* (Cambridge: Cambridge University Press, 1998).

26. Talal Asad, *On Suicide Bombing*, Wellek Library Lectures (New York: Columbia University Press, 2007), 86.

27. Phillipe Buc, *Holy War, Martyrdom, and Terror: Christianity, Violence, and the West* (Philadelphia: University of Pennsylvania Press, 2015); see also Jay Rubenstein, *Armies of Heaven: The First Crusade and the Quest for Apocalypse* (New York: Basic Books, 2011).

28. Buc, *Holy War, Martyrdom, and Terror*, 1–19.

29. Nicole Kelley, "Philosophy as Training for Death: Reading the Ancient Christian Martyr Acts as Spiritual Exercises," *Church History* 75, no. 4 (December 2006): 723–31; Daniel Boyarin, *Dying for God: Martyrdom and the Making of Christianity and Judaism* (Stanford, Calif.: Stanford University Press, 1999); R. D. Young, *In Procession before the World: Martyrdom as Public Liturgy in Early Christianity* (Milwaukee: Marquette University Press, 2001).

30. Judith Perkins, *The Suffering Self: Pain and Narrative Representation in the Early Christian Era* (London: Routledge, 1995), 3, 12, 17.

31. In 2 Cor Paul compares Christian sufferings to Roman triumphal processions: "But thanks be to God, who in Christ always leads us in triumphal procession, and through us spreads in every place the fragrance that comes from knowing him / For we are the aroma of Christ to God among those who are being saved and among those who are perishing / to the one a fragrance from death to death, to the other a fragrance from life to life. Who is sufficient for these things?"; 2 Cor 14–16, *New Revised Standard Version*. See also Andreas Hock, "Christ Is the Parade: A Comparative Study of the Triumphal Procession in 2 Cor 2:14 and Col 2:15," *Biblica* 88, no. 1 (January 1, 2007): 110.

32. In a letter to a female interlocutor, Jerome answered twelve questions she posed. Question 11 asks, "What is the meaning of 2 Cor. 2:16?" Jerome's full interpretation is as follows, *"Triumphus Dei est passio Martyrum; et pro Christi nomine cruoris effusio, et inter tormenta laetitia. Cum enim quis viderit tanta perseverantia stare Martyres, atque torqueri, et in suis cruciatibus gloriari, odor notitiae Dei disseminatur in gentes, et subit tacita cogitation quod nisi verum esset Evangelium, nunquam sanguine defenderater. Neque enim delicata et divitiis students ac secura confession est; sed in carceribus, in plagis, in persecutionibus, in fame, in nuditate et siti. Hic triumphus est Dei Apostolorumque Victoria."* The Latin text is from Epist. CXX. Ad Hedib. Cap. 11, in Migne, *Hieronymus-Epistolae Secundum Ordinem Temporum Distributae—Patrologia Latina*, Vol. 22: Col. 0325–1224, p. 262. from http://www.documentacatholicaomnia.eu/02m/03470420,_Hieronymus,_Epistolae_Secundum_Ordinem_Temporum_Distributae,_MLT.pdf\, accessed on March 3, 2016.

33. Perkins, *Suffering Self*, 12.

34. Elizabeth Castelli, *Martyrdom and Memory: Early Christian Culture Making* (New York: Columbia University Press, 2004), 32.

35. "First, using a hermeneutic of suspicion to 'unmask ideologies' destroys the very possibility of understanding historical difference. With arbitrary condescension, it pigeonholes the past according to contemporary values and assumptions, separating the 'ideological' from the 'authentic,' the 'reactionary' from the 'progressive.' Functioning as a presentist mirror, it predictably yields a history reflecting the interpreter's commitments"; Brad Gregory, *Salvation at Stake: Christian Martyrdom in Early Modern Europe* (Cambridge, Mass.: Harvard University Press, 1999), 14.

36. The death narratives of once celebrated missionaries like Isaac Jogues and Jean de Brébeuf, who along with six other Jesuits died in New France during the seventeenth century, have been plied for their "uses," provoking attention more for their "discursive constructs" and "community definitions" than their canonical details. Allan Greer and Emma Anderson have demonstrated the ways that both European and Indigenous conceptions of suffering framed understandings and presentations of coloniality for European audiences; Greer, "Colonial Saints: Gender, Race, and Hagiography in New France," *William and Mary Quarterly* 57, no. 2 (Apr. 2000): 323; Anderson, "Blood, Fire, and 'Baptism': Three Perspectives on the Death of Jean De Brébeuf, Seventeenth-Century Jesuit 'Martyr,'" in *Native Americans, Christianity, and the Reshaping of the American Religious Landscape*, ed. Joel W. Martin and Mark A. Nicholas (Chapel Hill: University of North Carolina Press, 2010), 125–58. Carole Blackburn offered a brief analysis of the connection between martyrdom and military aggression in Blackburn, *Harvest of Souls: The Jesuit Missions and Colonialism in North America, 1632–1650* (Montreal: McGill-

Queen's University Press, 2000), 64–69. Paul Perron's study of narrative constructs in the martyrologies of Isaac Jogues and Julia Boss's treatment of martyrological social locations nicely demonstrate the possibilities of this approach; Boss, "Writing a Relic: The Uses of Hagiography in New France," and Paul Perron, "Isaac Jogues: From Martyrdom to Sainthood," both in *Colonial Saints: Discovering the Holy in America, 1500–1800*, ed. Allan Greer and Jodi Bilinkoff (New York: Routledge, 2003), 153–68, 211–34, respectively. More recently, Timothy G. Pearson has analyzed how diverse men and women "became holy" in early Canada, studying well-known figures like Marie l'Incarnation as well as the lesser-known Algonquin martyr Joseph Onaharé. It is a model of the kind of embedded, contextualized analysis hagiographic narratives and idioms engaged in this book; Pearson, *Becoming Holy in Early Canada* (Montreal: McGill-Queen's University Press, 2014).

37. Gregory, *Salvation at Stake*, 12–15.

38. Anderson, *The Death and Afterlife of the North American Martyrs* (Cambridge, Mass.: Harvard University Press, 2013).

39. Cornelius Conover, "Saintly Biography and the Cult of San Felipe de Jesús in Mexico City, 1597–1697," *Americas* 67, no. 4 (April 2011): 441–66.

40. While this conception of Indigenous colonization separated into discrete tasks or phases traces to the early conquest and before that to Roman imperial practices, the Jesuits formed their own distinct descriptions of that process. The conquistador Bernal Díaz del Castillo claimed to "serve His majesty by discovering, conquering, pacifying, and settling" in the opening of his account of the Mexican conquest; Bernal Díaz del Castillo, *The Discovery and Conquest of Mexico, 1517–1521*, ed. Davíd Carrasco (Albuquerque: University of New Mexico Press, 2008), xxv, 1. Jesuits adapted this slightly, using the language of "reduction" and "conversion"; Polzer, *Rules and Precepts*.

41. David Sweet, "The Ibero-American Frontier in Native American History," in *The New Latin American Mission History*, ed. Erick D. Langer and Robert H. Jackson (Lincoln: University of Nebraska Press, 1995), 8.

42. Were the object of critical theory simply the "unmasking of ideologies" or suspicious hermeneutics, Gregory may have a point about the unbridgeable gap that separates unbelieving scholars and their believing subjects. It is my contention that critical theory is necessary to bridge just such gaps between the scholarly subject and historical and/or cultural "others." Surely, Gregory's assumptions of historical difference demand some sort of theoretical justification, else why not posit sameness between scholar and subject? On the other hand, works that fail to appreciate what Michel Foucault called the *episteme* of discursive knowledge—that is, the historical a priori and cultural assumptions that make received truths seem self-evident or "given" at a particular time and place and amongst a certain people and thereby provide the very conditions of

possibility for belief and action—run the risk of at once lacking sympathy for their subjects and making anachronistic assumptions about what that subject meant in its own context; Foucault, *The Order of Things: An Archaeology of the Human Sciences* (New York: Vintage, 1973), 344f.

43. For examples of Bolton's wide influence, see Herbert E. Bolton, *The Spanish Borderlands: A Chronicle of Old Florida and the Southwest* (Albuquerque: University of New Mexico Press, 1996); Bolton and John F. Bannon, *Bolton and the Spanish Borderlands* (Norman: University of Oklahoma Press, 1964). For contemporary critiques of Bolton and his influence on the study of the "borderlands," see Deeds, *Defiance and Deference*, 3–15; Robert H. Jackson, ed., *New Views of Borderlands History* (Albuquerque: University of New Mexico Press, 1998), 1–20; Sweet, *Ibero-American Frontier in Native American History*; Russell M. Magnaghi, *Herbert E. Bolton and the Historiography of the Americas* (Westport, Conn.: Greenwood, 1998), 211; David J. Weber, "Turner, the Boltonians, and the Borderlands," *American Historical Review* 91, no. 1 (February 1986): 66.

44. With this in mind, Sweet argues for a critical evaluation of missionary hagiographies: "We must reread their accounts more critically than has sometimes been done, with an eye primarily to what they have to say about the dimly viewed Indian 'other'; and we must learn to distinguish their high ideals and aspirations, the inflated claims of their fundraising appeals, and the well-meaning instructions regularly sent by their superiors from what we can reconstruct of their actual practice." Sweet and others urge extreme hermeneutical suspicion, ultimately dismissing the missionary documents as hopeless obstacles that need to be surmounted in order to arrive at "authentic" accounts of what *really* happened; Sweet, "Ibero-American Frontier in Native American History," 9

45. Deeds, *Defiance and Deference*; Ramon A. Gutiérrez, *When Jesus Came, the Corn Mothers Went Away: Marriage, Sexuality, and Power in New Mexico, 1500–1846* (Stanford, Calif.: Stanford University Press, 1991); Radding, *Wandering Peoples*; Thomas E. Sheridan, *Empire of Sand: The Seri Indians and the Struggle for Spanish Sonora, 1645–1803* (Tucson: University of Arizona Press, 1999); Juliana Barr, *Peace Came in the Form of a Woman: Indians and Spaniards in the Texas Borderlands* (Chapel Hill: University of North Carolina Press, 2007); José Refugio de la Torre Curiel, *Twilight of the Mission Frontier: Shifting Interethnic Alliances and Social Organization in Sonora, 1768–1855* (Stanford, Calif.: Stanford University Press, 2013).

46. Weber, *The Spanish Frontier in North America* (New Haven, Conn.: Yale University Press, 1994), 7–10, 353–60.

47. Barr, "Geographies of Power: Mapping Indian Borders in the 'Borderlands' of the Early Southwest," *William and Mary Quarterly* 68, no. 1 (January 2011): 5–46.

48. This list employs autonymous autochthonous terms for the Indigenous groups mentioned where possible. In the following, when colonial sources are being used, the tribal name used by the sources will be followed for the sake of clarity, while autonyms will be used to discuss identifiable contemporary communities.

49. For an example of a scholar who has tried to tell both sides of this encounter, see the work of Daniel T. Reff, whose comparative history of late antique Christian practice and the early modern Jesuit missions *Plagues, Priests, and Demons*, as well as his long introduction and extensive editorial notes for Pérez de Ribas's *History of the Triumphs*, attempt an evenhanded evaluation; Reff, *Plagues, Priests, and Demons: Sacred Narratives and the Rise of Christianity in the Old World and the New* (Cambridge: Cambridge University Press, 2005); Andrés Pérez de Ribas, *History of the Triumphs of Our Holy Faith Amongst the Most Barbarous and Fierce Peoples of the New World*, ed. Daniel T. Reff, trans. Daniel Reff, Maureen Ahern, and Richard Danford (Tucson: University of Arizona Press, 1999).

50. Pamela Klassen, "Secular Christian Power and the Spiritual Invention of Nations," *The Immanent Frame*, https://tif.ssrc.org/2017/06/06/secular-christian-power-and-the-spiritual-invention-of-nations/, accessed on July 28, 2018.

51. Linda Tuhiwai Smith, *Decolonizing Methodologies: Research and Indigenous Peoples* (London: Zed, 1999), 147.

52. On genealogical work and decolonization, see Edward Said, *Orientalism* (New York: Random House, 1979); Mignolo, *Darker Side of the Renaissance*.

53. Gutiérrez, *When Jesus Came, the Corn Mothers Went Away*, 135–37; Robert H. Jackson, *Missions and the Frontiers of Spanish America: A Comparative Study of the Impact of Environmental, Economic, Political, and Socio-Cultural Variations on the Missions in the Río de la Plata Region and on the Northern Frontier of New Spain* (Scottsdale, Ariz.: Pentacle, 2005), 246.

54. Contemporary Catholic theologians frequently cite death for "hatred of the faith," or "*in odium fidei*," as the central requirement for official recognition as a martyr. Though the idea that one must have died for faith hatred dates back to the early church, the phrase made its way into official church dogma only gradually. Seeking to discourage suicidal risk-taking and distinguish faithful deaths from accidental deaths, theologians like Augustine stressed the necessity of unprovoked suffering, not private instigation, for the sake of the faith. Medieval popes began the process of consolidating canonization in Rome in the eleventh and twelfth centuries; Michael Goodich, *Vita Perfecta: The Ideal of Sainthood in the Thirteenth Century*, Monographien Zur Geschichte Des Mittelalters 25 (Stuttgart: A. Hiersemann, 1982). For this reason, Sixtus V created the Congregation of Rites in 1588 in the Bull *Immensa Aeterni Dei* with accompanying prohibitions on unregulated cults or veneration of saints.

Though Sixtus did not use the term *odium fidei*, authors increasingly employed it throughout the sixteenth and seventeenth centuries in reference to true martyrs. For example, in 1634 Pope Urban VII prohibited any cult be given to any saints or martyrs without official recognition by the Holy Spirit via the Roman pontificate; Benedict XIV, *Doctrina de servorum dei beatificatione et beatorum canonizatione* (Bruxellis, 1840). By 1675 the Holy Office of the Inquisition had decided to apply this decree broadly, beginning investigations of improper cults and censoring books that promoted undue reverence of undeclared saints and martyrs. For a later confirmation of this position, see Pope Benedict XVI's encyclical letter to the Session of the Congregation for Sainthood Causes of April 24, 2006. In the latter, Benedict XVI reiterated Benedict XIV's requirement: "It is of course necessary to find irrefutable proof of readiness for martyrdom, such as the outpouring of blood and of its acceptance by the victim. It is likewise necessary, directly or indirectly but always in a morally certain way, to ascertain the '*odium fidei*' [hatred of the faith] of the persecutor. If this element is lacking there would be no true martyrdom according to the perennial theological and juridical doctrine of the Church. The concept of 'martyrdom' as applied to the saints and blessed martyrs should be understood, in conformity with Benedict XIV's teaching, as '*voluntaria mortis perpessio sive tolerantia propter Fidem Christi, velalium virtuti sactum in Deum relatum*.' This is the constant teaching of the Church." For a modern argument for the extension of martyrdom to include faithful deaths beyond "*odium fidei*," see Karl Rahner, "Dimensiones del Martirio," *Concilium* 183 (1983): 321–24. See also the arguments of Jon Sobrino about the Salvadoran martyrs of the 1980s; Sobrino, *Witnesses to the Kingdom: The Martyrs of El Salvador and the Crucified Peoples* (Maryknoll, N.Y.: Orbis, 2003), 121–23.

55. For a theory of the contact zone as a space of both asymmetrical violent confrontation and religious creativity, see David Carrasco, "Jaguar Christians in the Contact Zone," in *Beyond Primitivism: Indigenous Religious Traditions and Modernity*, ed. Jacob Olupona (New York: Routledge, 2003), 128–38.

56. Cynthia Radding, "Colonial Spaces in the Fragmented Communities of Northern New Spain," in *Contested Spaces of Early America* (Philadelphia: University of Pennsylvania Press, 2014), 135–38.

57. Ernest J. Burrus, *La obra cartográfica de la provincia mexicana de la Compañia de Jesús, 1567–1967* (Madrid: Ediciones José Porrua Turanzas, 1967), 1:55–75.

58. This multivalent sense of "confrontation," as both forceful struggle and inventive mixing, has roots in the term itself, which connotes hostile opposition in English, but encounter, comparison, and sometimes sympathy in the Spanish *confrontación*; Evelyn Hu-Dehart, "Introduction: Transpacific Con-

frontation / Confrontación transpacífica," *Review: Literature and Arts of the Americas* 39, no. 1 (2006): 3–12.

59. Radding, "Colonial Spaces."

60. Colonists and missionaries used the Spanish term *ranchería* to describe agriculturalist settlements of between fifty and a hundred people that typically operated as scattered, semipermanent dwellings for diverse Indigenous groups in New Spain and other parts of the Americas. Most of the groups with whom the Jesuits worked in northwestern New Spain were semiagricultural, gathered in small villages with five or six extended families. These groups rarely established wider forms of fixed political organization, except in the case of forming war parties and strategic alliances for survival; Gordon Curtis Baldwin, *Indians of the Southwest* (New York: Capricorn, 1973); Frank Russell and the Smithsonian Institution Bureau of American Ethnology, *The Pima Indians* (Tucson: University of Arizona Press, 1975); Edward H. Spicer, *Cycles of Conquest: The Impact of Spain, Mexico, and the United States on the Indians of the Southwest, 1533–1960* (Tucson: University of Arizona Press, 1962), 119.

61. See, for example, Juan Mateo Manje, *Kino and Manje, Explorers of Sonora and Arizona: Their Vision of the Future. A Study of their Expeditions and Plans with an Appendix of Thirty Documents*, ed. and trans. Ernest J. Burrus, Sources and Studies for the History of the Americas 10 (St. Louis: Jesuit Historical Institute, 1971); Manje, *Unknown Arizona and Sonora, 1693–1721: From the Francisco Fernández del Castillo Version of Luz de tierra incógnita*, trans. Francisco Fernández del Castillo and Harry J. Karns (Tucson: Arizona Silhouettes, 1954).

62. On the difficulty of reading for contrary purposes, see Saidiya Hartman, *Scenes of Subjection: Terror, Slavery, and Self-Making in Nineteenth-Century America* (New York: Oxford University Press, 1997), 10.

63. Marisa J. Fuentes, *Dispossessed Lives: Enslaved Women, Violence, and the Archive* (Philadelphia: University of Pennsylvania Press, 2016), 7–11, 78.

64. J. Michelle Molina, *To Overcome Oneself: The Jesuit Ethic and the Spirit of Global Expansion, 1520–1767* (Berkeley: University of California Press, 2013); Ivonne del Valle, *Escribiendo desde los márgenes: Colonialismo y jesuitas en el siglo XVIII* (México, D.F.: Siglo XXI Editores, 2009).

65. R. Po-Cha Hsia, *Jesuit in the Forbidden City: Matteo Ricci, 1552–1610* (Oxford: Oxford University Press, 2013); Ines Županov, *Catholic Orientalism: Portuguese Empire, Indian Knowledge, 16th–18th Centuries* (Oxford: Oxford University Press, 2014); John W. O'Malley, Gauvin Alexander Bailey, Steven J. Harris, and T. Frank Kennedy, eds., *The Jesuits II* (vol. 2), *Cultures, Sciences, and the Arts, 1540–1773* (Toronto: University of Toronto Press, 2006); Luke Clossey, *Salvation and Globalization in the Early Jesuit Missions* (New York: Cambridge University Press, 2008); Karin Vélez, *The Miraculous Flying House of Loreto: Spreading Catholicism in the Early Modern World* (Princeton, N.J.: Princeton

University Press, 2018); David Rex Galindo, *To Sin No More: Franciscans and Conversion in the Hispanic World, 1683–1830* (Stanford, Calif.: Stanford University Press, 2018).

66. Atanasio G. Saravia, *Los misioneros muertos en el norte de Nueva España* (México, D.F.: Ediciones Botas, 1943), 34–42.

67. Decorme, *Historia de la Compañia de Jesús en la República Mexicana durante el siglo XIX* (Chihuahua, Mexico: J. M. Yguiniz, 1959), 433–34. Jesuit tradition has designated Pascual and Martínez as "Tarahumara martyrs," but they actually were killed while working among the Guazapares; Pérez de Ribas, *History of the Triumphs*, 301–11.

68. "Tapia, Gonzalo de," *Pontificium Consilium de Cultura*, https://www.dhial.org/diccionario/index.php/TAPIA,_Gonzalo_de, accessed on August 15, 2017; Saravia, *Los misioneros Muertos*, 91–92.

69. "Cabeza del P. Gonzalo d Tapia, Primer Martyr y Fundador de las Misiones de Sinaloa," in *Gonzalo de Tapia (1561–1594): Founder of the First Permanent Jesuit Mission in North America*, by William Eugene Shiels, Monograph Series 14 (New York: United States Catholic Historical Society, 1934), 169–70, and *Mensajero del Sagrado Corazon* (México, D.F.: January 1901).

70. The historian and priest Mariano Cuevas later photographed and verified the pieces; Mariano Cuevas, *Historia de la iglesia de México* (Mexico, D.F.: Imprenta del Asilo "Patricio Sanz," 1922), 2:384–85; Shiels, *Gonzalo de Tapia (1561–1594)*, 168–70.

1. Seeds: Planting Conversions

1. Tapia's focus on learning Nahuatl and later Purépecha, Otomí, and Cahíta was part of a push by the Society in the 1580s and 1590s to better train priests in Indigenous languages in New Spain for the purpose of advancing the northern and western missions; Charlotte M. Gradie, *The Tepehuan Revolt of 1616: Militarism, Evangelism and Colonialism in Seventeenth-Century Nueva Vizcaya* (Salt Lake City: University of Utah Press, 2000), 87–90.

2. Juan de Albiçuri, *Historia de las Misiones Apostolicas que los Clerigos Regulares de la Compañia de Jesus an echo en las Indias Occidentales del Reyno de la Nueva Vizcaya y Vida y Martyrio del P. Gonzalo de Tápia fundador de las Dichas Missiones y Apostol de Cynaloas*, Bamupa, Mexico, 1633, M-M 7, Hubert Howe Bancroft Collection, Bancroft Library (BL), University of California, Berkeley, 231–32; Andrés Pérez de Ribas, *Historia de los triumphos de Nuestra Santa Fee entre Gentes las Mas Barbaras, y Fieras del Nueuo Orbe: Conseguidos por los soldados de la milicia de la Compañia de Iesus en las missiones de la provincia de Nueua-España; Refierense assimismo las costumbres, ritos, y supersticiones que vsauan estas gentes, sus puestos, y temples, las vitorias que de algunas dellas*

alcançaron con las armas los catolicos españoles, quando les obligaron à tomarlas, y las dichosas muertes de veinte religiosos de la Compañia, que en varios puestos, y a manos de varias naciones, dieron sus vidas por la predicación del Santo Euangelio (Madrid: Alonso de Paredes, junto a los estudios de la Compañia, 1645), 132–32.

3. William Eugene Shiels, *Gonzalo de Tapia (1561–1594): Founder of the First Permanent Jesuit Mission in North America*, Monograph Series 14 (New York: United States Catholic Historical Society, 1934), 50–57.

4. Valladolid was later renamed "Morelia," and is the contemporary capital of the Mexican state of Michoacán; Shiels, *Gonzalo de Tapia*, 60–62; Joseph de Guibert, *The Jesuits, Their Spiritual Doctrine and Practice: A Historical Study* [Spiritualité de la Compagnie de Jésus: Esquisse historique] (Chicago: Institute of Jesuit Sources, 1972), xxi, 236, 253, 267, 280–91.

5. Pérez de Ribas, *History of the Triumphs of Our Holy Faith Amongst the Most Barbarous and Fierce Peoples of the New World*, ed. Daniel T. Reff, trans. Daniel Reff, Maureen Ahern, and Richard Danford (Tucson: University of Arizona Press, 1999), 196.

6. Shiels, *Gonzalo de Tapia*, 66.

7. "Chichimeco, ca," in *Diccionario de la lengua española*, edición 22a (Madrid 2012), available at http://lema.rae.es/drae/?val=chichimeca, accessed on May 1, 2014; see also Gradie, "Discovering the Chichimecas," *Americas* 51, no. 1 (July 1994): 67–88.
San Luis de la Paz is now located in the modern Mexican state of Guanajuato; Pérez de Ribas, *History of the Triumphs*, 194–97.

8. Shiels, *Gonzalo de Tapia*, 66–81.

9. Susan M. Deeds, *Defiance and Deference in Mexico's Colonial North: Indians under Spanish Rule in Nueva Vizcaya* (Austin: University of Texas Press, 2003), 15–16; Sergio Ortega Noriega, *Breve historia de Sinaloa* (México, D.F.: Colegio de México, 1999), 90–96.

10. Ortega Noriega, *Breve historia de Sinaloa*, 70–74.

11. Albiçuri, *Historia de las misiones apostolicas*, 164. Relying on two different manuscripts, the Canadian scholar Jason Dyck is editing and preparing a critical edition of Juan de Albiçuri's *Historia de las misiones*, which will be the first publication of this crucial early source.

12. Pérez de Ribas, *Historia de los triumphos de Nuestra Santa Fee*, 49.

13. Albiçuri, *Historia de las misiones*, 164.

14. Pérez de Ribas, *History of Triumphs*, 125.

15. Both Albiçuri and Pérez de Ribas relied on investigations reported in letters from Fathers Martín Pérez, Pedro de Velasco, and Pedro Mendez and a formal investigative report of Father Martín Paláez; Francisco Zambrano, S.J., and Jose Gutiérrez Casillas, *Diccionário bio-bibliográfico de la Compánia de Jesus*,

14 vols. (México, D.F.: Editorial Tradicion, 1961–75), 400; Félix Zubillaga and Miguel Angel Rodríguez, eds., *Monumenta Mexicana* (Rome: Institutum Historicum Societatis Iesu, 1973), 5:270–93, 750–58.

16. Albiçuri, *Historia de las misiones*, 183–84.

17. Albiçuri, *Historia de las misiones*, 184–85.

18. Albiçuri, *Historia de las misiones*; Pérez de Ribas first published *Historia de los triumphos* in Madrid in 1645. There are two modern editions cited throughout this chapter. The first is a facsimile edition of the original, published in Mexico in 1992, and the second a critical English translation with introduction and annotation by Daniel Reff, Maureen Ahern, and Richard Danford; Pérez de Ribas, *Historia de los triumphos de Nuestra Santa Fee*, ed. Ignacio Guzmán Betancourt, edición facsimilar (México, D.F.: Siglo Veintiuno Editores, 1992); Pérez de Ribas, *History of the Triumphs*.

19. John 12:24, New Revised Standard Version Bible (New York: Division of Christian Education of the National Council of the Churches of Christ U.S.A, 1989).

20. Blake Leyerle, "Blood Is Seed," *Journal of Religion* 81, no. 1 (January 2001): 26–48; Stephanie Lynn Budin, "Fertility and Gender in the Ancient Near East," in *Sex in Antiquity: Exploring Gender and Sexuality in the Ancient World*, ed. Mark Masterson, Nancy Sorkin Rabinowitz, and James Robson (Abingdon: Routledge, 2011), 30–49; Gil Anidjar, *Blood: A Critique of Christianity* (New York: Columbia University Press, 2014), 175–87; Melissa Meyer, *Thicker Than Water: The Origins of Blood as Symbol and Ritual* (Abingdon: Routledge, 2005), 8.

21. Depending on the theory, blood was compared variously to both seed and water, the former based on the Aristotelian theory that blood constituted semen and therefore was the foundational element in seed; Anidjar, *Blood*, 182–87.

22. W. H. C. Frend, *Martyrdom and Persecution in the Early Church: A Study of a Conflict from the Maccabees to Donatus* (1967; repr. Grand Rapids, Mich.: Baker, 1981); Judith Perkins, *The Suffering Self: Pain and Narrative Representation in the Early Christian Era* (London: Routledge, 1995); Elizabeth Castelli, *Martyrdom and Memory: Early Christian Culture Making* (New York: Columbia University Press, 2004); Robin D. Young, *In Procession before the World: Martyrdom as Public Liturgy in Early Christianity* (Milwaukee: Marquette University Press, 2001); Daniel Boyarin, *Dying for God: Martyrdom and the Making of Christianity and Judaism* (Stanford, Calif.: Stanford University Press, 1999), 247.

23. Leyerle, "Blood Is Seed," 46–47; Joyce E. Salisbury, *The Blood of Martyrs: Unintended Consequences of Ancient Violence* (New York: Routledge, 2004), 44–49.

24. Frend, *Martyrdom and Persecution*. Philippe Buc argues that the hope that persecution would produce conversion was only one interpretation of martyrdom, which he calls the "universalist" interpretation. Others avowed an "apocalyptic" interpretation of suffering that foresaw judgment, condemnation, and the "purging" of enemies rather than their future conversion; Phillipe Buc, *Holy War, Martyrdom, and Terror: Christianity, Violence, and the West* (Philadelphia: University of Pennsylvania Press, 2015), 10, 152–76.

25. "The oftener we are mown down by you, the more in number we grow; the blood of Christians is seed"; Tertullian, *Apolegetica* 50.12–13, in *Ante-Nicene Fathers: The Writings of the Fathers Down to A.D. 325*, ed. Alexander Roberts, James Donaldson, and A. Cleveland Coxe (Peabody, Mass.: Hendrickson, 1995), 3:150. The Latin reads as follows: "[12] Sed hoc agite, boni praesides, meliores multo apud populum si illis Christianos immolaveritis, cruciate, torquete, damnate, atterite nos: probatio est enim innocentiae nostrae iniquitas vestra. Ideo nos haec pati deus patitur. Nam et proxime ad lenonem damnando Christianam potius quam ad leonem confessi estis labem pudicitiae apud nos atrociorem omni poena et omni morte reputari. [13] Nec quicquam tamen proficit exquisitior quaeque crudelitas vestra; inlecebra est magis sectae. Plures efficimur quotiens metimur a vobis; semen est sanguis Christianorum": http://www.tertullian.org/latin/apologeticus.htm (accessed on March 3, 2008).

26. Timothy Barnes, *Constantine: Dynasty, Religion, and Power in Later Roman Empire* (Oxford: Blackwell, 2011).

27. St. Augustine, *The City of God*, trans. Henry Bettenson (New York: Penguin Classics, 2004), 406, 422–23, 504–6, 591–98, 609.

28. Richard Fletcher, *The Barbarian Conversion: From Paganism to Christianity* (Berkeley: University of California Press, 1999), 31, 161; Buc, *Holy War, Martyrdom, and Terror*, 179, 260.

29. Anidjar, *Blood*, 58.

30. Luke Clossey, *Salvation and Globalization: Salvation and Globalization in the Early Jesuit Missions* (New York: Cambridge University Press, 2008), 225.

31. Ines G. Županov, *Missionary Tropics: The Catholic Frontier in India, 16th–17th Centuries*, History, Languages, and Cultures of the Spanish and Portuguese Worlds (Ann Arbor: University of Michigan Press, 2005), 6, 30, 75.

32. Bronwen McShea, *Apostles of Empire: The Jesuits of New France* (Lincoln: University of Nebraska Press, 2019).

33. Emma Anderson, *The Death and Afterlife of the North American Martyrs* (Cambridge, Mass.: Harvard University Press, 2013), 20, 45, 54–55, 65, 73, 138, 300.

34. Adrian Weimer, *Martyrs' Mirror: Persecution and Holiness in Early New England* (Oxford: Oxford University Press, 2011), 4, 36, 153.

35. The series of "bulls of donation," issued by Pope Alexander VI in the 1480s and '90s, set up the system of royal patronage of the Church (*patronato real* in Spanish, *padronado real* in Portuguese); "*Inter Caetera*, the Papal Bull of 1493," in *People and Issues in Latin American History from Independence to the Present: Sources and Interpretations*, ed. Lewis Hanke and Jane M. Rausch, 3rd ed. (Princeton, N.J.: Markus Wiener, 2006), 146–48; Shiels, *King and Church: The Rise and Fall of the Patronato Real* (Chicago: Loyola University Press, 1961), 195f; Ismael Sánchez Bella, *Iglesia y estado en la América Española*, vol. 16 (Pamplona: Ediciones Universidad de Navarra, 1990); Charles W. Polzer, *Rules and Precepts of the Jesuit Missions of Northwestern New Spain* (Tucson: University of Arizona Press, 1976), 6.

36. Allan Greer, "Towards a Comparative Study of Jesuit Missions and Indigenous Peoples," in *Native Christians: Modes and Effects of Christianity Among Indigenous People of the Americas*, ed. Aparecida Vilaça and Robin Wright (Farnham, UK: Ashgate, 2009), 27; Patricia Seed, *Ceremonies of Possession in Europe's Conquest of the New World, 1492–1640* (Cambridge: Cambridge University Press, 1995), 86, 187.

37. On Pérez de Ribas's life and the process of his writing, see Reff's "Introduction," in Pérez de Ribas, *History of the Triumphs*, 11–46; Maureen Ahern, "Visual and Verbal Sites: The Construction of Jesuit Martyrdom in Northwest New Spain in Andres Pérez De Ribas' *Historia de los triumphos de Nuestra Santa Fe* (1645)," *Colonial Latin American Review* 8, no. 1 (June 1999): 7–33; Peter Masten Dunne, *Andrés Pérez De Ribas, Pioneer Black Robe of the West Coast, Administrator, Historian* (New York: United States Catholic Historical Society, 1951), 25:175.

38. Francisco Javier Alegre and Carlos María de Bustamante, *Historia de la Compañía de Jesús en Nueva España, que estaba escribiendo el p. Francisco Javier Alegre al tiempo de su expulsión* (México: Impr. de J. M. Lara, 1841), 229–35; Mathias Tanner, *Societas Jesu usque ad sanguinis et vitae profusionem militans in Europa, Africa, Asia, et America* (Prague: Typis Universitatis Carolo-Ferdinandeae, 1675); Eusebio Francisco Kino, *Kino's Historical Memoir of Pimería Alta: A Contemporary Account of the Beginnings of California, Sonora, and Arizona*, ed., trans. Herbert Eugene Bolton (New York: AMS, 1976), 87, 223; Joseph Neumann, *Historia de las sublevaciones indias en la Tarahumara*, ed. Bohumír Roedl and Simona Binková (Prague: Universidad Carolina, 1994), 6:70.

39. For a thorough account of Pérez de Ribas's audience, purpose, and the use of "cosmic battle" themes, see Reff, "Critical Introduction," in Pérez de Ribas, *History of the Triumphs*, 11–46.

40. Pérez de Ribas, *History of the Triumphs*, 64. Pérez de Ribas cites *Hier. epist. ad Hebdil.*, q. 11. But he is probably referring to Jerome's letter to Hedibia,

"a lady of Gaul much interested in the study of scripture," usually noted as *Hier. epist.ad. Hedib.*, Epist. CXX. Ad Hedib. Cap. 11, in Migne, *Hieronymus-Epistolae Secundum Ordinem Temporum Distributae—Patrologia Latina*, vol. 22: col. 0325–1224, p. 262, from http://www.documentacatholicaomnia.eu/02m /03470420,_Hieronymus,_Epistolae_Secundum_Ordinem_Temporum _Distributae,_MLT.pdf\, accessed on March 3, 2008.

41. Boyarin, *Dying for God*, 94–95.

42. Flavius Josephus, *The Jewish War, Books V-VII*, translated by Henry St. John Thackeray, Loeb Classical Library (Cambridge, Mass.: Harvard University Press, 1971), 3.621–23; Buc, *Holy War, Martyrdom and Terror*, 21.

43. Boyarin, *Dying for God*, 16.

44. *The Martyrs of Lyons* 1.5, in Eusebius, *Eusebius' Ecclesiastical History Complete and Unabridged* (Peabody, Mass.: Hendrickson, 1998), 148. On the motif of spiritual warfare implicit in this letter, see Richard Valantasis, *Religions of Late Antiquity in Practice* (Princeton, N.J.: Princeton University Press, 2000), 399.

45. "[12] But go zealously on, good presidents, you will stand higher with the people if you sacrifice the Christians at their wish, kill us, torture us, condemn us, grind us to dust; your injustice is the proof that we are innocent. Therefore, God suffers that we thus suffer; for but very lately, in condemning a Christian woman to the *leno* rather than to the *leo* you made confession that a taint on our purity is considered among us something more terrible than any punishment and any death. [13] Nor does your cruelty, however exquisite, avail you; it is rather a temptation to us. The oftener we are mown down by you, the more in number we grow; *the blood of Christians is seed*"; Tertullian, *Apolegetica* 50.12–13, 3:150. The Latin reads as follows: "[12] Sed hoc agite, boni praesides, meliores multo apud populum si illis Christianos immolaveritis, cruciate, torquete, damnate, atterite nos: probatio est enim innocentiae nostrae iniquitas vestra. Ideo nos haec pati deus patitur. Nam et proxime ad lenonem damnando Christianam potius quam ad leonem confessi estis labem pudicitiae apud nos atrociorem omni poena et omni morte reputari. [13] Nec quicquam tamen proficit exquisitior quaeque crudelitas vestra; inlecebra est magis sectae. Plures efficimur quotiens metimur a vobis; semen est sanguis Christianorum"; http://www.tertullian.org/latin/apologeticus.htm (accessed on March 3, 2008).

46. For the martial language, see Tertullian, *Apolegetica* 1.50.1–4, 3:150.

47. Tertullian, *Apolegetica*, I.L.

48. Leyerle, *Blood Is Seed*, 47.

49. Reff, *Plagues, Priests, and Demons: Sacred Narratives and the Rise of Christianity in the Old World and the New* (Cambridge: Cambridge University Press, 2005), 136.

50. Frend, *Martyrdom and Persecution*, 268.

51. Pérez de Ribas, *Historia de los triumphos*, 73; Pérez de Ribas, *History of the Triumphs*, 76; Pérez de Ribas, *Historia de los triumphos*, 761.

52. Pérez de Ribas, *History of the Triumphs*, 461.

53. Pérez de Ribas, *History of the Triumphs*, 64.

54. On Jesuit conceptions of the hierarchy of civilizations, see Anthony Pagden, *The Fall of Natural Man: The American Indian and the Origins of Comparative Ethnology* (Cambridge: Cambridge University Press, 1982), 146–97.

55. On the biblical and hagiographic contexts that informed Pérez de Ribas and his readers, see Reff, "Critical Introduction," in *History of the Triumphs*, 19–23.

56. Pérez de Ribas, *History of the Triumphs*, 64.

57. Pérez de Ribas, *History of the Triumphs*, 53.

58. Pérez de Ribas, *History of the Triumphs*, 52.

59. Pérez de Ribas, *History of the Triumphs*, 65.

60. Pérez de Ribas, *History of the Triumphs*, 64; Benedict Anderson, *Imagined Communities: Reflections on the Origin and Spread of Nationalism*, rev. ed. (London: Verso, 2006). On the Jesuit imagined global mission, see Clossey, *Salvation and Globalization*, 68–89.

61. Pérez de Ribas, *History of the Triumphs*, 53.

62. Pérez de Ribas, *History of the Triumphs*, 323.

63. Pérez de Ribas, *History of the Triumphs*, 461.

64. Pérez de Ribas, *History of the Triumphs*, 244n52.

65. Pérez de Ribas, *History of the Triumphs*, 169–70.

66. Pérez de Ribas, *History of the Triumphs*, 461; Luke 8:5–8.

67. 1 Corinthians 1:18, 26–30.

68. Pérez de Ribas, *History of the Triumphs*, 461; Acts 16:13.

69. Pérez de Ribas, *History of the Triumphs*, 461.

70. Pérez de Ribas, *History of the Triumphs*, 206–7.

71. Pérez de Ribas, *Historia de los triumphos de Nuestra Santa Fee*, 340–41; Pérez de Ribas, *History of the Triumphs*, 376.

72. "Con ellos iva Dios entresacado los viejos, que suelen ser estorvo a la doctrina destas gentes contentandose de ganar a muchos dellos en el termino ultimo de su vida y dexando la juventud para que diese mas abundantes frutos la semilla del Evangelio, con su crianza"; Pérez de Ribas, *History of the Triumphs*, 100.

73. Pérez de Ribas, *History of the Triumphs*, 200; Maureen Ahern, "Visual and Verbal Sites: The Construction of Jesuit Martyrdom in Northwest New Spain in Andres Pérez De Ribas' *Historia de los Triumphos de Nuestra Santa Fe* (1645)," *Colonial Latin American Review* 8, no. 1 (June 1999): 16.

74. Pérez de Ribas, *History of the Triumphs*, 194–98. For Pérez's letter, see the *Carta Anua* of 1594 in Archivo General de la Nación (AGN), *Historia*, Tomo

15, fol. 42f, Mexico City, Mexico; see also Hubert Howe Bancroft et al., *The Works of Hubert Howe Bancroft*, vol. 1, *History of the North Mexican States and Texas* (San Francisco: History Company, 1886), 120; and Zubillaga and Rodríguez, *Monumenta Mexicana*, 5:44–46.

75. On the increasingly strict canonical restrictions against using the terms "saint," "holy," or "martyr" in hagiographies of the seventeenth century, see Chapter 4.

76. Albiçuri, *Historia de las Misiones*, 213; Shiels, *Gonzalo De Tapia*, 30–50.

77. Zambrano and Gutiérrez Casillas, *Diccionario bio-biobliográfico de la Compañía de Jesús en México*, vol. 2, 1566–1600, 684.

78. Albiçuri, *Historia de las misiones*, 213.

79. Albiçuri, *Historia de las misiones*, 217.

80. Albiçuri, *Historia de las misiones*, 219.

81. Albiçuri, *Historia de las misiones*, 214.

82. Cynthia Radding, "Indigenous Landscapes in Northwestern New Spain: Environmental History through Contested Boundaries and Colonial Land Claims," *Resilience: A Journal of the Environmental Humanities* 3 (Winter/Spring/Fall 2015–16): 315–17; Reff, *Plagues, Priests, and Demons*, 188–92; N. Ross Crumrine, *The Mayo Indians of Sonora: A People Who Refuse to Die* (Tucson: University of Arizona Press, 1977), 144–47.

83. Raphael Brewster Folsom, *The Yaquis and the Empire: Violence, Spanish Imperial Power, and Native Resilience in Colonial Mexico* (New Haven, Conn.: Yale University Press, 2014), 52; Reff, "Introduction," in Pérez de Ribas, *History of the Triumphs*, 39.

84. Albiçuri, *Historia de las misiones*, 174.

85. Albiçuri, *Historia de las misiones*, 165.

86. Albiçuri, *Historia de las misiones*, 176–77.

87. Pérez de Ribas, *History of the Triumphs*, 202.

88. For a similar example of Indigenous ritual inversion of Catholic sacrament in the torture and killing of a Jesuit missionary, see Emma Anderson, "Blood, Fire, and 'Baptism': Three Perspectives on the Death of Jean de Brebeuf, Seventeenth-Century Jesuit 'Martyr,'" in *Native Americans, Christianity, and the Reshaping of the American Religious Landscape*, ed. Joel W. Martin and Mark A. Nicholas (Chapel Hill: University of North Carolina Press, 2010), 126–27, 141–47.

89. Pérez de Ribas, *History of the Triumphs*, 126.

90. "This practice was so completely uprooted that it has never again been seen or heard among these people, and this is a most unique and miraculous thing, for you will not find among all the many nations in the extensive Kingdom of Nueva España a single one that is more abstinent or freer from this vice"; Pérez de Ribas, *History of the Triumphs*, 201.

91. Pérez de Ribas, *History of the Triumphs*, 202.
92. Pérez de Ribas, *History of the Triumphs*, 157.
93. Pérez de Ribas, *History of the Triumphs*, 125.
94. Pérez de Ribas, *History of the Triumphs*, 125.
95. Albiçuri, *Historia de las misiones*, 187.
96. Albiçuri, *Historia de las misiones*, 187.
97. Tanner, *Societas Jesu usque ad sanguinis et vitae*, 451–54.
98. Stolarova Lenka and Vlnas Vit, *Karel Skreta, 1610–1674: His Work and his Era* (Prague: National Gallery, 2010).
99. Pérez de Ribas, *Historia de los triumphos de Nuestra Santa Fee*, 52; Pérez de Ribas, *History of the Triumphs*, 128.
100. Pérez de Ribas, *History of the Triumphs*, 376.
101. Pérez de Ribas, *History of the Triumphs*, 163, n.150.
102. "Carta de los indios Tarascos escrita a los Tarascos de Michoacan sobre la muerte del Padre Gonzalo de Tapia, por relación que les dio el Indio Tarasco, que estava con el Padre quando lo mataron," in *Memorias para la historia de la provincia de Sinaloa*, Archivo General de la Nación (AGN), Historia, Legajo 15, Mexico City, Mexico, consulted on Microfilm; Office of Ethnohistorical Research, Arizona State Museum, University of Arizona, Tucson, Ariz. (AZTM, J-02-D-01 AGN), 40v–42; also consulted in *Memorias para la historia de Sinaloa*, Mexican Manuscripts (M-M) 224–27, Bancroft Library, University of California, Berkeley; see also Pérez de Ribas, *History of the Triumphs*, 199.
103. ARSI, Mex. 8, 264; see also Mex. 15, 260v; Mex. 8, 255v; Katherine McAllen, "Jesuit Martyrdom Imagery between Mexico and Rome," in *The New World in Early Modern Italy, 1492–1750*, ed. Elizabeth Hordowich (Cambridge: Cambridge University Press, 2017), 143.
104. Pérez de Ribas, *History of the Triumphs*, 68, 89–91.
105. "Case of Mexica Indian Lorenzo, Holy Life and Acceptance into Society of Jesus in his Death"; Pérez de Ribas, *History of the Triumphs*, 716–18.
106. He was forthright about the epidemic context of the mission and the ample *exempla* of affliction such disease environments could supply. In the mining town of Parras, for example, a priest encountered "a very old Indian who was so thin that he was a living portrait of death." And yet, God gave him enough life to hear the gospel, accept baptism, and give the priest an edifying account of his own spiritual journey. The difference between militant and triumphant was one of life and death, and Pérez de Ribas contended that the goal was for Indigenous converts to enter into glory, even if sorely afflicted in life and often experiencing death from European disease; Pérez de Ribas, *History of the Triumphs*, 52.
107. "El Padre Martin Pelaez al Padre Antonio de Mendoza, Asist., Sept. 1594," in Zubillaga and Rodríguez, *Monumenta Mexicana*, 5:293–95; "Carta

Annua of Pedro Mendez of 1594," in *Memorias para la historia de la provincia de Sinaloa*, 49.

2. Weeds: Ritual Confrontations

1. William Eugene Shiels, *Gonzalo de Tapia (1561–1594): Founder of the First Permanent Jesuit Mission in North America*, Monograph Series 14 (New York: United States Catholic Historical Society, 1934), 161.

2. Charlotte M. Gradie, *The Tepehuán Revolt of 1616: Militarism, Evangelism and Colonialism in Seventeenth-Century Nueva Vizcaya* (Salt Lake City: University of Utah Press, 2000), 92–94; Edward H. Spicer, *Cycles of Conquest: The Impact of Spain, Mexico, and the United States on the Indians of the Southwest, 1533–1960* (Tucson: University of Arizona Press, 1962), 46–47; Harry Prescott Johnson, "Diego Martínez de Hurdaide: Defender of the Northwestern Frontier of New Spain," *Pacific Historical Review* 11, no. 2 (June 1942): 169–85.

3. In some ways, they followed the model emphasized by the Dominican Bartolomé de las Casas, though already informed by challenging resistance in Florida, Ajacán (Virginia), and with the Chichímeca and other tribes in the near north of New Spain; Bartolome de las Casas, *The Only Way*, ed. Helen Rand Parish and Francis Park Sullivan, S.J. (Mahway, N.J.: Paulist Press, 1992); Fray Bartolomé de las Casas, *Del Unico Modo de atraer a todos los pueblos a la verdadera Religión*, ed. Agustín Millares Carlo and Atenógenes Santamaria (México, D.F.: Fondo de Cultura Económica, 1942).

4. Andrés Pérez de Ribas, *History of the Triumphs of Our Holy Faith Amongst the Most Barbarous and Fierce Peoples of the New World*, ed. Daniel T. Reff, trans. Daniel Reff, Maureen Ahern, and Richard Danford (Tucson: University of Arizona Press, 1999), 496f.

5. Hernando de Santarén, "Testimonio jurídico de las poblaciones y conversions de los serranos acaxes hechas por el Capitán Diego de Avila y el venerable Padre Hernando de Santarén por el año de 1600," AGN, Historia, Tomo 20, Exponiente 19, folios 183–294; Felix Zubillaga, ed., *Monumenta Mexicana* (Rome: Institutum Historicum Societatis Iesu, 1981), 7:268–352; Susan Deeds, *Defiance and Deference in Mexico's Colonial North: Indians under Spanish Rule in Nueva Vizcaya* (Austin: University of Texas Press, 2003), 21–22; José de la Cruz Pacheco Rojas, *Milenarismo tepehuán: Mesianismo y resistencia indígena en el norte novohispano* (México, D.F.: Siglo Veintiuno Editores, 2008), 76f.

6. On burial, cannibalism, and treatment of dead bodies amongst the Acaxee and other Sinaloans, see Ralph L. Beals, *The Acaxee: A Mountain Tribe of Durango and Sinaloa* (Berkeley: University of California Press, 1933), 6:153; Beals, *The Comparative Ethnology of Northern Mexico before 1750* (New York:

Cooper Square, 1973), 122–31; Luis González Rodríguez, "La etnografía Acaxee de Hernando de Santarén," in *Tlalocan* (México, D.F.: 1980), 8:375–80.

7. This accorded with contemporary Castilian usage, which, since *the Poema del Cid*, had described the *monte* as "*tierra inculta cubierta de árboles, arbustos o matas*," a hidden land, so blanketed with trees and bushes that wild and thieving people fled there to hide from justice; Francisco López Estrada, *Poema del Cid: Texto completo en Castellano actual*, Odres nuevos, ed. conmemorativa del VIII centenario del manuscrito de Per Abbat (Madrid: Editorial Castalia, 2007), 2,693. See also "Monte," in *Enciclopedia del Idioma: Diccionario histórico y moderno de la lengua española (siglos XII al XX): Etimológico, tecnológico, regional e hispanoamericano*, ed. Martín Alonso (Madrid: Aguilar, 1958), 2:2,885; "Monte," in *Diccionario Crítico Etimológico Castellano e Hispánico*, ed. Joan Corominas and Jose Pascual (Madrid: Editorial Gredos, 1980), 131.

8. Santarén, "Testimonio juridico," AGN, Historia, 20, 222v; Nicolas de Arnaya, "El Padre Nicolas de Arnaya al Padre Francisco Vaez, Prov, Guadiana, 8 de febrero, 1601," in Zubillaga, *Monumenta Mexicana*, 7:364.

9. Santarén, "Testimonio juridico," AGN, Historia, 20, 221r.

10. Santarén, "Testimonio juridico," AGN, Historia, 20, 224r.

11. Santarén, "Testimonio juridico," AGN, Historia, 20, 203r, 214v, 224r, 232r, 242r, 252r, 259v, 270r, 280v.

12. Pérez de Ribas, *History of the Triumphs*, 505–10.

13. Deeds, *Defiance and Deference*, 23–34.

14. Pérez de Ribas, *History of the Triumphs*, 505.

15. Pérez de Ribas, *History of the Triumphs*, 506.

16. Pérez de Ribas, *History of the Triumphs*, 507.

17. Pérez de Ribas, *History of the Triumphs*, 508.

18. Pérez de Ribas, *History of the Triumphs*, 508.

19. Zubillaga, *Monumenta mexicana*, 8:563.

20. Pérez de Ribas, History of the Triumphs, 511.

21. Pérez de Ribas, History of the Triumphs, 511.

22. Pérez de Ribas, *History of the Triumphs*, 81, 205–6, 229.

23. Though the dates are not mentioned in the text, Father Méndez (the priest who reported the scene to the Jesuit Provincial Andres Pérez de Ribas) entered the settlement with Captain Hurdaide in 1606 and fled for his life in 1611. On the location, language, and culture of Tehueco and other Cáhita speakers on the Fuerte River, see Spicer, *Cycles of Conquest*, 609.

24. On Méndez's *entrada*, see Peter Masten Dunne, *Andrés Pérez De Ribas, Pioneer Black Robe of the West Coast, Administrator, Historian* (New York: United States Catholic Historical Society, 1951), 25:175; Pérez de Ribas, *History of the Triumphs*, 228f.

25. Forgoing their hunt in the spring of 1607 may have been made possible by an increased yield in the mission crops or extra meat offered in the Pascal celebration. On Tehueco and the survival and cultural practices of other Cáhita-speaking groups, see Beals, *Comparative Ethnology*, 65; Beals, *The Aboriginal Culture of the Cáhita Indians* (New York: AMS, 1978), 17–24.

26. Pérez de Ribas, *History of the Triumphs*, 237. The donning of masks, travel from town to town, and banishment of illness and evil during Holy Week remain common practices of the Mayo in northern Sinaloa to this day. See James S. Griffith, "Images and Notes Concerning the Traditional Material Culture of the Easter Ceremony in Northern Sinaloa," *Journal of the Southwest* 32, no. 1 (Spring 1990): 36–67; Crumrine, *Mayo Indians*, 87–95.

27. Pérez de Ribas, *History of the Triumphs*, 237.

28. Pérez de Ribas, *Historia de los triumphos de Nuestra Santa Fee entre gentes las mas barbaras, y fieras del Nueuo Orbe: Conseguidos por los soldados de la Milicia de la Compañia de Iesus en las missiones de la prouincia de Nueua-España: Refierense assimismo las costumbres, ritos, y supersticiones que Vsauan estas gentes, sus puestos, y temples, las vitorias que de Algunas dellas Alcançaron con las armas los catolicos españoles, quando les obligaron à tomarlas, y las dichosas muertes de veinte religiosos de la Compañia, que en varios puestos, y a manos de varias naciones, dieron sus vidas por la predicacion del Santo Euangelio*, ed. Alonso de Paredes (Madrid: Alonso de Paredes, junto a los estudios de la Compañia, 1645), 195.

29. Ramon A. Gutiérrez, *When Jesus Came, the Corn Mothers Went Away: Marriage, Sexuality, and Power in New Mexico, 1500–1846* (Stanford, Calif.: Stanford University Press, 1991), 135–37; Robert H. Jackson, *Missions and the Frontiers of Spanish America: A Comparative Study of the Impact of Environmental, Economic, Political, and Socio-Cultural Variations on the Missions in the Rio de la Plata Region and on the Northern Frontier of New Spain* (Scottsdale, Ariz.: Pentacle, 2005), 246; David Sweet, "The Ibero-American Frontier Mission in Native American History," in *The New Latin American Mission History*, ed. Erick D. Langer and Robert H. Jackson (Lincoln: University of Nebraska Press, 1995), 39–46.

30. Pérez de Ribas, *History of the Triumphs*, 239; Thomas Naylor and Charles W. Polzer, eds., *The Presidio and Militia on the Northern Frontier of New Spain: A Documentary History* (Tucson: University of Arizona Press, 1986), 212. Decades later, the Visitor Juan Antonio Balthasar confirmed that the Fuerte River missions still struggled with Native mobility and ritual exclusivity; Balthasar, *Father Balthasar Visits the Sinaloa Missions, 1744–1745*, Rare Book, HL, trans. Jerry Patterson (printed by Frederick W. Beinecke, 1959), 14.

31. Pérez de Ribas, *History of the Triumphs*, 377.

32. On the variety of burial practices in Sinaloa, including bone bundles and cave platforms see Beals, *Acaxee*, 32; Beals, *Comparative Ethnology*, 122–23.

33. Pérez de Ribas, *History of the Triumphs*, 164. Debates over the method and location of proper burial not only dated back to early Christianity but were common to other Jesuit missions in Latin America; Peter Brown, *The Cult of the Saints: Its Rise and Function in Latin Christianity* (Chicago: University of Chicago Press, 1982), 24–27; Kenneth Mills, *Idolatry and Its Enemies: Colonial Andean Religion and Extirpation, 1640–1750* (Princeton, N.J.: Princeton University Press, 1997), 42, 75; Peter Gose, "Converting the Ancestors: Indirect Rule, Settlement Consolidation, and the Struggle over Burial in Colonial Peru, 1532–1614," in *Conversion: Old Worlds and New*, ed. Kenneth Mills and Anthony Grafton (Rochester, N.Y.: University of Rochestor Press, 2003), 140–74.

34. Matthew 13:29–30.

35. Pérez de Ribas, *History of the Triumphs*, 699. For a fascinating chronicle of the people called "Chichimec" by the Nahua of central Mexico as well as their association with migration and semi-sedentary practices, see David Carrasco and Scott Sessions, *Cave, City, and Eagle's Nest: An Interpretive Journey through the Mapa de Cuauhtinchan No. 2* (Albuquerque: University of New Mexico Press; published in collaboration with the David Rockefeller Center for Latin American Studies and the Peabody Museum of Archaeology and Ethnology, Cambridge, Mass: Harvard University, 2007), 161–69.

36. Daniel Reff interpreted the *"enfermedades de espinas"* as "probably malignant smallpox, measles, or typhus, each of which produces a rash that, from the Indians' perspective, may have been analogous to the inflammation and swelling that can occur with puncture wounds from cholla or other cacti that abound in the monte"; Pérez de Ribas, *History of the Triumphs*, 255n73.

37. Pérez de Ribas, *History of the Triumphs*, 255.

38. Pérez de Ribas, *History of the Triumphs*, 521.

39. Pérez de Ribas, *History of the Triumphs*, 521.

40. For an extensive discussion of the Jesuit approach to epidemic, baptism, infant mortality, and salvations, see Daniel T. Reff, *Plagues, Priests, and Demons: Sacred Narratives and the Rise of Christianity in the Old World and the New* (Cambridge: Cambridge University Press, 2005), 179–89.

41. Pérez de Ribas, *History of the Triumphs*, 521

42. Pérez de Ribas, *History of the Triumphs*, 521; Pérez de Ribas, *Historia de los triumphos de Nuestra Santa Fee*, 499–500. In the original, "habito de tantos años de sujeción al demonio y la tierra donde estamos de mucha occasion de padecer y merecer, por la variedad de temples y toseos y pocos mantenimientos; pero no se niegue, sino que a vezes, y muchas, nos paga Dios nuestro Señor de contado, viendo el fruto tan palbable, que quando yo me acuerdo que en estos años se han muerto al pie de mil niños bautizados por mis manos, sin edad para poder pecar."

43. Pérez de Ribas, *History of the Triumphs*, 262.

44. Pérez de Ribas, *History of the Triumphs*, 301.
45. Matthew 13:24–30, NRSV.
46. Pérez de Ribas, *History of the Triumphs*, 301.
47. Pérez de Ribas, *Historia de los triumphos de Nuestra Santa Fee*, 256–57.
48. Pérez de Ribas, *Historia de los triumphos de Nuestra Santa Fee*, 254.
49. Pérez de Ribas, *Historia de los triumphos de Nuestra Santa Fee*, 256.
50. Pérez de Ribas, *Historia de los triumphos de Nuestra Santa Fee*, 306.
51. Pérez de Ribas, *History of the Triumphs*, 301–11.
52. Pérez de Ribas, *History of the Triumphs*, 309; Matthew 27:35; Mark 15:24.
53. Pérez de Ribas, *History of the Triumphs*, 310; Genesis 4:10.
54. Pérez de Ribas, *History of the Triumphs*, 310.
55. Pérez de Ribas, *History of the Triumphs*, 310.
56. Pérez de Ribas, *History of the Triumphs*, 311.
57. Pérez de Ribas, *History of the Triumphs*, 310.
58. The later Jesuit historian Peter Masten Dunne confirmed that the heads were likely removed and sent to the college, since their skeletons were exhumed in 1907 and the skulls were missing. This also corresponds to the later account by Peláez that when he found the remains in 1906 they did not have skulls; Dunne and Herbert Eugene Bolton, *Pioneer Black Robes on the West Coast* (Berkeley: University of California Press, 1940), 261, f. 14; https://www.dhial.org/diccionario/index.php/TAPIA,_Gonzalo_de, accessed on August 15, 2017; Atanasio G. Saravia, *Los misioneros muertos en el norte de Nueva España* (México, D.F.: Ediciones Botas, 1943), 91–92.
59. Pérez de Ribas, *History of the Triumphs*, 311.
60. "Otros algunos se quedaron con Gentiles complices foragidos, y obstinados, que no toda la semilla que sembró el Labrador Evangelico se logró"; Pérez de Ribas, *Historia de los triumphos de Nuestra Santa Fee*, 268; Pérez de Ribas, *History of the Triumphs*, 312.
61. Pérez de Ribas, *History of the Triumphs*, 539. For other examples of bad seed or seed choked out by weeds, see 148, 348, 593, 689.
62. Pérez de Ribas, *History of the Triumphs*, 312.
63. Pérez de Ribas, *History of the Triumphs*, 301.
64. Pérez de Ribas, *Historia de los triumphos de Nuestra Santa Fee*, 254; Pérez de Ribas, *History of the Triumphs*, 301.
65. Daniel Reff has estimated the Tepehuán population at 21,000 in 1500, 14,000 in 1598, and down to 2,000 by 1625; Reff, *Disease, Depopulation, and Culture Change in Northwestern New Spain, 1518–1764* (Provo: University of Utah Press, 1991), 152, 204–5; Gradie, *Tepehuán Revolt*, 23–26.
66. Gradie, *Tepehuán Revolt*, 148; *Carta Anua de 1615*, Bolton Papers, Bancroft Library, UC Berkeley, MSS C-B 840, carton 23, folder 18.
67. Gradie, *Tepehuán Revolt*, 80–81.

68. "Carta Anua de 1596," *Monumenta mexicana*, ed. Félix Zubillaga (Rome: Institutum Historicum Societatis Iesu, 1976), 6: 234.

69. Gradie, *Tepeháun Revolt*, 101–2; On Mesoamerican sacrifice, agriculture, and rituals of reciprocity, see David Carrasco, *Religions of Mesoamerica*, 2nd ed. (Long Grove, Ill.: Waveland, 2013), 37–40, 105–12.

70. Pérez de Ribas, *History of the Triumphs*, 593.

71. The other missionaries killed in the Tepehuán Revolt were the Franciscan Pedro Gutierrez and Dominican Sebastian Montaño; Pérez de Ribas, *History of the Triumphs*, 607; Gradie, *Tepehuán Revolt*, 162, 166.

72. Francisco de Figueroa, *Memorial presentado a su magestad por el P. Francisco de Figueroa Procurador de la Provincias de las Indias de la Compañia de IESUS: Acerca del Martyrio de nueve religiosos de la misma compañia* (Barcelona: Lorenço Déu, 1617), 1.

73. Figueroa, *Memorial del martyrio de nueve religiosos*, 1v.

74. Figueroa, *Memorial del martyrio de nueve religiosos*, 1v–2.

75. Figueroa, *Memorial del martyrio de nueve religiosos*, 2.

76. Figueroa, *Memorial del martyrio de nueve religiosos*, 2–2v; Pérez de Ribas, *History of the Triumphs*, 594–95.

77. Gradie, *Tepehuán Revolt*, 22–26.

78. Figueroa, *Memorial del martyrio de nueve religiosos*, 3.

79. Figueroa, *Memorial del martyrio de nueve religiosos*, 3.

80. For a fascinating discussion of the 1616 rebellion at El Zape and Pérez de Ribas's representation of its statue of the Virgin's "miraculous salvation," see Clara Bargellini, "The Virgin of El Zape and Jesuit Missions in Nueva Vizcaya," in *Oxford Handbook of Borderlands of the Iberian World*, ed. Cynthia Radding and Dana Levin Rojo (Oxford: Oxford University Press, 2020), 489–508.

81. Pérez de Ribas, *History of the Triumphs*, 593.

82. Gradie, *Tepehuán Revolt*, 153–59.

83. Pérez de Ribas, *History of the Triumphs*, 601–3.

84. Figueroa, *Memorial del martyrio de nueve religiosos*, 5v–6.

85. Figueroa, *Memorial del martyrio de nueve religiosos*, 11.

86. Gose, "Converting the Ancestors, 140–74; Mills, *Idolatry and Its Enemies*; Inga Clendinnen, *Ambivalent Conquests: Maya and Spaniard in Yucatan, 1517–1570* (Cambridge: Cambridge University Press, 1987).

87. Figueroa, *Memorial del martyrio de nueve religiosos*, 5v.

88. Juan de Albiçuri (Albieuri), *Historia de la vida y martirio del venerable P. Hernando de Santaren de la compania de Jesus y de las cinco missiones apostolicas que fundo de Guazave, Topia, S Andres, Tecuchuapa y Xiximes por el P Juan de Albicuri, sacerdote de la misma compania y misionero en la mission de Topia*, ca. 1634, Beinecke Rare Book and Manuscript Library, Yale University, ca. 1634, Western Americana Collection, WA MSS S-769. Jason Dyck, who is at work on

a critical edition of both of Albiçuri's *Historias*, has argued that the date for the later *Historia* traces to 1640; author communication.

89. Katherine McAllen, "Jesuit Martyrdom Imagery between Mexico and Rome," in *The New World and Italian Religious Culture, 1492–1750*, ed. Elizabeth Horodowich and Lia Markeyl (Cambridge: Cambridge University Press, 2017), 143–66; Clara Bargellini and Michael Komanecky, *The Arts of the Missions of Northern New Spain, 1600–1821* (Mexico City: Antiguo Coloegio de San Ildefonso, 2009), 248–49. The Jesuit College of San Francisco Xavier is now the Museo Nacional del Virreinato in Tepotzatlan, Mexico. A description of these portraits and their place in the current headquarters of the Provincia Mexicana de la Sociedad de Jesus can be found in the Introduction to this book.

90. Luke Clossey, *Salvation and Globalization in the Early Jesuit Missions* (New York: Cambridge University Press, 2008), 154; Gauvin Alexander Bailey, *Between Renaissance and Baroque: Jesuit Art in Rome, 1565–1610* (Toronto: University of Toronto Press, 2003), 61, 67; Louis Richeôme, *La peinture spirituelle, ou, l'art d'admirer, aimer et louer Dieu en toutes ses oeuvres, et tirer de toutes profit saluterre* (Lyon, 1611), 153, 237.

91. McAllen, "Jesuit Martyrdom Imagery," 154; ARSI, Mex. 16, f. 204r.

92. McAllen, "Jesuit Martyrdoom Imagery," 144; ARSI, Mex. 2, f. 202f–204r.

93. McAllen, "Jesuit Martyrdoom Imagery," 157.

94. Francisco Xavier Saeta, "Carta al P. Thirso Gonzales, September 19, 1687," in Eusebio Francisco Kino, *Kino's Biography of Francisco Javier Saeta, S.J.*, ed. Ernest J. Burrus, trans. Charles W. Polzer (Rome: Jesuit Historical Institute; St. Louis: St. Louis University, 1971), 9, 332–33.

95. Kino, *Kino's Biography of Francisco Javier Saeta, S.J.*, 9:331–37.

3. Fruits: Passionate Expansion

1. The Jesuits branded this part of Sonora the "Pimería Alta," naming it after the Indigenous community that inhabited the region that they called the Pima Alta (Upper Pima). Unless quoting a colonial source that uses "Pima," this chapter employs the self-designation "O'odham" (the People), but Pimería Alta to refer to the territory that the Spaniards imagined in their writings. With between sixteen and thirty thousand inhabitants, the Pimería Alta was populated, but fairly isolated from other Spanish work. The region corresponds to parts of Arizona and Sonora (Mexico) on both sides of the current United States–Mexico border; see Edward Holland Spicer, *Cycles of Conquest: The Impact of Spain, Mexico, and the United States on the Indians of the Southwest, 1533–1960* (Tucson: University of Arizona Press, 1962), 12.

2. "Saeta to Kino, April 1, 1695," in Kino, *Kino's Biography of Francisco Javier Saeta, S.J.* (Rome: Jesuit Historical Institute; St. Louis: St. Louis University, 1971), 9:74–75; original manuscript consulted in the Biblioteca Nacional de México (BN), Fondo Reservado, Colección Archivo Franciscano, 1118, Ex. 13, ff. 139–98.

3. Although *flecha* is the more common Castilian word for "arrow," *saeta* had some use, especially in classical texts; "Saeta," in Sebastián de Covarrubias Orozco and Benito Remigio Noydens, *Tesoro de la lengua Castellana o Española, según la impresión de 1611, con las adiciones de Benito Remigio Noydens publicadas en la de 1674* (Barcelona: Horta, 1943), 2:167. The entry links the name to both Greek and Latin cognates (*sagitta*) as well as the Persian zodiac figure of Sagittarius. See also Isaiah 49:2: "Y me puso por *saeta* bruñida, me guardó en su aljaba," in Cipriano de Valera and Casiodoro de Reina, *La Biblia, que es, los sacros libros del Vieio y Nuevo Testamento: Revista y conferida con los textos hebreos y griegos y con diversas translaciones*, Segunda edición ed. (Amsterdam: En casa de Lorenço Iacobi, 1602).

4. Kino, *Kino's Biography of Francisco Javier Saeta, S.J.*, ed. Ernest J. Burrus, trans. Charles W. Polzer (Rome: Jesuit Historical Institute; St. Louis: St. Louis University, 1971), 9:180–81.

5. Kino, *Saeta*, 62–63.

6. Kino, *Saeta*, 77.

7. Kino, *Saeta*, 89–92. While Kino blamed the violence solely on residents of Tubutama and Oquitoa, others argued there was a wider revolt that incorporated residents of Pitiquito and Caborca; "Padre Guillermo de Burgos al Padre Provincial Diego de Almonazir," Vanamitzi, June 1, 1695, Archivo Historico de Hacienda, AGN, Mexico, Temporalidades, Legajo 972, no. 1, 2f; Juan Fernandez de la Fuente, "A Campaign against the Pimas," in *The Presidio and Militia on the Northern Frontier of New Spain*, vol. 1, 1570–1700, ed. Thomas H. Naylor and Charles W. Polzer (Tucson: University of Arizona Press, 1986), 582–718; Juan Mateo Manje, *Luz de tierra incógnita en la América septentrional y diario de las exploraciones en Sonora*, Publicaciones Archivo General de la Nación (México, D.F.: Talleres Gráficos de la Nación, 1926), 10:236–46; Manje, *Unknown Arizona and Sonora, 1693–1721: From the Francisco Fernández del Castillo Version of Luz de Tierra Incógnita* (Tucson: Arizona Silhouettes, 1954), 53–58; Francisco Xavier Mora, "Informe de Francisco Xavier de Mora al Provincial Juan de Palacios, 1698," in Kino: *¿Frustrado alguacil y mal misionero? Informe de Francisco Xavier de Mora SJ al Provincial Juan de Palacios, Arizpe, 28 de Mayo de 1628*, ed., trans. Gabriel Gomez Padilla, edición facsimilar (Guadalajara, México: Universidad de Guadalajara; Culiacán, México: Colegio de Sinaloa, 2004); Luis Xavier Velarde, "La Primera Relación de la Pimería Alta," in *Etnologia y mision en la Pimería Alta, 1715–1740: Informes y relaciones mision-*

eras de Luis Xavier Velarde, Giuseppe Maria Genovese, Daniel Januske, Jose Agustin de Campos y Cristobal de Cañas, ed. Luis R. Gonzalez (Mexico: Universidad Nacional Autonoma de Mexico, 1977), 27:69–79.

8. Charles W. Polzer, "An Epilogue to Kino's Biography of Saeta," in Kino, *Saeta*, 93–97, 258–65; Naylor and Polzer, *The Presidio and Militia*, 1:585–91.

9. Thomas Sheridan, *Landscapes of Fraud: Mission Tumacácori, the Baca Float, and the Betrayal of the O'odham* (Tucson: University of Arizona Press), 28–30.

10. Donald Weinstein and Rudolph Bell, *Saints and Society: The Two Worlds of Western Christendom, 1000–1700* (Chicago: University of Chicago Press, 1982), 147.

11. Luke Clossey, *Salvation and Globalization in the Early Jesuit Missions* (New York: Cambridge University Press, 2008), 88.

12. For the former, see Herbert E. Bolton, *Rim of Christendom: A Biography of Eusebio Francisco Kino, Pacific Coast Pioneer* (Tucson: University of Arizona Press, 1984), 293–318; Burrus, "A General Conspectus," in Kino, *Saeta*, 2–3. For the latter, see David Sweet, "The Ibero-American Frontier in Native American History," in *The New Latin American Mission History*, ed. Erick D. Langer and Robert H. Jackson (Lincoln: University of Nebraska Press, 1995), 8.

13. David J. Weber, *The Spanish Frontier in North America* (New Haven, Conn.: Yale University Press, 1994), 59–61.

14. For an extensive example of this conflict, see Ramon Gutiérrez, *When Jesus Came, the Corn Mothers Went Away: Marriage, Sexuality, and Power in New Mexico, 1500–1846* (Stanford, Calif.: Stanford University Press, 1991), 95–142.

15. James Lockhart and Stuart B. Schwartz, *Early Latin America* (New York: Cambridge University Press 1983), 340–49; Evelyn Hu-Dehart, *Missionaries, Miners, and Indians: History of Spanish Contact with the Yaqui Indians of Northwestern New Spain, 1533–1820* (Tucson: University of Arizona, 1981), 57–60; Weber, *Spanish Frontier in North America*, 117–19.

16. Juliana Barr, "Geographies of Power: Mapping Indian Borders in the 'Borderlands' of the Early Southwest," *William and Mary Quarterly* 68, no. 1 (January 2011): 5–46.

17. On the Pueblo Revolt, see Gutiérrez, *When Jesus Came*, 127–40; Matthew Liebmann, *Revolt: An Archeological History of Pueblo Resistance and Revitalization in 17th Century New Mexico* (Tucson: University of Arizona Press, 2012). On the Tarahumara rebellions, see Susan M. Deeds, *Defiance and Deference in Mexico's Colonial North: Indians under Spanish Rule in Nueva Vizcaya* (Austin: University of Texas Press, 2003), 86–103.

18. On equestrianism and the rise of raiding in the northwestern frontier, see Ned Blackhawk, "Towards an Indigenous Art History of the West: The Segesser Hide Paintings," in *Contested Spaces of Early America*, ed. Julianna

Barr and Edward Countryman (Philadelphia: University of Pennsylvania Press, 2014), 276–99.

19. The frequency and extent of these confrontations have led some scholars to term the violence "the Great Southwestern Revolt"; Jack Forbes, *Apache, Navajo, and Spaniard* (Norman: University of Oklahoma Press, 1960), 200–224; Matthew Babcock, *Apache Adaptation to Hispanic Rule* (Cambridge: Cambridge University Press, 2016), 34–47. While Babcock has recently pointed to evidence of coordination between these groups and the O'odham in the late 1680s and early 1690s, there is little evidence that the 1695 uprising had wider connections beyond the Altar River Valley.

20. Nuestro Señor del Pilar y Glorioso San José del Paso del Norte at El Paso (1683), San Pedro del Gallo north of the Río Nazas (1685), Concepción del Pasaje de Cuencamé northeast of Durango (1685), San Francisco de Conchos on the Río Conchos (1685), San Antonio de Casas Grandes (1686), San Felipe y Santiago de Janos, and the Presidio de las Fronteras de la Provincia de Sonora (1689); Sheridan, *Landscapes of Fraud*, 29.

21. Lauren E. Jelinek and Dale S. Brenneman, "Population Dynamics in the Pimería Alta, AD 1650–1750," in *New Mexico and the Pimería Alta: The Colonial Period in the American Southwest*, ed. John G. Douglass and William M. Graves (Boulder: University of Colorado Press, 2017), 170–73.

22. Kino, *Saeta*, 363.

23. Kino's friend and contemporary Lieutenant Juan Mateo Manje also employed the language of celestial "favors" to describe the spiritual intercession of Mary; Juan Mateo Manje, *Luz de tierra incógnita*, 7–9, 186–87.

24. Eusebio Francisco Kino, *Favores Celestiales de Jesús y de María SS. ma y del gloriosíssimo apostol de las Indias San Francisco Xavier*, Archivo General de la Nación, México, D.F. (AGN), Misiones, Legajo 27, 1–433. See also Kino, Francisco Fernández del Castillo, and Emil Böse, eds., *Las Misiones de Sonora y Arizona: comprendiendo; La rónica titulada: "Favores Celestiales" y la "relación diaria de la entrada al Noroeste"* (México, D.F.: Editorial "Cultura," 1913); Kino, *Kino's Historical Memoir of the Pimería Alta*, ed. Herbert Eugene Bolton (Cleveland: Arthur H. Clark, 1919).

25. Kino, *Favores celestiales*, 6–9; Kino, Castillo, and Böse, *Las Misiones de Sonora y Arizona*, 8–12.

26. Kino, Castillo, and Böse, *Las Misiones de Sonora y Arizona*, 44.

27. Notably, the Latin Vulgate translated the Greek phrase "polished arrow" as *sagittam electam*, or "chosen arrow," conveying an even more specific sense of divine election: "*Et posuitos meum quasi gladiumacutum in umbra manus suae protexit me et posuit me sicut sagitta me electam in faretra sua abscondit me*"; Is 49:2, Vulgate, http://www.fourmilab.ch/etexts/www/Vulgate/Isaiah.html, February 17, 2017; Kino, *Saeta*, 63; *Historical Memoir*, 157.

28. Éamonn Ó Carragáin, "Chosen Arrows, First Hidden Then Revealed: The Visitation-Archer Sequence as a Key to the Ruthwell Cross," in *Early Medieval Studies in Memory of Patrick Wormald*, ed. Stephen Baxter, Catherine Karkov, Janet L. Nelson, and David Pelteret (Routledge: New York, 2009), 192–96.

29. Rather, she was best known for her institutional reforms, meditations on suffering, and pursuit of mystic love through severe asceticism; "Saint Colette," in *The Oxford Dictionary of Saints*, ed. David Hugh Farmer, 4th ed. (Oxford: Oxford University Press, 1997), 107.

30. Kino, *Saeta*, 63.

31. Rv 2:10: "Do not fear what you are about to suffer. Beware, the devil is about to throw some of you into prison so that you may be tested, and for ten days you will have affliction. Be faithful until death, and I will give you the crown of life"; NRSV.

32. Kino, *Saeta*, 63–64.

33. "Tube la dicha de ayudar a recoger los huesos, zenicas y caveza que hallamos todavía con pelo del difunto Padre que encerramos en una mediana caja. Cerca de las quales halle tanvien una vitela de pergamino de una Monga (Según el Avito Pardo Y negro) hera venita o franelica con el titulo de Santa Coleta, Y un Angel enarcando una flecha, otra la clavada en el corazón de la Santa y otra en el intermedio de ella y el Angel que lleve al Padre Kino y la tenia por reliquia y registro en su rezo"; Manje, AGN, *Historia*, Tomo 393, Hoja 58.

34. Naylor and Polzer, *Presidio and Militia*, 1:584–656.

35. The theology of incorruptible or imperishable bodies in connection to the resurrection has roots in the New Testament, a major theme in Chapter 15 of Paul's First Letter to the Church of Corinth. The expectation of incorruptibility of martyrs' bodies dates back to the early-second-century account of the martyrdom of Polycarp, the bishop of Smyrna. In the narrative, Polycarp only died after his body displayed many signs of incorruptibility, most notably resisting reduction and giving off the odor of baking bread when his persecutors tried to burn it; "The Martyrdom of Polycarp," in *The Apostolic Fathers: Revised Greek Texts with Introductions and English Translations*, ed. Joseph Barber Lightfoot and J. R. Harmer (Grand Rapids, Mich.: Baker, 1984), 131–44.

36. On miraculous bodies and relics, see Weinstein and Bell, *Saints and Society*, 150. For examples of bodies resistant to burning, see Brad Gregory, *Salvation at Stake: Christian Martyrdom in Early Modern Europe* (Cambridge, Mass.: Harvard University Press, 1999), 176; Mathias Tanner, *Societas Jesu usque ad sanguinis et vitae profusionem militans in Europea, Africa, Asia, et America* (Prague: Typis Universitatis Carolo-Ferdinandeae, 1675), 333, 359, 485, 541.

37. Andrés Pérez de Ribas, *History of the Triumphs of Our Holy Faith Amongst the Most Barbarous and Fierce Peoples of the New World*, ed. Daniel T. Reff, trans. Daniel Reff, Maureen Ahern, and Richard Danford (Tucson: University of Arizona Press, 1999), 123; William Eugene Shiels, *Gonzalo de Tapia (1561–1594): Founder of the First Permanent Jesuit Mission in North America*, Monograph Series 14 (New York: United States Catholic Historical Society, 1934), 198.

38. Pérez de Ribas, *History of the Triumphs*, 647.

39. Pérez de Ribas, *History of the Triumphs*, 649.

40. On Indigenous use of poisoned arrows and the putrefaction of missionary bodies, see Joseph Neumann, *Historia de las rebeliones de la sierra tarahumara, 1626–1724*, ed. Luis González Rodríguez (Chihuahua: Editorial Camino, 1991), 98.

41. Manje, *Luz de tierra incógnita*, 238.

42. Kino, *Saeta*, 94–97.

43. Manje, "Luz de tierra incógnita," AGN, Historia, Tomo 393, 58; Manje, *Luz de tierra incógnita*, 239. Whether O'odham communities actually employed cremation in their mortuary practice in this period is unclear. Archeologists have evidence of earlier groups like the Hohokam and surrounding Quechan and Yoeme communities frequently burning the bodies and objects of the dead. Later Tohono O'odham ethnographies suggest the more widespread practice of cave burial; Michael Hellen, *Uncovering Identity in Mortuary Analysis: Community-Sensitive Methods for Identifying Group Affiliation in Historical Cemetaries* (Walnut Creek, Calif.: Left Coast, 2012), 54–55, 179–82. Evidence for O'odham practice of cremation is strongest in the context of warfare; Jessica I. Cerezo-Román, "Pathways to Personhood: Cremation as a Social Practice among the Tucson Basin Hohokam," in *Transformation by Fire: The Archeology of Cremation in Cultural Context*, ed. Ian Kujit, Colin P. Quinn, and Gabriel Cooney (Tucson: University of Arizona Press, 2014), 150–55.

44. Juan Mateo Manje, *Luz de tierra incógnita*, 10:52; Manje, *Luz de tierra incógnita*, 238; Velarde, "La Primera Relación," in González, *Etnología y misión*, 71.

45. Gonzalez, *Etnología y misión*, nn. 37, 73; Kino, *Saeta*, 97–98; *Historical Memoir*, 39–40.

46. Manje, *Luz de tierra incógnita*, 239.

47. Kino, *Saeta*, 98; Manje, *Luz de tierra incógnita*, 239; Velarde, "La Primera relación," in González, *Etnología y misión*, 73–74.

48. Velarde, "La Primera relación," chs. 9–11, in Manje, *Luz de tierra incógnita*, AGN, Historia, 393, 81v–92v; see also Velarde, "La Primera relación," in González, *Etnología y misión*, 66f.

49. Campos's "Life of Saeta" has not been located in any archive. González cites the Fondo Gesuitico 3601, which later was relocated to Biblioteca

NOTES TO PAGES 108-14   249

Nazionale Vittorio Emmanuele in Rome, 1472, Fasc. 2. However, that location contains only a later (post-1751), separate account of the missions of the Pimería Alta; Velarde, *Relación de la Pimería Alta*, in Manje, AGN, Historia, Tomo 393, 75; González, *Etnología y misión*, 72–73.

50. On the "sacred economy" of financial support, prayers, relics, "Vidas," between devout European patrons, Jesuit colleges, and global missionaries, see Clossey, *Salvation and Globalization*, 216–37.

51. Manje, *Luz de tierra incógnita*, 238–39.

52. Manje, *Luz de tierra incógnita*, 326.

53. Manje, *Luz de tierra incógnita*, 326.

54. On the "unfeeling tone" of colonial missionary discourse in reference to indigenous suffering, see Georges Sioui, *Histoires de Kanatha: Vues et contées* [Histories of Kanatha: Seen and Told] (Ottowa: Les Presses de l'Université d'Ottowa [University of Ottowa Press], 2008), 311.

55. "Even though you intended to do harm to me, God intended it for good, in order to preserve a numerous people, as he is doing today"; Gn 50:20 (NRSV).

56. "So that the blood of the martyrs might be the seed of Christians"; Kino, *Saeta*, 88. Kino repeats this interpretation in *Favores celestiales*, explicitly citing Tertullian, *Apolegeticus adversus gentes*, Cap. 1., L; Kino, *Historical Memoir*, 157. For another example of Jesuit citation of Tertullian's dictum, see Juan Eusebio Nieremberg, *Varones Ilustres de la Compania de Jesus* (Bilboa: Administracion del Mensajero del Corazon de Jesus, 1887), 280.

57. Kino, *Saeta*, 113.

58. Kino, *Saeta*, 103.

59. Kino, *Saeta*, 103.

60. Leal in Kino, *Saeta*, 106–7.

61. Kino, *Saeta*, 108–11.

62. Kino, *Saeta*, 111.

63. Kino, *Saeta*, 111.

64. Manje, *Luz de tierra incógnita*, 12–13.

65. Daniel Stolzenberg, "Four Trees, Some Amulets, and the Seventy-Two Names of God," in *Athanasius Kircher: The Last Man Who Knew Everything*, ed. Paula Findlen (New York: Routledge, 2004), 159–61; Clossey, *Salvation and Globalization*, 81; José Gabriel Martínez Serna, "Procurators and the Making of the Jesuit Atlantic Network," in *Soundings in Atlantic History, Latent Structures and Intellectual Currents, 1500–1830*, ed. Bernard Bailyn and Patricia L. Denault (Cambridge, Mass.: Harvard University, 2009), 183–85.

66. It is possible that, absent absolute confirmation for each martyrdom location, Kino, a famously fastidious cartographer, never completed his plan to mark each location with an "M." Ernest Burrus has made a strong argument

that this part of the map was never finished; "Introduction: The Manuscript," in Kino, *Saeta*, 29, 114–15. See Chapter 4 for a further analysis of the "Teatro de los Trabajos Apostolicos."

67. For a very close contemporaneous example of a Jesuit map that marks the time and place of missionary martyrdoms, see Samuel Fritz, S.J., *El Gran Rio Marañon, o Amazonas con la mission de la Compañia de Jesus*, 1707, Bibliohèque Nationale de France, Paris, BNF, *Cartes et plans*, Ge D 7855; Camila Loureiro Dias, "Jesuit Maps and Political Discourse: The Amazon River of Father Samuel Fritz," *Americas* 69, no. 1 (July 2012): 107–16; André Ferrand de Almeida, "Samuel Fritz and the Mapping of the Amazon," *Imago mundi* 55 (2003): 113–19. More famously, Jesuits in New Frances similarly paired cartography with martyrdom. See Francesco Giuseppe Bressani's *Novae Franciae accurata delineatio*, Jésuites, 1657, Bibliothèque nationale de France, *Cartes et plans*, CPL GE DD-2987.

68. Three years later, Kino himself would finally prove that California was not an island, but actually a peninsula; Burrus, *Kino and the Cartography of Northwestern New Spain* (Tucson: Arizona Pioneers' Historical Society, 1965), 46–50.

69. Kino had attempted to build a boat in Caborca to prove its strategic viability; Kino, *Historical Memoir*, 55.

70. Kino, *Saeta*, 81.

71. Jose de Ortega, *Apostolicos afanes de la Compañia de Jesus*, ed. Francisco X. Fluvia (Reimpreso en México: L. Alvarez y Alvarez de la Cadena, 1944), 263.

72. Reff, "Critical Introduction," in Pérez de Ribas, *History of the Triumphs*, 30–31; DeHart, *Missionaries, Miners, and Indians*, 40–49; Cynthia Radding, *Wandering Peoples: Colonialism Ethnic Spaces, and Ecological Frontiers in Northwestern Mexico, 1700–1850* (Durham, N.C.: Duke University Press, 1997), 40–42; Deeds, *Defiance and Deference*, 95.

73. "Kino a la Audiencia Real de Guadalajara" and "Auto de la Audiencia de Guadalajara," December 16, 1686, Archivo General de Indias (AGI), Guadalajara, 69; Bolton, *Rim of Christendom*, 234. Kino reproduced the entire Royal Cédula in his *Favores Celestiales*; Kino, *Historical Memoir*, 108–9.

74. Kino, Castillo, and Böse, *Las misiones de Sonora y Arizona*, 21; Kino, *Historical Memoir*, 98.

75. Augustine argued that, contrary to pagan deity rites, which often celebrated deceased emperors, the Christian cult did not celebrate martyrs in and of themselves, as if they were heroes praised for their deeds; instead, Christians venerated the faith to which they bore witness. Since miraculous power came from the faith, it was not inherent to the holy person, but was rather the object of their faith. The reason and motivation for the martyrdom

constituted its power, not the victim. In the culminating chapters of *The City of God*, the bishop of Hippo highlighted this kind of martyrdom as the defining mark of Christian triumph over pagan superstition. He explained that martyrdom by definition meant the testimony of a death suffered out of hatred for the faith: "For the martyrs themselves were martyrs, that is to say, witnesses of this faith, drawing upon themselves by their testimony (*martyrium*) the hatred of the world, and conquering the world not by resisting it, but by dying"; Philip Schaff, ed. *St. Augustine's City of God and Christian Doctrine*, Select Library of the Nicene and Post-Nicene Fathers of the Christian Church (New York: Christian Literature, 1886), 2:491.

76. Answering the objection that death may not prove essential for martyrdom, Aquinas cited Maximus, who had preached that "in dying for the faith he conquers who would have been vanquished in living without faith." Aquinas went on to conclude, "Therefore the perfect notion of martyrdom requires that a man suffer death for Christ's sake"; Thomas Aquinas, *Summa Theologica* II-II, q. 124, art. 4 (New York: Benziger Bros., 1947).

77. Simon Ditchfield has detailed the elaborate structures erected for the purpose of authorizing official hagiographic accounts and consolidating beatification procedures. By vetting martyr claims, the Vatican hoped to not only bring some unity within the diversity of increasingly global worship practices, but also gird up Catholic identity vis-à-vis Protestant challenges at home. While Ditchfield maintains that centralizing forces were mediated by local dynamics, the founding of the Congregation of Rites in 1588, the assertion of Inquisitional censorship of hagiographical accounts in 1625, and the issuing of papal decrees on canonization in 1642, nevertheless circumscribed both public worship and published claims of martyrdom; Ditchfield, "Tridentine Worship and the Cult of the Saints," in *Cambridge History of Christianity: Reform and Expansion 1500–1660*, ed. R. Po-chia Hsia (Cambridge: Cambridge University Press, 2007), 6:206–15. See also Simon Ditchfield, "Martyrs on the Move: Relics as Vindicators of Local Diversity in the Tridentine Church," in *Studies in Church History*, vol. 30, *Martyrs and Martyrologies* (Oxford: Oxford University Press; Cambridge, Mass.: Blackwell, 1993), 213f.

78. With specific regard to martyrs, the head of the Congregation of Rites and the Promoter of Faith Cardinal Prospero Lambertini (later Benedict XIV) inscribed the requirement of dying "*ex odio in fidem*" into the formal dogma of beatification a century later. In what became the standard work on canonization up until the twentieth century, Benedict XIV confirmed the Augustinian notion that true martyrdom required killing out of hatred of the faith; Benedict XIV, *Doctrina de Servorum Dei Beatificatione et Beatorum Canonizatione*, 118f. Benedict employs the ablative and accusative form "ex odio in fidem" instead of the dative genitive "ex odium fidei" throughout the section on martyrdom

(120–24), nevertheless underlining the Augustinian and Thomistic definitions of true martyrdom as willing death and knowing murder out of hatred for the faith.

79. In doing so, they often directly cited Urban VIII and vowed obedience; Pérez de Ribas, *Historia de los triumphos de Nuestra Santa Fee entre gentes las mas barbaras, y fieras del Nueuo Orbe: Conseguidos por los soldados de la milicia de la Compañia de Iesus en las missiones de la prouincia de Nueua-España: Refierense assimismo las costumbres, ritos, y supersticiones que Vsauan estas gentes, sus puestos, y temples, las vitorias que de Algunas dellas Alcançaron con las armas los catolicos españoles, quando les obligaron à Tomarlas, y las dichosas muertes de veinte religiosos de la Compañia, que en varios puestos, y a manos de varias naciones, dieron sus vidas por la predicacion del Santo Euangelio*, ed. Alonso de Paredes (Madrid: Alonso de Paredes, junto a los estudios de la Compañia, 1645), xiv; Velarde, "La Primera Relación," in González, *Etnología y misión*, 71.

80. Manje, *Luz de tierra incógnita*, 11.

81. Manje, *Luz de tierra incógnita*, 11.

82. Manje, *Luz de tierra incógnita*, 238.

83. Velarde, "La Primera relación," in González, *Etnología y mission*, 71.

84. On Jesuit martyrology as *exempla* and models for fellow Jesuits, see Jane ten Brink Goldsmith, "Jesuit Iconography," in *Jesuit Art in North American Collections: Exhibition 7 March–16 June 1991*, ed. Jane ten Brink Goldsmith (Milwaukee: Patrick and Beatrice Haggerty Museum of Art, Marquette University, 1991), 16f.; Pérez de Ribas, *History of the Triumphs*, 761; Charles W. Polzer, *Rules and Precepts of the Jesuit Missions of Northwestern New Spain* (Tucson: University of Arizona Press, 1976), 141.

85. Kino, *Saeta*, 41–45. For a similar declaration, see Pérez de Ribas's distinction between personal and public veneration. He argues that there is a difference between reverence shown to those "who, with good and prudent reasoning, the individual judges to have been of distinguished sanctity," and the "public veneration," by the faithful of saint's relics, which the "Supreme Vicar alone declares and certifies for the Catholic Church"; Pérez de Ribas, *History of the Triumphs*, 200.

86. Reff, "Critical Introduction," in Pérez de Ribas, *History of the Triumphs*, 25–27.

87. For a full treatment of these disputes, see Brandon Bayne, "Willy-Nilly Baptisms and Chichimeca Freedoms: Missionary Disputes and Indigenous Desires in the O'odham Revolt of 1695," *Journal of Early Modern History* 21, no. 1 (2017): 9–37.

88. Convinced that the "barbarous" tribes must be taught a lesson, Solís pressed for stronger military control of the O'odham and resented the missionary's dominance of Indigenous relations; Bolton, *Rim of Christendom*, 331f;

Francisco Xavier Mora and Juan de Palacios, *Kino: ¿Frustrado aguacil y mal misionero? Informe de Francisco Xavier de Mora SJ Al Provincial Juan de Palacios, Arizpe, 28 de Mayo de 1698*, ed., trans. Gabriel Gómez Padilla, Edición facsimilar (Guadalajara, Mexico: Universidad de Guadalajara; Culiacán, Mexico: Colegio de Sinaloa, 2004), 173; Bayne, "Willy-Nilly Baptisms," 17–23.

89. For more on Kappus, see Janez Stanonik, "Letters of Marcus Antonius Kappus from Colonial America," *Acta neophilologica* 19 (1995): 33–43.

90. Padre Marcos Antonio Kappus al Padre Provincial Diego de Almonazir (hereafter Kappus al Almonazir), Curcurpe, 28 de Julio de 1695, Beinecke Rare Book and Manuscript Library, Yale University, Western Americana, MSS S-956 K142.

91. Kappus al Almonazir, 1.

92. Kappus al Almonazir, 2.

93. Kappus al Almonazir, 2.

94. Kappus al Almonazir, 2.

95. Kappus al Almonazir, 3.

96. Kappus al Almonazir, 3.

97. Donald M. Bahr, "Pima and Papago Social Organization," in *Handbook of North American Indians: Southwest*, ed. Alfonso Ortiz (Washington, D.C.: Smithsonian Institution, 1983), 10:187–92; Carl Lumholtz, *New Trails in Mexico: An Account of One Year's Exploration in North-Western Sonora, Mexico, and South-Western Arizona* (New York: Charles Scribner's Sons, 1912), 164–65.

98. Rich Lewis, *Neither Wolf nor Dog: American Indians, Environment, and Agrarian Change* (Oxford: Oxford University Press, 1994), 123, 135, 160.

99. Radding, *Wandering Peoples*, 59.

100. Kino, *Saeta*, 78–83.

101. Kino, *Saeta*, 80–81.

102. Kino, *Saeta*, 157.

103. Kino, *Saeta*, 134–35.

104. Kino, *Saeta*, 89.

105. Kino, *Saeta*, 182–217.

106. Kino, *Saeta*, 185.

107. Rv 19:17; Kino, *Saeta*, 185.

108. Kino, *Saeta*, 81. While the notion that residents of Oquitoa might have killed Saeta out of jealousy for such an invitation deserves skepticism, Daniel Reff has charted this common combination of desire and frustration with communities awaiting missions in other parts of northern New Spain; Reff, *Plagues, Priests and Demons*, 162. For skeptics of this explanation, see Sweet, "Ibero-American Frontier in Native American History," 39–46.

109. On Castrioto's harsh treatment of the Tubutamans, see Manje, *Luz de tierra incógnita*, 45–46; Bayne, "Willy-Nilly Baptisms," 28.

110. Manje, *Luz de tierra incógnita*, 45–46.

111. Some believe he went as far as execution; see Bolton, *Rim of Christendom*, 289–96, and Sheridan, *Landscapes of Fraud*, 30. For those who believe it was something less, see Charles Polzer, S.J., "Epilogue: The Situation," in Kino, *Saeta*, 262.

112. Kino, *Saeta*, 81.

113. Later in the eighteenth and nineteenth centuries, Spanish demand for Native servants drove a thriving economy of raiding and trading in Indigenous captives, collectively labeled *nijoras*; Henry F. Dobyns, Paul H. Ezell, Alden W. Jones, and Greta S. Ezell, "What Were Nixoras?," *Southwestern Journal of Anthropology* 16, no. 2 (Summer 1960): 230–58; Natale A. Zappia, *Traders and Raiders: The Indigenous World of the Colorado Basin, 1540–1859* (Chapel Hill: University of North Carolina Press, 2014), 2–4, 63, 160.

114. Bolton, *Rim of Christendom*, 298.

115. Kino, *Saeta*, 92–93, 249.

116. *Autos criminales contra Nicolas de Higuera por homicidios contra indios Pimas*, San Joseph del Parral, 31August 1688, Archive of the Diocese of Parral, Parral, Chihuahua, Mf. rl. 1688c fr. 1481–1599. Consulted at the Office of Ethnohistory, Arizona State Museum, Tucson Arizona.

117. Bolton, *Rim of Christendom*, 259, 358, 498; Naylor and Polzer, *Presidio and Militia*, 1:575, 594.

118. Laura E. Matthew and Michel R. Oudijk, eds., *Indian Conquistadors: Indigenous Allies in the Conquest of Mesoamerica* (Norman: University of Oklahoma Press, 2007).

119. "Relación de nuestra Señora de los Remedios en su nueva capilla de su nuevo pueblo de las nuevas conversiones de la Pimería en 19 de Setiembre de 1698," AGN, *Misiones* 26, no. 74; consulted in *Materiales para la historia de Sonora* 16, no. 17, Microfilm, Mexican Manuscripts (M-M) 229, Bancroft Library, Berkeley, California, 323–24. See also *Documentos para la historia de Mexico*, Ser. 3 (Mexico City, 1856), 4:814–16; Bolton, *Rim of Christendom*, 390–92; Fay Jackson Smith, John Kessell, and Francis J. Fox, *Father Kino in Arizona* (Phoenix: Arizona Historical Foundation, 1966), 142.

120. Kino, *Saeta*, 81–83.

121. Kino, *Saeta*, 136–37.

122. Kino, *Saeta*, 136–37.

123. Padre Oracio Polici, "Del Estado grasias al Nss. pasifico iquieto deesta dilatada Pimeria y dela prova de Sonora, 1698," in The Beinecke Rare Book and Manuscript Library, Yale University, Western Americana, MSS S-968 P759.

124. Gomez Padilla, ed., *Kino: ¿Frustrado aguacíl?*, 28–31; Bayne, "Willy-Nilly," 23–24.

125. Polici, "Del Estado grasias al Nss. pasifico," 6.

126. Polici, "Del Estado grasias al Nss. pasifico," 6; The first part of the quote, "Plantaberit Ecclesiam Suam Sanguine Suo," seems to be a variation of Acts 20:28, "God has obtained his church with his blood" (NRSV).

127. Polici, "Del Estado grasias al Nss. pasifico," 6. For a comprehensive archeological and historical account of the battle, see Deni J. Seymour, *A Fateful Day in 1698: The Remarkable Sobaipuri-O'odham Victory of the Apaches and Their Allies* (Salt Lake City: University of Utah Press, 2014).

128. Polici, "Del Estado grasias al Nss. pasifico," 7.

129. Polici, "Del Estado grasias al Nss. pasifico," 1–4.

130. Eusebio Kino, "Breve relación de la insigne Victoria que los Pimas, Sobaipuris en 30 de marzo del año de 1698, han consequido contra los enemigos de la provincial de Sonora," in *Materiales para la historia de Sonora*, ed. Rafael Pérez-Taylor and Miguel Ángel Paz Frayre (Universidad Nacional Autónoma de Méxcio, 2007), 101–4.

131. For examples of Indigenous children named after Francis Xavier, Juan Maria Salvatierra, and even Kino himself, see Kino, *Historical Memoir*, 131; Polzer, "Epilogue," in Kino, *Saeta*, 312.

132. Kino, "Breve relación de la insigne Victoria," 103.

133. Kino, *Saeta*, 82–83.

4. Deserted: Prolonged Isolation

1. Diego de Almonazír in Eusebio Francisco Kino, *Kino's Biography of Francisco Javier Saeta, S.J.*, ed. Ernest J. Burrus, trans. Charles W. Polzer (Rome: Jesuit Historical Institute; St. Louis: St. Louis University, 1971), 9, 37.

2. Kino, *Saeta*, 37.

3. Ramon A. Gutiérrez, *When Jesus Came, the Corn Mothers Went Away: Marriage, Sexuality, and Power in New Mexico, 1500–1846* (Stanford, Calif.: Stanford University Press, 1991), 136–37; David J. Weber, *The Spanish Frontier in North America* (New Haven, Conn.: Yale University Press, 1994), 136.

4. For alternative readings of Pueblo approaches to Catholic images and rituals, see Matthew Liebmann, *Revolt: An Archaeological History of Pueblo Resistance and Revitalization in 17th Century New Mexico* (Tucson: University of Arizona Press, 2012), 29–68.

5. On Franciscan martyrology and missionary motivation in New Spain, see David Rex Galindo, *To Sin No More: Franciscans and Conversion in the Hispanic World, 1683–1830* (Stanford, Calif.: Stanford University Press, 2018), 101–5.

6. "Funeral Oration over the Twenty-One Franciscan Missionaries Killed by the Pueblo Indians, August 10, 1680, Preached by Doctor Ysidro Sariña y Cuenca March 20, 1681," Historical Society of New Mexico, no. 7, Santa Fe,

1906, in Wagner, *The Spanish Southwest*, no. 54, microfilm (New Haven, Conn.: Research Publications, 1975), Western Americana, reel 473, no. 4768), 20; Isidro Sariñana y Cuenca, *Oracion funebre, que dixo el doctor D. Ysidro Sariñana y cuenca en las exequias de veinte y un religiosos de la regular ovservancia del seraphico P.s. Francisco, que murieron a manos de los indio apostatas de la Nuevo Mexico, en diez de Agosto de 1681* (México, D.F.: la Viuda de Bernardo Calderon, 1681), 20; Gutiérrez, *When Jesus Came*, 136–37.

7. On the transition from providential framing of natural events to scientific explanation in global European discourse in the eighteenth century, see Bentley B. Allan, *Scientific Cosmology and International Orders* (Cambridge: Cambridge University Press, 2018), 35–38.

8. Jesuits from the provinces of Austria, Germany, and Bohemia had been prohibited from working as missionaries in Spanish colonies until 1664, when a special agreement between the Castilian crown and Jesuit General Paul Oliva allowed up to one-fourth of the total missionaries to come from parts of the Holy Roman Empire. In the eighteenth century, this proportional guard was lifted, and German-speaking Jesuits became a majority of the northern missionaries; Ivonne del Valle, *Escribiendo desde los márgenes: Colonialismo y Jesuitas en el siglo XVIII* (México, D.F.: Siglo XXI editores, 2009), 57–59; Karl Kohut and Maria Cristina Torales Pacheco, *Desde los confines de los imperios Ibéricos: Los Jesuitas de habla alemana en las misiones Americanas, simposio "Diversidad en la unidad: Los Jesuitas de habla alemana en Iberoamérica, siglos XVI–XVIII en Mexico City, 2005"* (Madrid and Frankfurt am Main: Iberoamericana and Vervuert, 2007), 16:xxi; Luke Clossey, *Salvation and Globalization in the Early Jesuit Missions* (New York: Cambridge University Press, 2008), 150–52, 172; John Francis Bannon, *The Mission Frontier in Sonora, 1620–1687* (Philadelphia: United States Catholic Historical Society, 1955); Thomas DaCosta Kaufmann, "East and West: Jesuit Art and Artists in Central Europe and Central European Art in the Americas," in *The Jesuits: Cultures, Sciences, and the Arts, 1540–1773*, ed. John W. O'Malley, Gauvin Alexander Bailey, Steven J. Harris, and T. Frank Kennedy (Toronto: University of Toronto Press, 1999), 1:294–95; Albrecht Classen, *Early History of the Southwest through the Eyes of German-Speaking Jesuit Missionaries: A Transcultural Experience in the Eighteenth Century* (Lanham, Md.: Lexington, 2013), 12.

9. Ignacio del Río, *A la diestra mano de las Indias: Descubrimiento y ocupación colonial de la Baja California* (México, D.F.: Universidad Nacionál Autónoma de México, 1990), 20, 36, 51–60, 74–99; del Río, *Conquista y aculturación en la California Jesuítica, 1697–1768* (México, D.F.: Universidad nacional autónoma de México instituto de investigaciones históricas, 1998); del Río, *El Régimen Jesuítico de la antingua California* (México, D.F.: Universidad Nacionál Autónoma de México, 2003), 17–25, 30–39.

10. Harry Crosby, *Antigua California: Mission and Colony on the Peninsular Frontier, 1697–1768* (Albuquerque: University of New Mexico Press, 1994), 20–26; William E. McDonald, "The Pious Fund of the Californias," *Catholic Historical Review* 19, no. 4 (January 1934): 427–36; Francis W. Weber, "The Pious Fund of the Californias," *Hispanic American Historical Review* 43, no. 1 (February 1963): 78–94.

11. Francisco Maria Piccolo, *Informe del estado de la nueva Cristiandad de California 1702 y otros documentos*, ed. Ernest J. Burrus (Madrid: Ediciones Jose Porrua Turanzas, 1967).

12. Jesuits who considered themselves German came from a wide variety of areas that mostly constituted parts of the Holy Roman Empire, including Austria, Switzerland, Slovenia, Bohemia, Croatia, and northern Italy; Classen, *Early History of the Southwest*, 8.

13. On the O'odham uprising of 1751 and the prolonged hostilities between Spaniards, O'odham, and Seris in the 1740s and '50s, see Ignacio Martínez, "The Paradox of Friendship: Loyalty and Betrayal on the Sonoran Frontier," *Journal of the Southwest* 56, no. 2 (Summer 2014): 319–44; José Luis Mirafuentes Galván, *Las rebeliones de los Seris, 1748–1750* México, D.F.: Universidad Nacional Autónoma de México, 1979); Mirafuentes Galván, *Movimientos de resistencia y rebeliones indígenas en el norte de México, 1680–1821, Guia documentales* I–III (Universidad Nacional Autónoma de México, 1989, 1992 2004); Mirafuentes Galván, "El 'enemigo de las casas de adobe': Luis del Sáric y la rebelión de los pimas altos en 1751," in *Memoria del xiii Simposio de historia y antropología de Sonora* (Hermosillo: Instituto de Investigaciones Históricas de la Unison, 1988), 105–24; Mirafuentes Galván, "El 'enemigo de las casas de adobe,'" in *Organización y liderazgo en los movimientos populares novohispanos* (México, D.F.: Universidad Nacional Autónoma de México, 1992), 147–71.

14. David Brakke, *Demons and the Making of the Monk: Spiritual Combat in Early Christianity* (Cambridge, Mass.: Harvard University Press, 2005), 10–11, 23–47. For a complication of the martyr to monasticism theory, see Elizabeth A. Clark, *Reading Renunciation: Asceticism and Scripture in Early Christianity* (Princeton, N.J.: Princeton University Press, 1999), 23.

15. Andrew Louth, *The Origins of the Christian Mystical Tradition: From Plato to Denys*, 2nd ed. (Oxford: Oxford University Press, 2007), 95.

16. Elizabeth Castelli, *Martyrdom and Memory: Early Christian Culture Making* (New York: Columbia University Press, 2004), 69–77.

17. Richard Fletcher, *The Barbarian Conversions: From Paganism to Christianity* (Berkeley: University of California Press, 1999), 22–44, 153, 314–25.

18. Fletcher, *Barbarian Conversions*, 22, 232; Olivia Remie Constable and Damian Zurro, ed., *Medieval Iberia: Readings from Christian, Muslim, and Jewish Sources* (Philadelphia: University of Pennsylvania Press, 2012), 61–66, 119,

184–89; Joyce E. Salisbury, *The Blood of the Martyrs: The Unintended Consequences of Ancient Violence* (New York: Routledge, 2004), 34–45, 70–79.

19. Brad Gregory, *Salvation at Stake: Christian Martyrdom in Early Modern Europe* (Cambridge, Mass.: Harvard University Press, 1999), 41–62.

20. Maximilian von Habsburg, *Catholic and Protestant Translations of the Imitatio Christi, 1425–1650* (London: Routledge, 2011), 160–70; Carlos Eire, *From Madrid to Purgatory: The Art and Craft of Dying in Sixteenth-Century Spain* (Cambridge: Cambridge University Press, 1995), 24–29.

21. John of the Cross, *The Ascent of Mount Carmel*, bk. II, ch. 15, ed. David Lewis and Benedict Zimmerman (London: T. Baker, 1928), 165.

22. Guibert, *The Jesuits, Their Spiritual Doctrine and Practice: A Historical Study* [Spiritualité de la Compagnie de Jésus: Esquisse historique] (Chicago: Institute of Jesuit Sources, 1972), 28–29, 137–38.

23. Terence O'Reilly, *From Ignatius Loyola to John of the Cross: Spirituality and Literature in Sixteenth-Century Spain* (New York: Routledge, 1995); Ignatius of Loyola, *Ignatius of Loyola: The Spiritual Exercises and Selected Works*, ed. George Ganns, S.J. (New York: Paulist Press, 1991), 123–24, 202–4, 426.

24. John O'Malley, *The First Jesuits* (Cambridge, Mass.: Harvard University Press, 1993), 38–48; Maureen Ahern, "Visual and Verbal Sites": The Construction of Jesuit Martyrdom in Northwest New Spain in Andres Perez De Ribas' *Historia de los triumphos de Nuestra Santa Fe* (1645)," *Colonial Latin American Review* 8, no. 1 (June 1999): 9; Guibert, *The Jesuits, Their Spiritual Doctrine and Practice*, 128–39.

25. Katherine McAllen, "Jesuit Martyrdom Imagery between Mexico and Rome," in *The New World and Italian Religious Culture, 1492–1750*, ed. Elizabeth Horodowich and Lia Markey (Cambridge: Cambridge University Press, 2017), 153–61.

26. Ahern, "Visual and Verbal Sites," 9; James D. Ryan, "Missionary Saints of the High Middle Ages: Martyrdom, Popular Veneration, and Canonization," *Catholic Historical Review* 90, no. 1 (January 2004); O'Malley, *First Jesuits*, 457.

27. Jane ten Brink Goldsmith, ed. *Jesuit Art in North American Collections: Exhibition 7 March–16 June, 1991* (Milwaukee: Patrick and Beatrice Haggerty Museum of Art, Marquette University, 1991), 19; Marcus B. Burke and Saint Peter's College Art Gallery, *Jesuit Art and Iconography, 1550–1800: Introductory Essay and Exhibition Catalogue* (Jersey City, N.J.: Saint Peter's College, Art Gallery, 1993), 3.

28. Even as they ate and relaxed, Jesuit novices might look to frescoes on walls and ceilings that depicted the Society's fallen heroes, who had given their lives in evangelistic service; Clossey, *Salvation and Globalization*, 82–83; Ahern,

"Visual and Verbal Sites," 72; Burke and Saint Peter's College Art Gallery, *Jesuit Art and Iconography*.

29. Daniel T. Reff, *Plagues, Priests, and Demons: Sacred Narratives and the Rise of Christianity in the Old World and the New* (Cambridge: Cambridge University Press, 2005), 133.

30. Clossey, *Salvation and Globalization*, 83.

31. Félix Zubillaga, *Monumenta antiquae Floridae (1566–1572)*, Monumenta Missionum Societatis Iesu 3 (Rome: Monumenta Historica Soc. Iesu, 1946), 107, 692.

32. Andrés Pérez de Ribas, *History of the Triumphs of Our Holy Faith Amongst the Most Barbarous and Fierce Peoples of the New World*, ed. Daniel T. Reff, trans. Daniel Reff, Maureen Ahern, and Richard Danford (Tucson: University of Arizona Press, 1999), 719–22.

33. "De un genero de martirio, que si no con derramiento de sangre, que a vezes en breve passa, por lo menos de otro triunfo, y vitoria de inumerables y prologados trabajos, y linage de martirio de mucho sanos"; Pérez de Ribas, *Historia de los triumphos de Nuestra Santa Fee de Nuestra Santa Fee entre gentes las mas barbaras, y fieras del nueuo orbe*, ed. Alonso de Paredes (Madrid: Alonso de Paredes, junto a los estudios de la Compañia, 1645), 419; Juan Eusebio Nieremberg, *Varones ilustres de la Compañia de Jesus* (Bilbao: Administración del mensajero del corazón de Dios, 1890), 6:405, 420, 678; Guy Rozat, *América, imperio del demonio: cuentos y recuentos* (México, D.F.: Universidad Iberoamericana, 1995), 155–58.

34. "Eusebio Kino, Cadiz, to Maria de Guadalupe Lancastre, Duchess of Aveiro," December 6, 1680, Kino Letters, Huntington Manuscripts (HM) 9984, Huntington Library (HL), San Marino, Calif.; see also Kino and Maria de Guadalupe, the duchess of Aveiro, *Kino Writes to the Duchess: Letters of Eusebio Francisco Kino, S.J., to the Duchess of Aveiro; An Annotated English Translation, and the Text of the Non-Spanish Documents*, ed., trans. Ernest J. Burrus (St. Louis: Jesuit Historical Institute, 1965), 87; Kino referred to a circular letter written by the astronomer and mathematician Ferdinand Verbiest to his Jesuit colleagues in Europe on August 15, 1678. For an account of the letter and Verbiest's ideal of the "mathematician as martyr," see Florence C. Hsia, *Sojourners in a Strange Land: Jesuits and their Scientific Missions in Late Imperial China* (Chicago: University of Chicago Press, 2009), 30–33; R. Po-chia Hsia, *The World of Catholic Renewal, 1540–1770* (New York: Cambridge University Press, 1998), 1; Ferdinand Verbiest, Henri Josson, and Léopold Willaert, *Correspondance de Ferdinand Verbiest de la Compagnie de Jésus (1623–1688) Directeur de l'observatoire de Pékin*, Académie Royale des Sciences, des Lettres et des Beaux-Arts de Belgique, Brussels, Commission Royale d'

Histoire, Publications in-Octavo (Brusells: Palais des académies, 1938), 49:232–50.

35. For his mathematical, cartographical, and linguistic skills, the Flemish Jesuit had achieved a high place at court and become an intimate advisor and friend of the Kangxi emperor; Hsia, *Sojourners in a Strange Land*, 28.

36. Hsia, *Sojourners in a Strange Land*, 28; "Epistola ad socios Europae ("Letter to fellow fathers in Europe") of August, 15th, 1678," quoted in Noël Golvers, "The Missionary and His Concern about Consolidation and Continuity," in *A Lifelong Dedication to the China Mission: Essays Presented in Honor of Father Jeroom Heyndrickx, CICM*, ed. Noël Golvers and Sara Lievens, Leuven Chinese Studies 17 (Leuven: Ferdinand Verbiest Institute, 2000), 358–60; Ferdinand Verbiest, "Lettre du P. Ferdinand Verbiest, vice-provincial de la mission de Chine, a ses confreres de la Societe en Europe, le 15 aout 1678, de la residence imperial de Beijing," trans. Noel Golvers, *Courier Verbiest* (Leuven: Ferdinand Verbiest Institute, 1993), 5:5–6.

37. On China's ranking as the highest comparable "civilization" in Jesuit misionary discourse, see José de Acosta, *Natural and Moral History of the Indies* [Historia natural y moral de las Indias], ed., trans. Jane Mangan, Walter Mignolo, and Frances M. Lopez-Morillas (Durham, N.C.: Duke University Press, 2002), 336–39; R. Po-Cha Hsia, *Jesuit in the Forbidden City: Matteo Ricci, 1552–1610* (Oxford: Oxford University Press, 2013), 75–78.

38. Florence C Hsia, *Sojourners in a Strange Land*, 32; Florence C. Hsia, "Mathematical Martyrs, Mandarin Missionaries, and Apostolic Academicians: Telling Institutional Lives," in *Institutional Culture in Early Modern Society*, ed. Anne Goldgar and Robert I. Frost (Leiden: Brill, 2004), 17–21.

39. The Chinese Rites controversy centered on a series of debates between Jesuit, Dominican, and Franciscan missionaries in Asia over the extent to which the Catholic Church should accommodate practices associated with Confucian, Buddhist, and ancestral religious traditions. In general, Jesuits like Martíni favored accommodation, while Dominican opponents regarded ancestral rites as "idolatry." Each side scored victories with Rome in the seventeenth century, but the rites were ultimately condemned in the eighteenth century and subsequently led to Chinese prohibition of Catholic missions; Paul Rule, "Towards a History of the Chinese Rites Controversy," in *The Chinese Rites Controversy*, ed. D. E. Mungello (Bonn: Monumenta Serica, 1994), 249–66; R. Po-Cha Hsia, *The World of Catholic Renewal*, 91–105. On Martini's *Novus atlas sinensis*, see David Mungello, *Curious Land: Jesuit Accommodation and the Origin of Sinology* (Honolulu: University of Hawaii Press, 1989), 108.

40. "I have always had an especially strong leaning toward the conversions of Great China, and at the suggestion of the superiors I applied myself to the

mathematical sciences, which are very general there, and in the beginning, I asked to go to the missions there, because in that great vineyard of the Lord had lived and worked my relative, Father Martin Martini, who wrote those celebrated volumes and geographical maps of the great empire and monarch of Great China"; Kino, *Historical Memoir of the Pimería Alta: A Contemporary Account of the Beginnings of California, Sonora, and Arizona*, ed., trans. Herbert Bolton (Cleveland: Arthur H. Clark, 1919), 2:77–78; Ernest J. Burrus, "Kino's Relative, Father Martino Martini, S.J.: A Comparison of Two Outstanding Missionaries," *Neue Zeitschrift für Missionswissenschaft* 31 (1975): 100–109.

41. Clossey, *Salvation and Globalization*, 139; Herbert E. Bolton, *Rim of Christendom: A Biography of Eusebio Francisco Kino, Pacific Coast Pioneer* (Tucson: University of Arizona Press, 1984), 32.

42. Bolton, *Rim of Christendom*, 37–39.

43. "Ni parece me podrá ser que Nuestro Señor desampare aquella Cristiandad, ya sembrada con la preciosa sangre de los mártires"; Kino to Lancastre, Cadiz, September 15, 1680, Huntington Library, 9980; *Kino Writes to the Duchess*, 73–74.

44. Kino, *Historical Memoir*, 1:333.

45. On Jesuit missionaries and their use of female aristocratic patrons, see R. Po-Cha Hsia, *Noble Patronage and Jesuit Missions: Maria Theresia von Fugger-Wellenburg (1690–1762) and Jesuit Missionaries in China and Vietnam*, Monumenta Historica Societatis Iesu 2 (Rome: Institutum Historicum Societatis Iesu, 2006); on Aveiro and her extensive patronage of Catholic causes, see George Anthony Thomas, "The Death of the Duchess of Aveiro: The Life and Legacy of María de Guadalupe Lencastre," *Dieciocho* 39, no. 1 (Spring 2016): 29–42.

46. *Kino Writes to the Duchess*, 75; 1 Samuel 15:22.

47. "Kino to Lancastre, Cadiz, December 6, 1680," in *Kino Writes to the Duchess*, 225.

48. Kino, *Historical Memoir*, 2:78.

49. Benoît Vermander, S.J., "Jesuits and China," *Oxford Handbooks Online*, accessed on October 15, 2017, http://www.oxfordhandbooks.com/view/10.1093/oxfordhb/9780199935420.001.0001/oxfordhb-9780199935420-e-53.

50. "Father Pedro Van Hamme, Letter to Father Guilielmo y Cinzer, Haquan, December 17, 1700," in Kino, *Historical Memoir*, 2:78–79.

51. Kino built chapels to Xavier in all the churches constructed under his supervision and often dedicated them on his saint's day, Dec. 3; Kino, *Historical Memoir*, 1:378, and 2:230; Kino, *Saeta*, 217.

52. Kino, *Saeta*, 27; Burrus, *Kino and the Cartography of Northwestern New Spain* (Tucson: Arizona Pioneers' Historical Society, 1965), 3.

53. On Xavier's status as a bloodless martyr and role in ramping up Jesuit practices of self-mortification, see Patricia W. Manning, *Voicing Dissent in*

Seventeenth-century Spain: Inquisition, Social Criticism and Theology in the Case of El Criticón (Leiden: Brill, 2009), 270–71.

54. Kino, *Saeta*, 217.

55. In the late seventeenth and early eighteenth centuries, most geographers considered California to be an island (although several sixteenth-century maps showed a peninsula). Kino played a crucial role in overturning the island theory through his exploration and maps; Burrus, *Kino and the Cartography*, 68.

56. Kino, *Historical Memoir*, 2:139–42.

57. Burrus, *Kino and the Cartography*, 143.

58. Kino, *Historical Memoir*, 2:145–46.

59. Kino, *Historical Memoir*, 2:144: "And let there be one fold and one Shepherd" (John 10:16). The imagery of arches and the triumphal car refers to ancient Roman parades for returning conquerers, an image picked up by the author of the New Testament epistle to the Colossians (2:16) and subsequently invoked as a frequent motif in Jesuit art of the seventeenth and eighteenth centuries in which Jesuit leaders, missionaries, and martyrs led a triumphal wagon across the world; cf. José Rodríguez Carnero's eighteenth-century mural *Carro triunfal de la iglesia guiado por los jesuitas*, Iglesia del espíritu santo, Puebla, Mexico; María Bernal Martín, "El triunfo de S. Ignacio y S. Francisco Javier," *TeatrEsco: Revista del Antiguo Teatro Escolar Hispánico*, no. 1 (2005), accessed July 15, 2015, http://parnaseo.uv.es/ars/teatresco/revista/Revista1/MBernalTriunfodeIgnacioySFcoJ.htm; Alcalá, *Fundaciones Jesuíticas*, 305–6.

60. Though overly ambitious in retrospect, Kino's 1703 plan outlined much of what Franciscans would execute in California almost seven decades later under Father Junipero Serra; Kino, *Plan for the Development of Pimería Alta, Arizona and Upper California: A Report to the Mexican Viceroy*, ed., trans., Ernest J. Burrus, S.J. (Tucson: Arizona Pioneers' Historical Society, 1961), 24, 33.

61. On the early modern Jesuit transpacific network, see Brandon Bayne, "Converting the Pacific: Jesuit Networks between New Spain and Asia," *Oxford Handbook of Borderlands of the Iberian World*, ed. Danna L. Rojo and Cynthia Radding (Oxford: Oxford University Press, 2019), 786–816.
On the legacy of Jesuit, Franciscan, and Spanish plans for expansion in the north and its complicated relationship to indigenous inhabitants of Sonora, the Pimeria, and California, as well as their cartographic expression, see Jose Refugio de la Torre Curiel, "Santidad y martirio en testimonios jesuitas y franciscanos sobre la cristianización del noroeste novohispano, Siglos XVII y XVIII," *Relaciones* 37, no. 145 (Winter 2016): 63–107.

62. Kino, *Saeta*, 39.

63. Kino, *Saeta*, 217.

64. Kino, *Saeta*, 127.

65. Monica Matei-Chesnoiu, *Re-imagining Western European Geography in English Renaissance Drama* (London: Palgrave Macmillan, 2012), 13–39.

66. Cf. "Trabajos de la Compania de Jesu en N. Espana," in *Los PP. Jesuitas Juan Bautista Velasco y Hermano Francisco de Castro: Tapaguis y conicaris; Conversion de los Mayos, reduccion de Chinipa y Guazapares, elogios a los PP. Julio Pascual y Manuel Martinez, conquista del Hiaqui, Capitan Diego Martinez de Hurdaide*, Ex. 648, Ms. (32/648), no. 1960, Archivo Franciscano, Biblioteca Nacional de México.

67. Miguel Venegas, *Noticia de la California, y de su conquista temporal, y espiritual hasta el tiempo presente: Sacada de la historia manuscrita, formada en México año de 1739 por el Padre Miguèl Venegas, de la Compañía de Jesús; y de otras noticias, y relaciones antiguas, y modernas. Añadida de algunos mapas particulares, y uno general de la América septentrional, Assia oriental, y Mar del Sùr intermedio, formados sobre las memorias mas recientes, y exactas, que se publìcan juntamente. Dedicada al Rey Ntro. Señor por la provincia de Nueva-España, de la Compañía de Jesus*, ed. Andrés Marcos Burriel, S.J., 3 vols. (Madrid: Imprenta de la Viuda de Manuel Fernández, y del Supremo Consejo de la Inquisición, 1757, Wilson Library (WL), Rare Book Collection, University of North Carolina at Chapel Hill). Venegas's original manuscript, *Empresas apostólicas de los misioneros de la Compañía de Jesús de la Nueva España en la conquista de las Californias*, was completed in Mexico in 1739 and sent to Spain but was left unpublished until Burriel's edition.

68. Instead, Burriel had taken up the life of a successful scholar, and after several academic appointments as a professor of philosophy and theology, he had been appointed the head of the comisión de archivos by Ferdinand VI and the Real academia de la historia in 1750; Alfonso Echánove Tuero, *La preparación intelectual del P. Andrés Marcos Burriel, S.J., 1731–1750* (Madrid: CSIC, 1971). On Burriel's possible motive of securing Jesuit royal patronage over and against Creole Spaniards in New Spain, see Jorge Cañizares-Esguerra, *How to Write the History of the New World* (Palo Alto, Calif.: Stanford University Press, 2002), 145f. In a similar attempt to catalog Spain's imperial dominion, the criollo scholar José Antonio Villaseñor y Sánchez dedicated his *Theatro americano* to Felipe V and Fernando VI in 1746; Villaseñor y Sánchez, *Theatro americano, descripción general de los reinos y provincias de la Nueva España y sus jurisdicciones (1746–1748)*, 2 vols., 2nd ed. (México, D.F.: Editora Nacional, 1952).

69. Burriel, "Sobre los mapas de Baja California," in Burrus, *La obra cartográfica de la Provincia Mexicana de la Compañía de Jesús, 1567–1967* (Madrid: Ediciones José Porrúa Turanzas, 1967), 210.

70. Venegas, *Noticia de la California*, 1:21–22, 39–30; 2:551–52; 3:279, 287–92.

71. Derived from the Greek word *marturos*, the term "martyr" literally means "witness." Burriel's *Map of California* marked Jesuit witnessing through both scientific contribution and sacrificial action; "Μάρτυς, μάρτυρος," in Frederick William Banker and Walter Bauer, *A Greek-English Lexicon of the New Testament and Other Early Christian Literature* (Chicago: University of Chicago Press, 2000).

72. Venegas, *Noticia*, 1:70.

73. Venegas, *Noticia*, 1:71.

74. Venegas, *Noticia*, 1:74–75.

75. Venegas, *Noticia*, 2:2.

76. Venegas, *Noticia*, 2:450–52.

77. Venegas, *Noticia*, 2:457–58.

78. Venegas, *Noticia*, 2:461–62.

79. On Pericú strategies of warfare, see W. Michael Mathes, "Violence in Eden: Indigenous Warfare in Peninsular Baja California," *Pacific Coast Archeological Society Quarterly* 45, nos. 1 & 2 (August 2011):1–12.

80. Venegas, *Noticia*, 2:468–69.

81. Venegas, *Noticia*, 2:471.

82. Sigismundo Taraval, *Historia de las misiones Jesuitas en California Baja desde su establecimiento hasta 1737*, "Journal Recounting Indian Uprisings in Baja California: 1734–1737," NL, Edward E. Ayer Collection, MS 1240, http://collections.carli.illinois.edu/cdm/ref/collection/nby_eeayer/id/36199, accessed October 2, 2017.

83. Taraval, *Historia de las misiones*, NL 17, 38.

84. Matthew 4:1–11.

85. Taraval, *Historia de las misiones*, NL 250, 144.

86. Joseph Barba, "Informe del padre Joseph Barba sobre el alzamiento de las Californias del año 1734 al Virrey Arzobispo Juan Antonio de Vizarrón y Eguiarreta April 26, 1735," BL, University of California, Berkeley, M-M 1717.

87. Joseph Barba, "Informe sobre el alzamiento," BL, 1v.

88. Joseph Barba, "Informe sobre el alzamiento," BL, 2.

89. Joseph Barba, "Informe sobre el alzamiento," BL, 1.

90. Joseph Barba, "Informe sobre el alzamiento," BL, 3v.

91. Francisco Zambrano and Jose Gutiérrez Casillas, *Diccionario bio-bibliográfico* (Mexico: Editorial Tradicion, 1975), 14:295–302.

92. Both Kino and Pérez de Ribas cited Tutino as the ideal response to the tales of martyrdom: Kino, *Saeta*, 129; Pérez de Ribas, *History of the Triumphs*, 610–11.

93. "Reciban, pues, este opúsculo, prueba de mi estimación por ustedes, e impetren para mí en sus oraciones el feliz y anhelado termino de mi vida. Nunca merecí alcanzarlo aunque lo hay esperado en las tres rebeliones que aquí

narro; pero no pierdo la esperanza de lograrlo con la ayuda divina, pues nos rodean aquí graves y constants peligros, de modo que podría darse la ocasión de ofrendar la vidapor la gloria de Dios, ya sea derramando mi sangre o de otro modo como el Señor disponga"; Joseph Neumann, *Historia de las rebeliones en la sierra tarahumara, 1626–1724*, ed. Luis González Rodríguez (Chihuahua: Editorial Camino, 1991), 16.

94. Thomas E. Sheridan, *Landscapes of Fraud: Mission Tumacácori, the Baca Float, and the Betrayal of the O'odham* (Tucson: University of Arizona Press, 2006), 46–54; John L. Kessell, *Mission of Sorrows: Jesuit Guevavi and the Pimas, 1691–1767* (Tucson: University of Arizona Press, 1970), 102–18; Roberto Mario Salmón, "A Marginal Man: Luis of Saric and the Pima Revolt of 1751, *Americas* 45, no. 1 (July 1988): 61–77; Alberto Francisco Pradeau, "Los Jesuitas en Sonora y el alzamiento Pima de 1751," 491–519, Alberto Francisco Pradeau Collection 1551–1980, MSS-67, box 1, folder 17, Chicano Research Collection, Arizona State University.

95. Joseph Och, *Missionary in Sonora: The Travel Reports of Joseph Och, S.J., 1755–1767*, trans., ed. Theodore Treutlein (San Francisco: California Historical Society, 1965), 43–44.

96. Och, *Missionary in Sonora*, 44.

97. See Chapter 5 for a description of the sickness and how it shaped Och's account of the Jesuit expulsion.

98. Phlipp Segesser, "Letter to His Brother from Seville, December 26, 1729," in *A Jesuit Missionary in Eighteenth-Century Sonora: The Family Correspondence of Philipp Segesser*, ed. Raymond H. Thompson, trans. Werner S. Zimmt and Robert E. Dahlquist (Albuquerque: University of New Mexico Press, 2014), 59.

99. Segesser, *Jesuit Missionary in Eighteenth-Century Sonora*, 59.

100. Segesser, *Jesuit Missionary in Eighteenth-Century Sonora*, 157.

101. Segesser, *Jesuit Missionary in Eighteenth-Century Sonora*, 155.

102. On Bohemian Jesuit letters and descriptions of New Spain, see Markéta Křížová, "Meeting the Other in the New World: Jesuit Missionaries from the Bohemian Province in America," *Historie—Otázky—Problémy: European Civilisation and the World between Conflicts, Cooperation, and Dialogue* 2 (2016): 35–46.

103. AGN, *Historia*, 21, 188–91; Wenceslaus Linck, "1762 Report," in *Wenceslaus Linck's Reports and Letters, 1762–1778*, ed. Ernest Burrus (Los Angeles: Dawson's Books, 1967), 45.

104. Ernest Burrus, ed., *Wenceslaus Linck's Reports and Letters*, 46.

105. Linck, "1763 Report," 67.

106. Linck, "Observation on Lower California," in Burrus, *Wenceslaus Linck's Reports and Letters*, 65.

107. Linck, "Observation on Lower California," 72.

108. Cañizares-Esguerra, *How to Write the History*, 235–49.

109. On accusations of Jesuit wealth and the calumnies that led to their expulsion in 1767, see Chapter 5.

110. Linck, "Observation on Lower California," 72.

111. Linck, "Observation on Lower California," 65.

112. Cynthia Radding, *Wandering Peoples: Colonialism Ethnic Spaces, and Ecological Frontiers in Northwestern Mexico, 1700–1850* (Durham, N.C.: Duke University Press, 1997).

113. Linck, "Letter to Benno Ducrue, Olmütz, 1778," in Burrus, *Wenceslaus Linck's Reports and Letters*, 60.

114. Ignacio Tirsch, "Plate VI, VIII, IX," in *The Drawings of Ignacio Tirsch: A Jesuit Missionary in Baja California*, ed. Doyce B. Nunis (Los Angeles: Dawson's Book Shop, 1972), 41–47.

115. Jacob Baegert, *The Letters of Jacob Baegert, 1749–1761: Jesuit Missionary in Baja California*, ed. Doyce B. Nunis Jr., trans. Elsbeth Schulz-Bischof (Los Angeles: Dawson's Books, 1982), 123; Sky Michel Johnston, "What Is California? Nothing but Innumerable Stones: German Jesuits, Salvation, and Landscape Building in the California Missions," *Journal of Jesuit Studies* 2 (2015): 41–42.

116. Miguel Venegas, *A Natural and Civil History of California*, 2 Vols. (London: Rivington and Fletcher, 1759); Baegert, *Observations in Lower California* (Berkeley: University of California Press, 1952), 5–8.

117. Baegert, *Observations*, 14, 168.

118. Baegert, *Observations*, 5.

119. Baegert, *Observations*, 95.

120. Baegert, *Observations*, 173f.

121. Juan Antonio Balthasar, *Carta del padre provincial Juan Antonio Balthasar en que de noticia de la exemplar vida, reliogosas virtudes, y apostolicos trabajos del fervoroso misionero el venerable P. Francisco Maria Picolo*, México, HL, 44103, Rare Books, Mexico, 1752, 46.

122. Balthasar, *Carta del padre provincial Juan Antonio Balthasar*, 83.

123. Balthasar, *Carta del padre provincial Juan Antonio Balthasar*, 84–85.

5. Uprooted: Missionary Expulsion

1. Alberto Francisco Pradeau, *La expulsión de los Jesuitas de las provincias de Sonora, Ostimuri y Sinaloa en 1767* (México, D.F.: José Porrúa e Hijos, 1959), 24, 26–46.

2. Pineda tried to follow guidelines laid out by the president of the Council of Castile, Don Pedro Pablo Albeca de Bolea, the conde de Aranda: "Instruc-

ción de lo que deberán ejecutar," in Pradeau, *La expulsion*, 30–39. For a Sonoran Jesuit account of this process, see Bernardo Middendorff, "Diario de la Expulsión, 1767–1776," in *Cartas e informes de misioneros Jesuitas extranjeros en hispanoamérica, 1751–1778*, quinta parte, ed. Mauro Matthei, O.S.B., and Rodrigo Moreno Jeria (Santiago: Pontificia universidad Católica de Chile, 2001), 224–27.

3. Miguel Mathes, *Los padres expulsos de Sonora y Sinaloa*, vol. 51, serie Cuadernos (Culiacán, Sinaloa Mexico: El Colegio de Sinaloa, 1999), 7.

4. Jaime Mateu, S.J. (attributed to Antonio Sterkianowski, S.J.), "Destierro de los misioneros de la America septentrional española por Don A. S. olim misionero de Norogachic," Bancroft Library, University of California Berkeley, Bolton papers, C-B 840, container 29, folder 22–23, 108–9. Large sections of this text are cited and summarized in Pradeau as the work of the Moravian missionary Antonio Sterkianowski. This follows the assumptions of Herbert Bolton and Peter Masten Dunne; cf. Peter Masten Dunne, "The Expulsion of the Jesuits from New Spain," *Mid-America: An Historical Review* 19, no. 8 (January 1937): 13n30. All of these scholars based this conclusion on the signed initials "A.S." cited in the title. However, Ernest Burrus has persuasively argued that the Spanish missionary to the Tarahumara, Jaime Mateu, was the true author as attested by the Jesuit cataloguer Ramón Diosdado Caballero, who met Mateu in Spain during the exile, as well as Mateu's own signature on the Latin translation; Ernest J. Burrus, "Mexican Historical Documents in the Central Jesuit Archives," *Manuscripta: A Journal for Manuscript Research* 12, no. 3 (November 1968): 139; Pradeau, *La expulsión*, 64.

5. Technically, Palomino was the second death during the process of the expulsion. The former superior of the Sinaloa mission, Father Andres Ignacio González, died in the Jesuit college at Bamoa, Sinaloa, on September 7. Since he was moribund at the time of the expulsion, he had been allowed to stay behind, under the care of Palomino, for a couple of weeks after their other colleagues had departed. Dávila y Arrillaga, Pradeau, and Julio César Montané Marti all count González as the first deceased amongst the exiles; José Mariano Dávila y Arrillaga and Francisco Javier Alegre, *Continuación de la historia de la Compañia de Jesús en Nueva España del P. Francisco Javier Alegre* (Puebla: Imp. del Colegio pio de artes y oficios, 1888), 1:309; Pradeau, *La expulsión*, 165, 189; Julio César Montané Marti, *La expulsión de los Jesuitas de Sonora* (México, D.F.: Contrapunto, 1999), available online at http://www.monografias.com/trabajos27/jesuitas-sonora/jesuitas-sonora.shtml, accessed November 11, 2016.

6. Mateu, "Destierro de los misioneros," 115; Dunne, "Expulsion of the Jesuits," 22; Middendorff, *Vertreibung und Gefangenschaft* (Munster, 1845), 2:33.

7. Middendorff, "Diario de la expulsión," 239.

8. Several secondary sources provide a basic narrative of the expulsion, including Dunne, "Expulsion of the Jesuits," and Pradeau, *La expulsión*; Eva María St. Clair Segurado, *Expulsión y exilio de la provincial jesuíta mexicana (1767–1820)* (Alicante: Publicaciones Universidad de Alicante, 2005); Mathes, *Los padres expulsos de Sonora y Sinaloa*; John J. Martínez, *Not Counting the Cost: Jesuit Missionaries in Colonial Mexico; A Story of Struggle, Commitment, and Sacrifice* (Chicago: Jesuit Way, 2001); Martí, *La expulsión de los Jesuitas*; Salvador Bernabéu Albert, *Expulsados del Infierno: El exilio de los misioneros Jesuitas de la península de California, 1767–1768* (Madrid: Consejo Superior de investigaciones científicas, 2008). For English translations of primary sources, see Benno F. Ducrue, *Ducrue's Account of the Expulsion of the Jesuits from Lower California (1767–1769): An Annotated English Translation of Benno Ducrue's Relatio Expulsionis*, ed. Ernest J. Burrus, S.J., Sources and Studies for the History of the Americas 2 (St. Louis: Jesuit Historical Institute, 1967); Joseph Och, *Missionary in Sonora: The Travel Reports of Joseph Och, S.J., 1755–1767*, ed. Theodore Treutlein (San Francisco: California Historical Society, 1965); Baegert, *Observations in Lower California*, ed. Doyce B. Nunis Jr., trans. Elsbeth Schulz-Bischof, Baja California Travels Series 45 (Los Angeles: Dawson's Book Shop, 1982). In German, see Johann Jacob Baegert, *Nachrichten von der Amerikanischen Halbinsel Californien: Mit einem Zweyfachen Anhang falscher Nachrichten* (Mannheim: Gedruckt in der Churfürstl. Hof- und Academie-Buchdruckerey, 1772). In Spanish, see Middendorff, "Diario de la Expulsión, 1767–1776," 223–46; Antonio Lopez de Priego, Rafael Zelis, and Francesco Saverio Clavigero, *Tesoros documentales de México, siglo XVIII*, ed. Mariano Cuevas (México, D.F.: Editorial Galatea, 1944); Francisco Javier Alegre and Carlos María de Bustamante, *Historia de la Compañia de Jesus en Nueva-España, que estaba escribiendo el P. Francisco Javier Alegre al tiempo de su expulsión* (México, D.F.: Impr. de J. M. Lara, 1841).

9. Dunne, "Expulsion of the Jesuits," 3.

10. Dunne, "Expulsion of the Jesuits," 5. For accounts of exile from other territories, see Nicholas P. Cushner, *Philippine Jesuits in Exile: The Journals of Francisco Puig, S.J., 1768–1770*, vol. 24 (Rome: Institutum Historicum, 1964); José del Rey Fajardo, *La expulsión de los Jesuítas de Venezuela, 1767–1768* (San Cristóbal: Universidad Católica del Tachira, 1990), 398; Magnus Mörner, ed., *The Expulsion of the Jesuits from Latin America* (New York: Knopf, 1965), 207; Florence C. Hsia, *Sojourners in a Strange Land: Jesuits and their Scientific Missions in Late Imperial China* (Chicago: University of Chicago Press, 2009); Francisco Javier Alegre et al., *Testimonios del exilio*, Clásicos Cristianos 12 (Mexico: Jus, 2000), 156.

11. Alma Montero Alarcón, *Jesuitas de Tepotzotlán: La expulsión y el amargo destierro*, 1st ed. (Tepotzotlán, Mexico: Museo Nacional del Virreinato; México, D.F.: Plaza y Valdes, 2009), 39–41.

12. For a dated, but helpful summary of the papal suppression, see Giovanni Battista Nicolini, *History of the Jesuits: Their Origin, Progress, Doctrines, and Designs* (London: H. G. Bohn, 1854), 362.

13. Andrés Pérez de Ribas, *History of the Triumphs of Our Holy Faith amongst the Most Barbarous and Fierce Peoples of the New World*, ed. Daniel T. Reff, trans. Daniel Reff, Maureen Ahern, and Richard Danford (Tucson: University of Arizona Press, 1999), 443; Pérez de Ribas, *Historia de los triumphos de Nuestra Santa Fee entre gentes las mas barbaras, y fieras del Nueuo Orbe: Conseguidos por los soldados de la milicia de la Compañia de Iesus en las missiones de la prouincia de Nueua-España: Refierense assimismo las costumbres, ritos, y supersticiones que vsauan estas gentes, sus puestos, y temples, las Vitorias que de algunas dellas Alcançaron con las armas los catolicos españoles, quando les obligaron à Tomarlas, y las dichosas muertes de veinte religiosos de la Compañia, que en varios puestos, y a manos de varias naciones, dieron sus vidas por la predicacion del Santo Euangelio*, ed. Alonso de Paredes (Madrid: Alonso de Paredes, junto a los estudios de la Compañia, 1645), 418.

14. Pérez de Ribas, *History of the Triumphs*, 443; Pérez de Ribas, *Historia de los triumphos*, 418.

15. Father Lambert Hostell, S.J., "The Second Short Letter of Father Lambert Hostell, S.J., to his religious sister," *Welt-Bott*, no. 761, translated in Ducrue, *Account of the Expulsion*, 169.

16. Jesuits from the provinces of Austria, Germany, and Bohemia had been prohibited from working as missionaries in Spanish colonies off and on until 1664, when a special agreement between the Castilian crown and Jesuit general Paul Oliva allowed up to one-fourth of the total missionaries to come from parts of the Holy Roman Empire. In the eighteenth century even this proportional guard was lifted, and Germans became a majority of the northern missionaries; del Valle, *Escribiendo desde los márgenes: Colonialismo y Jesuitas en el siglo XVIII* (Mexico, D.F.: Siglo XXI editores, 2009), 57–59; Karl Kohut and Maria Cristina Torales Pacheco, eds., *Desde los confines de los imperios Ibéricos: Los Jesuitas de habla alemana en las misiones Americanas*, simposio "Diversidad en la unidad: Los Jesuitas de habla alemana en Iberoamérica, siglos XVI–XVIII en Mexico City, 2005" (Madrid and Frankfurt am Main: Iberoamericana and Vervuert, 2007), 16:xxi; Luke Clossey, *Salvation and Globalization in the Early Jesuit Missions* (New York: Cambridge University Press, 2008), 172; John Francis Bannon, "The Mission Frontier in Sonora (1620–1687)," in Charles W. Polzer, *The Jesuit Missions of Northern Mexico* (New York: Garland, 1991), 164–70.

17. Clossey, *Salvation and Globalization*, 35; Eusebio Francisco Kino and and Maria de Guadalupe, the Duchess of Aveiro, *Kino escribe a la duquesa: Correspondencia del P. Eusebio Francisco Kino con la duquesa de Aveiro y otros documentos*, ed. Ernest J. Burrus (Madrid: J. Porrúa Turanzas, 1964), 105–15.

18. Marcus Kappus, "Letters of Marcus Antonius Kappus from Colonial America," in *Acta neophilologica XIX*, Part 1, ed. Janez Stanonick (Slovenia: University of Ljubljana, 1986), 35–36.

19. Marcus Kappus, "Letter of Father Marcus Kappus to His Aunt, Lady Francisca Adlmanin, a Nun at Skofja Loka, April 30, 1689," *Acta neophilologica XIX*, Part 1, ed. Janez Stanonick (Ljubljana, Slovenia: University of Ljubljana University, 1986), 55–56.

20. Marcus Kappus, "Letter of Father Marcus to His Brother, Johann," *Acta neophilologica XXII*, Part 4, ed. Janez Stanonick (Ljubljana, Slovenia: University of Ljubljana Press, 1989), 48–50.

21. Hostell, "Second Short Letter of Rev. Fr. Lambert Hostell," no. 761; trans. in Ducrue, *Account of the Expulsion*, 176–77.

22. Segesser, "Letter 22: Letter to His Brother from Genoa, June 21, 1729," in Raymond H. Thompson, ed., *A Jesuit Missionary in Eighteenth-Century Sonora: The Family Correspondence of Philipp Segesser*, trans. Werner S. Zimmt and Robert E. Dahlquist (Albuquerque: University of New Mexico Press, 2014), 46–47. On German and Spanish differences, see "Letters 25–28," 74–78, and "Letter 39," 105.

23. Segesser, "Letter 37: Letter to My Highly Born Honorable Mother, Puerto de Santa Maria, 1730," in Thompson, *Jesuit Missionary in Eighteenth-Century Sonora*, 105.

24. "Letter 41: Letter to His Mother Anna Maria Catharina Segesser, née Rusconi, Havana, April 3, 1731," in Thompson, *Jesuit Missionary in Eighteenth-Century Sonora*, 117–19.

25. "Letter 53," in Thompson, *Jesuit Missionary in Eighteenth-Century Sonora*, 170.

26. "Letter 62," in Thompson, *Jesuit Missionary in Eighteenth-Century Sonora*, 271.

27. "Letter 62," in Thompson, *Jesuit Missionary in Eighteenth-Century Sonora*, 269.

28. Father Franz Inama, "Letter of Reverend Father Franz Inama, S.J., Missionary in California, from the Austrian Province to His Reverend Sister, a Carmelite in Cologne on the Rhine, written from Mission San José on October 14, 1755," in Ducrue, *Account of the Expulsion*, 152.

29. Hostell, "The First Letter of Rev. Fr. Lambert Hostell, S.J., Missionary in California of the Lower Rhine Province Addressed to his Father from the Mission of San Luis Gonzaga, September 27, 1743," in Ducrue, *Account of the Expulsion*, 163–65.

30. Hostell, "The Fourth Letter of Rev. Fr. Lambert Hostell, S.J., Missionary in California of the Lower Rhine Province, to Rev. Fr. Josef Burscheid of the Same Order and Province," in Ducrue, *Account of the Expulsion*, 166–67.

31. Hostell died just after the suppression in the former Jesuit College of Dusseldorf in 1773; Burrus, "Introduction," in Ducrue, *Account of the Expulsion*, 163–65.

32. Kino, *Saeta*, 114–29; Jose Gutierrez Casillas, S.J., *Martires Jesuitas de la provincia de Mexico*, 2nd ed. (México, D.F.: Tradición, 1981).

33. Och, *Missionary in Sonora*, 65.

34. Och, *Missionary in Sonora*, 65.

35. The New Testament presents two different accounts of Judas's death, with the Gospel of Matthew suggesting he hung himself out of guilt (Matthew 27:1–10), while the Acts of the Apostles presents Judas falling in a field and splitting open to spill his guts (Acts 1:18).

36. Theodore Treutlein, "Translator's Introduction," in Och, *Missionary in Sonora*, xii–xiii.

37. Och, *Missionary in Sonora*, 34–38.

38. Treutlein, "Translator's Introduction," in Och, *Missionary in Sonora*, xii–xiii.

39. Och, *Missionary in Sonora*, 115.

40. Mateu, "Destierro de los misioneros," 111.

41. Mateu, "Destierro de los misioneros," 112.

42. On the authorship and audience for Jesuit natural histories, see Bryan Green, "Apostles and Men of Learning: Miguel Venegas, Andrés Marcos Burriel, and the Jesuit Vocation for Natural History," *Journal of Jesuit Studies* 4 (2017): 28–55.

43. José de Acosta, *Natural and Moral History of the Indies* [*Historia natural y moral de las Indias*], ed. Jane E. Mangan, Walter Mignolo, and Frances M. López-Morillas (Durham, N.C.: Duke University Press, 2002), 76f; Anthony Pagden, *The Fall of Natural Man: The American Indian and the Origins of Comparative Ethnology* (Cambridge: Cambridge University Press, 1982), 161–65.

44. Baegert, *Observations in Lower California*; Baegert, *Nachrichten von der Amerikanischen Halbinsel Californien*, 8; Jacob Baegert, *Noticias de la peninsula Americana de California*, Primera española ed., ed. Paul Kirchhoff and Pedro R. Hendrichs (S.L.: Antigua Librería Robredo de José Porrúa e hijos, 1942).

45. Baegert, *Observations in Lower California*, 157.

46. Baegert, *Observations in Lower California*, 155.

47. Baegert, *Observations in Lower California*, 172.

48. Ignaz Pfefferkorn, *Sonora: A Description of the Province* (Tucson: University of Arizona Press, 1989), 169, 175, 248f; Och *Missionary in Sonora*, 153.

49. Baegert did not see the defects as inherent or natural, but rather blamed them on the environment, which he described as hell (*infierno*); Baegert, *Observations in Lower California*, 80.

50. Ducrue, *Account of the Expulsion*, 51.

51. Ducrue, *Account of the Expulsion*, 51.

52. Emma Anderson, "Blood, Fire, and 'Baptism': Three Perspectives on the Death of Jean De Brébeuf, Seventeenth-Century Jesuit 'Martyr,'" in *Native Americans, Christianity, and the Reshaping of the American Religious Landscape*, ed. Joel W. Martin and Mark A. Nicholas (Chapel Hill: University of North Carolina Press, 2010), 63.

53. Ducrue, *Account of the Expulsion*, 66.

54. Ducrue, *Account of the Expulsion*, 68.

55. On the importance of disciplined imagination in Jesuit spiritual formation, see John W. O'Malley, *The First Jesuits* (Cambridge, Mass.: Harvard University Press, 1993), 37–50.

56. Mateu, "Destierro de los misioneros," 126.

57. Middendorff, "Diario de la expulsión," 225.

58. Middendorff, "Diario de la expulsión," 226.

59. Middendorff, "Diario de la expulsión," 227.

60. Middendorff, "Diario de la expulsión," 229.

61. Middendorff, "Diario de la expulsión," 230.

62. Middendorff, "Diario de la expulsión," 231.

63. Middendorff, "Diario de la expulsión," 234.

64. Middendorff puts the number of deceased missionaries in Nayarit at 24; Middendorff, "Diario de la expulsión," 235. Mateu and Ita put the number at twenty, which most historians have followed since they have had better access to the latter source; Pradeau, *La expulsión*, 99–100.

65. Fathers Enrique Kurtzel, Sebastian Cava, and Vicente Rubio all died in Aquacatlán; Mateu, "Destierro de los misioneros," 132; Pradeau, *La expulsión*, 96.

66. Middendorff, "Diario de la expulsión," 235.

67. Julio César Montané, in Aarón Grageda Bustamante, *Seis expulsiones y un adiós: Despojos y exclusiones en Sonora*, Primera ed. (Mexico, D.F.: Plaza y Valdés, 2003), 50.

68. Mateu, "Destierro de los misioneros," 136–37: "Pero tambien murieron, como los otros, que habian quedado en Istlan, y entre todos fueron 20 los muertos, habian perdido la vida a fuerza de trabajos padecidos por Dios, quedando 30 vivos para glorificar tambien al mismos Dios con la vida trabajosa que les esperaba."

69. Middendorff, "Diario de la expulsión," 236.

70. Ita, quoted in Mateu, "Destierro de los misioneros," 137–38.

71. David Brading, *Church and State in Bourbon Mexico: The Diocese of Michoacán, 1749–1810* (Cambridge: Cambridge University Press, 1994), 3–7.

72. Raphael Brewster Folsom, *The Yaquis and the Empire: Violence, Spanish Imperial Power, and Native Resilience in Colonial Mexico* (New Haven, Conn.: Yale University Press, 2014), 194.

73. Ducrue, *Account of the Expulsion*, 78–79; Martínez, *Not Counting the Cost*, 236–39.

74. Ducrue, *Account of the Expulsion*, 42.

75. Ducrue, *Account of the Expulsion*, 58.

76. Ducrue, *Account of the Expulsion*, 58.

77. Ducrue, *Account of the Expulsion*, 86–87.

78. Ducrue, *Account of the Expulsion*, 116–18.

Epilogue: Civilization and Savagery

1. Bob Thomas, "Kino's Grave Believed Located in Magdalena," *Arizona Daily Star*, May 24, 1966, 1.

2. Thomas, "Grave of Father Kino Found in Magdalena," *Arizona Daily Star*, May 25, 1966, 1.

3. "Kino Remains Discovered in Mexico," *Arizona Republic*, May 25, 1966, 16.

4. "Hallaron Los Restos de Kino," *El Sonorense* (Hermosillo, Sonora, Mexico), May 25, 1966, 1–8.

5. Bob Thomas, "Diggers Lucky to Find Kino's Bones Intact," *Arizona Daily Star*, B, 1.

6. Cruz G. Acuña, "Para los que duden," in *El Encuentro de los restos del Padre Kino*, ed. Aristides Prat (Magdalena, Sonora: Publicaciones del Comité del Tricentenario del Arribo de Eusebio Francisco Kino a Sonora, 1987), 50.

7. William W. Wasley, "Archeological Notes on the Discovery of Father Eusebio Francisco Kino," 1966, http://padrekino.com/kino-s-legacy/chapel-discovery/, accessed on May 12, 2017.

8. Thomas, "Diggers Lucky," 2.

9. Ernest J. Burrus, "La Autoridad máxima reconoce los restos del Padre Kino," in *El Encuentro de los restos*, 26.

10. Burrus, "La Autoridad máxima reconoce los restos del Padre Kino," in *El Encuentro de los restos*, 26.

11. Governor Luis Encinas Johnson, "Aquel que fue constructor de Pueblos," in *El Encuentro de los restos de Padre Kino*, ed. Arístides Prat (Magdalena, Sonora: Publicaciones del comité del tricentenario del arribo de Eusebio Francisco Kino a Sonora, 1987), 14.

12. Carlos Argüelles, "Plena indentificación del gran civilizador," *El Sonorense*, May 25, 1966, 5.

13. Rubén Parodi, "Hoy: Eusebio Kino," *El Sonorense*, May 25, 1966, 7.

14. Enriqueta de Parodi, "Atena hacia el noroeste, Magdalena de Kino," *El Nacional*, June 16, 1966.

15. Dr. Joaquin Antonio Peñalosa, "El Padre Kino, insigne forjador de la civilización del noroeste del país," *El Sol de Mexico*, July 19, 1966.

16. Humberto W. Lopez Campbell, *El Sonorense*, July 11, 1966, 11.

17. Bernard Fontana, "Afterword," in Jorge H. Olvera, *Finding Father Kino: The Discovery of the Remains of Father Eusebio Francisco Kino, S.J., 1965–1966* (Tucson: Southwestern Mission Research Center, 1998), 252.

18. Andrae M. Marak, "Little House on the Prairie in Sonora: Borderlands, the Comcáac, and World History," World History Connected 18, no. 1 (February 2021): 11–12.

19. "Presentation of Statue by Honorable Samuel P. Goddard, Jr., Governor of Arizona," in *Acceptance of the Statue of Eusebio Francisco Kino: Presented by the State of Arizona*. United States Congress (89th 1st session: 1965) (Washington, D.C.: U.S. Government Printing Office, 1965), 26.

20. For a full description of the production of the statue and other speeches that day, see Brandon Bayne, "Recalling Kino: Remembering a Pimería Past, Reimagining an Arizona Present," *Southwestern Mission Research Center Revista* 164–65 (Fall–Winter 2010): 35–43.

21. J. Brett Hill, *From Huhugam to Hohokam: Heritage and Archaeology in the American Southwest* (Lanham, Md.: Lexington, 2019); M. Kyle Woodson, *The Social Organization of Hohokam Irrigation in the Middle Gila River Valley, Arizona* (Sacaton, Ariz.: Gila River Indian Community, 2016); Suzanne K. Fish and Paul R. Fish, *The Hohokam Millennium* (Santa Fe, N.M.: School for Advanced Research Press, 2007).

22. Kino, *Kino's Historical Memoir of Pimería Alta: A Contemporary Account of the Beginnings of California, Sonora, and Arizona*, ed., trans. Herbert Eugene Bolton (New York: AMS, 1976), 1:127–29.

23. James S. Griffith, *Belief and Holy Places: A Spiritual Geography of the Pimería Alta* (Tucson: University of Arizona Press, 1992); Seth Schermerhorn, *Walking to Magdalena: Personhood and Place in Tohono O'odham Songs, Sticks, and Stories* (Lincoln: University of Nebraska Press, 2019).

24. Frederick Jackson Turner, "The Significance of the Frontier in American History," *Proceedings of the State Historical Society of Wisconsin*, December 14, 1893.

25. Goddard, "Presentationf of Statue," in *Acceptance of Statue*, 27.

26. "Grave of Father Kino Found in Magdalena," *Arizona Daily Star* (Tucson), May 25, 1966, 1; "Identificaron los restos," *El Imparcial*, 2; "Monumento y museo a la memoria de Kino," *El Imparcial*, May 26, 1966, 1. Encinas mistakenly called Kino "Fray," though Kino was not a Friar.

27. "Yañez y Salvat Viene a Sonora esta semana, interés nacional por el hallazgo de los restos de Fray Eusebio Kino," *El Regional*, May 25, 1966, 1.

28. Lic. Luis Encinas, "Kino continua su obra civilizadora," *El Sonorense*, June 10, 1966, 1, 6.

29. Agustin Yañez, "Lección de Kino: Trabajo Constante," *El Sonorense*, June 10, 1966, 7.

30. The sentiment, expressed in Spanish, clearly suffers in the journalist's unwieldy translation; "Throng Hails Sonora Chief," *Arizona Republic*, August 23, 1967, 1, 12.

31. "Statue Given, 'Neighbors and Good Brothers,'" *Phoenix Gazette*, August 23, 1967, 19.

32. "Ford and Mexico Meet for Day of Diplomacy," *Arizona Republic*, October 22, 1974, A 18–19.

33. Gerald R. Ford, "Toasts of President Ford and President Echeverria of Mexico at a Luncheon in Tubac, Arizona, October 21, 1974," in Gerhard Peters and John T. Woolley, "The American Presidency Project," http://www.presidency.ucsb.edu/ws/?pid=4496, accessed on August 13, 2016.

34. Luis Echeverría, "Toasts of President Ford and President Echeverría."

35. Lisa Blee and Jean M. O'Brien, *Monumental Mobility: The Memory Work of Massasoit* (Chapel Hill: University of North Carolina Press, 2019), 13–14.

36. Roxanne Dunbar-Ortiz, *An Indigenous Peoples' History of the United States* (Boston: Beacon Press, 2014), 178.

37. W. Fitzhugh Brundage, *The Southern Past: A Clash of Race and Memory* (Cambridge, Mass.: Harvard University Press, 2005), 4.

38. Brundage, *Southern Past*, 5–6.

39. Sacred spaces are "battlefields," by necessity implicated in conflict because they involved the "politics of position, property, exclusion, and exile." Creating a sacred locale involves locating (position), possessing (property), demarcating (exclusion), and differentiating (exile) specific places, all of which entail forms of conflict over and against other people and places; David Chidester and Edward Tabor Linenthal, eds., *American Sacred Space* (Bloomington: Indiana University Press, 1995), 7–10, 16–20.

40. On the institutional strategies, see Michel de Certeau, *The Practice of Everyday Life*, trans. Steven Rendell (Berkeley: University of California Press, 2011).

41. Talal Asad, *On Suicide Bombing*, Wellek Library Lectures (New York: Columbia University Press, 2007), 16–20.

42. This conversation was conducted as part of the O'odham-Pee Posh Documentary History Project, which is a collaboration between the Documentary Relations of the Southwest (DRSW) program of the Arizona State Museum's Office of Ethnohistorical Reseach and the four O'odham and

O'odham-Pee Posh (Maricopa) communities of southern Arizona. For a further description of the project and their publications, see Dale S. Brenneman, "Bringing O'odham into the 'Pimeria Alta': Introduction," in *Journal of the Southwest* 56, no. 2 (Summer 2014): 205–18.

43. Office of Ethnohistorical Research, Arizona State Museum, June 21, 2013. Used with speaker's permission and request of anonymity.

Bibliography

Abbreviations

AGN	Archivo Géneral de la Nación, Mexico City, Mexico
AHF	Arizona Historical Foundation, Arizona State University, Phoenix
AHPMSJ	Archivo Histórico de la Provincia Méxicana de la Sociedad de Jesús, Mexico City, Mexico
AHS	Arizona Historical Society, Tucson
AZTM	Arizona State Museum, Office of Ethnohistorical Research, Tucson
BL	Bancroft Library, University of California at Berkeley
BN	Biblioteca Nacionál de Mexico, UNAM, Mexico City
CRC	Chicana/Chicano Research Collection, Arizona State University
HL	Huntington Library, Pasadena, California
JCB	John Carter Brown Library, Brown University
NL	Newberry Library, Chicago, Illinois
VSL	Vatican Film Library, St. Louis University
YBL	Beineke Library, New Haven, Connecticut

Primary Sources

Acosta, José de. *Natural and Moral History of the Indies* [Historia natural y moral de las Indias]. Edited by Jane E. Mangan, Walter Mignolo, and Frances M. López-Morillas. Durham, N.C.: Duke University Press, 2002.

Albiçuri, Juan de. *Historia de las misiones apostolicas que los clerigos regulares de la Compañia de Jesus an echo en las Indias occidentales del Reyno de la nueva vizcaya y vida y martyrio del P. Gonzalo de Tápia fundador de las dichas missiones y apostol de Cynaloas*. Bamupa, Mexico, 1633, M-M 7, Hubert Howe Bancroft Collection, Bancroft Library, University of California, Berkeley.

Alegre, Francisco Javier. *Historia de la provincia de la Compañia de Jesús de Nueva España*. Bibliotheca Instituti Historici Societatis Jesu. Edited by Ernest J. Burrus and Félix Zubillaga. Vols. 9, 13, 16–17. Rome: Institutum Historicum S.J., 1956.

Alegre, Francisco Javier, and José Mariano Dávila y Arrillaga. *Continuación de la historia de la Compañia de Jesús en Nueva España del P. Francisco Javier Alegre*. Puebla: Imp. del Colegio pio de artes y oficios, 1888.

Alegre, Francisco Javier, and Carlos María de Bustamante. *Historia de la Compañía de Jesús en Nueva España, que estaba escribiendo el padre Francisco Javier Alegre al tiempo de su expulsión*. México, D.F.: Impr. de J. M. Lara, 1841.

Alegre, Francisco Javier, Rafael de Zelis, Antonio López de Priego, and Elsa Cecilia Frost. *Testimonios del exilio*. Clásicos Cristianos 12. México, D.F.: Jus, 2000.

Alegre, Francisco Javier, and Jacinto Jijón y Caamaño. *Memorias para la historia de la provincia que tuvo la Compañía de Jesús en Nueva España*. México, D.F.: Talleres tipográficos modelo, s.a., 1940.

Arizona Dept. of Library Archives and Public Records. Museum Division. *Wesley Bolin Memorial Plaza: Memorial Descriptions*. Phoenix, Ariz.: The Division, 2001.

Augustine of Hippo. *The City of God*. Translated by Henry Bettenson. New York: Penguin Classics, 2004.

———. *St. Augustine's City of God and Christian Doctrine*. Edited by Philip Schaff. Select Library of the Nicene and Post-Nicene Fathers of the Christian Church 2. New York: Christian Literature, 1886.

Baegert, Jacob. *The Letters of Jacob Baegert, 1749–1761: Jesuit Missionary in Baja California*. Edited by Doyce B. Nunis Jr. Translated by Elsbeth Schulz-Bischof. Baja California Travels Series 45. Los Angeles: Dawson's Book Shop, 1982.

———. *Nachrichten von der amerikanischen Halbinsel Californien: Mit einem Zweyfachen Anhang falscher Nachrichten*. Mannheim: Gedruckt in der Churfürstl. Hof- und Academie-Buchdruckerey, 1772.

———. *Noticias de la peninsula Americana de California*. Primera Española ed. Edited by Paul Kirchhoff and Pedro R. Hendrichs. S.L.: Antigua Librería Robredo de José Porrúa e hijos, 1942.

———. *Observations in Lower California*. Berkeley: University of California Press, 1952.

Baegert, Jacob, Paul Kirchhoff, and Pedro R. Hendrichs. *Noticias de la peninsula americana de California*. Primera Española ed. S.L.: Antigua librería Robredo de José Porrúa e hijos, 1942.

Baltasar, Juan Antonio. *Carta de p. provincial Juan Antonio Balthassar, en que dà noticia de la exemplar vida, religiosas virtudes, y apostolicos trabajos del . . . p.*

Francisco Maria Picolo. MS 44103, Huntington Library, Rare Books. México, D.F.: 1752.

———. *Father Balthasar Visits the Sinaloa Missions, 1744–1745,* Rare Book, HL. Translated by Jerry Patterson. Frederick Beinecke, 1959.

Barba, Joseph. "Informe del padre Joseph Barba sobre el alzamiento de las Californias del año 1734 al Virrey Arzobispo Juan Antonio de Vizarrón y Eguiarreta April 26, 1735." BL, University of California, Berkeley, M-M 1717.

Barco, Miguel del, and Miguel Venegas. *Historia natural y crónica de la Antigua California.* Serie de historiadores y cronistas de Indias. First ed. Vol. 3. México, D.F.: Universidad Nacional Autónoma de Mexico, Instituto de Investigaciones Historicas, 1973.

Benedict XIV. *Doctrina de servorum Dei beatificatione et beatorum canonizatione.* Bruxellis: 1840.

Covarrubias Orozco, Sebastián de, Benito Remigio Noydens, and Martín de Riguer. *Tesoro de la lengua Castellana o Española.* Madrid: Luiz Sanchez, 1611. http://fondosdigitales.us.es/fondos/libros/765/1252/tesoro-de-la-lengua-castellana-o-espanola/. Accessed on May 8, 2017.

de la Vega, Garcilaso. *La Florida del Inca: Historia del Adelantado, Hernando de Soto, governador, y capitan general del Reino de la Florida. Y de otros heroicos caballeros, espanoles, e Indios.* Madrid: En la Oficina Real, y à Costa de Nicolas Rodriguez Franco, 1723.

Díaz del Castillo, Bernal. *The Discovery and Conquest of Mexico, 1517–1521.* Edited by Davíd Carrasco. Albuquerque: University of New Mexico Press, 2008.

El Nuevo Testamento de nuestro Señor Jesucristo que contiene los escritos evangélicos y apostólicos: Antigua versión de Casiodoro de Reina (1569), revisada por Cipriano de Valera (1602) y cotejada posteriormente con diversas traducciones, y con el texto griego: El libro de los Salmos. Madrid: Deposito Central de la Sociedad Bíblica, 1937.

Eusebius. *Eusebius' Ecclesiastical History Complete and Unabridged.* Peabody, Mass.: Hendrickson, 1998.

Figueroa, Francisco de. *Memorial presentado a su Magestad por el P. Francisco de Figueroa procurador de la provincias de las Indias de la Compañia de IESUS: Acerca del martyrio de nueve religiosos de la misma compañia.* Barcelona: Lorenço Déu, 1617.

Ford, Gerald R. "Toasts of President Ford and President Echeverria of Mexico at a Luncheon in Tubac, Arizona, October 21, 1974." In Gerhard Peters and John T. Woolley, eds. "The American Presidency Project." http://www.presidency.ucsb.edu/ws/?pid=4496, accessed on August 13, 2016.

Goddard, Samuel P., Jr. "Presentation of Statue, Honorable Samuel P. Goddard, Jr., Governor of Arizona" In United States Congress (89th 1st session:

1965). *Acceptance of the Statue of Eusebio Francisco Kino: Presented by the State of Arizona*. Washington, D.C.: U.S. Government Printing Office, 1965, 25–28.

Gonzalez, Luis, ed. *Etnologia y mision en la Pimeria Alta, 1715–1740: Informes y relaciones misioneras de Luis Xavier Velarde, Giuseppe Maria Genovese, Daniel Januske, Jose Agustin de Campos y Cristobal de Cañas*. Vol. 27. México, D.F.: Universidad Nacional Autonoma de Mexico, 1977.

Hurdaide, Capitan Diego Martínez. *Los PP. Jesuitas Juan Bautista Velasco y Hermano Francisco de Castro: Tapaguis y Conicaris; Conversion de los Mayos; Reduccion de Chinipa y Guazapares; Elogios a los PP. Julio Pascual y Manuel Martinez; Conquista del Hiaqui*, Ex. 648, Ms. (32/648), no. 1960, Archivo Franciscano, Biblioteca naciónal de Mexico (BN).

Ignatius of Loyola. *Ignatius of Loyola: The Spiritual Exercises and Selected Works*. Edited by George Ganns, S.J. New York: Paulist Press, 1991.

John of the Cross. *The Ascent of Mount Carmel*. Edited by David Lewis and Benedict Zimmerman. London: T. Baker, 1928.

Josephus, Flavius. *The Jewish War, Books V–VII*. Translated by Henry St. John Thackeray. Loeb Classical Library. Cambridge, Mass.: Harvard University Press, 1971.

Kappus, Marcus. "Letters of Marcus Antonius Kappus from Colonial America." In *Acta Neophilologica XXII*, Part 4, ed. Janez Stanonick. Ljubljana, Slovenia: University of Ljubljana, 1989.

———. "Letters of Marcus Antonius Kappus from Colonial America." In *Acta Neophilologica XIX*, Part 1. Edited by Janez Stanonick. Ljubljana, Slovenia: University of Ljubljana, 1986.

———. "Padre Eusebio Francisco Kino." *Libro de entierros de Santa María de Magdalena*, 1711, 15–16. Pinart Collection, BANC MSS M-M 414, Bancroft Library, University of California.

Kino, Eusebio Francisco. *Correspondencia del P. Kino con los generales de la Companía de Jesús, 1682–1707*. Edited by Ernest J. Burrus. Vol. 5. México, D.F.: Editorial Jus, 1961.

———. "Eusebio Kino, Cadiz, to Maria de Guadalupe Lancastre, Duchess of Aveiro." December 6, 1680. Kino Letters, Huntington Manuscripts, 9984. Huntington Library. San Marino, Calif.

———. *A Kino Keepsake: Facsimile of an Original Eusebio Francisco Kino Field Diary, Preserved at the University of Arizona Library, Describing Southern Arizona in 1699*. Tucson: Friends of the University of Arizona Library, 1991.

———. *Kino Reports to Headquarters: Supplement Facsimiles of Documents and Kino's 1683 Map of Lower California*. Edited by Ernest J. Burrus. Rome: Institutum Historicum Societatis Jesu, 1954.

———. *Kino's Biography of Francisco Javier Saeta, S.J.* Edited by Ernest J. Burrus. Translated by Charles W. Polzer. Vol. 9. Rome: Jesuit Historical Institute; St. Louis: St. Louis University, 1971.

———. *Kino's Historical Memoir of Pimería Alta: A Contemporary Account of the Beginnings of California, Sonora, and Arizona.* Edited and translated by Herbert Eugene Bolton. 2 Vols. New York: AMS, 1976. Originally published in Cleveland by Arthur H. Clark, 1919.

———. *Plan for the Development of Pimería Alta, Arizona and Upper California: A Report to the Mexican Viceroy.* Edited and translated by Ernest J. Burrus. Tucson: Arizona Pioneers' Historical Society, 1961.

———. *Vida del P. Francisco J. Saeta, S.J.: Sangre misionera en Sonora.* Figuras y episodios de la historia de Mexico. Edited by Ernest J. Burrus. México, D.F.: Editorial Jus, 1961.

Kino, Eusebio Francisco, and Maria de Guadalupe, the Duchess Aveiro. *Kino Writes to the Duchess: Letters of Eusebio Francisco Kino, S.J., to the Duchess of Aveiro; An Annotated English Translation, and the Text of the Non-Spanish Documents.* Edited and translated by Ernest J. Burrus. St. Louis: Jesuit Historical Institute, 1965.

———. *Kino escribe a la Duquesa: Correspondencia del P. Eusebio Francisco Kino con la duquesa de Aveiro y otros documentos.* Edited by Ernest J. Burrus. Madrid: J. Porrúa Turanzas, 1964.

Kino, Eusebio Francisco, and Juan Mateo Manje. *Kino and Manje, Explorers of Sonora and Arizona: Their Vision of the Future and a Study of Their Expeditions and Plans with an Appendix of Thirty Documents.* Edited and translated by Ernest J. Burrus. St. Louis: Jesuit Historical Institute, 1971.

Kino, Eusebio Francisco, and Isidro Otondo y Antillón. *First from the Gulf to the Pacific: The Diary of the Kino-Atondo Peninsular Expedition, December 14, 1684–January 13, 1685.* Jesuit Relations of Baja California. Vol. 16. Los Angeles: Dawson's Book Shop, 1969.

Kino, Eusebio Francisco, Robert L. Stevenson, and Jose de Estrada. *Stevenson and Kino* (Letters to the Duchess of Aveiro). Beinecke Rare Book and Manuscript Library. New Haven, Conn.: 1963.

Kino, Eusebio Francisco, Francisco Fernández del Castillo, and Emil Bóse. *Las misiones de Sonora y Arizona: Comprendiendo; La crónica titulada: "Favores celestiales" y la "relación diaria de la entrada al norueste."* Publicaciones del archivo general de la nacion 8. México, D.F.: Editorial "Cultura," 1913.

Kino Memorial Statue Committee. *The Kino Memorial Statue Competition: Prospectus for Sculptors.* Tucson, Ariz.: The Committee, 1963.

Linck, Wenceslaus. *Wenceslaus Linck's Reports and Letters, 1762–1778.* Edited by Ernest Burrus. Los Angeles: Dawson's Books, 1967.

Manje, Juan Mateo. *Diario de las exploraciones en Sonora: Luz de tierra incógnita*. Hermosillo: Gobierno del Estado de Sonora, 1985.

———. *Kino and Manje, Explorers of Sonora and Arizona: Their Vision of the Future; A Study of Their Expeditions and Plans with an Appendix of Thirty Documents*. Edited and translated by Ernest J. Burrus. Sources and Studies for the History of the Americas 10. St. Louis: Jesuit Historical Institute, 1971.

———. *Luz de tierra incógnita en la America septéntrional y diario de las exploraciones en Sonora*. Edited by Francisco Fernandez del Castillo. Publicaciones del archivo general de la nación 10. México, D.F.: Talleres Graficos de la Nacion, 1926.

———. *Unknown Arizona and Sonora, 1693–1721: From the Francisco Fernández Del Castillo Version of Luz de tierra incógnita*. Tucson: Arizona Silhouettes, 1954.

"Maps of the Jesuit Mission in Spanish America, 18th Century. Archives of the Society of Jesus, Rome, Hist. Soc. 150, I." *Imago Mundi* 15 (1960): 14–118.

"The Martyrdom of Polycarp." In *The Apostolic Fathers: Revised Greek Texts with Introductions and English Translations*, edited by Joseph Barber Lightfoot and J. R. Harmer, 131–44. Grand Rapids, Mich.: Baker, 1984.

Mateu, Jaime. "Destierro de los misioneros de la America septentrional española por Don A. S. olim misionero de Norogachic." Unpublished manuscript, Bolton papers, C-B 840, container 29, folder 22–23, Bancroft Library, University of California Berkeley.

Matthei, Mauro, O.S.B., and Rodrigo Moreno Jeria, eds. *Cartas e informes de misioneros Jesuitas extranjeros en hispanoamérica, 1751–1778*, quinta parte. Santiago: Pontificia Universidad Católica de Chile, 2001.

Mensajero del Sagrado Corazon. México, D.F., January 1901.

Middendorff, Bernhard (Bernardo). "Diario de la expulsión, 1767–1776." In *Cartas e informes de misioneros Jesuitas extranjeros en hispanoamérica, 1751–1778*, quinta parte, edited by Mauro Matthei, O.S.B., and Rodrigo Moreno Jeria, 224–27. Santiago: Pontificia Universidad Católica de Chile, 2001.

———. *Vertreibung und Gefangenschaft*. Vol. 2. Munster, 1845.

Mora, Francisco Xavier. "Informe de Francisco Xavier de Mora SJ al provincial Juan de Palacios, Arizpe, 1698." In *Kino: ¿Frustrado alguacil y mal misionero?* Edited and translated by Gabriel Gómez Padilla. Edición facsimilar. Guadalajara, Mexico: Universidad de Guadalajara; Culiacán, Mexico: Colegio de Sinaloa, 2004.

Nentvig, Juan. *Rudo Ensayo: A Description of Sonora and Arizona in 1764*. Edited and Translated by Albert F. Pradeau and Robert R. Rasmussen. Tucson: University of Arizona Press, 1980.

Neumann, Joseph. *Historia de las rebeliones de la sierra tarahumara, 1626–1724*. Edited by Luis González Rodríguez. Chihuahua: Editorial Camino, 1991.

———. *Historia de las sublevaciones Indias en la Tarahumara*. Edited by Bohumír Roedl and Simona Binková. Vol. 6. Prague: Universidad Carolina, 1994.
Nieremberg, Juan Eusebio. *Varones ilustres de la Compañia de Jesus*. Vol. 6. Bilboa: Administración del Mensajero del Corazon de Jesus, 1890.
Och, Joseph. *Missionary in Sonora: The Travel Reports of Joseph Och, S. J., 1755–1767*. Edited by Theodore Treutlein. San Francisco: California Historical Society, 1965.
Ortega, José de. *Apostolicos afanes de la Compañia de Jesus*. Edited by Francisco X. Fluvia. Reimpreso en Mexico: L. Alvarez y Alvarez de la Cadena, 1944.
———. *Historia del Nayarit, Sonora, Sinaloa y Ambas Californias: Que con el titulo de "Apostólicos afanes de la Compañia De Jesus, en la America septentrional" se Publicó anónima en Barcelona el año de 1754*. Mexico, D.F.: Tipografía de E. Abadiano, 1887.
Ortega, José de, Juan Antonio Baltasar, Francisco J. Fluviá, Juan F. López, Eusebio F. Kino, Ferdinand Konsag, Thomas Calvo, and Jesus Jáuregui. *Apostólicos afanes de la Compañía de Jesús en su provincia de Mexico*. México, D.F.: Centro Francés de Estudios Mexicanos y Centroamericanos: Instituto Nacional Indigenista, 1996.
Pérez de Ribas, Andrés. *Historia de los triumphos de Nuestra Santa Fee entre gentes las mas barbaras, y fieras del nueuo orbe: Conseguidos por los soldados de la milicia de la Compañia de Iesus en las missiones de la prouincia de Nueua-España; Refierense assimismo las costumbres, ritos, y supersticiones que vsauan estas gentes, sus puestos, y temples, las vitorias que de Algunas dellas Alcançaron con las armas los catolicos españoles, quando les obligaron à tomarlas, y las dichosas muertes de veinte religiosos de la Compañia, que en varios puestos, y a manos de varias naciones, dieron sus vidas por la predicacion del santo euangelio*. Edited by Alonso de Paredes. Madrid: Alonso de Paredes, Junto a los Estudios de la Compañia, 1645.
———. *History of the Triumphs of Our Holy Faith amongst the Most Barbarous and Fierce Peoples of the New World*. Edited by Daniel T. Reff. Translated by Daniel Reff, Maureen Ahern, and Richard Danford. Tucson: University of Arizona Press, 1999.
Pfefferkorn, Ignaz. *Sonora: A Description of the Province*. Tucson: University of Arizona Press, 1989.
Píccolo, Francisco Maria. *Informe del estado de la nueva Cristiandad de California, 1702, Y otros documentos*. Edited by Ernest J. Burrus. Mexico City: Ediciones Jose Porrúa Turanzas, 1967.
Píccolo, Francesco Maria, and Juan Manuel Basaldúa. *Copia de una carta que el P[adre] Francisco María Piccolo misionero de California escribió al P[Adre] Juan Manuel de Bassaldua rector del colegio de raum su fecha en Santa Rosalia a 10*

de enero del año de 1717, MS 1880. Edward E. Ayer Manuscript Collection and Newberry Library.

Priego, Antonio Lopez de, Rafael Zelis, and Francesco Saverio Clavigero. *Tesoros documentales de Mexico, siglo XVIII*. Edited by Mariano Cuevas. México, D.F.: Editorial Galatea, 1944.

Reina, Casiodoro de, and Cipriano de Valera. *La santa biblia: Antiguo y Nuevo Testamento*. Asunción Paraguay: Sociedades Bíblicas en América Latina, 1977.

Richeôme, Louis. *La peinture spirituelle, ou, l'art d'admirer, aimer et louer Dieu en toutes ses oeuvres, et tirer de toutes profit saluterre*. Lyon, 1611.

Sariñana y Cuenca, Isidro. *The Franciscan Martyrs of 1680*. Historical Society of New Mexico. Vol. 7. Santa Fe, N.M.: New Mexican Printing Company, 1906.

———. *Oración funebre, que dijo el Doctor D. Ysidro Sariñana, y Cuenca en las exequias de veinte y un religiosos de la regular ovservancia del seraphico P.s. Francisco, que murieron a manos de los indio apostatas de la Nuevo Mexico, en diez de Agosto de 1681*. México, D.F.: La Viuda de Bernardo Calderon, 1681.

Taraval, Sigismundo. "Elogios dee misioneros de Baja California: Baja California 1737." M-M 233A–33B, Bancroft Library, University of California Berkeley

———. *Historia de las misiones Jesuitas en California Baja desde su establecimiento hasta 1737*. "Journal Recounting Indian Uprisings in Baja California: 1734–1737." MS 1240. NL, Edward E. Ayer Manuscript Collection.

Taraval, Sigismundo, Charles Fletcher Lummis, William Gordon, and Edward E. Ayer. *Journal Recounting Indian Uprisings in Baja California, 1734*. Manuscript Collection and Newberry Library.

Thompson, Raymond H., ed. *A Jesuit Missionary in Eighteenth-Century Sonora: The Family Correspondence of Philipp Segesser*. Translated by Werner S. Zimmt and Robert E. Dahlquist. Albuquerque: University of New Mexico Press, 2014.

Tirsch, Ignacio. *The Drawings of Ignacio Tirsch: A Jesuit Missionary in Baja California*. Edited by Doyce B. Nunis. Los Angeles: Dawson's Book Shop, 1972.

United States Congress (89th Cong., 1st session: 1965). *Acceptance of the Statue of Eusebio Francisco Kino: Presented by the State of Arizona*. Washington, D.C.: U.S. Government Printing Office, 1965.

Venegas, Miguel. *A Natural and Civil History of California*. 2 vols. London: Rivington and Fletcher, 1759.

———. *Noticia de la California, y de su conquista temporal, y espiritual hasta el tiempo presente: Sacada de la historia manuscrita, formada en Mexico año de 1739 por el padre Miguèl Venegas, de la Compañía de Jesús; y de otras noticias, y relaciones antiguas, y modernas. Añadida de algunos mapas particulares, y uno general de la América septentrional, Assia oriental, y Mar del Sùr intermedio, formados sobre las memorias mas recientes, y exactas, que se publìcan juntamente. Dedicada al Rey Ntro. Señor por la provincia de Nueva-España, de la Compañia de Jesus,* edited by Andrés Marcos Burriel, S.J. 3 vols. Madrid: Imprenta de la viuda de Manuel Fernández, y del supremo consejo de la inquisición, 1757, Wilson Library (WL), Rare Book Collection, University of North Carolina at Chapel Hill.

Venegas, Miguel, Vivian C. Fisher, and W. Michael Mathes. *Obras Californianas del Padre Miguel Venegas, S.J.* La Paz, Mexico: Universidad Autónoma de Baja California Sur, 1978.

Venegas, Miguel, Ferdinand Konsag, Sebastián Vizcaino, and Andrés Marcos Burriel. *Noticia de la California y de su conquista temporal y espiritual hasta el tiempo presente: Sacada de la historia manuscrita, formada en Mexico a de 1739.* México, D.F.: Reimpreso por L. Alvarez y Alvarez de la Cadena, 1943.

Verbiest, Ferdinand. "Lettre du P. Ferdinand Verbiest, vice-provincial de la mission de Chine, a ses confreres de la Societe en Europe, le 15 aout 1678, de la residence imperial de Beijing." In *Courier Verbiest*, translated by Noel Golvers, vol. 5. Leuven: Ferdinand Verbiest Institute, 1993.

Verbiest, Ferdinand, Henri Josson, and Léopold Willaert. *Correspondance de Ferdinand Verbiest de la Compagnie de Jésus (1623–1688) directeur de l'Observatoire de Pékin.* Académie Royale des Sciences, des Lettres et des Beaux-Arts de Belgique, Brussels. Commission Royale d' Histoire. Publications in-Octavo. Vol. 49. Brussells: Palais des Académies, 1938.

Villaseñor y Sánchez. *Theatro americano, descripción general de los reinos y provincias de la Nueva España y sus jurisdicciones.* 2 vols. 2nd ed. México, D.F.: Editora Nacional, 1952.

Zambrano, Francisco, and Jose Gutiérrez Casillas. *Diccionario bio-bibliográfico de la Compánia de Jesus.* 14 Vols. México, D.F.: Editorial Tradicion, 1961–75.

Zubillaga, Félix, ed. *Monumenta Antiquae Floridae (1566–1572).* Monumenta Missionum Societatis Iesu 3. Rome: Monumenta Historica Societatis Iesu, 1946.

———. *Monumenta Mexicana.* Vol. 5. Rome: Institutum Historicum Societatis Iesu, 1981.

Zubillaga, Félix, and Miguel Angel Rodríguez, eds. *Monumenta Mexicana.* Vol. 5, 1592–1596. Rome: Monumenta Historica Soc. Iesu, 1973.

Secondary Sources

Acuña, Cruz G. *El Romance del Padre Kino.* Hermosillo, Sonora: Imprenta Regional, 1972.

Ahern, Maureen. "Visual and Verbal Sites: The Construction of Jesuit Martyrdom in Northwest New Spain in Andres Perez De Ribas' *Historia de los triumphos de Nuestra Santa Fe* (1645)." *Colonial Latin American Review* 8, no. 1 (June 1999): 7–33.

Alarcón, Alma Montero. *Jesuitas de Tepotzotlán: La expulsión y el amargo destierro.* Mexico City: Plaza y Valdes, 2009.

Albert, Salvador Bernabéu. *Expulsados del Infierno: El exilio de los misioneros Jesuitas de la península de California, 1767–1768.* Madrid: Consejo Superior de Investigaciones Científicas, 2008.

Alden, Dauril. *The Making of an Enterprise: The Society of Jesus in Portugal, Its Empire, and Beyond: 1540–1750.* Stanford, Calif.: Stanford University Press, 1996.

Allan, Bentley B. *Scientific Cosmology and International Orders.* Cambridge: Cambridge University Press, 2018.

Alonso, Martín, ed. *Enciclopedia del Idioma: Diccionario histórico y moderno de la lengua española (siglos XII al XX): Etimológico, tecnológico, regional e hispanoamericano.* Madrid: Aguilar, 1958.

Anderson, Benedict. *Imagined Communities: Reflections on the Origin and Spread of Nationalism.* Rev. ed. London: Verso, 2006.

Anderson, Emma. "Blood, Fire, and 'Baptism': Three Perspectives on the Death of Jean De Brébeuf, Seventeenth-Century Jesuit 'Martyr.'" In *Native Americans, Christianity, and the Reshaping of the American Religious Landscape,* edited by Joel W. Martin and Mark A. Nicholas, 125–58. Chapel Hill: University of North Carolina Press, 2010.

———. *The Death and Afterlife of the North American Martyrs.* Cambridge, Mass.: Harvard University Press, 2013.

Anidjar, Gil. *Blood: A Critique of Christianity.* New York: Columbia University Press, 2014.

Asad, Talal. *Genealogies of Religion: Discipline and Reasons of Power in Christianity and Islam.* Baltimore: Johns Hopkins University Press, 1993.

———. *On Suicide Bombing.* Wellek Library Lectures. New York: Columbia University Press, 2007.

Babcock, Matthew. *Apache Adaptation to Hispanic Rule.* Cambridge: Cambridge University Press, 2016.

Bahr, Donald M. "Pima and Papago Social Organization." In *Handbook of North American Indians: Southwest,* ed. Alfonso Ortiz, 10:187–92. Washington, D.C.: Smithsonian Institution, 1983.

Bailey, Gauvin Alexander. *Between Renaissance and Baroque: Jesuit Art in Rome, 1565–1610.* Toronto: University of Toronto Press, 2003.

Baldwin, Gordon Curtis. *Indians of the Southwest.* New York: Capricorn, 1973.

Bancroft, Hubert Howe, Henry Lebbeus Oak, J. J. Peatfield, and William Nemos. *The Works of Hubert Howe Bancroft*. Vol. 1, *History of the North Mexican States and Texas*. San Francisco: History Company, 1886.

Banker, Frederick William, and Walter Bauer. *A Greek-English Lexicon of the New Testament and Other Early Christian Literature*. Chicago: University of Chicago Press, 2000.

Bannon, John Francis. *Herbert Eugene Bolton: The Historian and the Man*. Tucson: University of Arizona Press, 1978.

———. "The Mission Frontier in Sonora (1620–1687)." In Charles W. Polzer, *The Jesuit Missions of Northern Mexico*, 164–70. New York: Garland, 1991.

———. *The Mission Frontier in Sonora, 1620–1687*. Philadelphia: United States Catholic Historical Society, 1955

Bargellini, Clara. "The Virgin of El Zape and Jesuit Missions in Nueva Vizcaya." In *The Oxford Handbook of Borderlands of the Iberian World*, edited by Danna L. Rojo and Cynthia Radding, 489–508. New York: Oxford University Press, 2019.

Bargellini, Clara, and Michael Komanecky. *The Arts of the Missions of Northern New Spain, 1600–1821*. Mexico City: Antiguo Coloegio de San Ildefonso, 2009.

Barnes, Timothy. *Constantine: Dynasty, Religion, and Power in the Later Roman Empire*. Oxford: Blackwell, 2011.

Barr, Juliana. "Geographies of Power: Mapping Indian Borders in the 'Borderlands' of the Early Southwest." *William and Mary Quarterly* 68, no. 1 (January 2011): 5–46.

———. *Peace Came in the Form of a Woman: Indians and Spaniards in the Texas Borderlands*. Chapel Hill: University of North Carolina Press, 2007.

Barr, Julianna, and Edward Countryman, eds. *Contested Spaces of Early America*. Philadelphia: University of Pennsylvania Press, 2014.

Bayne, Brandon. "Converting the Pacific: Jesuit Networks between New Spain and Asia." In *The Oxford Handbook of Borderlands of the Iberian World*, edited by Danna L. Rojo and Cynthia Radding, 786–816. New York: Oxford University Press, 2019.

———. "Recalling Kino: Remembering a Pimería Past, Reimagining an Arizona Present." *Southwestern Mission Research Center Revista* 164–65 (Fall–Winter 2010): 35–43.

———. "Willy-Nilly Baptisms and Chichimeca Freedoms: Jesuit Disputations, Indigenous Desires, and the O'odham Revolt of 1695." *Journal of Early Modern History* 21, no. 1 (January 2017): 9–37.

Beals, Ralph L. *The Aboriginal Culture of the Cáhita Indians*. New York: AMS, 1978.

———. *The Acaxee: A Mountain Tribe of Durango and Sinaloa.* Vol. 6. Berkeley, Calif.: University of California Press, 1933.

———. *The Comparative Ethnology of Northern Mexico before 1750.* New York: Cooper Square, 1973.

Binfield, Clyde. *Sainthood Revisioned: Studies in Hagiography and Biography.* Sheffield: Sheffield Academic, 1995.

Blackburn, Carole. *Harvest of Souls: The Jesuit Missions and Colonialism in North America, 1632–1650.* Montreal: McGill-Queen's University Press, 2000.

Blackhawk, Ned. "Towards an Indigenous Art History of the West: The Segesser Hide Paintings." In *Contested Spaces of Early America*, edited by Julianna Barr and Edward Countryman, 276–99. Philadelphia: University of Pennsylvania Press, 2014.

Blee, Lisa, and Jean M. O'Brien. *Monumental Mobility: The Memory Work of Massasoit.* Chapel Hill: University of North Carolina Press, 2019.

Bohme, Frederick G. "The Italians in Mexico: A Minority's Contribution." *Pacific Historical Review* 28, no. 1 (February 1959): 1–18.

Bolognani, Boniface. *Padre e Pioniere: Eusebio Francesco Chini, S.J., missionario, scrittore, geografo (1645–1711).* Trento: Biblioteca PP. Francescani, 1983.

———. *Pioneer Padre: A Biography of Eusebio Francisco Kino S.J., Missionary, Discoverer, Scientist, 1645–1711.* Sherbrooke: Editions Paulines, 1968.

Bolton, Herbert E. *The Padre on Horseback: A Sketch of Eusebio Francisco Kino, S.J., Apostle to the Pimas.* Chicago: Loyola University Press, 1986.

———. *Rim of Christendom: A Biography of Eusebio Francisco Kino, Pacific Coast Pioneer.* Tucson: University of Arizona Press, 1984.

———. *The Spanish Borderlands: A Chronicle of Old Florida and the Southwest.* Albuquerque: University of New Mexico Press, 1996.

Bolton, Herbert E., and John F. Bannon. *Bolton and the Spanish Borderlands.* Norman: University of Oklahoma Press, 1964.

Borges Morán, Pedro. *El envío de misioneros a América durante la época española.* Bibliotheca salmanticensis 20. Salamanca: Universidad Pontificia, 1977.

Boss, Julia. "Writing a Relic: The Uses of Hagiography in New France." In *Colonial Saints: Discovering the Holy in America, 1500–1800*, edited by Allan Greer and Jodi Bilinkoff, 153–68. New York: Routledge, 2003.

Boyarin, Daniel. *Dying for God: Martyrdom and the Making of Christianity and Judaism.* Stanford, Calif.: Stanford University Press, 1999.

Boyarin, Jonathan. *The Unconverted Self: Jews, Indians, and the Identity of Christian Europe.* Chicago: University of Chicago Press, 2009.

Brading, David. *Church and State in Bourbon Mexico: The Diocese of Michoacán, 1749–1810.* Cambridge: Cambridge University Press, 1994.

Brakke, David. *Demons and the Making of the Monk: Spiritual Combat in Early Christianity.* Cambridge, Mass.: Harvard University Press, 2005.

Brenneman, Dale S. "Bringing O'odham into the 'Pimeria Alta': Introduction." *Journal of the Southwest* 56, no. 2 (Summer 2014): 205–18.

Brown, Peter. *The Cult of the Saints: Its Rise and Fall in Late Antiquity.* Chicago: University of Chicago Press, 1982.

Brundage, W. Fitzhugh. *The Southern Past: A Clash of Race and Memory.* Cambridge, Mass.: Harvard University Press, 2005.

Buc, Phillipe. *Holy War, Martyrdom, and Terror: Christianity, Violence, and the West.* Philadelphia: University of Pennsylvania Press, 2015.

Budin, Stephanie Lynn. "Fertility and Gender in the Ancient Near East." In *Sex in Antiquity: Exploring Gender and Sexuality in the Ancient World*, edited by Mark Masterson, Nancy Sorkin Rabinowitz, and James Robson, 30–49. Abingdon: Routledge, 2011.

Burke, Marcus B., and Saint Peter's College Art Gallery. *Jesuit Art and Iconography, 1550–1800: Introductory Essay and Exhibition Catalogue.* Jersey City, N.J.: Saint Peter's College, Art Gallery, 1993.

Burrus, Ernest J. "La Autoridad máxima reconoce los restos del Padre Kino." In *El encuentro de los restos del Padre Kino.* Edited by Aristides Prat. Magdalena, Sonora: Publicaciones del Comité del Tricentenario del Arribo de Eusebio Francisco Kino a Sonora, 1987.

———, ed. *Francisco Javier Alegre: Historian of the Jesuits in New Spain, 1729–1788.* Rome: Institutum Historicum S.I, 1953.

———. "A General Conspectus." In *Kino's Biography of Francisco Javier Saeta, S.J.*, edited by Ernest J. Burrus, translated by Charles W. Polzer. Vol. 9. Rome: Jesuit Historical Institute; St. Louis: St. Louis University, 1971.

———, ed. *Jesuit Relations: Baja California, 1716–1762.* Los Angeles: Dawson's Book Shop, 1984.

———. *Kino and the Cartography of Northwestern New Spain.* Tucson: Arizona Pioneers' Historical Society, 1965.

———. "Kino, Historian's Historian." *Arizona and the West* 4, no. 2 (Summer 1962): 145–56.

———. "Kino's Relative, Father Martino Martini, S. J.: A Comparison of Two Outstanding Missionaries." *Neue Zeitschrift für Missionswissenschaft* 31 (1975): 100–109.

———. *La obra cartográfica de la provincia mexicana de la Compañía de Jesús, 1567–1967.* Madrid: Ediciones José Porrúa Turanzas, 1967.

———. "Mexican Historical Documents in the Central Jesuit Archives." *Manuscripta: A Journal for Manuscript Research* 12, no. 3 (November 1968).

Burrus, Ernest J., and Felix Zubillaga, eds. *El Noroeste de Mexico: Documentos sobre las misiones Jesuíticas, 1600–1769.* Mexico, D.F.: Universidad Nacional Autónoma de Mexico Instituto de Investigaciones Históricas, 1986.

———. *Misiones Mexicanas de la Compañía de Jesús, 1618–1745: Cartas e informes conservados en la "Colección Mateu."* Vol. 41. Madrid: J. Porrúa Turanzas, 1982.

Bustamante, Aarón Grageda. *Seis expulsiones y un Adiós: Despojos y exclusiones en Sonora*. Primera ed. México, D.F.: Plaza y Valdés, 2003.

Canny, Nicholas P. "The Ideology of English Colonization: From Ireland to America." *William and Mary Quarterly* 30, no. 4 (October 1973): 575–98.

Casillas, Jose Gutiérrez, S.J. *Martires Jesuitas de la provincia de Mexico*. 2nd ed. México, D.F.: Tradición, 1981.

Cañizares-Esguerra, Jorge. *How to Write the History of the New World*. Palo Alto, Calif.: Stanford University Press, 2002.

———. *Puritan Conquistadors: Iberianizing the Atlantic, 1550–1700*. Stanford, Calif.: Stanford University Press, 2006.

Carrasco, David. "Jaguar Christians in the Contact Zone." In *Beyond Primitivism: Indigenous Religious Traditions and Modernity*, edited by Jacob Olupona, 128–38. New York: Routledge, 2003.

———. *Religions of Mesoamerica*. 2nd ed. Long Grove, Ill.: Waveland, 2013.

Carrasco, David, Leonardo López Luján, and Eduardo Matos Moctezuma. *Breaking through Mexico's Past: Digging the Aztecs with Eduardo Matos Moctezuma*. Albuquerque: University of New Mexico Press, 2007.

Carrasco, David, and Scott Sessions. *Cave, City, and Eagle's Nest: An Interpretive Journey through the Mapa de Cuauhtinchan no. 2*. Albuquerque: University of New Mexico Press. Published in collaboration with the David Rockefeller Center for Latin American Studies and the Peabody Museum of Archaeology and Ethnology, Cambridge, Mass.: Harvard University, 2007.

Castelli, Elizabeth. *Martyrdom and Memory: Early Christian Culture Making*. New York: Columbia University Press, 2004.

Cerezo-Román, Jessica I. "Pathways to Personhood: Cremation as a Social Practice among the Tucson Basin Hohokam." In *Transformation by Fire: The Archeology of Cremation in Cultural Context*, edited by Ian Kujit, Colin P. Quinn, and Gabriel Cooney, 150–55. Tucson: University of Arizona Press, 2014.

Certeau, Michel de. *The Practice of Everyday Life*. Translated by Steven Rendell. Berkeley: University of California Press, 2011.

Chidester, David, and Edward Tabor Linenthal, eds. *American Sacred Space*. Bloomington: Indiana University Press, 1995

Clark, Elizabeth A. *Reading Renunciation: Asceticism and Scripture in Early Christianity*. Princeton, N.J.: Princeton University Press, 1999.

Classen, Albrecht. *Early History of the Southwest through the Eyes of German-Speaking Jesuit Missionaries: A Transcultural Experience in the Eighteenth Century*. Lanham, Md.: Lexington, 2013.

Clendinnen, Inga. *Ambivalent Conquests: Maya and Spaniard in Yucatan, 1517–1570*. Cambridge: Cambridge University Press, 1987.
Clossey, Luke. *Salvation and Globalization in the Early Jesuit Missions*. New York: Cambridge University Press, 2008.
Comaroff, Jean, and John L. Comaroff. *Of Revelation and Revolution*. Chicago: University of Chicago Press, 1991.
Conover, Cornelius. "Saintly Biography and the Cult of San Felipe de Jesús in Mexico City, 1597–1697." *Americas* 67, no. 4 (April 2011): 441–66.
Constable, Olivia Remie, and Damian Zurro, ed. *Medieval Iberia: Readings from Christian, Muslim, and Jewish Sources*. Philadelphia: University of Pennsylvania Press, 2012.
Cook, Noble David. *Born to Die: Disease and New World Conquest, 1492–1650*. Cambridge: Cambridge University Press, 1998.
Corominas, Joan, and José Pascual, eds. *Diccionario crítico etimológico castellano e hispánico*. Madrid: Editorial Gredos, 1980, 131.
Coronado, Moisés E. *Kino y Salvatierra en la conquista de las Californias*. La Paz, B.C. Sur: Fonapas, 1981.
Cronin, Michael. *Translation and Globalization*. New York: Routledge, 2003.
Crosby, Harry. *Antigua California: Mission and Colony on the Peninsular Frontier, 1697–1768*. Albuquerque: University of New Mexico Press, 1994.
Crumrine, N. Ross. *The Mayo Indians of Sonora: A People Who Refuse to Die*. Tucson: University of Arizona Press, 1977.
Cuello, José. "Beyond the 'Borderlands' Is the North of Colonial Mexico: A Latin-Americanist Perspective to the Study of the Mexican North and the United States Southwest." *Proceedings of the Pacific Coast Council on Latin American Studies* 9 (1982): 1–24.
Cuevas, Mariano. *Historia de la iglesia de Mexico*. Vol. 2. Mexico City: Imprenta del Asilo "Patricio Sanz," 1922.
Cushner, Nicholas P. *Jesuit Ranches and the Agrarian Development of Colonial Argentina, 1650–1767*. Albany: State University of New York Press, 1983.
———. *Philippine Jesuits in Exile: The Journals of Francisco Puig, S.J., 1768–1770*. Vol. 24. Rome: Institutum Historicum, 1964.
Davidson, Chandler. Review of *Red Scare! Right-Wing Hysteria, Fifties Fanaticism, and Their Legacy in Texas*. *Journal of Southern History* 52, no. 2 (May 1986): 327–28.
Dávila y Arrillaga, José Mariano, and Francisco Javier Alegre. *Continuación de la historia de la Compañia de Jesús en Nueva España del P. Francisco Javier Alegre*. Puebla: Imp. del Colegio Pio de Artes y Oficios, 1888.
de Grazia, Ted. *De Grazia and Padre Kino: Depicting Memorable Events in the Life and Times of the Heroic, Historic and Immortal Priest-Colonizer of the Southwestern Desert*. Tucson, Ariz.: DeGrazia Gallery in the Sun, 1979.

de Guibert, Joseph. *The Jesuits, their Spiritual Doctrine and Practice: A Historical Study* [Spiritualité de la Compagnie de Jésus: Esquisse historique]. Chicago: Institute of Jesuit Sources, 1972.

de las Casas, (Frey) Bartolome. *Del unico modo de atraer a todos los pueblos a la verdadera Religión*. Edited by Agustín Millares Carlo and Atenógenes Santamaria. México, D.F.: Fondo de Cultura Económica, 1942.

———. *The Only Way*. Edited by Helen Rand Parish and Francis Park Sullivan, S.J. Mahway, N.J.: Paulist Press, 1992.

de la Teja, Jesus F., and Ross Frank, eds. *Choice, Persuasion, and Coercion: Social Control on Spain's North American Frontiers*. Albuquerque: University of New Mexico Press, 2005.

de la Torre Curiel, José Refugio. "Santidad y martirio en testimonios jesuitas y franciscanos sobre la cristianización del noroeste novohispano, siglos XVII y XVIII." *Relaciones* 37, no. 145 (Winter 2016): 63–107.

———. *Twilight of the Mission Frontier: Shifting Interethnic Alliances and Social Organization in Sonora, 1768–1855*. Stanford, Calif.: Stanford University Press, 2013.

Deck, Allan Figueroa. *Francisco Javier Alegre: A Study in Mexican Literary Criticism*. Sources and Studies for the History of the Americas 13. Rome and Tucson: Jesuit Historical Institute, 1976.

Decorme, Gerard. *Historia de la Compañia de Jesús en la República mexicana durante el siglo XIX*. Chihuahua, Mexico: J. M. Yguiniz, 1959.

———. *La Obra de los Jesuítas mexicanos durante la época colonial, 1572–1767*. México, D.F.: Antigua Librería Robredo de J. Porrúa e Hijos, 1941.

———. *Mártires Jesuitas de la provincia de Mexico*. Guadalajara: E. Acevez, 1957.

Deeds, Susan M. *Defiance and Deference in Mexico's Colonial North: Indians under Spanish Rule in Nueva Vizcaya*. Austin: University of Texas Press, 2003.

del Río, Ignacio. *A la diestra mano de las Indias: Descubrimiento y ocupación colonial de la Baja California*. México, D.F.: Universidad Nacionál Autónoma de Mexico, 1990.

———. *Conquista y aculturación en la California Jesuítica, 1697–1768*. México, D.F.: Universidad Nacional Autónoma de Mexico Instituto de Investigaciones Históricas, 1998.

———. *Crónicas Jesuíticas de la antigua California*. Biblioteca del estudiante universitario. Vol. 132. México, D.F.: Universidad Nacionál Autónoma de México, 2000.

———. *El Régimen Jesuítico de la antingua California*. México, D.F.: Universidad Nacionál Autónoma de México, 2003.

del Río, Ignacio, and María Eugenia Altable Fernández. *Breve historia de Baja California Sur*. México, D.F.: El Colegio de México, 200.

del Valle, Ivonne. *Escribiendo desde los márgenes: Colonialismo y Jesuitas en el siglo XVIII*. México, D.F.: Siglo XXI Editores, 2009.

di Peso, Charles C., and Jonathan E. Reyman. *The Gran Chichimeca: Essays on the Archaeology and Ethnohistory of Northern Mesoamerica*. Worldwide Archaeology Series 12. Aldershot, Hampshire, UK: Avebury, 1995.

di Peso, Charles C., Anne I. Woosley, and John C. Ravesloot. *Culture and Contact: Charles C. Di Peso's Gran Chichimeca*. 1st ed. Vol. 2. Albuquerque: Amerind Foundation and University of New Mexico Press, 1993.

Ditchfield, Simon. "Martyrs on the Move: Relics as Vindicators of Local Diversity in the Tridentine Church." In *Studies in Church History* 30 (1993): 283–94.

———. "Tridentine Worship and the Cult of the Saints." In *Cambridge History of Christianity: Reform and Expansion 1500–1660*, edited by R. Po-chia Hsia, 6:206–15. Cambridge: Cambridge University Press, 2007.

Dobyns, Henry F., Paul H. Ezell, Alden W. Jones, and Greta S. Ezell. "What Were Nixoras?" *Southwestern Journal of Anthropology* 16, no. 2 (Summer 1960): 230–58.

Domby, Adam. *The False Cause: Fraud, Fabrication, and White Supremacy in Confederate Memory*. Charlottesville: University of Virginia Press, 2020.

Donohue, John A. *After Kino: Jesuit Missions in Northwestern New Spain, 1711–1767*. St. Louis: Jesuit Historical Institute, 1969.

Ducrue, Benno F. *Ducrue's Account of the Expulsion of the Jesuits from Lower California (1767–1769): An Annotated English Translation of Benno Ducrue's Relatio Expulsionis*. Edited by Ernest J. Burrus. Sources and Studies for the History of the Americas 2. St. Louis: Jesuit Historical Institute, 1967.

Dunbar-Ortiz, Roxanne. *An Indigenous Peoples' History of the United States*. Boston: Beacon Press, 2014.

Dunne, Peter Masten. *Andrés Pérez De Ribas, Pioneer Black Robe of the West Coast, Administrator, Historian*. Vol. 25. New York: United States Catholic Historical Society, 1951.

———. *Black Robes in Lower California*. Berkeley: University of California Press, 1968.

———. "The Expulsion of the Jesuits from New Spain." *Mid-America: An Historical Review* 19, no. 8 (January 1937): 13n30.

———. *Jacobo Sedelmayr: Missionary, Frontiersman, Explorer in Arizona and Sonora*. Tucson: Arizona Pioneers' Historical Society, 1955.

———. "Jesuits Begin the West Coast Missions." *Pacific Historical Review* 4, no. 2 (June 1935): 131–42.

———. *Las Antiguas misiones de la Tarahumara*. México, D.F.: Editorial Jus, 1958.

———. *Pioneer Jesuits in Northern Mexico*. Westport, Conn.: Greenwood, 1979. Originally published in 1944 in Berkeley: University of California Press.

Dunne, Peter Masten, and Juan Antonio Baltasar. *Juan Antonio Balthasar: Padre Visitador to the Sonora Frontier, 1744–1745; Two Original Reports*. Tucson: Arizona Pioneers' Historical Society, 1957.

Dunne, Peter Masten, and Herbert Eugene Bolton. *Pioneer Black Robes on the West Coast*. Berkeley: University of California Press, 1940.

Duval, Kathleen. *The Native Ground: Indians and Colonists in the Heart of the Continent*. Philadelphia: University of Pennsylvania Press, 2006.

Edgerton, Samuel Y., and Jorge Pérez de Lara. *Theaters of Conversion: Religious Architecture and Indian Artisans in Colonial Mexico*. 1st ed. Albuquerque: University of New Mexico Press, 2001.

Eire, Carlos. *From Madrid to Purgatory: The Art and Craft of Dying in Sixteenth-Century Spain*. Cambridge: Cambridge University Press, 1995.

Fajardo, José del Rey. *La expulsión de los Jesuítas de Venezuela, 1767–1768*. San Cristóbal: Universidad Católica del Tachira, 1990.

Farmer, David Hugh, ed. *The Oxford Dictionary of Saints*. 4th ed. Oxford: Oxford University Press, 1997.

Fernandez de la Fuente, Juan. "A Campaign against the Pimas." In *The Presidio and Militia on the Northern Frontier of New Spain*. Vol. 1, 1570–1700, edited by Thomas H. Naylor and Charles W. Polzer, 582–718. Tucson: University of Arizona Press, 1986.

Ferrand de Almeida, André. "Samuel Fritz and the Mapping of the Amazon." *Imago Mundi* 55 (2003): 113–19.

Findlen, Paula. *Athanasius Kircher: The Last Man Who Knew Everything*. New York: Routledge, 2004.

Fish, Suzanne K., and Paul R. Fish. *The Hohokam Millennium*. Santa Fe, N.M.: School for Advanced Research Press, 2007.

Fletcher, Richard. *The Barbarian Conversion: From Paganism to Christianity*. Berkeley: University of California Press, 1999.

Folsom, Raphael Brewster. *The Yaquis and the Empire: Violence, Spanish Imperial Power, and Native Resilience in Colonial Mexico*. New Haven, Conn.: Yale University Press, 2014.

Fontana, Bernard. "Afterword." In Jorge H. Olvera, *Finding Father Kino: The Discovery of the Remains of Father Eusebio Francisco Kino, S.J., 1965–1966*, 245–52. Tucson: Southwestern Mission Research Center, 1998.

Forbes, Jack. *Apache, Navajo, and Spaniard*. Norman: University of Oklahoma Press, 1960.

Foucault, Michel. *The Order of Things: An Archaeology of the Human Sciences*. New York: Vintage, 1973.

France, Peter, and William St. Clair. *Mapping Lives: The Uses of Biography*. British Academy Centenary Monographs. Oxford: Oxford University Press for the British Academy, 2002.

Frend, W. H. C. *Martyrdom and Persecution in the Early Church: A Study of a Conflict from the Maccabees to Donatus*. New York: New York University Press, 1967.

Freeman, Charles. *Holy Bones, Holy Dust: How Relics Shaped the History of Medieval Europe*. New Haven, Conn.: Yale University Press, 2011.

Fuentes, Marisa J. *Dispossessed Lives: Enslaved Women, Violence, and the Archive*. Philadelphia: University of Pennsylvania Press, 2016.

Galindo, David Rex. *To Sin No More: Franciscans and Conversion in the Hispanic World, 1683–1830*. Stanford, Calif.: Stanford University Press, 2018.

Gillingham, Paul. *Cuahtémoc's Bones: Forging National Identity in Modern Mexico*. Albuquerque: University of New Mexico Press, 2011.

Green, Bryan. "Apostles and Men of Learning: Miguel Venegas, Andrés Marcos Burriel, and the Jesuit Vocation for Natural History." *Journal of Jesuit Studies* 4 (2017): 28–55.

Gregory, Brad. *Salvation at Stake: Christian Martyrdom in Early Modern Europe*. Cambridge, Mass.: Harvard University Press, 1999.

Goldsmith, Jane ten Brink, ed. *Jesuit Art in North American Collections: Exhibition 7 March–16 June 1991*. Milwaukee: Patrick and Beatrice Haggerty Museum of Art, Marquette University, 1991.

Golvers, Noël. *The Christian Mission in China in the Verbiest Era: Some Aspects of the Missionary Approach*. Louvain Chinese Studies 6. Leuven: Ferdinand Verbiest Foundation, K. U. Leuven, 1999.

———. "The Missionary and His Concern about Consolidation and Continuity." In *A Lifelong Dedication to the China Mission: Essays Presented in Honor of Father Jeroom Heyndrickx, CICM*. Edited by Noel Golvers and Sara Lievens. Leuven Chinese Studies 17. Leuven: Ferdinand Verbiest Institute, 2000.

González Rodríguez, Luis. "La etnografía Acaxee de Hernando de Santarén." *Tlalocan* 8 (1980): 355–94.

Goodich, Michael. *Vita Perfecta: The Ideal of Sainthood in the Thirteenth Century*. Monographien zur Geschichte des Mittelalters 25. Stuttgart: A. Hiersemann, 1982.

Gose, Peter. "Converting the Ancestors: Indirect Rule, Settlement Consolidation, and the Struggle over Burial in Colonial Peru, 1532–1614." In *Conversion: Old Worlds and New*, edited by Kenneth Mills and Anthony Grafton, 140–74. Rochester, N.Y.: University of Rochester Press, 2003.

Gradie, Charlotte M. "Discovering the Chichimecas." *Americas* 51, no. 1 (July 1994): 67–88.

———. *The Tepehuan Revolt of 1616: Militarism, Evangelism and Colonialism in Seventeenth-Century Nueva Vizcaya*. Salt Lake City: University of Utah Press, 2000.

Grafton, Anthony, April Shelford, and Nancy G. Siraisi. *New Worlds, Ancient Texts: The Power of Tradition and the Shock of Discovery.* Cambridge, Mass.: Belknap Press of Harvard University Press, 1992.

Greer, Allan. "Colonial Saints: Gender, Race, and Hagiography in New France." *William and Mary Quarterly* 57, no. 2. (April 2000): 323.

———. "Towards a Comparative Study of Jesuit Missions and Indigenous Peoples." In *Native Christians: Modes and Effects of Christianity among Indigenous People of the Americas*, edited by Aparecida Vilaça and Robin Wright. Farnham, UK: Ashgate, 2009.

Greer, Allan, and Jodi Bilinkoff, eds. *Colonial Saints: Discovering the Holy in America, 1500–1800.* New York: Routledge, 2003.

Griffith, James S. *Beliefs and Holy Places: A Spiritual Geography of the Pimería Alta.* Tucson: University of Arizona Press, 1992.

———. "Images and Notes Concerning the Traditional Material Culture of the Easter Ceremony in Northern Sinaloa." *Journal of the Southwest* 32, no. 1 (Spring 1990): 36–67.

Guibert, Joseph, de. *The Jesuits, Their Spiritual Doctrine and Practice: A Historical Study* [Spiritualité de la Compagnie de Jésus: Esquisse historique]. Chicago: Institute of Jesuit Sources, 1972.

Gutiérrez, Ramon A. *When Jesus Came, the Corn Mothers Went Away: Marriage, Sexuality, and Power in New Mexico, 1500–1846.* Stanford, Calif.: Stanford University Press, 1991.

Hackel, Steven W. *Children of Coyote, Missionaries of Saint Francis: Indian-Spanish Relations in Colonial California, 1769–1850.* Chapel Hill: Omohundro Institute and University of North Carolina Press, 2005.

Hanke, Lewis, and Jane M. Rausch, eds. *People and Issues in Latin American History from Independence to the Present: Sources and Interpretations.* 3rd ed. Princeton, N.J.: Markus Wiener, 2006.

Hartman, Saidiya. *Scenes of Subjection: Terror, Slavery, and Self-Making in Nineteenth-Century America.* New York: Oxford University Press, 1997.

Hellen, Michael. *Uncovering Identity in Mortuary Analysis: Community-Sensitive Methods for Identifying Group Affiliation in Historical Cemeteries.* Walnut Creek, Calif.: Left Coast, 2012.

Hill, J. Brett. *From Huhugam to Hohokam: Heritage and Archaeology in the American Southwest.* Lanham, Md.: Lexington, 2019.

Hills, Helen. "Demure Transgression: Portraying Female Saints in Post-Tridentine Italy." *Early Modern Women: An Interdisciplinary Journal* 3 (2008): 153–208.

Hock, Andreas. "Christ Is the Parade: A Comparative Study of the Triumphal Procession in 2 Cor 2:14 and Col 2:15." *Biblica* 88, no. 1 (January 1, 2007): 110.

Hsia, Florence C. "Mathematical Martyrs, Mandarin Missionaries, and Apostolic Academicians: Telling Institutional Lives." In *Institutional Culture in Early Modern Society*, edited by Anne Goldgar and Robert I. Frost, 17–21. Leiden: Brill, 2004.

———. *Sojourners in a Strange Land: Jesuits and their Scientific Missions in Late Imperial China*. Chicago: University of Chicago Press, 2009.

Hsia, R. Po-Cha. *Jesuit in the Forbidden City: Matteo Ricci, 1552–1610*. Oxford: Oxford University Press, 2013.

———. *Noble Patronage and Jesuit Missions: Maria Theresia von Fugger-Wellenburg (1690–1762) and Jesuit Missionaries in China and Vietnam*. Monumenta Historica Societatis Iesu 2. Rome: Institutum Historicum Societatis Iesu, 2006.

———. *Reform and Expansion 1500–1660*. Cambridge History of Christianity 6. Cambridge: Cambridge University Press, 2007.

———. *The World of Catholic Renewal, 1540–1770*. New York: Cambridge University Press, 1998.

Horn, Rebecca. *Postconquest Coyoacán: Nahua-Spanish Relations in Central Mexico, 1519–1650*. Stanford, Calif.: Stanford University Press, 1997.

Hu-DeHart, Evelyn. "Introduction: Transpacific Confrontation / Confrontación transpacífica." *Review: Literature and Arts of the Americas* 39, no. 1 (2006): 3–12.

———. *Missionaries, Miners, and Indians: Spanish Contact with the Yaqui Nation of Northwestern New Spain, 1533–1820*. Tucson: University of Arizona Press, 1981.

Hurtado, Albert. "Parkmanizing the Spanish Borderlands: Bolton, Turner, and the Historians' World." *Western Historical Quarterly* 26, no. 2 (Summer 1995): 149–67.

Ives, Ronald L. "Father Kino's 1697 Entrada to the Casa Grande Ruin in Arizona: A Reconstruction." *Arizona and the West* 15, no. 4 (Winter 1973): 345–70.

Jackson, Robert H. *Missions and the Frontiers of Spanish America: A Comparative Study of the Impact of Environmental, Economic, Political, and Socio-Cultural Variations on the Missions in the Rio de la Plata Region and on the Northern Frontier of New Spain*. Scottsdale, Ariz.: Pentacle, 2005.

———, ed. *New Views of Borderlands History*. Albuquerque: University of New Mexico Press, 1998.

Jacobs, Andrew S. *Remains of the Jews: The Holy Land and Christian Empire in Late Antiquity*. Stanford, Calif.: Stanford University Press, 2004.

Jelinek, Lauren E., and Dale S. Brenneman. "Population Dynamics in the Pimería Alta, AD 1650–1750." In *New Mexico and the Pimería Alta: The Colonial Period in the American Southwest*, edited by John G. Douglass and William M. Graves, 170–73. Boulder: University of Colorado Press, 2017.

Johnson, Harry Prescott. "Diego Martínez de Hurdaide: Defender of the Northwestern Frontier of New Spain." *Pacific Historical Review* 11, no. 2 (June 1942): 169–85.

Johnson, Luis Encinas. "Aquel que fue constructor de Pueblos." In *El Encuentro de los restos de Padre Kino*, ed. Arístides Prat, 14. Magdalena, Sonora: Publicaciones del Comité del Tricentenario del Arribo de Eusebio Francisco Kino a Sonora, 1987.

Kelley, Nicole. "Philosophy as Training for Death: Reading the Ancient Christian Martyr Acts as Spiritual Exercises." *Church History* 75, no. 4 (December 2006): 723–31.

Kessell, John L. *Mission of Sorrows: Jesuit Guevavi and the Pimas, 1691–1767.* Tucson: University of Arizona Press, 1970.

Klassen, Pamela. "Secular Christian Power and the Spiritual Invention of Nations." *The Immanent Frame*, https://tif.ssrc.org/2017/06/06/secular-christian-power-and-the-spiritual-invention-of-nations/. Accessed on July 28, 2018.

Knobloch, Frieda. *The Culture of Wilderness: Agriculture as Colonization in the American West.* Chapel Hill: University of North Carolina Press, 1996.

Kohut, Karl, and Maria Cristina Torales Pacheco. *Desde los confines de los imperios Ibéricos: Los Jesuitas de habla alemana en las misiones Americanas, Simposio "Diversidad en la unidad: Los Jesuitas e habla alemana en Iberoamérica, siglos XVI–XVIII en Mexico City, 2005."* Vol. 16. Madrid and Frankfurt am Main: Iberoamericana and Vervuert, 2007.

Křížová, Markéta. "Meeting the Other in the New World: Jesuit Missionaries from the Bohemian Province in America." *Historie—Otázky—Problémy: European Civilisation and the World between Conflicts, Cooperation, and Dialogue* 2 (2016): 35–46.

Lenka, Stolarova, and Vlnas Vit. *Karel Skreta, 1610–1674: His Work and his Era.* Prague: National Gallery, 2010.

León de la Barra, L. *Vida y obra del padre Kino.* México, D.F: Secretaría de Educación Pública Subsecretaría de Asuntos Culturales, 1965.

León García, Ricardo. *Misiones Jesuitas en la Tarahumara (siglo XVIII).* Vol. 6. Ciudad Juárez, Chihuahua: Universidad Autónoma de Ciudad Juárez, 1992.

Lewis, Clifford Merle, Albert J. Loomie, and Virginia Historical Society. *The Spanish Jesuit Mission in Virginia, 1570–1572.* Chapel Hill: Published for the Virginia Historical Society by the University of North Carolina Press, 1953.

Leyerle, Blake. "Blood Is Seed." *Journal of Religion* 81, no. 1 (January 2001): 26–48.

Liebmann, Matthew. *Revolt: An Archeological History of Pueblo Resistance and Revitalization in 17th Century New Mexico.* Tucson: University of Arizona Press, 2012.

Lockhart, James, and Stuart B. Schwartz. *Early Latin America*. New York: Cambridge University Press 1983.
Lockwood, Frank C. *Story of the Spanish Missions of the Middle Southwest: Being a Complete Survey of the Missions Founded by Padre Eusebio Francisco Kino in the Seventeenth Century and Later Enlarged and Beautified by the Franciscan Fathers during the Last Part of the Eighteenth Century*. Santa Ana, Calif.: Fine Arts Press, 1934.
———. *With Padre Kino on the Trail*. Tucson: University of Arizona, 1934.
Lomnitz, Claudio. *Death and the Idea of Mexico*. New York: Zone, 2005.
López Estrada, Francisco. *Poema del Cid: Texto completo en Castellano actual*. Odres Nuevos. Ed. conmemorativa del VIII centenario del manuscrito de Per Abbat ed. Madrid: Editorial Castalia, 2007.
———. *Poema del Cid: Texto completo en Castellano actual*. Ed. conmemorativa del VIII centenario del manuscrito de Per Abbat. Madrid: Editorial Castalia, 2007.
López-Menéndez, Marisol. *Miguel Pro: Martyrdom, Politics, and Society in Twentieth-Century Mexico*. Lanham, Md.: Lexington, 2016.
Loureiro Dias, Camila. "Jesuit Maps and Political Discourse: The Amazon River of Father Samuel Fritz." *Americas* 69, no. 1 (July 2012): 107–16.
Louth, Andrew. *The Origins of the Christian Mystical Tradition: From Plato to Denys*. 2nd ed. Oxford: Oxford University Press, 2007.
Lumholtz, Carl. *New Trails in Mexico: An Account of One Year's Exploration in North-Western Sonora, Mexico, and South-Western Arizona*. New York: Charles Scribner's Sons, 1912.
Luo, Robert Fang. *Accommodating Jesuit Successes in China: Evaluating Matteo Ricci's Mission House and Ferdinand Verbiest's Calendar*. Cambridge, Mass.: Harvard University Press, 2001.
MacCormack, Sabine. *On the Wings of Time: Rome, the Incas, Spain, and Peru*. Princeton, N.J.: Princeton University Press, 2006.
Maggs Bros. *Bibliotheca Americana et Philippina*. London: Maggs Brothers, 1922.
Magnaghi, Russell M. *Herbert E. Bolton and the Historiography of the Americas*. Westport, Conn.: Greenwood, 1998.
Manning, Patricia W. *Voicing Dissent in Seventeenth-century Spain: Inquisition, Social Criticism and Theology in the Case of El Criticón*. Leiden: Brill, 2009.
Marak, Andrae M. "Little House on the Prairie in Sonora: Borderlands, the Comcáac, and World History." *World History Connected* 18, no. 1 (February 2021): 11–12.
Marti, Julio César Montané. *La expulsión de los Jesuitas de Sonora*. México, D.F.: Contrapunto, 1999. Available online at http://www.monografias.com/trabajos27/jesuitas-sonora/jesuitas-sonora.shtml. Accessed November 11, 2016.

Martin, Joel W., and Mark A. Nicholas, eds. *Native Americans, Christianity, and the Reshaping of the American Religious Landscape*. Chapel Hill: University of North Carolina Press, 2010.

Martín, María Bernal. "El triunfo de S. Ignacio y S. Francisco Javier." *Revista del antiguo teatro escolar hispánico*, no. 1 (2005): 305–6. Accessed July 15, 2015. http://parnaseo.uv.es/ars/teatresco/revista/Revista1/MBernalTriunfodeIgnacioySFcoJ.htm.

Martínez, Ignacio. "The Paradox of Friendship: Loyalty and Betrayal on the Sonoran Frontier." *Journal of the Southwest* 56, no. 2 (Summer 2014): 319–44.

Martínez, John J. *Not Counting the Cost: Jesuit Missionaries in Colonial Mexico; A Story of Struggle, Commitment, and Sacrifice*. Chicago: Jesuit Way, 2001.

Martínez Serna, José Gabriel. "Procurators and the Making of the Jesuit Atlantic Network." In *Soundings in Atlantic History, Latent Structures and Intellectual Currents, 1500–1830*, edited by Bernard Bailyn and Patricia L. Denault, 183–85. Cambridge, Mass.: Harvard University, 2009.

———. *Viñedos e indios del desierto: Fundación, auge y secularización de una misión jesuita en la frontera noreste de la Nueva España*. Monterrey, Mexico: Museo de Historia Mexicana, 2014.

Matei-Chesnoiu, Monica. *Re-imagining Western European Geography in English Renaissance Drama*. London: Palgrave Macmillan, 2012.

Mathes, Miguel. *Jesuitica Californiana 1681–1764: Impresos de los RR. PP. Eusebio Francisco Kino, Fernando Consag, Juan Antonio Balthasar, Juan Joseph de Villavicencio, y Francisco Zevallos de la Compañia de Jesus*. Madrid: J. Porrua Turanzas, 1998.

———. *Los padres expulsos de Sonora y Sinaloa*. Serie Cuadernos 51. Culiacán, Sinaloa Mexico: El Colegio de Sinaloa, 1999.

Mathes, W. Michael. "Violence in Eden: Indigenous Warfare in Peninsular Baja California." *Pacific Coast Archeological Society Quarterly* 45, nos. 1 & 2 (August 2011): 1–12.

Matthew, Laura E., and Michel R. Oudijk, eds. *Indian Conquistadors: Indigenous Allies in the Conquest of Mesoamerica*. Norman: University of Oklahoma Press, 2007.

McAllen, Katherine. "Jesuit Martyrdom Imagery between Mexico and Rome." In *The New World and Italian Religious Culture, 1492–1750*, edited by Elizabeth Horodowich and Lia Markeyl. Cambridge: Cambridge University Press, 2017.

McCarty, Kieran R. "A Song of Roland in Northwest Mexico." *Arizona and the West* 28, no. 4 (Winter 1986): 378–90.

McCormick, Michael. *Origins of the European Economy: Communication and Commerce, AD 300–900*. Cambridge: Cambridge University Press, 2001.

McDonald, William E. "The Pious Fund of the Californias." *Catholic Historical Review* 19, no. 4 (January 1934): 427–36.
Mclynn, Neil B. *Ambrose of Milan: Church and Court in a Christian Capital.* Berkeley: University of California Press, 1994.
McShea, Bronwen. *Apostles of Empire: The Jesuits of New France.* Lincoln: University of Nebraska Press, 2019.
Meyer, Melissa. *Thicker Than Water: The Origins of Blood as Symbol and Ritual.* Abingdon: Routledge, 2005.
Mignolo, Walter. *The Darker Side of the Renaissance: Literacy, Territoriality, and Colonization.* Ann Arbor: University of Michigan Press, 1995.
Mills, Kenneth. *An Evil Lost to View? An Investigation of Post-Evangelisation Andean Religion in Mid-Colonial Peru.* Liverpool: University of Liverpool, Institute of Latin American Studies, 1994.
———. *Idolatry and Its Enemies: Colonial Andean Religion and Extirpation, 1640–1750.* Princeton, N.J.: Princeton University Press, 1997.
Mills, Kenneth, and Anthony Grafton, eds. *Conversion in Late Antiquity and the Early Middle Ages: Seeing and Believing.* Rochester, N.Y.: University of Rochester Press, 2003.
Mirafuentes Galván, José Luis. "El 'enemigo de las casas de adobe': Luis del Sáric y la rebelión de los pimas altos en 1751." In *Memoria del xiii simposio de historia y antropología de Sonora*, 105–24. Hermosillo: Instituto de Investigaciones Históricas de la Unison, 1988. Also published in *Organización y liderazgo en los movimientos populares novohispanos.* México, D.F.: Universidad Nacional Autónoma de Mexico, 1992), 147–171.
———. *Las rebeliones de los Seris, 1748–1750.* Universidad Nacional Autónoma de Mexico, 1979.
———. *Movimientos de resistencia y rebeliiones indígenas en el norte de Mexico, 1680–1821, guia documentales* I–III. Universidade Nacional Autónoma de Mexico, 1989, 1992, 2004.
Molina, J. Michelle. *To Overcome Oneself: The Jesuit Ethic and the Spirit of Global Expansion, 1520–1767.* Berkeley: University of California Press, 2013.
Montero Alarcón, Alma. *Jesuitas de Tepotzotlán: La expulsión y el amargo destierro.* 1st ed. Tepotzotlán: Mexico, D.F.: Museo Nacional del Virreinato; Plaza y Valdes, 2009.
Mörner, Magnus, ed. *The Expulsion of the Jesuits from Latin America.* New York: Knopf, 1965.
Muldoon, James, ed. *The Spiritual Conversion of the Americas.* Gainesville: University Press of Florida, 2004.
Mungello, David. *Curious Land: Jesuit Accommodation and the Origin of Sinology.* Honolulu: University of Hawaii Press, 1989.

Naylor, Thomas, and Charles W. Polzer, eds. *The Presidio and Militia on the Northern Frontier of New Spain: A Documentary History*. Tucson: University of Arizona Press, 1986.

Nicolini, Giovanni Battista. *History of the Jesuits: Their Origin, Progress, Doctrines, and Designs*. London: H. G. Bohn, 1854.

Noble, Thomas F. X., and Thomas Head. *Soldiers of Christ: Saints and Saints' Lives from Late Antiquity and the Early Middle Ages*. University Park: Pennsylvania State University Press, 1995.

Ó Carragáin, Éamonn. "Chosen Arrows, First Hidden Then Revealed: The Visitation-Archer Sequence as a Key to the Ruthwell Cross." In *Early Medieval Studies in Memory of Patrick Wormald*, edited by Stephen Baxter, Catherine Karkov, Janet L. Nelson, and David Pelteret. New York; Routledge, 2009.

Olin, John C. *Catholic Reform: From Cardinal Ximenes to the Council of Trent, 1495–1563: An Essay with Illustrative Documents and a Brief Study of St. Ignatius Loyola*. New York: Fordham University Press, 1990.

Olvera, Jorge H. *Finding Father Kino: The Discovery of the Remains of Father Eusebio Francisco Kino, S.J., 1965–1966*. Tucson, Ariz.: Southwestern Mission Research Center, 1998.

O'Malley, John W. *The First Jesuits*. Cambridge, Mass.: Harvard University Press, 1993.

O'Malley, John W., Gauvin Alexander Bailey, Steven J. Harris, and T. Frank Kennedy, eds. *The Jesuits*. Vol. 1, *Cultures, Sciences, and the Arts, 1540–1773*. Toronto: University of Toronto Press, 1999.

———. *The Jesuits II*. Vol. 2, *Cultures, Sciences, and the Arts, 1540–1773*. Toronto: University of Toronto Press, 2006.

O'Malley, John W., John W. Padberg, and Vincent T. O'Keefe. *Jesuit Spirituality: A Now and Future Resource*. Campion Book. Chicago: Loyola University Press, 1990.

O'Reilly, Terence. *From Ignatius Loyola to John of the Cross: Spirituality and Literature in Sixteenth-Century Spain*. New York: Routledge, 1995.

Ortega Noriega, Sergio. *Breve historia de Sinaloa*. México, D.F.: Colegio de México, 1999.

Pacheco Rojas, José de la Cruz. *Milenarismo tepehuán: Mesianismo y resistencia indígena en el norte novohispano*. México, D.F.: Siglo Veintiuno Editores, 2008.

Pagden, Anthony. *The Fall of Natural Man: The American Indian and the Origins of Comparative Ethnology*. Cambridge: Cambridge University Press, 1982.

Paquette, Gabriel. *Enlightenment, Governance, and Reform in Spain and its Empire, 1759–1808*. New York: Palgrave Macmillan, 2008.

Pawling, Perla Chinchilla. "Jesuit Restoration in Mexico." In *Jesuit Survival and Restoration: A Global History, 1773–1900*, edited by Robert A. Maryks and Jonathan Wright. Leiden: Brill, 2014.
Paylore, Patricia. *Kino: A Commemoration*. Tucson: Arizona Pioneers' Historical Society, 1961.
Pearson, Timothy G. *Becoming Holy in Early Canada*. Montreal: McGill-Queen's University Press, 2014.
Perkins, Judith. *The Suffering Self: Pain and Narrative Representation in the Early Christian Era*. London: Routledge, 1995.
Perron, Paul. "Isaac Jogues: From Martyrdom to Sainthood." In *Colonial Saints: Discovering the Holy in America, 1500–1800*, edited by Allan Greer and Jodi Bilinkoff, 211–34. New York: Routledge, 2003.
Pesqueira, Fernando, and Herbert E. Bolton. *Síntesis biográfica de Eusebio Francisco Kino*. Cananea, Sonora: Imprenta de Cananea, 1945.
Peters, Gerhard, and John T. Woolley. "The American Presidency Project." http://www.presidency.ucsb.edu/ws/?pid=4496. Accessed on August 13, 2016.
Pickens, Buford. *The Missions of Northern Sonora: A 1935 Field Documentation*. Tucson: University of Arizona Press, 1993.
Polzer, Charles W. "An Epilogue to Kino's Biography of Saeta." In Eusebio Kino, *Kino's Biography of Francisco Javier Saeta, S.J.*, edited by Ernest J. Burrus, translated by Charles W. Polzer. Vol. 9. Rome: Jesuit Historical Institute; St. Louis: St. Louis University, 1971.
——. *Eusebio Kino, S.J.: Padre de la Pimería Alta: Biografía de Eusebio Francisco Kino, civilizador de Sonora, explorador de Arizona, misionero en la Pimería Alta, y una guia a sus misiones y monumentos*. Tucson, Ariz.: Southwestern Mission Research Center, 1972.
——. "The Evolution of the Jesuit Mission System in Northwestern New Spain, 1600–1767." Ph.D. diss. University of Arizona, 1972.
——. *The Jesuit Missions of Northern Mexico*. New York: Garland, 1991.
——. *A Kino Guide: A Life of Eusebio Francisco Kino, Arizona's First Pioneer and a Guide to His Missions and Monuments*. Tucson: Southwestern Mission Research Center, 1976.
——. *Kino Guide II: A Life of Eusebio Francisco Kino, S.J., Arizona's First Pioneer and a Guide to His Missions and Monuments*. Tucson, Ariz.: Southwestern Mission Research Center, 1982.
——. *Rules and Precepts of the Jesuit Missions of Northwestern New Spain*. Tucson: University of Arizona Press, 1976.
Pradeau, Alberto Francisco. *La expulsión de los Jesuitas de las provincias de Sonora, Ostimuri y Sinaloa en 1767*. Disertacion documentada y anotada. México, D.F.: José Porrúa e Hijos, 1959.

———. "Los Jesuitas en Sonora y el alzamiento Pima de 1751," 491–519. Alberto Francisco Pradeau Collection 1551–1980, MSS-67, box 1, folder 17, Chicano Research Collection, Arizona State University.

Prat, Arístides, ed. *El encuentro de los restos de Padre Kino*. Magdalena, Sonora: Publicaciones del Comité del Tricentenario del Arribo de Eusebio Francisco Kino a Sonora, 1987.

Provost-Smith, Patrick. "Macao, Manila, Mexico, and Madrid: Jesuit Controversies over Strategies for the Christianization of China (1580–1600)." Ph.D. diss. Johns Hopkins University, 2002.

Radding, Cynthia. "Colonial Spaces in the Fragmented Communities of Northern New Spain." In *Contested Spaces of Early America*, 135–38. Philadelphia: University of Pennsylvania Press, 2014.

———. "Indigenous Landscapes in Northwestern New Spain: Environmental History through Contested Boundaries and Colonial Land Claims." *Resilience: A Journal of the Environmental Humanities* 3 (Winter/Spring/Fall 2015–16): 315–17.

———. *Landscapes of Power and Identity: Comparative Histories in the Sonoran Desert and the Forests of Amazonia from Colony to Republic*. Durham, N.C.: Duke University Press, 2005.

———. *Wandering Peoples: Colonialism, Ethnic Spaces, and Ecological Frontiers in Northwestern Mexico, 1700–1850*. Durham, N.C.: Duke University Press, 1997.

Rafael, Vicente L. *Contracting Colonialism: Translation and Christian Conversion in Tagalog Society under Early Spanish Rule*. Ithaca: Cornell University Press, 1988.

Rahner, Karl. "Dimensiones del Martirio." *Concilium* 183 (1983): 321–24.

Rajchenberg, Enrique, and Catherine Heau-Lambert. "El septentrión mexicano entre el destino manifiesto y el imaginario territorial." *Journal of Iberian and Latin American Research* 11, no. 1 (2005): 1–40.

Reff, Daniel T. *Disease, Depopulation, and Culture Change in Northwestern New Spain, 1518–1764*. Provo: University of Utah Press, 1991.

———. "Making the Land Holy: The Mission Frontier in Early Medieval Europe and Colonial Mexico." In *The Spiritual Conversion of the Americas*, edited by James Muldoon. Gainesville: University Press of Florida, 2004.

———. *Plagues, Priests, and Demons: Sacred Narratives and the Rise of Christianity in the Old World and the New*. Cambridge: Cambridge University Press, 2005.

Richter, Daniel K. *Facing East from Indian Country: A Native History of Early America*. Cambridge, Mass.: Harvard University Press, 2001.

Roberts, Alexander, James Donaldson, and A. Cleveland Coxe, eds. *Ante-Nicene Fathers: The Writings of the Fathers Down to A.D. 325*. Peabody, Mass.: Hendrickson, 1995.

Roehner, Bertrand M. "Jesuits and the State: A Comparative Study of Their Expulsions (1590–1990)." *Religion* 27, no. 2 (1997): 165–82.

Rollason, David W. "Le corps incorruptible de Saint Cuthbert et l'eglise de Durham vers l'an 1100." In *Reliques*, 313–20. Turnhout: Brepols, 1999.

Ross, Andrew. *A Vision Betrayed: The Jesuits in Japan and China 1542–1742*. Edinburgh: Edinburgh University Press, 1994.

Rozat, Guy. *América, imperio del demonio: Cuentos y recuentos*. México, D.F.: Universidad Iberoamericana, 1995.

Rubenstein, Jay. *Armies of Heaven: The First Crusade and the Quest for Apocalypse*. New York: Basic Books, 2011.

Rule, Paul. "Towards a History of the Chinese Rites Controversy." In *The Chinese Rites Controversy*, edited by D. E. Mungello. Bonn: Monumenta Serica, 1994.

Russell, Frank, and the Smithsonian Institution Bureau of American Ethnology. *The Pima Indians*. Tucson: University of Arizona Press, 1975.

Ryan, James D. "Missionary Saints of the High Middle Ages: Martyrdom, Popular Veneration, and Canonization." *Catholic Historical Review* 90, no. 1 (January 2004).

Sagarena, Roberto Ramón Lint. *Aztlán and Arcadia: Religion, Ethnicity, and the Creation of Place*. New York: NYU Press, 2014.

Said, Edward. *Orientalism*. New York: Random House, 1979.

Salisbury, Joyce E. *The Blood of Martyrs: Unintended Consequences of Ancient Violence*. New York: Routledge, 2004.

Salmón, Roberto Mario. "A Marginal Man: Luis of Saric and the Pima Revolt of 1751." *Americas* 45, no. 1 (July 1988): 61–77.

Salvador, Bernabéu Albert. *El gran norte mexicano: Indios, misioneros y pobladores entre el mito y la historia*. Madrid.: Consejo Superior de Investigaciones Científicas, 2009.

Sánchez Bella, Ismael. *Iglesia y estado en la América Española*. Vol. 16. Pamplona: Ediciones Universidad de Navarra, 1990.

Saravia, Atanasio G. *Los misioneros muertos en el norte de Nueva España*. México, D.F.: Ediciones Botas, 1943.

Schermerhorn, Seth. "Walkers and Their Staffs: O'odham Walking Sticks by Way of Calendar Sticks and Scraping Sticks." *Material Religion: The Journal of Objects, Art and Belief* 12, no. 4 (October 10, 2016): 476–500.

———. *Walking to Magdalena: Place and Person in Tohono O'odham Songs, Sticks, and Stories*. Lincoln: University of Nebraska Press, 2019.

Schroeder, Susan, and Stafford Poole. *Religion in New Spain*. Albuquerque: University of New Mexico Press, 2007.

Seed, Patricia. *Ceremonies of Possession in Europe's Conquest of the New World, 1492–1640*. Cambridge: Cambridge University Press, 1995.

Seymour, Deni J. *A Fateful Day in 1698: The Remarkable Sobaipuri-O'odham Victory of the Apaches and Their Allies.* Salt Lake City: University of Utah Press, 2014.

Sheridan, Thomas E. *Empire of Sand: The Seri Indians and the Struggle for Spanish Sonora, 1645–1803.* Tucson: University of Arizona Press, 1999.

———. *Landscapes of Fraud: Mission Tumacácori, the Baca Float, and the Betrayal of the O'odham.* Tucson: University of Arizona Press, 2006.

Shermer, Elizabeth Tandy. *Barry Goldwater and the Remaking of the American Political Landscape.* Tucson: University of Arizona Press, 2013.

Shiels, William Eugene. "Cabeza del P. Gonzalo d Tapia, primer martyr y fundador de las misiones de Sinaloa." In *Gonzalo de Tapia (1561–1594): Founder of the First Permanent Jesuit Mission in North America.* Monograph Series 14. New York: United States Catholic Historical Society, 1934.

———. *King and Church: The Rise and Fall of the Patronato Real.* Chicago: Loyola University Press, 1961.

Silverman, David J. *Faith and Boundaries: Colonists, Christianity, and Community among the Wampanoag Indians of Martha's Vineyard, 1600–1871.* Studies in North American Indian History. New York: Cambridge University Press, 2005.

Simposio Binacional de estudios sobre Eusebio Francisco Kino: Memoria, Mayo de 1987. Hermosillo: Gobierno del Estado de Sonora Secretaría de Fomento Educativo y Cultura, 1987.

Sioui, Georges. *Histoires de Kanatha: Vues et contées* [Histories of Kanatha: Seen and Told]. Ottowa: Les Presses de l'Université d'Ottowa [University of Ottowa Press], 2008.

Smith, Fay Jackson. *Captain of the Phantom Presidio: A History of the Presidio of Fronteras, Sonora, New Spain, 1686–1735, Including the Inspection by Brigadier Pedro de Rivera, 1726.* Spain in the West Series 14. Spokane, Wash.: A. H. Clark, 1993.

Smith, Fay Jackson, John Kessell, and Francis J. Fox. *Father Kino in Arizona.* Phoenix: Arizona Historical Foundation, 1966.

Smith, Linda Tuhiwai. *Decolonizing Methodologies: Research and Indigenous Peoples.* London: Zed, 1999.

Sobrino, Jon. *Witnesses to the Kingdom: The Martyrs of El Salvador and the Crucified Peoples.* Maryknoll, N.Y.: Orbis, 2003.

Stanonik, Janez. "Letters of Marcus Antonius Kappus from Colonial America." *Acta neophilologica* 19 (1995): 33–43.

Southwest Museum (Los Angeles Calif.). *Padre Kino: Memorable Events in the Life and Times of the Immortal Priest-Colonizer of the Southwest.* Los Angeles, Calif.: Southwest Museum, 1962.

Spicer, Edward H. *Cycles of Conquest: The Impact of Spain, Mexico, and the United States on the Indians of the Southwest, 1533–1960*. Tucson: University of Arizona Press, 1962.

St. Clair Segurado, Eva Maria. *Expulsión y exilio de la provincia Jesuita mexicana, 1767–1820*. Alicante, Spain: Publicaciones Universidad de Alicante, 2005.

Stewart, Charles, and Rosalind Shaw. *Syncretism/Anti-Syncretism: The Politics of Religious Synthesis*. European Association of Social Anthropologists. New York: Routledge, 1994.

Stolzenberg, Daniel. "Four Trees, Some Amulets, and the Seventy-Two Names of God." In *Athanasius Kircher: The Last Man Who Knew Everything*, edited by Paula Findlen, 159–61. New York: Routledge, 2004.

Sweet, David. "The Ibero-American Frontier in Native American History." In *The New Latin American Mission History*, edited by Erick D. Langer and Robert H. Jackson. Lincoln: University of Nebraska Press, 1995.

Tanner, Mathias. *Societas Jesu usque ad sanguinis et vitae profusionem militans in Europa, Africa, Asia, et America*. Prague: Typis Universitatis Carolo-Ferdinandeae, 1675.

Thomas, George Anthony. "The Death of the Duchess of Aveiro: The Life and Legacy of María de Guadalupe Lencastre." *Dieciocho* 39, no. 1 (Spring 2016): 29–42.

Trueba, Alfonso. *El Padre Kino: Misionero itinerante y ecuestre*. México, D.F.: Editorial Jus, 1960.

Truett, Samuel, and Elliott Young. *Continental Crossroads: Remapping U.S.-Mexico Borderlands History*. William P. Clements Center for Southwest Studies. Durham, N.C.: Duke University Press, 2004.

Tuero, Alfonso Echánove. *La preparación intelectual del P. Andrés Marcos Burriel, S.J., 1731–1750*. Madrid: CSIC, 1971.

Turner, Frederick Jackson. "The Significance of the Frontier in American History." In *Proceedings of the State Historical Society of Wisconsin*, December 14, 1893.

Valantasis, Richard. *Religions of Late Antiquity in Practice*. Princeton Readings in Religions. Princeton, N.J.: Princeton University Press, 2000.

Valera, Cipriano de, and Casiodoro de Reina. *La biblia, que es, los sacros libros del Vieio y Nuevo Testamento: Revista y conferida con los textos hebreos y griegos y con diversas translaciones*. Segunda edición ed. Amsterdam: En Casa de Lorenço Iacobi, 1602.

Varagine, Jacobus. *Legenda aurea, vulgo historia lombardica dicta*. 2nd ed. Edited by Johann Georg Grässe. Liepzig, 1850.

Velarde, Luis Xavier. "La primera relación de la Pimería Alta." In *Etnologia y mision en la Pimería Alta, 1715–1740: Informes y relaciones misioneras de Luis

Xavier Velarde, Giuseppe Maria Genovese, Daniel Januske, Jose Agustin de Campos, y Cristobal de Cañas, edited by Luis R. Gonzàlez, 27:69–79. México, D.F.: Universidad Nacional Autonoma de México, 1977.

Vélez, Karin. *The Miraculous Flying House of Loreto: Spreading Catholicism in the Early Modern World*. Princeton, N.J.: Princeton University Press, 2018.

Vermander, Benoît, S.J. "Jesuits and China." *Oxford Handbooks Online*. Accessed on October 15, 2017, http://www.oxfordhandbooks.com/view/10.1093/oxfordhb/9780199935420.001.0001/oxfordhb-9780199935420-e-53.

von Habsburg, Maximilian. *Catholic and Protestant Translations of the Imitatio Christi, 1425–1650*. London: Routledge, 2011.

Wasley, William W. "Archeological Notes on the Discovery of Father Eusebio Francisco Kino." 1966. http://padrekino.com/kino-s-legacy/chapel-discovery/. Accessed on May 12, 2017.

Weber, David J. *The Spanish Frontier in North America*. New Haven, Conn.: Yale University Press, 1994.

———. "Turner, the Boltonians, and the Borderlands." *American Historical Review* 91, no. 1 (February 1986): 66–81.

———, ed. *What Caused the Pueblo Revolt of 1680?* Boston: Bedford and St. Martin's, 1999.

Weber, Francis W. "The Pious Fund of the Californias." *Hispanic American Historical Review* 43, no. 1 (February 1963): 78–94.

Weimer, Adrian. *Martyrs' Mirror: Persecution and Holiness in Early New England*. Oxford: Oxford University Press, 2011.

Weinstein, Donald, and Rudolph Bell. *Saints and Society: The Two Worlds of Western Christendom, 1000–1700*. Chicago: University of Chicago Press, 1982.

Whalen, Brett E. "The Discovery of the Holy Patriarchs: Relics, Ecclesiastical Politics and Sacred History in Twelfth-Century Crusader Palestine." *Historical Reflections/Réflexions Historiques* 27, no. 1 (Spring 2001): 139–76.

Witek, John W. *Ferdinand Verbiest (1623–1688): Jesuit Missionary, Scientist, Engineer and Diplomat*. Monumenta Serica Monograph Series 30. Nettetal: Steyler Verlag, 1994.

Wittkower, Rudolf, and Irma B. Jaffe. *Baroque Art: The Jesuit Contribution*. New York: Fordham University Press, 1972.

Woodson, M. Kyle. *The Social Organization of Hohokam Irrigation in the Middle Gila River, Valley, Arizona*. Sacaton, Ariz.: Gila River Indian Community, 2016.

Wyllys, Rufus K. *Pioneer Padre: The Life and Times of Eusebio Francisco Kino*. Dallas: Southwest Press, 1935.

Velazquez, Maria del Carmen. *Establecimiento y pérdida del septentrión de Nueva España*. México, D.F.: Colego de México, 1997.

Young, Robin D. *In Procession before the World: Martyrdom as Public Liturgy in Early Christianity*. Milwaukee: Marquette University Press, 2001.

Zappia, Natale A. *Traders and Raiders: The Indigenous World of the Colorado Basin, 1540–1859*. Chapel Hill: University of North Carolina Press, 2014.

Županov, Ines. *Catholic Orientalism: Portuguese Empire, Indian Knowledge, 16th–18th Centuries*. History, Languages, and Cultures of the Spanish and Portuguese Worlds. Oxford: Oxford University Press, 2014.

———. *Missionary Tropics: The Catholic Frontier in India, 16th–17th Centuries*. Ann Arbor: University of Michigan Press, 2005.

Index

Acaxee: 1601 rebellion, 18, 65–66; and disease, 86; post-Santarén missions to, 85; Santarén's ritual confrontations, 61–69, 73, 75–76, 9; on the Sierra Madres Occidental, 19, 84. *See also* Perico
Acevedo, Diego de, 75, 76
Acevedo, Laureano Veres, 26
Adlmanin, Francisca, 174
Africa, 36, 40, 55, 161
Africans, 66, 68, 175, 212
agrarian metaphor, 7–8, 34
Ahome, 19, 47–48
Aigenler, Adam, 143
Alavés, Luis de, 88, 104
Albiçuri, Juan de: cosmic war, 101; missionary deaths as seed, 22, 33, 34, 35, 49–52, 54, 60; narrates Tapia's death, 32–33; on Santarén, 92; on Tapia, 31
alcohol, 3, 53, 78
Alegre, Francisco Javier, 3, 40
Alexander VI, 98
Almonazír, Diego de, 117, 120, 125, 133–34
Ambrose of Milan, 36, 41, 141, 168
Amrhyn, Beatus, 143
Anahuacalli Museum, 1
Anaya, Nicolás de, 84
ancestry.com, 9
Apache, 6, 20, 96, 99, 107, 117, 126, 129–30, 132, 149, 159, 176, 211
Aquinas, Thomas, 118–19
Aristotle, 9
ars moriendi, 13, 139, 168
atonement, 10, 151
Augustine of Hippo, 36–37, 118–19, 141, 168
Avila, Diego de, 62–65, 99
Awgin in Syria, 138

Baegert, Johann Jacob, 23–24, 136, 164–66, 172, 183–86, 188, 196
Balthasar, Juan Antonio, 158–59, 166–67
baptism: of children, 57, 69, 76–77, 109, 124, 158; Indigenous, 47, 58, 67, 81, 83, 86, 111, 113, 121–23, 130, 174, 186; Indigenous objection to, 31, 75–76, 91; Indigenous rebaptism, 65; Indigenous renouncement of, 87; and sickness, 109, 167
Barba, Joseph, 155–56
Basilio, Antonio, 110
Battle of Pamplona, 140
beatification, 5, 102, 104
Benedict of Nursia, 138
Beudin, Cornelius, 110
blood: bloodless martyrdom, 23, 133, 141, 145–46, 148, 168; bloodthirstiness, 67–68; Indigenous Christians shed, 24, 128, 195, 197; innocent, 80, 112; martyrs' as seed, 5, 7–10, 35–37, 40–44, 47–48, 50, 57, 64, 68, 83, 85–86, 94, 109–14, 117, 129, 144, 156–57, 168, 177, 212; processions, 67–68, 77; and relics, 82, 141; of Tapia, 33, 52, 54–55
Bolton, Herbert, 15–16, 25
bone bundles, 23, 62–64, 73, 91
borderlands, 1, 5–6, 15–20, 60, 90, 99–100, 113, 168, 176, 197, 204, 210–11, 213
Borgia (Borja), Francis, 3, 113
bourbon reforms, 194
Burgos, Juan Muñoz de, 111
Burriel, Andrés Marcos, 24, 149–56, 165
Burrus, Ernest J., 200

Caddo, 99
Cahita (language), 31, 51, 68
California: Indigenous, 163–67, 176–77, 185–87, 190; Jesuit expulsion from, 171, 173, 183–84, 190–91, 194–95; landscape, 23–24, 135–37, 160–62, 169; map of, 150–51, 153
Campos, Agustín, 106–9
canonization, 11, 14, 119–20
Carranco, Lorenzo, 24, 136–37, 150, 152, 153, 154–56, 168, 183
Castner, Gaspar, 145
Castrioto, Juan Nicolás, 125–27, 132
Castro, Francisco de, 57
Cava, Sebastián, 191
Charles II (Spain), 99
Chichimeca (Chichimeca/o), 30, 74, 84
China (Chinese), 38, 43, 45, 47, 113, 142–47; Chinese Rites, 143
Chínipa, 16, 19, 64, 77, 91; Christians, 78, 80–82, 126
Chrysostom, 141
Cisneros, Bernardo de, 85, 88
civilization discourse: Christian mission, 10, 15–18, 25, 31, 60, 63, 74, 132, 152, 162–64, 167, 176–77; cultivated, 45–46, 142, 151, 183; frontier, 20; Jesuit discourse on, 7–8; in Kino's grave discourse, 200–13; *reducción*, 14
Clavijero, Francisco Javier, 3
Clement XIV, 172
Cobameai, 78–79, 91
Cochimí, 16, 152, 166–67
Cocomaricopas, 117
Cocopá, 149
Colette of Corbie (Santa Coleta), 102–3, 106
Comanche, 99
Comcaác (Seri), 96, 99, 174, 201, 211
Consag, Ferdinand (Fernando), 19–20, 150
Constantine, 36, 38, 137
converso, 9
Copotiari, 130
Coro, 130
Cortes, Hernán, 1
Cristero War, 3
Croix, Carlos Francisco Marqués de, 170

Cruzate, Domingo Jironza Petris de, 96–97, 103
Cundari, Antonio, 146

death: holy, 15, 41, 49, 119, 140, 144; pious, 138; redemptive, 10–11, 110, 212
Decorme, Gerard, 5–6
Deve, 16
Dionysius the Areopagite, 45
dissension, 38, 120
Dominicans, 178–79
Duchess of Aveiro, 144, 174
Ducrue, Benito, 24, 160, 172, 184, 186–88, 194–97

Echeverría Álvarez, Luis, 25, 207–9, 209
Edict of Milan, 36, 137
Encinas Johnson, Luis, 200–2, 204–6
Encomenderos, 62, 66–67
epidemics, 7, 9–10, 31–32, 35, 40, 48, 57–60, 65, 69–70, 72, 74–78, 83–91, 109, 166, 188–89, 191–92
Eucharist, 3, 37, 58, 88, 154
euthanasia, 72
exile, 6, 23–24, 91, 136. *See also* Chapter 5
expansion: Christian, 6, 13, 37–38, 97, 138, 147; imperial, 7, 11, 13, 18–19, 22, 112, 117, 149

Faronda, Diego Ortiz de, 110
Feast: of the Apostle Saint Andrew, 195; of the Discovery of the Holy Cross, 106; of the Presentation of the Blessed Virgin Mary, 87
Felipe de Jesus, 14
Figueroa, Francisco, 85–86, 89–90, 92, 101
Flying Company (*La Compañia Volante*), 96–97, 100, 103
Fontana, Bernard, 201
Fonte, Juan, 88, 159
Ford, Gerald, 25, 207–9, 209
Franciscans, 14, 133–34, 137; alter Christus, 134

Gerstner, Miguel, 158
Glandorf, Franz Hermann, 5

INDEX   313

Goddard, Samuel, 202–6
Goldwater, Barry, 25
González, Tirso, 94, 117, 131–32, 136
Guaycura, 16, 156, 165–66, 185
Guazapares, 19, 26, 64, 78–82, 86, 91; uprising (1632), 6, 26
Guilielmo y Cinzer, 145
Guzapares, 16

Hapsburg family, 99
hatred of the faith (Odio de la fe), 5, 14, 18, 32, 44, 49, 80, 89, 106, 117–20, 124, 133, 138, 141, 154, 156, 159–60, 168, 189–90
Havasupai, 149
Higuera, Nicolás de, 99, 127, 132
Hlawa, Francis, 158
holy jealousy, 137, 193
Hopi, 149
Hostell, Lambert, 23, 136, 166, 173–77
Hurdaide, Diego Martínez de, 61, 71, 99
holy death, 15, 41, 49, 119, 140, 144

idolatry, 3, 9, 23, 29, 31, 41–42, 45, 49, 53–54, 60, 151, 165, 178, 174; Jesuit ritual confrontations (*see* Chapter 2)
Ignatius of Loyola, 3, 12, 30, 101, 113, 131, 139, 142, 152, 168
imitatio Christi, 13, 102, 106, 134, 139, 168, 186, 196
imperialism, 7, 11, 13–14, 17, 22, 37–39, 41, 133–34, 154, 165, 211
Inama, Franz, 176
Inde, 16
Indies, 29, 44, 50, 54, 85, 94, 180–81
Inquisition, Holy Office of the, 9, 49, 119–20, 180
Isidore of Seville, 37
Islam (Muslim), 37, 138; Morisco, 9
Ita, Francisco, 172, 191–93, 196
Italy (Italian), 120, 136–37, 149–50, 167, 174

Janos, 99, 107, 126–27, 129–30, 132
Januske, Daniel, 96, 125–27
Japan, 14, 38, 43, 45, 113, 140, 142, 145, 147
Jerusalem, 41, 195
Jesuits. *See* Society of Jesus

Jesus, 59, 87, 89, 102–3, 143, 148, 155; death, 139, 196; desolation, 139; martyrdom, 35, 54, 113, 139, 156, 168; suffering, 42–43, 138, 172, 187, 195–96
Jew (Jewish), 36–37, 41–42; *converso*, 9
Jiménez, Wigberto, 200
Jocomes, 96, 126–27, 129–32
John Paul II, 5
John the Baptist, 101–2
Jova, 16, 19
Jumanos, 99

Kahlo, Frida, 1
Kappus, Johann, 174–75
Kappus, Marcos Antonio (Marcus), 106, 110–11, 120–23, 125, 127, 129, 132, 174–75
Keller, Ignacio, 19
Kino, Eusebio Francisco: blamed for O'odham revolt, 121–23; and bloodless martyrdom, 133, 145–49, 156, 159, 174; bones, 25, 27, 199–211, 213; early life, 142–45; explanations for violence, 98, 110–14, 116–17, 123–29, 134; *Favores Celestiales*, 40, 101, 145; *Inocente muerte de Saeta*, 23, 100, 125, 145, 148 (*see also* chapter 3); *Mapa de California*, 150, 153; maps, 116, 131, 149; Mission Route, 202, 213; opposition to, 117–18, 129, 132; and Saeta, 95–96; Saeta's relics, 103–8; teaches *odium fidei*, 120; *Teatro de los trabajos*, 114, 116, 148, 149
Kircher, Athanasius, 114, 115
Kürtzel, Enrique, 191

Leal, Antonio, 111–12
León, Francisco, 178–79
Licinius, 137
Linck, Wenceslaus, 136, 160–64
López Campbell, Humberto W., 201
Loyola, Marcos de, 111–12
Lyons martyrs, 12, 41

Maccabees, 10, 41–42
Maldanado, Miguel, 32
Mancuso, Visitor Luis, 107–9

Manje, Juan Mateo, 98–99, 103, 103–9, 112–14, 117, 119–20, 125, 129, 131, 136
maps: 5, 7, 11, 14, 16, 18, 20, 23–24, 98, 114, 137, 169, 197, 202–3; *Mapa de California*, 150, 153; *Teatro de los trabajos*, 114, 116, 131, 148, 149
Maricopa (Pii-Pash), 19–20, 149, 211
Martínez, Manuel, 6, 26, 79, 81–83, 110
Martínez, Pedro, 5, 141–42
Martini, Martino, 143
martyrdom: bloodless, 23, 133, 141, 145–46, 148, 168; *imitatio Christi*, 13, 102, 106, 134, 139, 168, 186, 196; protomartyrdom, 33, 48, 55, 58, 61, 86, 101, 104, 108–10, 141, 195; red, 23–24, 44, 57, 133–34, 137–39, 157, 168, 192; white, 23–25, 44, 50, 57, 133–34, 137–42, 145, 147–48, 155, 158–59, 168, 173, 184, 190, 192, 213
Martyrology of Christmas Eve, 196
martyrs, as suffering servants, 39, 48, 102, 139, 196
Massachusetts Bay, 38–39
Mateu, Jaime, 24, 172, 181–84, 186, 191–94, 196
Mayo, 9, 19, 69, 71, 110
measles, 74, 83
medicine work (*hechiceros*), 62–63, 65, 70, 75–76, 86, 155, 167
Méndez, Pedro, 44, 48, 55, 57, 69
Menendez, Antonio, 8–9, 110
Mensajero del Sagrado Corazon, 26
mestizos, 84, 88, 152, 178, 191
Middendorf, Bernardo, 24, 172, 188–92, 196
Middle Ages, 10, 13, 37, 46–47, 104
mitote, 31, 51, 53, 70
Mohawk, 39
monte: idols, 91; Indigenous movement from, 20, 23, 68–71, 73, 86, 163, 166–67; Indigenous stronghold, 62–63, 65–66, 74, 76, 87
Mora, Francisco Xavier, 120, 125, 129, 132
Moranta, Gerónimo de, 88, 104, 159
morisco, 9
Mota y Escobar, Alfonso de la, 65
Mototicachi: Lucía, 127; massacre, 127, 129
Museo Manuel Ignacio Perez Alonso, 2, 4

Naáyarite (Cora), 193
Nacabeba, 31–32, 60, 78
Nahuatl (language), 29–30
Natives: Native, extirpation, 23, 53–54, 64, 73, 76, 90–91, 151, 166; land, 7–8, 59, 118; relocation, 8, 17, 70, 167; suffering, 8, 33, 48, 68, 81, 86, 97, 99, 186, 211–12; as weeds, 72
natural histories, 18, 23–24, 135, 137, 150–51, 163–66, 169, 172, 182–83, 185, 196
Navajo, 149
Neumann, José (Joseph), 40, 137, 157
New France, 13–14, 38–39, 147, 186
Nicolas, Adolfo, 3
Nieremberg, Eusebio, 141
None (liturgical hour), 196
Noyelle, Charles de, 94
Nuestra Señora de Dolores (Our Lady of Sorrows), 106, 121
Nueva Vizcaya, 19, 31

O'odham: 1695 revolt, 9, 18, 23, 95–97, 100, 103, 105, 121, 126–28, 133, 213; 1751 revolt, 137, 157; Akimel, 19, 214; Christianity (Christians), 100–1, 105–6, 108–9, 111, 117–18, 122, 124, 132, 180; El Tupo meeting, 97, 128; Papago, 19; Sobaipuri, 113, 126, 130; Tohono, 19, 123, 214
observation, 135, 160–66, 168–69, 183–84, 196–97
Och, Joseph, 24, 137, 157–58, 172, 178–82, 184, 186, 196
odio de la fe (hatred of the faith), 5, 14, 18, 32, 44, 49, 80, 89, 106, 117–20, 124, 133, 138, 141, 154, 156, 159–60, 168, 189–90
Oliva, Giovanni Paolo, 143
Ópata, 19, 96–97, 100, 106, 126; Christians, 109, 121, 127, 174–75; Fernando, 96; Francis Xavier, 126; Martín, 96; Tomás, 126
Oquitoa, 96, 124
Ordinances Concerning Discovery, 98
Orozco, Diego de, 88
Otomí, 30, 194–95
Oto-Pamean, 74

Pachomius of Egypt, 138
Palomino, José (Joseph), 171, 189–90

Papago (Tohono O'odham), 19
Papal States, 170, 171, 179
Papasquiaro, Santiago, 88–89
Parable of the Sower, 46–47, 82–83
Parable of the Tares, 73, 78
Parodi, Enriqueta de, 201
Parodi, Rubén, 200–1
Pascual, Julio, 6, 26, 77–83, 90, 99, 110
patronato real (royal patronage), 14, 31, 39, 98
Pelaez, Martín, 3, 25
Peñalosa, Joaquin Antonio, 201
peninsula, 19–20, 135, 152, 161–63, 165, 173–74, 184
Pereira, Nicolás, 191
Perez, Martín, 3, 25
Pérez de Ribas, Andrés: on Chinípa and Guazápare converts, 81–83; defines Indigenous ritual as evil, 69–77, 79; disease as conversion accelerant, 57; *History of the Triumphs*, 22, 33, 40, 43, 48, 81, 92; on lonely suffering, 141, 147–48, 173; suffering as cosmic warfare, 22, 33, 35, 40–49, 53, 55, 59–60, 66, 79–80, 101; on Tepehuán, 85, 87–88; on Tapia, 29–30, 52
Perico, 65–66, 87, 91
Pericu, 16, 152, 165–67, 185; Pericu Revolt (1734), 24, 137, 150, 154–55
Perpetua, 12
Pfefferkrrorn, Ignaz, 24
Philippines, 94, 113, 147, 152, 171
Phillip II (Spain), 49, 98
Phillip IV (Spain), 43
Piccolo, Francisco María, 19, 136, 146, 166–67
Picondo, Pascual de, 112
Pii-Paash (Maricopa), 19
Pima (O'odham), 19, 113, 121, 128–31, 214; Pima fathers, 112
Piñan, Manuel, 26
Pineda, Juan Claudio, 170
Pious Fund of the Californias, 136
Pitquin, 96
Polici, Horacio, 128–31
Polycarp, 12, 104
polygamy, 31, 51, 60, 62
presidio, 100–1, 127
Pro, Miguel, 3, 5, 27
protomartyrs, 33, 48, 55, 58, 61, 86, 101, 104, 108–10, 141, 195

Psalm Sunday, 196
Pueblo Revolt (1680), 99, 133, 147; Popé (Pueblo), 133
Purépecha (Tarascan), 16, 29–30, 58
Puritan, 38–39

Quakers, 38–39
Quechan (Yumans), 19–20, 149, 211

Ramirez, Francisco de, 30
Rancheria, 20, 62–63, 69, 71, 86, 96, 124, 127, 130, 157, 167
Rarámuri (Tarahumara), 16, 19
reductions (*reducciones*), 8, 11, 22–23, 30, 35, 39, 64, 67–71, 74–76, 78, 84–86, 149, 151, 166, 169
relics, 6–7, 11, 27, 40, 58, 60, 74, 90–91, 141, 193–94, 200; bleeding, 37; bone bundles (*see* bone bundles); of Kino, 201–2, 213; of Pascual and Martínez, 80–82; of Saeta, 98, 103–9; of Tapia, 3, 23, 25–26, 50, 52–55, 61, 64
Ribadeneyra, Pedro de, 45
Ricci, Mateo, 142
ritual: bone bundles (*see* bone bundles); Catholic, 18; and conversion, 20, 122, 132; funerary practices, 103, 105, 107; herbs, 72–73; Indigenous, 1, 3, 151, 190, 203–4, 213; and martyrdom, 17, 36, 44, 147; *mitote*, 31, 51, 53, 70; *níari*, 123. *See also* baptism; Chapter 2
Romano, Arturo, 199
royal patronage (*patronato real*), 14, 31, 39, 98
Rubio, Vicente, 191
Ruhen, Enrique, 137, 157–58, 168
Ruhen, Heinrich, 157–58, 180
Ruiz, Alonso, 66, 68

sacraments, 31, 37, 48, 52–53, 57–58, 60, 121, 125, 132, 158, 186, 188–89. *See also chapter 2*
Saeta, Francisco Javier: Abel figure, 112–13; blood would promote success, 110–13, 125, 129, 133–34; "chosen arrow," 95, 97, 101–2; death of assistants, 95, 126, 131; martyrdom, 9, 95–96, 99–100, 116, 128, 133, 147–48, 168; natural

Saeta, Francisco Javier (cont.) explanations for martyrdom, 23, 100–3, 109–17; in *odium fidei*, 118–20, 124; premonition of death, 97; relics, 103–9; student life, 94–95. *See also* Kino, Eusebio Francisco: *Favores Celestiales*; Kino, Eusebio Francisco: *Inocente muerte de Saeta*
Salvatierra, Juan Maria, 19, 124, 131, 136
Sánchez, Manuel, 110
San Jose revolt (1734), 168
Santarén, Hernando de: and Acaxee, 64–68; church and military relations, 99; martyrdom, 75, 89–90, 92–93, 93, 110, 156, 168; and Native material objects, 61–64, 73, 76, 91–92; relics, 6; and Xixime, 75
Sarah of the Desert, 138
Sariñana y Cuenca, Ysidro, 134
Satan, 18, 41–42, 53, 65, 72, 76
savagery, 10, 17–18, 43, 52, 72, 74, 82, 132, 167, 176, 182, 200, 203–5, 209–11, 213
Schall, Adam, 142
Sedelmeyer, Jacobo (Jacob), 150
seeding, 8, 22, 36–37, 57, 60, 100
Segesser, Phiip, 24, 137, 158–59, 163, 175–76
Seri (Comcaác), 96, 99, 106, 159, 174, 201
shaman, 31, 63, 76, 78, 83, 86, 91, 168; Andrés (Tepehuán), 84
shrine, 5, 151, 205, 207–8
silver, 44, 68, 118, 160
Sivemeai, Crisanto, 80–81
Škréta, Karel, 55, 56
slavery, 212
smallpox, 69, 71, 74, 83, 166
Sobaipuri, 113, 126, 130
Society of Jesus (Jesuits): annual reports (carta annua), 57, 67, 75, 84–85; Company of Jesus, 44, 59, 114, 148, 193; converts as sheep, 83, 172, 184–85, 188–89; expulsion, 1, 19–20, 24, 170–71, 178, 194, 197; expulsion from California, 171, 173, 183–84, 190–91 (*see also chapter 5*); Germanic, 55, 136–37, 157, 160, 163–64, 166, 169, 173–76, 178, 184, 186, 188; imprisonment, 5, 142, 170–71, 188–91, 194; Jesuit college, 11, 25, 29, 49–50, 82, 111; paternalism (children), 24, 47, 52, 67, 69, 95, 131, 163, 172, 176, 184–86, 188, 193–94, 196, 210; visitor, 107–8, 111, 124, 128–29
Solís, Antonio, 97, 99, 106–7, 126–28, 132
Sonoita, 157–58
sorcery. *See* medicine work (*hechiceros*)
Spinola, Charles, 142
St. Andrew, 195–96
St. Anthony, 138
St. Eusebius, 41
St. Francis Xavier, 3, 101, 113, 145
St. Jerome, 12, 35, 40–41, 102
St. John of the Cross, 139, 168
St. Paul, 12, 40, 45–47, 59, 168, 173, 185
St. Peter, 12
St. Sebastian, 79
St. Stephen, 195–96
Stiger, Gaspar, 19, 180
Sumas, 99, 107
Syncletica in Egypt, 138

Tamaral, Nicolás, 24, 137, 150, 152, 153, 154–56, 167–68, 183
Tanner, Mathias, 40, 49, 55, 56
Tapia, Gonzalo de: arrival in Sinaloa, 19; martyrdom, 5, 15, 22, 32–35, 34, 44, 48–55, 56, 57–60, 61, 80, 85–86, 110, 168; and Pedro Méndez, 48; military relationships, 99; relics, 3, 4, 23, 25–26, 61, 64, 80–82, 90, 92, 104; Sinaoloan ministry, 29–32, 62, 64, 77; skull of, 3, 4, 25–26, 52–53, 55, 82, 86, 154; strictness, 30, 51–52, 54
Tarahamura (Rarámuri), 5, 99, 107, 110, 145, 157, 174, 181, 184
Tarasca, 22–23, 29, 58–59, 81, 127
Taraval, Sigismundo, 19, 152, 154–56
Tegüima, 16, 19
Tehueco, 19, 64, 68–71, 84
Tello, Tomás, 137, 157, 168, 180
Tepehuán: extirpation, 19; martyrs, 92, 104, 110, 113; Quautlatas, 87, 91; Revolt (1616), 6, 85–90, 140, 156, 159; ritual, 84–87
Tertullian, 35–36, 38, 41–42, 59, 110, 129

Theodosius I, 36
Thomas, Bob, 199–200
Tirsch, Ignacio, 163, *164*
Titus, 41
torture, 80, 127–28, 172, 195
Tovar, Hernando de, 88
Tridentine, 13, 19, 140
triumphs, 12, 35, 37, 42, 54, 57, 59, 79, 105, 119, 141, 146–47, 151; *History of the Triumphs*, 22, 33, 40–41, 43, 48, 81
Tubutama, 96–97, 111, 116, 119, 124–28
Tutino, Andrés, 88–89, 156–57
Typhus, 74

Upper Pima (Aakimel O'odham), 94
Urban VIII, 119

Valle, Juan del, 88, 104
Van Hamme, Pedro, 145–46
Velarde, Luis, 98, 107–9, 119–20, 129, 136
Velasco, Juan Bautista, 57–58
Venegas, Miguel, 136–37, 149–50, 165; *Noticia*, 149–52, *153*, 165
veneration, 22, 27, 58–59, 64, 81–82, 84, 89, 104–8, 110, 119

Verbiest, Ferdinand, 142–43
Vergara, Jose, 188–89
Vespasian, 41
vestment, 6, 96, 119, 129, 156, 173
viceroyalty, 19–20, 33, 62, 85, 129, 147, 149, 152, 155–56, 170–71
Villafañe, Hernando de, 57
Virgin Mary, 55, 87–88, 101, 133, 146
Vitelleschi, Mutio, 58, 92–93
Vivar, José Romo de, 112

war: cosmic warfare, 23, 40–42, 55, 59, 71, 101, 138; Cristero, 3; and redemptive death, 10; of religion, 13, 43; trophies, 23, 74, 91; Spanish, 1, 10, 129, 132; Spanish Succession, 99
Wasley, William, 199
witches, 38, 167

Xavier, Francis, 3, 93, 101, 113, 145

Yaqui, 19, 25
Yavapai, 149, 211
Yoeme (Yaqui), 16, 19, 211
Yoreme, 16, 211

Zuaque, 19, 31, 56, 60, 78, 80, 104

BRANDON BAYNE is Associate Professor of Religious Studies at the University of North Carolina, Chapel Hill.

CATHOLIC PRACTICE IN NORTH AMERICA

James T. Fisher and Margaret M. McGuinness (eds.), *The Catholic Studies Reader*

Jeremy Bonner, Christopher D. Denny, and Mary Beth Fraser Connolly (eds.), *Empowering the People of God: Catholic Action before and after Vatican II*

Christine Firer Hinze and J. Patrick Hornbeck II (eds.), *More than a Monologue: Sexual Diversity and the Catholic Church. Volume I: Voices of Our Times*

J. Patrick Hornbeck II and Michael A. Norko (eds.), *More than a Monologue: Sexual Diversity and the Catholic Church. Volume II: Inquiry, Thought, and Expression*

Jack Lee Downey, *The Bread of the Strong: Lacouturisme and the Folly of the Cross, 1910–1985*

Michael McGregor, *Pure Act: The Uncommon Life of Robert Lax*

Mary Dunn, *The Cruelest of All Mothers: Marie de l'Incarnation, Motherhood, and Christian Tradition*

Dorothy Day and the Catholic Worker: The Miracle of Our Continuance. Photographs by Vivian Cherry, Text by Dorothy Day, Edited, with an Introduction and Additional Text by Kate Hennessy

Nicholas K. Rademacher, *Paul Hanly Furfey: Priest, Scientist, Social Reformer*

Margaret M. McGuinness and James T. Fisher (eds.), *Roman Catholicism in the United States: A Thematic History*

Gary J. Adler Jr., Tricia C. Bruce, and Brian Starks (eds.), *American Parishes: Remaking Local Catholicism*

Stephanie N. Brehm, *America's Most Famous Catholic (According to Himself): Stephen Colbert and American Religion in the Twenty-First Century*

Matthew T. Eggemeier and Peter Joseph Fritz, *Send Lazarus: Catholicism and the Crises of Liberalism*

John C. Seitz and Christine Firer Hinze (eds.), *Working Alternatives: American and Catholic Experiments in Work and Economy*

Gerald J. Beyer, *Just Universities: Catholic Social Teaching Confronts Corporatized Higher Education*

www.ingramcontent.com/pod-product-compliance
Lightning Source LLC
Chambersburg PA
CBHW030433300426
44112CB00009B/987